A NATION UPSIDE DOWN

From Sovereignty to Serfdom . . . Enslavement of the People

PART 1

Kenneth Thomas Carter

A NATION UPSIDE DOWN

From Sovereignty to Serfdom . . . Enslavement of the People
PART 1

Kenneth Thomas Carter

Copyright 2021 by Kenneth Thomas Carter
All rights reserved
ISBN 9781948323130

Turning the Tide Publishing
6256 Bullet Drive • Crestview • Florida • 32536
(850) 689-8989
turningthetidepublishing.com

Reproduction Policy. Portions of this book may be reproduced without prior permission in critical reviews and other papers if credit is given to author, full book title is listed, and full contact information is given for publisher. No other reproduction of any portion of this book is allowed without permission.

Cover note: The upside-down U.S. flag is an official signal of distress. It is not meant to be or recognized as any type of disrespect when displayed for the right reasons. Public Law 77-623 SEC. 4. (a) approved June 22, 1942.
The Flag Code: Title 36, U.S.C., Chapter 10, as amended by P.L. 344, 94th Congress, approved July 7, 1976:

> §176. Respect for flag: No disrespect should be shown to the flag of the United States of America . . .
> (a) The flag should never be displayed with the union down, except as a signal of dire distress in instances of extreme danger to life or property.

Printed in the United States of America

This book is dedicated to

John Carol Jennings Sr.

My Mentor, my Teacher, my Friend . . .
One of the brightest minds I have ever met; with a heart that shone even brighter. A brilliant ray of Light shining through the mist on a cool, foggy morning; a Beacon of Hope to many in their hour of darkness. Rest in Peace, my Friend, basking in the luminous light of Truth only found in heavenly places. May God richly Bless you.

"The purpose of life is not to be happy— but to matter, to be productive, to be useful, to have it make some difference that you lived at all."
—Leo Rosten

"It is given to some to work for immediate results, and from year to year they can reckon up a balance of success. But the men and women who get no stimulus from any visible reward, whose lives pass while the objects for which they toil are too far away to comfort them, the individuals who hold aloof from dazzling schemes and earn the misunderstanding of the crowd because they foresee remoter issues, who even oppose a seeming good because a deeper evil lurks beyond; these are the true statesmen of the world."
—Henry Drummond

John, you made a difference. You were a true statesman of the world.

TABLE OF CONTENTS

PART 1

	Preface	xi
I	"... Of the People, By the People, For the People?"	1
II	From Sovereignty to Serfdom	17
III	"Preservation" of the Union and the Birth of Corporate Government	49
IV	Lincoln's Redemption	73
V	The "Global Elite"	83
VI	Treason on Our Shores: The End of the Republic	129
VII	Corporatism, a.k.a. Socialism/Fascism, in America	187
VIII	A Shadow Darkens the Land ... Reconstruction • 14th Amendment • Act of 1871	213
IX	The Darkness Deepens ... Trading with the Enemy Act and Federal Reserve Act	253
	Appendix A: The 10 Planks of *The Communist Manifesto*	307
	Appendix B: Excerpts from *Our War: An Account of the Civil War in Bedford, Virginia*	311
	Appendix C: Credit River Township Case	319
	Appendix D: Membership List of the Committee of 300	328

Disclaimer

The information contained within the pages of this book is for educational purposes only. Nothing set forth herein is intended to be legal advice or should be construed as such. Anyone acting on any of the contents herein does so solely on the basis of their own volition and at their own risk. Everyone has the duty and absolute right to think, evaluate, research, learn, and act independently and autonomously.

COPYRIGHT DISCLAIMER UNDER SECTION 107 OF THE COPYRIGHT ACT 1976: Allowance is made for "fair use" for purposes such as criticism, comment, news reporting, teaching, scholarship, and research. Fair use is a use permitted by copyright statute that might otherwise be infringing. Educational or personal use tips the balance in favor of fair use.

FAIR USE ACT 1976 NOTICE: This book may contain copyrighted material, the use of which has not always been specifically authorized by the copyright owner. Such material is made available to advance understanding of political, human rights, economic, scientific, moral, ethical, and social justice issues. This constitutes a "fair use" of any such copyrighted material as provided for in Section 107 of the 1976 U.S. Fair Use Copyright Act.

Acknowledgment

A heartfelt thank you to the many, many researchers and patriotic Americans who have worked diligently and tirelessly to shine the light of truth on the darkness. Many of you are quoted and/or sourced in this work. Your enduring perseverance and determination in the seemingly never-ending fight for Liberty and Truth is to be admired. The American people owe a great debt of gratitude to you. I am deeply humbled and honored to assume a place beside you on the front lines of the enduring fight for Freedom. May God bless you abundantly.

Foreword

I have known Ken Carter for many years and have found him to be a "Seeker of Truth." He is willing to follow the facts like a roadmap to a destination called discovery, even when it means shedding light on things concealed in darkness. He reminds me of the pioneers who set out to explore and discover the wonders and beauty of this great nation. Those who blazed the trail and demonstrated great courage every step of the way. They were willing to face danger in their quest for discovery. The book you are about to read chronicles Ken's journey and reveals his findings. It is a journey that he has been on for all the years I have known him. With each turning of the page you will see sights that you have never seen before and be exposed to things that will likely take your breath away. A weekly television show I grew up watching had a famous catchline, "Just the facts ma'am, just the facts." By following the facts, Ken arrives at a destination of discovery, one that says we have become "A Nation Upside Down."

Ed Russo
Life Church
Wesley Chapel, Florida

Preface

*"Should I keep back my opinions at such a time, through fear of giving offense . . .
I should consider myself as guilty of treason toward my country."*
—Patrick Henry

"In a time of universal deceit, telling the truth is a revolutionary act."
—Unknown

This is a book about truth. Not half-truths or twisted truths. Not conspiracy theories or unproven postulates. Not opinion, bias, phobias, or wishful thinking. Just the plain, unadulterated truth . . . based on verifiable facts. It seems that even truth has succumbed to the age of relativism: One man's truth is not necessarily another man's truth. And the mere *appearance* of truth is often accepted as truth. But ultimately, truth is undeniable. It does not change with the ages. It does not yield to man's perception. It does not change because of a man's belief. Truth has no *appearance*. Truth simply IS.

Black's Law Dictionary (sixth edition) tells us: "There are three conceptions as to what constitutes 'truth': agreement of thought and reality; eventual verification; and consistency of thought with itself." *Webster's Dictionary* (1913) defines truth as:

> 1. The quality or being true; as: (a) Conformity to fact or reality; exact accordance with that which is, or has been; or shall be. (b) Conformity to rule; exactness; close correspondence with an example, mood, object of imitation, or the like. (c) Fidelity; constancy; steadfastness; faithfulness. (d) The practice of speaking what is true; freedom from falsehood; veracity. 2. That which is true or certain concerning

any matter or subject, or generally on all subjects; real state of things; fact; verity; reality. 3. A true thing; a verified fact; a true statement or proposition; an established principle, fixed law, or the like; as, the great truths of morals.

Truth, therefore, conforms to reality, not the perception of realty. Truth may be obscured by illusion. It may be distorted by deception. It may be obnubilated by lies. But ultimately, truth is verified by uncorrupted facts. Truth is not subject to interpretation. Truth does not fade with time. There is not my truth; there is not your truth. There is only THE Truth. Truth is incorrigible. Truth is absolute.

Tragically, the American people have been fed lies by their government leaders for over 150 years. Truth has been buried deep in the muck of egregious falsehoods and deception. The government of today bears little resemblance to the Republic of the Founding Fathers. Constitutional rights no longer exist, merely the appearance of Constitutional rights. The Constitution itself is no longer honored. The United States of America has been turned upside down. Nothing is as it appears. But, no matter how deep the muck, truth is still there. No matter how many eulogies are spoken as truth is buried deep in the graveyard of antiquity, truth does not concede. Truth will simply not die. Truth does not change because of man's will, no matter how strong the will to ameliorate deception. Like peeling back the layers of an onion, truth will finally be exposed. Lies and illusion will, in the end, succumb to the light of truth. As Stephen Hawking expressed: "The greatest enemy of knowledge [truth] is not ignorance; it is the illusion of knowledge [truth]."

This work is the culmination of over 15 years of research . . . 15 years of digging deep into the muck; digging to within inches of the ceiling of Hell until the nuggets of truth were unearthed. There are no labels that apply to this work. This book is not about politics. It is not about religion. It is not about not about left—right, liberal —conservative, Republican—Democrat, Christian—atheist, right or wrong. There is only truth. There are only Facts. Facts well-documented. In the end, you must decide for yourself whether or not to believe the truth. To those living a lie, truth is most inconvenient. The answers are not hard to find; but they are often hard to accept. Tragically, truth is treason to the imperium of lies.

This book is also about freedom. But freedom is often confused with autonomy. Autonomy is doing whatever you want when you want. But autonomy is merely the illusion of freedom. Autonomy always leads to tyranny. Freedom, however, is doing not only what you want, but what you *should*. In other words, freedom is governed by moral law. Thomas Jefferson, author of the Declaration of Independence, wisely wrote: "Rightful liberty is unobstructed action according to our will within limits drawn around us by the equal rights of others. I do not add 'within the limits of the law' because law is often but the tyrant's will, and always so when it violates the rights of the individual."

Freedom, like truth, is being buried deeper and deeper in the muck, under the pretense of the government's "concern" for the "safety" of the people. Freedom has become an ethereal concept in America today. Yet freedom was the bulwark our country was founded upon. The rights of the people were unalienable. The people were sovereign. But today, the Bill of Rights is toothless, worthy of little more than lip service. And amazingly, the Bill of Rights has no standing in the courts of today. The ignorance of the people has led to freedom's demise.

At one time, in the early days of our history, the people were leery and distrustful of power in government, particularly a national government. Today, their trust in government is implicit. The people willingly accede, without questioning, to whatever demands the government makes upon them. That is not freedom. That is tyranny. The ignorance of the people abounds as they are blindly and unwarily led by their government into dungeons of darkness.

Freedom and ignorance can never coexist. As aptly expressed by Robert Hugh Benson: "Ignorance may be bliss, but it certainly is not freedom, except in the minds of those who prefer darkness to light and chains to liberty. The more truth we can acquire, the better for our enfranchisement." (*Intellectual Slavery*). And the words of George Bernard Shaw: "Beware of false knowledge; it is more dangerous than ignorance." For freedom to flourish, truth must be sacrosanct. But as truth has been obscured, freedom has yielded more and more to the brutal hand of the master, the federal government.

Indeed, the tide of socialism has washed up on our shores. As the waters of socialism rise with the waxing of the Moon, it is eroding more and more the very foundation of liberty in our country. It is only a matter of time before the tsunami comes, and the land is inundated with the flood waters of communism, i.e., Marxism.

In August of 1918, Bernard Baruch stated: "We are living in a highly, organized state of socialism. The state is all; the individual is of importance only as he contributes to the welfare of the state. His property is only [his] as the state does not need it. He must hold his life and his possessions at the call of the state." (*The Knickerbocker Press*, Albany, NY, August 8, 1918). And that was *1918*. What would he say today? Is that the Republic of our Founding Fathers?

My goal in writing this book has been to uncover truth, free of bias, prejudice, delusion, illusion, or agenda. *Testimonium veritatis* (truth through evidence). My purpose has been to render light to the path back to freedom. Much of what you are about to read may seem unbelievable. But I assure you, every word is the truth. I encourage you, do your own research. To that end, the book is profusely documented with over 1,000 footnotes. Many of the footnotes document sources; some are original sources. Other footnotes add clarification or more explanatory information. And other footnotes expound further on the subject with greater detail and vital information. Still other footnotes refer to additional resources for further study. My aim has been to make the work eminently readable without getting too bogged down in detail, a daunting task in light of the subject matter and the need for verity. Therefore, footnotes seemed to be the best way to add additional, but critical, explanatory information in a way that would not encumber the main body. Footnotes include quotes from the Founding Fathers and other well-known authors, philosophers, and prominent Americans or world leaders; cites from well-known court cases; definitions; and information from researchers who are experts in their field. Footnotes are also provided as a source of further study for the truly inquisitive. I recommend that you first read the book completely through without reading the footnotes. Then go back a second time and read the text with the footnotes. However, I am fully aware of the temptation of curiosity.

I realize there will be skeptics. There will be cynics. But then I remember these words from an article by Dexter Nelson:

> The modern revolutionist (or the eternal skeptic) . . . is the person that reverts to asking endless questions about your sources, not to verify what you've said, but to find a reason to discredit your source. This is also the person that despite any evidence will not believe anything. This is also the type of person that will continue to argue on a moot point and beat the proverbial dead horse with the proverbial stick . . . The problem I have is not so much with that type of debater, but the eternal skeptic or the modern revolutionist, who doubts everything on principle. For a long time I've said that a person who doubts everything, has to doubt their own arguments and, even doubts the logic in which they use; so they don't really have any solid ground beneath them to argue in the first place. They are essentially trying to build a house in quick sand.

And the wisdom of G.K. Chesterton, written in 1909: "But the new rebel is a skeptic, and will not entirely trust anything. He has no loyalty; therefore he can never be really a revolutionist. And the fact that he doubts everything really gets in his way when he wants to denounce anything (*Orthodoxy*)." The skeptic lives in a world of illusion, deluded by his own thoughts. The cynic is a prisoner of his own motives. They spew forth lies and deceptions to justify their phantasmagorical beliefs. They cling to their imaginary world as a toddler clings to his blankie. Illusion is the pacifier of their soul. But ultimately, their voice is silenced. When confronted with truth, they have no answer. The facts betray them. Realty eludes them. Tragedy awaits them.

Please read the book with an open mind and without judgment. Put aside pre-conceived notions, skepticism, or cynicism. At the conclusion, you will decide the veracity of these words for yourself. But those who resist the truth are those who live perpetually in the shadows. They are guilty of what Dr. Dallas Willard calls "irresponsible disbelief." They willingly choose to disbelieve in spite of the evidence before them. Their world of delusion gives them comfort. They perceive they have too much to lose by acquiescing to truth. They are so deep in the sticky muck they are unable to extricate themselves. They see no escape from the illusion. Pity. In the end, by clinging to their wealth, power, vanity, and illusions, they will lose the most valuable possession of all . . . their soul.

You must choose your destiny. I encourage you . . . take the words on these pages and compare them to what is happening in the world today. Connect the dots that are seemingly unconnected. You will be confronted with truth; reality staring directly in your face. And then it will be incumbent upon you to act. Or perish. Choose your destiny. Only you can make that choice. And ultimately, collectively, the people are choosing the fate of generations to come.

There are thousands of Americans, perhaps hundreds of thousands, who already know much of the material in this book. It is time for the "silent majority" to be silent no more, to wake up to the truth, and let the truth guide mankind to a new era of freedom and prosperity. My fervent prayer is that you will be one of the Americans that history will remember kindly. Let history record that you were part of a mighty force that ushered in a new generation of liberty for all mankind.

"And you will know the truth, and the truth will make you free."
—John 8:32

"The simple step of a courageous individual is not to take part in the lie. One word of truth outweighs the world."
—Aleksandr Solzhenitsyn

Chapter I

"... of the People, by the People, for the People?"

"Resolved, That the General Assembly of Virginia, doth unequivocally express a firm resolution to maintain and defend the Constitution of the United States, and the Constitution of this State, against every aggression either foreign or domestic ... That this Assembly doth explicitly and peremptorily declare, that it views the powers of the federal government, as resulting from the compact, to which the states are parties; as limited by the plain sense and intention of the instrument constituting the compact; as no further valid than they are authorized by the grants enumerated in that compact; and that in case of deliberate, palpable, and dangerous exercise of other powers, not granted by the said compact, the states who are parties thereto, have the right, and are in duty bound, to interpose for arresting the progress of the evil, and for maintaining within their respective limits, the authorities, rights and liberties appertaining to them."
—James Madison (1799)

The United States of America ... the greatest country on Earth, and perhaps the greatest country in the history of the world. The people of this country enjoy more freedom and liberty than the peoples of any nation that has ever existed. We owe a great debt of gratitude to our Founding Fathers for the wisdom, insight, and, I believe, spiritual guidance from a higher power, that they exhibited in drafting the greatest documents that have ever been conceived by the mind of man, documents that created "government of the People, by the People, and for the People."[1]

---

[1] Note that a lower case "u" will be used in this work when referencing the *de jure* Constitution for the united States of America. Although the Founding Fathers referred to the emerging country as the United States of America (capital "U"), for purposes of this work, I believe that the lower case "u" is more descriptive of what the Founding Fathers intended. By using the lower case, the word is changed from a

1

But somewhere along the way, something has gone terribly wrong. The freedoms we enjoy have been gradually eroded over the years. We can no longer say our rights are guaranteed. The stark reality is that we no longer have rights, merely privileges. The government has gained more and more control over the people. Our society has become more and more a socialist society, where the good of the masses takes precedence over the rights of the individual. The government has assumed the role of "big brother" over its people. The voice of the people has steadily diminished until it is now but barely a whisper.

What has gone wrong? How have the cherished beliefs, ideals, and principles of our forefathers, so eloquently stated in their speeches and writings, beliefs, ideals, and principles that formed the solid foundation of the Republic, become so distorted? It seems that the nation has been turned upside down. To begin to understand what has happened, we first need to understand where we have come from . . .

In 1606, the Virginia Company (originally called the London Company in the first charter) and the Plymouth Company were granted royal charters from King James I to establish colonies in the New World which came to be known as America. The charters granted them the right to coin money, raise revenue, and make laws in the new colonies, but reserved much power to the King. The Virginia Company was the first of the companies to act. On December 20, 1606, three ships of the Virginia Company, commanded by Captain Christopher Newport, set sail for shores of America bearing 108 colonists. By the spring of 1607, the long and dreary voyage was complete, and the settlement of Jamestown was established.

The Virginia Company was a joint stock corporation charged with the settlement of Virginia. It had the power to establish a government by appointing the Council of Virginia, the governor and other officials, and the responsibility to provide settlers, supplies, and ships for the venture. The new settlement initially generated

---

noun to an adjective, and is therefore more reflective of the fact that the States of the Union were intended to be sovereign entities, but *united* under a Constitution for specific purposes. They are States *united*. In the present-day government, the States are no longer sovereign, but subservient to an all-powerful federal government, which will be clearly set forth in the following pages.

CHAPTER I "... OF THE PEOPLE, BY THE PEOPLE, FOR THE PEOPLE?"

much excitement, but the task of colonization proved to be much more daunting a task than anticipated. Life in Jamestown was far more difficult than they could have imagined. The first colonists, being primarily "gentlemen," were ill-suited to taming the wild land and dealing with the unfriendly natives they encountered. The mortality rate was high, and the prospect for profits grew dimmer with each passing year. The leadership resorted to lotteries, searching for gold, and silkworm production to increase profits. The charter was finally revoked in 1624 and Virginia became a Crown colony.

The first colonists were primarily Englishmen who came to this continent to escape religious persecution in their homeland. The vast majority were Christian Protestants, with a strong belief in God, whose lives were characterized by a passionate and fervent belief in the Bible. Virtually every aspect of their lives was influenced, even dominated, by their religious beliefs and values. Thus, the Biblical worldview of the Protestant, orthodox, reformed Christian formed the backbone of the emerging government of the colonies.

The Bible was the basis of law among the earliest colonists. They had no "government" per se, but looked to the Holy Scriptures to govern the actions of the people. The people, having been denied religious liberty by King George III and suffering other egregious repressions, were understandably suspect of power in government. Most had come to the New World to escape the religious persecution and tyranny of the King. They gave up everything they had to make the dangerous journey from England to the shores of an untamed land, not knowing what would greet them when they landed. And many gave of their lives.

The most memorable year in the early history of this country, and in particular Virginia, was 1619. It was this year that witnessed the beginning of two institutions, strikingly opposite in character but equally important in impact. Each was destined to play a significant role in the development of the new nation that would eventually emerge from the roots of colonization.

The first significant event was government by the people. In November of 1618, the Virginia Company issued an order limiting the power of the governor of the colony and establishing a legislature of burgesses to be elected by the people. The first House of Burgesses, composed of 22 delegates, met in July 1619, and before long the people were living under the laws of their own making, and a "government of the People, by the People, and for the People" thus gained its first foothold on American soil. The granting of a share in the government to the people attracted new settlers, who, from this time forward, came to America's shores in ever-increasing numbers. From these humble beginnings, self-rule by the people would grow and expand until it developed into the greatest self-governing nation in the history of the world.

The second significant event was the beginning of the institution of slavery, which would fasten itself like a blight on the free institutions of the same people, and ultimately would be responsible for bringing about the enslavement of all the people. In that year, a Dutch vessel brought 20 Africans to the colonies and sold them to the colonists as slaves. So began a trafficking in slaves that continued till long after the American Revolution and independence from the British.

In the meantime, the colonies were growing in numbers and flourishing. Self-rule began to gain an even stronger foothold as distractions at home and abroad preoccupied the British government, not the least of which was the French and Indian War.

The first constitution drafted by the colonies was the Constitution of the Commonwealth of Massachusetts, adopted in 1766. It was written by John Adams, Samuel Adams, and James Bowdoin. It is noteworthy because it established six underlying principles that would become the foundational basis of each of the colonial constitutions of the colonies to follow, and eventually the united States Constitution. These six principles had their roots in orthodox Christian belief:

> (1) The first and perhaps most important principle is an acknowledgement of the sovereignty of God (or "the Great Legislator of the Universe," as John Adams phrased it).
> (2) Secondly, the principle that "all People are born free and equal, and have certain natural, essential, and unalienable rights; among which may be reckoned the right of enjoying

and defending their lives and liberties; . . . that of seeking and obtaining their safety and happiness."

(3) The third principle is closely tied to the second principle, ". . . that of acquiring, possessing, and protecting property." This principle was clearly set forth as an inviolate right that no government can interfere with.

(4) Fourth, the principle of the sovereignty of the People over the government (". . . whenever these great objects are not obtained, the People have a right to alter the government, and to take measures necessary for their safety, prosperity and happiness . . .").

(5) Fifth is the principle of representation in government, which was inspired by representative church governments, as modeled in 1 Timothy 3, Exodus 18:13-21.

(6) Finally, the principle of separation of powers. The authors recognized that in all governments there are three types of power; legislative, executive, and judicial. Isaiah 33:22 provided God's model for this principle (*"For the Lord is our judge; the Lord is our lawgiver, the Lord is our King"*).

The British victory in the French and Indian War proved to be very costly for the Crown. The conclusion of the war in 1763 allowed King George III time to redirect more of his attention to the American colonies. As a way to recoup the war costs, he began to tax heavily the American colonies. But he also sought to use the power of taxation to re-establish control over the colonial governments that had become increasingly independent while the British were engaged in the war and preoccupied with other political and civil matters at home. The series of events that followed, however, including the Stamp Act in 1765, the Townsend Act in 1767, and the Boston Massacre in 1770, only served to further alienate the colonists toward the Crown and strained relations with the Mother Country to the breaking point, fostering the seeds of rebellion.

The Boston Tea Party was the first deliberate act of defiance toward the Mother Country:

The colonies refused to pay the levies required by the Townsend Acts claiming they had no obligation to pay taxes imposed by a Parliament in which they had no representation. In response, Parliament retracted the taxes with the exception of a duty on tea—a demonstration of Parliament's ability and right to tax the colonies. In May of 1773, Parliament concocted a clever plan. They gave the struggling East India Company a monopoly on the importation of tea to America. Additionally, Parliament reduced the duty the colonies would have to pay for the imported tea. The Americans would now get their tea at a cheaper price than ever before. However, if the colonies paid the duty tax on the imported tea, they would be acknowledging Parliament's right to tax them. Tea was a staple of colonial life—it was assumed the colonists would rather pay the tax than deny themselves the pleasure of a cup of tea.

The colonists were not fooled by Parliament's ploy. When the East India Company sent shipments of tea to Philadelphia and New York the ships were not allowed to land. In Charleston, the tea was consigned to warehouses and allowed to rot. Only Boston permitted three tea-laden ships to dock, igniting furious reaction among the towns People.

The crisis came to a head on December 16, 1773 when as many as 7,000 agitated locals milled about the wharf where the ships docked. A mass meeting at the Old South Meeting House that morning resolved that the tea ships should leave the harbor without payment of any duty. A committee was selected to take this message to the Customs House to force release of the ships out of the harbor. The Collector of Customs refused to allow the ships to leave without payment of the duty. Stalemate ensued. The committee reported back to the mass meeting and a loud outcry erupted from the meeting hall. It was now early evening and a group of about 200 men disguised as Indians assembled on a near-by hill. Whopping war chants, the crowd marched two-by-two to the wharf, descended upon the three ships and dumped their offending cargos of tea into the harbor waters.[2]

Britain responded to the Boston Tea Party in 1774 by passing several laws that became known in America as the Intolerable Acts. One law closed Boston Harbor until Bostonians paid for the destroyed tea. Another law restricted the activities of the Massachusetts legislature and gave added powers to the governor of Massachusetts. Those powers in effect made him a dictator. The American colonists were very angered by these forceful acts. In response to these actions and laws, the colonist banded together to fight back. Several committees of colonists called for a convention of delegates from the colonies to organize resistance to the Intolerable Acts. The convention was later to be called the Continental Congress.

The sentiment of Thomas Paine was felt throughout the colonies: "Society in every state is a blessing, but Government, even in its best state, is but a necessary evil; in its worst state an intolerable one: for when we suffer, or are exposed to the same miseries by a government, which we might expect in a country without government, our calamity is heightened by reflecting that we furnish the means by which we suffer. Government, like dress, is the badge of lost innocence; the palaces of kings are built upon the ruins of the bowers of paradise."[3]

The First Continental Congress met in Philadelphia from September 5 to October 26, 1774, to protest the Intolerable Acts. Representatives attended from all the colonies except Georgia. The leaders included Samuel Adams and John Adams of Massachusetts and George Washington and Patrick Henry of Virginia. The Congress voted to cut off colonial trade with Great Britain unless Parliament abolished the Intolerable Acts. It approved resolutions advising the colonies to begin training their citizens for war. They also attempted to define America's rights, place limits on Parliament's power, and agree on tactics for resisting the aggressive acts of the English government. It also set up the Continental

---

[2] *eyewitnesstohistory.com/teaparty.htm*
[3] Paine, Thomas, *Common Sense*, chapter 1 (February 14, 1776).

Association to enforce an embargo against England. By the time the first meeting of the Continental Congress ended, hostilities had begun between Britain and the colonies.

The Virginia Constitution was another milestone along the road to self-rule. Adopted June 29, 1776, it was written by Thomas Jefferson, a delegate to the Continental Congress, and became the predecessor to the Declaration of Independence. The document establishes more clearly and emphatically than the previous constitutions of the colonies the foundational principles that would later become a part of the united States Constitution. The first part is titled "Bill of Rights" and is written in 16 sections. The second part contained a litany of abuses by King George III, accusing him of establishing a "detestable and insupportable tyranny."

The basic foundational principles established in the Virginia Constitution are strikingly similar to those of the Massachusetts Constitution:

> (1) That all men are by nature equally free and independent, and have certain inherent rights, of which, when they enter into a state of society, they cannot, by any compact, deprive or divest their posterity, namely, the enjoyment of life and liberty, with the means of acquiring and possessing property, and pursuing and obtaining happiness and safety.
> (2) That all power is vested in, and consequently derived from, the people . . .
> (3) That government is, or ought to be, instituted for the common benefit, protection, and security of the people, nation, or community . . . when any government shall be found inadequate or contrary to these purposes, a majority of the community hath an indubitable, inalienable, and indefeasible right to reform, alter, or abolish it, in such manner as shall be judged most conducive to the public weal.
> (4) That no man, or set of men, are entitled to exclusive or separate emoluments or privileges from the community.
> (5) That the legislative and executive powers of the State should be separate and distinct from the judiciary; and that

the members of the two first may be restrained from oppression, by feeling and participating in the burdens of the people . . .

(6) That elections of members to serve as representatives of the people, in assembly, ought to be free; and that all men, having sufficient evidence of permanent common interest with, and attachment to, the community, have the right of suffrage, and cannot be taxed or deprived of their property for public uses, without their own consent, or that of their representatives so elected, nor bound by any law to which they have not, in like manner, assembled, for the public good.

(7) That all power of suspending laws, or the execution of laws, by any authority, without consent of the representatives of the people, is injurious to their rights, and ought not to be exercised.

(8) That in all capital or criminal prosecutions a man hath a right to demand the cause and nature of his accusation, to be confronted with the accusers and witnesses . . .

(9) That a well-regulated militia, composed of the body of the people, trained to arms, is the proper, natural, and safe defence of a free State; that standing armies, in time of peace, should be avoided, as dangerous to liberty; and that in all cases the military should be under strict subordination to, and governed by, the civil power.

(10) That no free government, or the blessings of liberty, can be preserved to any people, but by a firm adherence to justice, moderation, temperance, frugality, and virtue, and by frequent recurrence to fundamental principles.

(11) That religion, or the duty which we owe to our Creator, and the manner of discharging it, can be directed only by reason and conviction, not by force or violence; and therefore all men are equally entitled to the free exercise of religion, according to the dictates of conscience; and that it is the mutual duty of all to practice Christian forbearance, love, and charity towards each other.

On June 7, 1776, the seeds of rebellion, which had long ago been planted, finally sprouted. Richard Henry Lee introduced a resolution that urged the Continental Congress to declare independence. On June 7, Thomas Jefferson, John Adams, Benjamin Franklin, Roger Sherman, and Robert R. Livingston were appointed to a committee to draft a declaration of independence.

Thomas Jefferson was the principal author. Working from the Virginia Constitution and an extensive knowledge of political theory, Jefferson wrote the document in under three weeks. An author at heart, Jefferson squirmed in resentment as the document was redacted during the final week of June 1776 by his fellow delegates to the Second Continental Congress.

Finally, on July 4, 1776, on the morning of a bright and sunny, but cool, Philadelphia day, Congress adopted the Declaration of Independence. John Dunlap was given the task of printing the document. These original prints are now called the "Dunlap Broadsides." Twenty-four copies are known to still exist, two of which are in the Library of Congress.

The Declaration of Independence begins with the following words:

> When in the Course of human events it becomes necessary for one People to dissolve the political bands which have connected them with another and to assume among the powers of the earth, the separate and equal station to which the Laws of Nature and of Nature's God entitle them, a decent respect to the opinions of mankind requires that they should declare the causes which impel them to the separation.
>
> We hold these truths to be self-evident, that all men are created equal, that **they are endowed by their Creator with certain unalienable Rights, that among these are Life, Liberty and the pursuit of Happiness**. That to secure these rights, **Governments are instituted among Men, deriving their just powers from the consent of the governed**, That whenever any Form of Government becomes destructive of these ends, it is the Right of the People to alter or to abolish

it, and to institute new Government, laying its foundation on such principles and organizing its powers in such form, as to them shall seem most likely to effect their Safety and Happiness. Prudence, indeed, will dictate that Governments long established should not be changed for light and transient causes; and accordingly all experience hath shewn that mankind are more disposed to suffer, while evils are sufferable than to right themselves by abolishing the forms to which they are accustomed. But when a long train of abuses and usurpations, pursuing invariably the same Object evinces a design to reduce them under absolute Despotism, it is their right, it is their duty, to throw off such Government, and to provide new Guards for their future security. Such has been the patient sufferance of these Colonies; and such is now the necessity which constrains them to alter their former Systems of Government. [Emphasis added]

The Declaration of Independence is arguably the most important document in the history of this country, if not the world. It clearly establishes the belief that the people are sovereign, subject only to the sovereignty of God. To our Founding Fathers and the colonists at the time, these truths were "self-evident." A sovereign God has given the people unalienable rights which no government can abrogate, and the government's primary purpose is to secure those rights. And that all government power is derived from the people.[4]

With the signing of the Declaration of Independence, the united States became the only country in the history of the world to politically recognize the unalienable *nature* of a people's rights. John Locke (1632-1704), the English philosopher and physician, had significant influence on the beliefs of the Founding Fathers,

---

[4] *Bouvier's Law Dictionary* (14th edition): "A sovereign is answerable for his acts only to his God and his own conscience." See, *Billings v. Hall*, 7 Cal 1: "Under our form of government, the **legislature is not supreme**. It is only one of the organs of that absolute **sovereignty which resides in the whole body of the people**; like other bodies of government, it can only exercise such powers as have been delegated to it, and **when it steps beyond that boundary**, its acts . . . are utterly **void**." [Emphasis added]

particularly Thomas Jefferson. His "life, liberty, and property" appears three times in the Constitution for the united States of America.[5] The unalienable rights of the people derive from natural law and natural liberty. Natural liberty is the "power of acting as one thinks fit, **without restraint or control**, except by the **law of nature** (1 Bl. Comm. 125)."[6] [Emphasis added] Natural law is *unwritten law*, i.e., common law.

As Thomas Jefferson so eloquently stated in later years: "God who gave us life gave us liberty. And can the liberties of a nation be thought secure when we have removed their only firm basis, a conviction in the minds of the People that these liberties are the Gift of God? That they are not to be violated but with His wrath? Indeed, I tremble for my country when I reflect that God is just; that His justice cannot sleep forever." John Adams reiterated the same belief when he stated: "You have rights antecedent to all earthly governments; rights that cannot be repealed or restrained by human laws; rights derived from the Great Legislator of the Universe."

Under British rule and the tyranny of the British throne, the people were *subjects*, not sovereign. They had no rights, only *privileges* granted them at the mercy of the king. Ultimately, they had no say in government—the king had absolute power. Against this tyranny, the colonies rebelled. And the beliefs and principles set forth in the Declaration of Independence and the state constitutions that preceded it would form the foundation of the government of a new and independent nation.

The Continental Congress felt the need for a stronger union, even before the Declaration of Independence was written. The Battles of Lexington and Concord took place on April 19, 1775. The urgency of impending war against Great Britain compelled the colonies to act quickly to draft a constitution for the purpose of

---

[5] The Constitution was named by the Founding Fathers in the preamble to the Constitution. The *de jure* Constitution is not to be confused with the Constitution of the United States of America, which will be discussed in subsequent chapters. See also, "without some such declaration of rights the government would assume, and might be held to possess, the power to trespass upon those rights of persons and property, **which by the Declaration of Independence were affirmed to be unalienable rights**." *U.S. v. Twin City Power Co.*, 350 U.S. 222 (1956). [Emphasis added]

[6] *Black's Law Dictionary* (4th edition) p. 1066.

Chapter I ". . . of the People, by the People, for the People?"

unifying the emerging nation. The new government would be based on principles clearly established in the first constitutions of the colonies. It would be instituted to protect the rights of the people and the sovereignty of the individual states. It is important to note that each of the 13 colonies were sovereign, separate from each other, governed by laws of their own making that were unique and distinct to a particular colony. The laws of Virginia, for example, had no effect in Massachusetts or Maryland. The people of one colony had no say in the laws and rules of another colony. Maintaining the autonomy and independence of each state was of paramount importance in establishing the new national government. Each state could be thought of as an independent nation.

The Articles of Confederation was finally completed in 1777. However, the Articles would go through six drafts before the final version was agreed to by the Continental Congress for submission to the states. The biggest obstacle to finalizing the draft of the Articles was a fear of too much power in a central government. By 1779, all states except Maryland approved the Articles. Finally, on March 1, 1781, Maryland ratified the document, and the new government was formed.

The Articles named the new nation "The United States of America." Article III described the confederation as "a firm league of friendship of states for their common defence, the security of their liberties, and their mutual and general welfare." Of overriding importance in the Articles, the states remained *sovereign* and *independent*. The new government was given limited, delegated powers. It was formed for specific, enumerated purposes, including the authority to "make treaties and alliances, to maintain armed forces, and coin money." However, the central government lacked the authority to levy taxes and regulate commerce, two of the issues that would ultimately lead to the Constitutional Convention in 1787.

One surprising provision of the Articles was the "perpetual union" clause. Surprising because the states were in the throes of a war to gain their independence from tyrannical rule. Surprising in light of Thomas Jefferson's words in the Declaration of Independence: ". . . it is their right; it is their duty, to throw off such Government, and to provide new Guards for their future security."

And surprising considering the reticence of the states to ratify the Articles of Confederation because of the people's wariness of too much power in a central government. The fear that a powerful national government may eventually devolve into tyranny was almost too much to overcome.

Another weakness of the Articles was that Congress was the sole governing body. There was no executive or judicial branch to balance the powers of the legislature. This omission from the Articles was also surprising since the first constitutions, among them the constitutions of the Commonwealth of Massachusetts and Virginia, were established with three equal branches of government; legislative, executive, and judicial, based upon Isaiah 33:22.

On October 19, 1781, General Cornwallis surrendered the British Army to General George Washington. The colonies had won their independence. The exciting journey of a new nation would begin.

After the cessation of hostilities, the weaknesses of the Articles of Confederation became more apparent. A constitutional convention was formed. On September 17, 1787, the new Constitution for the united States of America was signed by the delegates to the convention. The preamble to the Constitution reads:

"We the People of the United States, in Order to form a more perfect Union, establish Justice, insure domestic Tranquility, provide for the common defence, promote the general Welfare, and secure the Blessings of Liberty to ourselves and our Posterity, do ordain and establish this Constitution for the United States of America."

The new Constitution did not include the perpetual union clause. The sovereign states reserved the right to withdraw from the Union, if ". . . any Form of Government becomes destructive of these ends [to secure Life, Liberty and the pursuit of Happiness to the people], it is the Right of the People to alter or to abolish it, and to institute new Government, laying its foundation on such principles and organizing its powers in such form, as to them shall seem most likely to effect their Safety and Happiness."

With the signing of the Constitution for the united States of America in 1787, a new permanent form of government was created. Government *"of the People, by the People, and for the*

People" was permanently birthed . . . a government based on the principles of the sovereignty of the people, the government as servant of the people, the God-given unalienable rights of man, and the common law. No other government in the history of the world has venerated the people and exalted natural law as the supreme law of the land as was affirmed in the Constitution of the new Republic. Much more will be written about the Constitution in the following pages.

But, over the years, the Republic of the Founding Fathers has somewhat enigmatically disappeared. The U.S. government of today bears little resemblance to the government established by the Founders. "Government of the People, by the People, for the People," has morphed into "government of the Government, by the Government, for the Government." Sovereignty today rests in the federal government, not the people. The government has become the master. Unalienable rights are no longer extant; all "rights" of man are at the pleasure of government. Common law has been replaced by man-made statutes and regulations. The scales of justice are no longer balanced, heavily weighted in favor of the state, often bordering on tyranny. The cherished ideals established in the *de jure* Constitution have mysteriously vanished. The great American experiment has suffered a slow and inconspicuous death. Almost inexplicably, the Republic of our Founding Fathers no longer exists. How could this possibly have happened? And perhaps more importantly, why? Prepare yourself for a wild journey through the portals of time. But brace yourself . . . it will be a bumpy ride; at times harrowing, at times exhilarating; at times depressing, yet always hopeful.

"Necessity is the plea for every infringement of human freedom. It is the argument of tyrants; it is the creed of slaves."
—William Pitt the Younger (1759-1806), British prime minister

Chapter II

From Sovereignty to Serfdom

"I believe there are more instances of abridgement of freedom of the people by gradual and silent encroachments of those in power than by violent and sudden usurpations . . ."
—James Madison

"But we also need to remember that the struggle is a never-ending process. Freedom is never really won. You earn it and win it in every generation."
—Coretta Scott King

The causes of the Civil War have deep roots, extending as far back as the early days of the new Republic. And it is impossible to fully comprehend how the People surreptitiously lost their Sovereignty, without a basic knowledge of the truth concerning the events that led the South to take the drastic action of seceding from the Union. Sinister seeds of malice had been planted decades earlier by men such as Alexander Hamilton, John Jay, and Mayer Amschel Rothschild. The seeds germinated during this epic struggle . . . a war fought over man's right to rule as Sovereign over his government. The blood-soaked soil of a brutal war, shaded from the light by ominous clouds of inequity, would provide fertile ground for the germinated seeds to blossom into black orchids of death . . . death to the Republic.

The events leading up to and surrounding the Civil War, or more appropriately the War Between the States, marked the end of the *de jure* (right, legitimate, lawful) Constitutional Republic created by our Founding Fathers, and the beginning of the *de facto* (in fact, in deed, actually) corporate federal government, and along with that change, the loss of the Sovereignty of the People. The People, White Americans in both the North and South, entered the war free Sovereigns, masters over their own destiny, endowed by their Creator with unalienable rights. They ended the war subjects, "slaves" to a new Master in an all-powerful corporate federal government. And the former slave fared little better, merely subjected to a new Master.

Yes, history does indeed repeat itself. The times may be different, modern technology dramatically transforming the age in which we live. But the once proud Sovereign American has been relegated, as in medieval times, to the status of a mere serf, serving fealty to a lord and king in the federal government, his God exchanged for his government. At least in medieval times, the serfs were cognizant of their servant status. Today, Americans go about their daily lives oblivious to their serfdom. The evolution of this tragic transformation begins with a brief journey through the War Between the States. The tale reads like a mystery novel, an intricate web of betrayal, lies, treachery, and deceit. I caution you; much of what you are about to read seems unbelievable, even unfathomable; a tale worthy of an Orwellian bestseller. What you will read is contrary to what Americans have been taught and believe to be truth. It will stir feelings of disbelief, anger, denial, gloom, despair, depression, and yes, even hope . . . hope that once armed with the light of truth, Americans will change the course of history. But I assure you; chilling as it may seem, every word is true. We are indeed a nation that has been turned upside down. Nothing is as it appears.

The journey begins with two widespread misconceptions, quite purposely intended as we shall see, that have been promulgated over the years. First, that the War Between the States was fought over the issue of slavery; and, second, that the South started the war. These two myths have been taught in public schools and colleges as fact. This is grossly inaccurate and a blatant distortion of the truth; the South did **not** start the war. In fact, the South did not **want** war. And slavery was **not** the primary issue in the secession from the Union by the Southern States. However, to the winner goes the spoils, and along with victory, the privilege to rewrite history according to its purpose. And its purpose has been to enshroud the truth in a malefic self-serving deception worthy of

CHAPTER II FROM SOVEREIGNTY TO SERFDOM

the darkest mysteries of the ages. Yes, nothing is as it appears. Confederate Major General Patrick R. Cleburne accurately predicted in 1864: "Surrender means that the history of this heroic struggle will be written off by the enemy, that our youths will be taught by Northern school teachers; learn from Northern school books *their* version of the war, will be impressed by the influences of history and education to regard our gallant dead as traitors, and our maimed veterans as fit objects for derision . . ."[1] [Emphasis added] How right he was; his words a prophetical vision of the future. And his prescience foreshadowed the words of Karl Marx years later, as communism began to infiltrate American politics during Lincoln's presidency: "The first battlefield is the re-writing of history."

The web of deception continues with a third myth that has been proclaimed over the years; the South did not have the lawful right to secede, and the North was therefore justified in taking military action to "preserve" the Union. Anyone with a true knowledge and understanding of the Constitution for the united States of America will know that this is simply not true. Yet the myth has been propagated in the halls of our learning institutions and in the voluminous pages written by so-called "scholars" and "historians." In giving credence to these myths, Americans have been deceived for 150 years into believing a Big Lie. They have unquestioningly accepted this Lie as "truth," choosing to believe a convenient fantasy rather than assuming the responsibility of seeking verity. Americans have, without evident protest, accepted the veil of deception that has distorted their perception of reality, and in doing so, have willingly adorned the yoke of slavery. Yes; the roots of modern serfdom go back that far.

Alas, the ignorance of the People has led to their cryptic

---

[1] From a January 2, 1864 letter to General Joseph E. Johnston, Cleburne's superior officer. Patrick Ronayne Cleburne was born in Ireland on March 17, 1828. He immigrated to the U.S. with his family in 1849, settling in Helena, Arkansas. In Helena, he worked as a druggist and a lawyer. He joined the Confederate Army in April 1861. Major General Cleburne was a brilliant military tactician and one of the Confederate Army's most capable officers. He fought with valor and honor in the Battle of Shiloh, the Kentucky Campaign, and the Atlanta Campaign, among others. He was killed in the Battle of Franklin on November 30, 1864. He led the charge on the Union bulwarks, sword raised, into a hail of bullets after two horses had been shot out from under him.

undoing. Through their ignorance, Americans have unwittingly embraced their serfdom. As so eloquently prophesied by Thomas Jefferson: "If a nation expects to be ignorant and free, in a state of civilization, it expects what never was and never will be."[2] James Madison, the Father of the Constitution, echoed Jefferson's truth: "Knowledge will forever govern ignorance: and a People who mean to be their own governors, must arm themselves with the power which knowledge gives."[3] But, truth is light, deceit is darkness. And darkness must yield to the light of truth, regardless of the depth of the deception. "For nothing is hidden that will not be made manifest, nor is anything secret that will not be known and come to light." (Luke 8:17 ESV, also Mark 4:22) Along our journey we will traverse from the depths of darkness into the brilliant light of truth. And along the way, we will discover how the People have been so egregiously deceived by their government, and robbed of their God-given sovereignty and unalienable rights.

We begin unraveling the web of intrigue by dispelling Myth No. 1, that the war was fought over the issue of slavery. The truth is that slavery couldn't possibly have been an issue in secession, because it was specifically protected by the united States Constitution, in fact *guaranteed* until 1808, and that protection could be removed only by an amendment ratified by three-quarters of the states.[4] In 1860 there were 15 Slave states and 18 Free states. With the states so evenly divided, the possibility of a Constitutional amendment abolishing slavery was virtually nil for the foreseeable future.

In fact, many Northerners in the Union states of Delaware, Maryland, Kentucky, Missouri, and West Virginia owned slaves prior to and during the war. The U.S. government did not require those Northerners to free their slaves after the outbreak of

---

[2] January 6, 1816 letter to Charles Yancey.
[3] August 4, 1822 letter to W.T. Barry.
[4] To ensure ratification of the U.S. constitution, delegates from the North and South reached a number of compromises, which included the Slave-Trade clause. The Slave-Trade clause permitted the continued importation of slaves until at least 1808. The Fugitive-Slave clause protected slavery even in Free states. If a slave escaped to a Free state, his status remained that of a slave. Article 1, Section 9, Clause 1, is one of a handful of provisions in the original Constitution related to slavery. This clause prohibited the federal government from limiting the importation of "persons," understood at the time to mean enslaved Africans.

hostilities. Why, if the war was fought over slavery? The answer is simple: the war was not about slavery. And, as previously stated, the U.S. government could *not* require the Northern slaveholders to free their slaves, because slavery was protected by the Constitution.

Northerners who owned slaves were among the most widely recognized names on the Union side. General Ulysses S. Grant's family owned slaves, and Grant himself had a personal slave who accompanied him throughout the War. In a letter to the *Chicago Tribune* in 1862, Grant wrote: "The sole object of this War is to restore the Union. Should I be convinced it has any other object, or that the government designs using its soldiers to execute the wishes of the abolitionists, I pledge to you my honor as a man and a soldier I would resign my commission and carry my sword to the other side." Many Northerners, soldier and citizen alike, shared Grant's sentiment. Union General William T. Sherman was a slave holder, and had no disposition toward freeing them. Although an avowed abolitionist himself, Secretary of State William Seward's family was slave owners. Abraham Lincoln's father-in-law was among other prominent Northerners who owned slaves. And it should also be pointed out that Northern slaves were not included in the Emancipation Proclamation.[5] Such attitudes, widespread in the North, were hardly conducive to a war over slavery.

Yes, there was widespread and growing sentiment throughout the nation that slavery was morally wrong. But freeing the slaves was a different matter. The abolitionists were but a small radical minority at the outbreak of hostilities. In the North's war effort

---

[5] The Emancipation Proclamation was an *executive order* issued by President Lincoln on January 1, 1863, using war powers under his authority as "Commander in Chief," pursuant to Article II, section 2 of the U.S. Constitution. The Proclamation was not a law passed by Congress. It did not outlaw slavery and did not make the ex-slaves citizens. The order suspended civil law and proclaimed the freedom of slaves in the areas of the South that Lincoln considered to be in rebellion, where Lincoln had *no authority* to enforce it. Those "states" were in reality states of a separate, independent nation, the Confederate States of America. It did not free slaves in the North or in any of the regions of the South that were then under Union control. Slavery continued in the Northern states and in the South until the end of hostilities. If, as Lincoln claimed, the Southern States were still a part of the Union, then the Emancipation Proclamation was unconstitutional. Neither Lincoln nor Congress had the right to abolish slavery in any state. The only legal way to abolish slavery would have been by a Constitutional amendment or by the states abolishing it on their own. Slavery was not outlawed until the passage of the 13th Amendment in 1865.

against the South, slavery was, at least in the beginning of the War, a mere afterthought. The claim that the War was fought over slavery was a vain attempt on the part of a few Northerners, in particular the bankers and capitalists who supported war for their own enrichment, to cleanse their souls of their sins and to cover-up, as we shall see, a far more baleful agenda.

Another lie that has been promoted through the years is the comparative treatment of Blacks in the Northern versus the Southern States. The perception has been widely held that Blacks were welcomed in the North, treated with compassion, dignity, and respect, and considered to be almost equals of White Americans. On the other hand, the impression persists of the cruel plantation owner and overseer, who supposedly beat their slaves, forced them to live in squalid conditions, and treated them little better than animals. Stories of the Underground Railroad have perhaps helped to perpetuate this viewpoint. Perception and reality, however, are often quite different.

By 1860 there were 488,000 free Blacks in the U.S., the majority in the South. As many as 90,000 Blacks, slave and free, were employed in some capacity by the Confederate Army during the War. And the preponderance of the Southern Blacks were loyal to the independence of the Confederacy. At first thought, that may seem a paradox, but the loyalty was shared by both free and slave Blacks alike. They viewed the Union troops as invaders. Free Blacks fought with the Confederacy fearing the loss of their livelihood and property. They realized a Union victory would mean the destruction of the South's economy and the likely loss of everything they had achieved in gaining their freedom. Slaves supported the War out of loyalty to masters who treated them well, and knowing that in time, they, too, could gain their freedom, just as many Southern Blacks had already done. The reality is that Southerners were far more inclined to grant freedom to their slaves than Northern slave holders. And, contrary to the Union Army, Blacks served alongside Whites in the Confederacy.

Initially, Blacks served in the Confederate Army as military laborers or body servants. However, Blacks were armed as early as 1861 and fought in combat alongside Whites. They fought with the infantry, drove supply wagons, were employed as sharpshooters, and manned heavy artillery. They fulfilled a vital role in the Confederate army. As reported by Frederick Douglass, an African American abolitionist, in 1861: "There are at present many Coloured men in the Confederate Army doing duty not only as cooks, servants and labourers, but real soldiers, having muskets on their shoulders, and bullets in their pockets."[6]

Company E, 4th U.S. Colored Troops at Fort Lincoln, November 17, 1865

New York officers on patrol on December 22, 1861, near New Market, Virginia, reported they were attacked by Confederate cavalry and a group of 700 armed Blacks. The Northerners killed six of the Blacks before retreating.[7] The Northerners were taken aback, stupefied at the color of their adversary's skin. Upon returning to camp, they complained to their commanding officer that if the Confederate Army was employing Blacks, perhaps the Union Army should as well. In the Battle of Bull Run, the "Richmond Howitzers" was partially manned by Black militiamen. Two Black regiments, one free and one slave, also fought at the Battle of Bull Run. Confederate General Nathan Bedford Forrest

---

[6] Douglass, Frederick, *Douglass' Monthly, IV*, p. 516 (September 1861).
[7] Jordan, Ervin L., *Black Confederates and Afro-Yankees in Civil War Virginia* (University of Virginia, 1995). See also, Wiley, Bell, *Southern Negroes; 1861-1865* (Yale, 1938).

had slaves and free Blacks serving in units under his command, and said of them: "These boys stayed with me . . . and better Confederates did not live." Three thousand Black Confederates served as soldiers in Stonewall Jackson's army, and it was reported those soldiers were "manifestly an integral portion of the Southern Confederate Army."[8] In an article on July 11, 1863, the *New York Herald* reported: ". . . And after the battle of Gettysburg in July 1863 . . . reported among the rebel prisoners were seven Blacks in Confederate uniforms fully armed as soldiers . . ." Many other instances of Blacks serving in the Confederate Army are recorded in the annals of history.

Blacks in the Union Army, however, were treated quite differently. Both Grant and Sherman refused to allow them to serve in their armies, and they were generally relegated to segregated all-Black regiments. Thomas DiLorenzo wrote:

> Many slaves who ended up in the hands of the Federal army were not set free but were put to work doing the most unpleasant tasks in and around army encampments. Others were sent back to their owners. Congress passed several "confiscation acts" in the early years of the war that allowed Federal troops to confiscate the slaves and other property in conquered rebel territory. As one Illinois lieutenant wrote, "I have 11 Negroes in my company now. They do every particle of the dirty work. Two women among them do the washing for the company.[9]

Slaves were often conscripted for use as slave laborers for Union projects. In the Union slave state of Kentucky, "federal gunboats raided plantations, carrying off slaves to help build

---

[8] Segars, J.H. and Barrow, Charles Kelly, editors, *Black Southerners in Confederate Armies: A Collection of Historical Accounts* (Southern Lion Books, Atlanta, GA, 2001).

[9] DiLorenzo, Thomas J., *The Real Lincoln: A New Look at Abraham Lincoln, His Agenda, and an Unnecessary War* (Forum/Prima, Roseville, CA, 2002). Also, DiLorenzo, Thomas J., *Lincoln Unmasked* (Crown Publishing Group, Random House, NY, 2006). DiLorenzo was born August 8, 1954 and is an author and economics professor at Loyola University Maryland's Joseph A. Sellinger, S.J. School of Business and Management. He is a research fellow at the Independent Institute, a senior fellow of the Ludwig von Mises Institute, Board of Advisors member at CFACT, and an associate of the Abbeville Institute. He holds a Ph.D. in economics from Virginia Tech.

military railroads, fortifications, and wagon roads."[10] So much for Northern compassion for the Southern slave and the myth of a war to abolish slavery. Captured Southern slaves fared no better, or worse, in the hands of their Northern "liberators" then on the plantations from which they were "liberated." They remained slaves, only to a new master in the Union Army.[11]

The fact is that by the time the War Between the States started, many Southern landowners had already freed their slaves. Some Southern plantation owners freed their slaves as far back as the 1790s.[12]

And many of those freed slaves chose to stay on the plantations and work in exchange for a place to live and a plot of ground to raise their own gardens, and perhaps even a share of the crops. Though free, former slaves continued to provide a valuable source of labor and skilled craftsmanship on the plantation. Others departed the plantations to make their own way in life, utilizing skills learned on the plantation and contributing value to Southern society.

Robert E. Lee wrote in a December 27, 1856 letter: "There are few, I believe, in this enlightened age, who will not acknowledge that slavery as an institution is a moral and political evil." Following the death of his father-in-law in 1862, Lee freed all of his slaves. Many Southerners followed his example. Early in the War, James Alcorn, a powerful plantation owner from Mississippi,

---

[10] Klingaman, William, *Abraham Lincoln and the Road to Emancipation* (Viking Press, NY, 2001).

[11] For numerous accounts of atrocities and mistreatment of slaves by the Union Army, see, James and Walter Kennedy, *The South Was Right!* (Pelican Publishing Company, Gretna, LA, 1994), and David Edmonds, editor, *The Conduct of Federal Troops in Louisiana* (The Acadiana Press, Lafayette, LA, 1988).

[12] Robert Carter III of Nomini Hall was known as "The First Emancipator" and freed 500 slaves beginning in 1791. As the grandson of Robert "King" Carter, he was born into the highest circles of Virginia's Colonial aristocracy. He was neighbor and kin to the Washington and Lee families, and a friend and peer to Thomas Jefferson, James Madison, George Mason, and many other prominent Americans of the time. At the beginning of the Revolutionary War, Carter was one of the wealthiest men in America. He owned tens of thousands of acres of land, factories, ironworks, and hundreds of slaves. Yet personal convictions and a religious conversion led him to take action in the freeing of his slaves that was considered drastic for the time. See, Andrew Levy, *The First Emancipator: The Forgotten Story of Robert Carter, the Founding Father Who Freed His Slaves* (Random House, NY: April, 2005). Also, George Washington's will specified that all of his slaves be freed within two years after his death. Washington died on December 14, 1799, from pneumonia. Within one year, Martha freed all of her husband's slaves. When she died in 1802, she had only one slave in her name.

talked openly about emancipation. Duncan Kenner, one of the most powerful slaveholders in the South and a chairman in the Confederate Congress, urged that slavery be abolished. The Confederate Secretary of State Judah Benjamin and Governor William Smith of Virginia, both supported ending slavery.

Major General Cleburne, in his January 1864 letter to General Joseph E. Johnston, quoted from earlier in this chapter, urged enlisting more slaves into the Confederate Army in order to bolster the Confederacy's waning War effort, offering them freedom upon their discharge. Cleburne went on to write in his letter:

> As between the loss of independence and the loss of slavery, we assume that every patriot will freely give up the latter—give up the Negro slave rather than be a slave himself... It is said slavery is all we are fighting for, and if we give it up we give up all. Even if this were true, which we deny, slavery is not all our enemies are fighting for. It is merely the pretense to establish sectional superiority and a more centralized form of government, and to deprive us of our rights and liberties.

By late 1864, President Jefferson Davis was prepared to support abolishing slavery in all of the Confederate States in order to gain European diplomatic recognition and aid. His action clearly established that independence was far more important to the South than preserving slavery. Echoing Lee's sentiment, slavery would certainly have ended eventually for many diverse social, religious, and economic reasons, even if the War had not been fought or without the ensuing 13th Amendment to the Constitution. And the attitude of the South was far more disposed toward emancipation than that of the North.[13]

President Lincoln addressed slavery in his inaugural address

---

[13] The Amendments are styled, i.e., "Amendment I" in the original Constitution (*de jure*). All amendments of the original Constitution will be styled as such in this book (Amendments I through the original Amendment XIII). Amendments of the *de facto* Constitution will be styled as is more common in everyday usage; i.e., "14th Amendment," to distinguish between the amendments of the *de jure* and *de facto* Constitutions. The difference between the Constitutions will be discussed in detail in subsequent pages.

on March 4, 1861, making it clear he had no intention to change the status of slavery in the states where it existed, and that he had no constitutional authority to do so. Several years earlier, in his first debate with Stephen Douglas on August 21, 1858, he stated: ". . . I have no purpose, directly or indirectly, to interfere with the institution of slavery in the States where it exists. I believe I have no lawful right to do so, and I have no inclination to do so."

In 1861, among other efforts to "preserve" the Union, Congress proposed a Constitutional amendment guaranteeing the Southern States that slavery would never be abolished in exchange for a 40% tariff rate on imported goods.[14] The tariff, as will be shown later, was one of the main reasons the Southern States seceded. Lincoln wholeheartedly supported the measure. His response to the amendment was: "I understand a proposed amendment to the Constitution . . . has passed Congress, to the effect that the Federal Government shall never interfere with the domestic institutions of the States, including that of persons held to service . . . Holding such a provision to now be implied Constitutional law, I have no objection to its being made express and irrevocable."

The Confederate States, however, refused the offer. To the South, the issue was *not* slavery, but a crushing tax placed on them by the federal government without their consent, and the right to self-determination. It seems eerily reminiscent of Boston Harbor in December, 1773.

Exasperated, in a final attempt to avoid war, the Confederate States offered to free all of their slaves in exchange for a peaceful

---

[14] The proposed 13th Amendment, also known as the Corwin Amendment, was drafted at the urging of Abraham Lincoln after the 1860 presidential election in an attempt to reassure the Southern States that the incoming administration would not interfere with slavery. The Amendment was signed by outgoing President James Buchanan, the only proposed amendment to be signed by a president. In Lincoln's words: "Do the people of the South really entertain fears that a Republican administration would directly, or indirectly, interfere with their slaves, or with them, about their slaves? If they do, I wish to assure you, as once a friend, and still, I hope, not an enemy, that there is no cause for such fears. The South would be in no more danger in this respect than it was in the days of Washington." The proposed amendment was written in March 1861, the text of which avoided the use of the word "slavery," but stated: "No amendment shall be made to the Constitution which will authorize or give Congress the power to abolish or interfere within any state with the domestic institutions thereof, including that a person's held to labor or service by laws of said State." Only one state, Illinois, ratified the Amendment before the outbreak of war. Kentucky, Rhode Island, Ohio, and Maryland subsequently ratified it, although Ohio and Maryland later rescinded their ratifications.

separation. Clearly, independence and the right to self-determination were far more important to the emerging nation than slavery. This should not be surprising, considering that approximately 75% of Southerners did not own slaves.[15] Furthermore, the Confederate Constitution gave each state in the Confederacy the right to abolish slavery within their state, and permitted new states to be admitted as Free States.[16] But Lincoln would not agree to the South's offer. To him, the idea of the Southern States leaving the Union was unacceptable.

And finally, Congress later defeated a Constitutional amendment to abolish slavery, *after* all of the Southern representatives had left Congress to form their own nation. How could the Northern states possibly be fighting a war over slavery when they would not free their own, or when proposing a Constitutional amendment to ensure the perpetuity of slavery, and then defeating a Constitutional amendment to abolish it? Slavery obviously was not the primary motivating factor that led the South to secede. Nor was slavery the reason behind the North's invasion of the independent Southern States. Slavery was merely a cover-up for far more sinister motives.

The South saw no alternative but secession. They only wanted a peaceful separation. They were willing to give up slavery if bloodshed could be averted. And if Lincoln's primary motive for war was freeing the slaves, why would he not agree to the South's proposal? When asked why he would not let the South depart in peace, Lincoln tersely replied: "I can't let them go. Who would pay for the government? What then will become of my tariff?"[17]

With those words, Lincoln's motives began to surface. Money. Throughout all of history, money has been the source of much human suffering. The truth is the South provided the vast majority of the government's revenue. According to Senator Thomas Hart Benton:

---

[15] Niven, John, *The Coming of the Civil War: 1837-1861*, p. 34 (Harlan Davidson, Inc., Arlington Heights, IL, 1990). See also, the 1860 Census.
[16] McDonald, Forrest, *States' Rights and the Union*, p. 204 (University of Kansas Press, 2000)
[17] Abraham Lincoln to the Virginia compromise delegation (March 1861).

Chapter II From Sovereignty to Serfdom

> Under Federal Legislation, the exports of the South have been the basis of the Federal Revenue. Virginia, the two Carolina's, and Georgia may be said to defray three fourths of the annual expense of supporting the Federal Government; and of this great sum, annually furnished by them, nothing or next to nothing is returned to them, in the shape of government expenditures. That expenditure flows in the opposite direction—it flows North, in one uniform, uninterrupted and perennial stream. This is why wealth disappears from the South and rises up in the North. Federal legislation does this.

Thus, the web of deceit begins to unravel. Money, and the power that goes with it, is indeed the root of much evil and source of corruption.

On August 22, 1862, in a letter written to Horace Greeley, published in the *New York Tribune*, Lincoln acknowledged his primary purpose for the War:

> My paramount object in this struggle is to save the Union, and is not either to save or to destroy slavery. If I could save the Union without freeing any slave I would do it, and if I could save it by freeing all the slaves I would do it; and if I could save it by freeing some and leaving others alone I would also do that. What I do about slavery and the colored race I do because I believe it helps to save this Union. And what I forbear, I forbear because I do not believe it would help to save the Union.[18]

That statement unabashedly revealed Lincoln's motivation was the preservation of the Union, not slavery. However, in a much larger sense, the issue was slavery; or rather more aptly put, subjugation . . . the subjugation of the Southern States to an all-controlling federal government and the dictates of the Northern bankers.

---

[18] The letter was also printed in *Harper's Weekly*, p. 563 (September 6, 1862).

Finally, Congress itself dispelled any myth the War was fought over the issue of slavery. By Resolution passed July 23, 1861: "The War is waged by the government of the United States, not in the spirit of conquest or subjugation, nor for the purpose of overthrowing or interfering with the rights or institutions of the states, but to defend and protect the Union."

A War over slavery? No; not by any stretch of the imagination. And the depth of deceit will shatter perceptions and even the most skeptical of cynics as our sordid journey continues . . .

The true meaning of the term "free state" essentially meant "free from Blacks." Yes, the abolitionists wanted to see all slaves freed, but they and the majority of Northerners did not want to live with Blacks, slave or free. Many Northern states and territories passed laws prohibiting free Blacks from entering into them as far back as 1786. Alexis de Tocqueville,[19] in his highly acclaimed book, *Democracy in America* (1835), wrote:

> So the Negro [in the North] is free, but he cannot share the rights, pleasures, labors, griefs [sic], or even the tomb of him whose equal he has been declared; there is nowhere where he can meet him, neither in life nor in death . . . In the South, where slavery still exists, less trouble is taken to keep the Negro apart: they sometimes share the labors and the pleasures of the White men; people are prepared to mix with them to some extent; legislation is more harsh against them, but customs are more tolerant and gentle.

As an unbiased observer, French aristocrat, and visitor from France, he concluded in the book: ". . . race prejudice seems stronger in those states that have abolished slavery than in those where it still exists, and nowhere is it more intolerant than in those states

---

[19] Alexis de Tocqueville was a political free thinker and historian born into the French aristocracy. He came to the United States in 1831, and spent nine months traveling throughout the emerging nation, observing America's political and social systems. During his travels, he interviewed Americans from all walks of life, including the nation's presidents, settlers, politicians, bankers, and lawyers. He even met with Charles Carroll of Maryland, the sole surviving signer of the Declaration of Independence. He recorded his observations in *Democracy in America*, a highly acclaimed two-volume study of the American people and their social and political systems, written in 1835 and 1840.

where slavery was never known."

African American scholars John Franklin and Alfred Moss, wrote:

> There can be no doubt that many Blacks were sorely mistreated in the North and West. Observers like Fanny Kemble and Frederick L. Olmsted mentioned incidents in their writings. Kemble said of Northern Blacks, "They are not slaves indeed, but they are pariahs, debarred from every fellowship save with their own despised race . . . All hands are extended to thrust them out, all fingers point at their dusky skin, all tongues . . . have learned to turn the very name of their race into an insult and a reproach." Olmsted seems to have believed the Louisiana Black who told him that they could associate with Whites more freely in the South than in the North and that he preferred to live in the South because he was less likely to be insulted there.[20]

Lincoln shared the conviction of most Northerners of his time, and of many prominent statesmen before and after him, that Blacks could not be assimilated into White society. He rejected the notion of social equality of the races, and held to the view that Blacks should be resettled abroad. Lincoln was an avowed supporter of colonization. In his speech on the Dred Scott decision on June 26, 1857, he chastened both parties for not taking up the cause:

> I have said that the separation of the races is the only perfect preventative of amalgamation. I have no right to say all the members of the Republican Party are in favor of this, nor to say that as a party they are in favor of it. There is nothing in their platform directly on the subject. But I can say a very large proportion of its members are for it, and that the chief plank in their platform—opposition

---

[20] Franklin, John and Moss, Alfred, *From Slavery to Freedom: A History of African Americans*, p. 185 (Alfred A. Knopf, NY, 2000).

to the spread of slavery—is most favorable to that separation. Such separation, if ever effected at all, must be effected by colonization; and no political party, as such, is now doing anything directly for colonization. Party operations at present only favor or retard colonization incidentally. The enterprise is a difficult one . . .

Lincoln reiterated his position in a speech given in 1858, stating:

> I will say, then, that I am not nor ever have been in favor of bringing about in any way, the social and political equality of the White and Black races; that I am not nor ever have been in favor of making voters of the free negroes, or jurors, or qualifying them to hold office, or having them to marry White people. I will say in addition, that there is a physical difference between the White and Black races, which, I suppose, will forever forbid the two races living together upon terms of social and political equality, and inasmuch as they cannot so live, that while they do remain together, there must be the position of superior and inferior, that I as much as any other man am in favor of the superior position being assigned to the White man.[21]

As president, Lincoln supported projects to remove Blacks from the U.S. During a meeting with a group of Black leaders during the War, Lincoln stated the opinion of the Northern people, saying:

> There is unwillingness on the part of our people [Northern Whites] to live with you free colored people. Whether this is right or wrong, I am not prepared to discuss, but it is a fact with which we must deal . . . Your race suffers very

---

[21] Fehrenbacher, Don (ed), *Abraham Lincoln: Speeches and Writings 1832-1858*, p. 751 (The Library of America, NY, 1989).

CHAPTER II FROM SOVEREIGNTY TO SERFDOM

greatly, many of them, by living among us, while ours suffers from your presence. In a word, we suffer on each side. If this is admitted, it affords a reason, at least, why we should be separated. You here are freemen, I suppose? Perhaps you have been long free, or all your lives. Your race is suffering, in my judgment, the greatest wrong inflicted on any people. But even when you cease to be slaves, you are yet far removed from being placed on an equality with the White race. The aspiration of men is to enjoy equality with the best when free, but on this broad continent not a single man of your race is made the equal of a single man of our race . . . Therefore, I think it best for us to separate.[22]

Acting upon this sentiment, Abraham Lincoln and the U.S. Congress purchased land, passed laws, and set aside $600,000 for colonizing free Northern Blacks to the Caribbean basin and elsewhere. Some were shipped to poverty-stricken Haiti. A group of 400 were relocated to Liberia. Lincoln and Congress put together several other schemes to remove free Blacks from the U.S. Plans were discussed to send some to Central and South America, and other parts of Africa.[23]

An article entitled "The President's Plan" appeared in the September 6, 1862 edition of *Harper's Weekly*. The article read:

Senator Pomeroy, on behalf of the President, has issued an appeal to the colored population, inviting 500 of them to accompany him to Chiriqui, in New Granada, with a view to a permanent settlement there. The Senator assures them of the good-will and protection of the Government of New Granada, in which country Chiriqui is situated. He, like Mr. Lincoln, draws pleasing pictures of the prosperity which the exiles may enjoy in their new home, and earnestly

---

[22] Speech given by Lincoln to a group of Northern Black leaders at the White House (August 14, 1862).
[23] See, Magness, Phillip W. and Page, Sebastian N., *Colonization After Emancipation: Lincoln and the Movement for Black Resettlement* (University of Missouri Press, Columbia, MO, 2011)

urges them to give one more proof of their regard for the White man by getting out of his way.

The article went on to state:

That his scheme of colonization is impracticable and undesirable does not detract in the least from the honest good-will with which he urges it . . . With the President the question, as with all sensible men, is a practical one. What is the best thing to do under the circumstances? is what he asks. His reply is that, in view of the strong distaste of the dominant race in this country to the other, it is better that the latter should withdraw and settle elsewhere.[24]

At the end of the War, a few weeks before Lincoln was assassinated, Union General Benjamin Butler asked him what he was going to do with all the recently freed Southern Blacks. Lincoln replied: "I can hardly believe that the South and North can live in peace, unless we can get rid of the Negroes . . . I think we should deport them all."[25] This certainly brings into question Lincoln's true feelings regarding the slavery issue and civil rights. The enigmatic Lincoln was not "The Great Emancipator" history has portrayed him to be. Lincoln's legacy became that of "freeing the slaves," but it is a legacy obtained by subterfuge and obfuscation. He is perhaps the most mendacious president to hold the office right up to Barack Obama, his eloquent oratory tarnished by his minacious intentions.

A War over slavery? To even suggest so is the height of hypocrisy. And it is evident that the attitude of the South toward Blacks was far more compassionate and humanistic than that of the people of the North. Nothing is as it appears. The North has rewritten the history books to cover the darkness and shame of its own sin. And it has fabricated a scheming hero in a martyred president to champion its cause. Perhaps a more malicious and

---

[24] *Harper's Weekly*, p. 562 (September 6, 1862)
[25] Id. Magness, p. 109.

fallacious web has not been spun in the all the annals of history. As expressed by Jefferson Davis: "We are not fighting for slavery. We are fighting for independence . . . The assertion that the South fought for slavery is Yankee propaganda and a monstrous distortion." An unknown soldier in the Confederate Army is remembered as saying, "I was a soldier in Virginia in the campaigns of Lee and Jackson, and I declare I never met a Southern soldier who had drawn his sword to perpetuate slavery . . . What he had chiefly at heart was the preservation of the supreme and sacred right of self-government . . ." However, as Thomas Paine expressed over 200 years ago: "a long habit of not thinking a thing wrong, gives it a superficial appearance of being right, and raises at first a formidable outcry in defense of custom . . ."[26] Thus, the lie has been perpetuated as truth. But mere belief in a lie does not make it truth, only the perception of truth. And the tale becomes even more squalid as we travel further along our path.

The journey of intrigue continues with Myth No. 2, that the South was the aggressor. In reality, the North started the War. The North was the aggressor by invading the territory of a sovereign, independent nation, the Confederate States of America (CSA), as will be elucidated in the next Chapter.

And finally, Myth No. 3: The Southern States had no lawful right to secede, and the North was justified in taking military action. In fact, the Southern States seceded from the Union quite lawfully.

The Constitution for the united States of America does not have the "Perpetual Union" clause of the Articles of Confederation adopted in 1781. It was intentionally left out of the Constitution by the Founding Fathers. The Constitution is the document that formed the government of the collective States united and served as the national government charter. It provided the framework and served as the model for the individual state constitutions. According to the Constitution, any state was entitled to secede lawfully at any time.[27]

---

[26] Paine, Thomas, *Common Sense*, first published January 10, 1776, the most commonly reproduced edition is the third edition, published on February 14, 1776.
[27] See, Albert Taylor Bledsoe's *Is Davis a Traitor? Secession as a Constitutional Right Prior to the War of 1861* (Crown Rights, 1907).

The notion that secession was unconstitutional is blatantly preposterous; ludicrous to the point of absurdity.

To say the Southern States did not have the right to secede is to say the colonies did not have the right to separate from England. The principle of secession was clearly established with the Declaration of Independence, and our forefathers sought to preserve, in the Constitution, the sovereignty of the People over the state, the sovereignty of the states over the federal government, and the right of the People to change the form of government, if that government no longer served the Sovereignty of the People and the state. In Federalist No. 39, titled "The conformity of the Plan to Republican Principles," James Madison, the Father of the Constitution, succinctly defined the meaning of "the People," stating that the proposed Constitution would be subject to ratification by "the People," not as individuals composing one entire nation, but as composing the distinct and independent states to which they respectively belonged. The states were sovereign; the federal government was a creation, an agent, a servant of the states. In Madison's words, the Constitution was "the act of the people, as forming so many independent states, not as forming one aggregate nation." Madison, as the chief author of the Constitution, understood most acutely the intent of the Founding Fathers in forging the nation's charter. In later years, the U.S. Supreme Court (SCOTUS) reiterated Mr. Madison's purpose in stating: "[The Constitution] declares that it is ordained and established by the People of the United States. So far from saying that it is established by the governments of the several states, it does not even say that it is established by the people of the several states. But it pronounces that it was established by the people of the United States in the aggregate."[28]

The Declaration of Independence emphatically affirms the right of secession:

> When, in the course of human events, it becomes necessary for one people to *dissolve the political bands* which have connected them with another, and to assume among the

---

[28] *Downes v. Bidwell*, 182 U.S. 244 (1901).

CHAPTER II FROM SOVEREIGNTY TO SERFDOM

powers of the earth, the separate and equal station to which the laws of nature and of nature's God entitle them, a decent respect to the opinions of mankind requires that they should declare the causes which impel them to the separation. [Emphasis added]

And the Declaration continues: "But when a long train of abuses and usurpations, pursuing invariably the same object evinces a design to reduce them under absolute despotism, *it is their right, it is their duty, to throw off such government*, and to provide new guards for their future security." [Emphasis added]

The right of self-government and self-determination was a sacred principle to the Founding Fathers. The oppressive and despotic rule of the English monarchy was too deep and too recent a wound at the time the Constitution was forged. The states had sacrificed too much in their war for independence to relinquish what they considered an inviolable sacred right. Government only has the right to govern "with the consent of the governed."

Indeed, secession was the principle that led the colonies to rise up against England. It was a principle implicit in the 13 states ratifying the Constitution in 1789. And New York and Rhode Island *specifically reserved the right* to withdraw from the Union in their ratifying documents. Virginia ratified the Constitution by a slim margin (89-79). But they also passed a resolution that would allow them to secede if the national government became too tyrannical.[29] Secession was a principle that was unquestioned, understood to be available to any state at any time, right up to 1861. The philosophy of the Founding Fathers was that the nation was a *voluntary* union of sovereign states, each possessing as much right to depart from as they had to *voluntarily* join the Union of States. They saw no difference between the right of a state to secede and the right of the colonies to separate (or secede from) England.

During the Constitutional Convention, a proposal was made that would allow the federal government to quell any attempt by a

---

[29] Virginia Ratification Convention, Resolution: ". . . that the powers granted under the Constitution being derived from the People of the United States may be resumed by them whensoever the same shall be perverted to injury or oppression."

state to secede. James Madison tersely proclaimed: "A Union of States containing such an ingredient seemed to provide for its own destruction. The use of force against a State, would look more like a declaration of war, than an infliction of punishment, and would be considered by the Party attacked as a dissolution of all previous compacts by which it might be bound."[30] The Convention accepted Madison's proposal to not include the provision.

Thomas Jefferson, the author of the Declaration of Independence, in his First Inaugural Address in 1801, declared: "If there be any among us who would wish to dissolve this Union or to change its republican form, let them stand undisturbed as monuments of the safety with which error of opinion may be tolerated where reason is left free to combat it." Jefferson later wrote in a letter to William Crawford in 1816, that if a state wanted to leave the Union, he would not hesitate to say, "Let us separate." Alexis de Tocqueville, the French historian and political thinker, observed the principle of secession, expressing in his monumental work, *Democracy in America* (1835): "The Union was formed by the voluntary agreement of the States; and these, in uniting together, have not forfeited their Nationality, nor have they been reduced to the condition of one and the same people. If one of the States chose to withdraw its name from the contract, it would be difficult to disprove its right of doing so, and the Federal Government would have no means of maintaining its claims directly either by force or right."

SCOTUS completely agreed: "The people made the Constitution, and the people can unmake it. It is the creature of their own will, and lives only by their will."[31]

The early American constitutional scholar William Rawle understood the right of secession. He was a contemporary of Thomas Jefferson and James Madison, and frequently corresponded with these Founding Fathers. He was appointed by President George Washington as the first U.S. Attorney for Pennsylvania. In

---

[30] Vile, John R., *The Constitutional Convention of 1787*, p. 481 (ABC-CLIO, Inc., Santa Barbara, CA, 2005).

[31] *Cohens v. Virginia*, 19 U.S. (6 Wheaton) 264, 387 (1821).

supporting the right of secession, he stated: "It depends on the state itself to retain or abolish the principle of representation, because it depends on itself whether it will continue a member of the Union. To deny this right would be inconsistent with the principle on which all our political systems are founded, which is, that the people have in all cases, a right to determine how they will be governed. This right must be considered as an ingredient in the original composition of the general government, which, though not expressed, was mutually understood . . ."[32]

Another brilliant legal mind of the early Republic was George Tucker of Virginia. He, too, was a contemporary of Jefferson and Madison. He was a professor of law and moral philosophy at the University of Virginia and William and Mary College, and maintained a prominent law practice in Richmond, Virginia. He served in Congress from 1815 to 1819, served as Chief Justice of the Virginia Supreme Court, and had the reputation of being the "American Blackstone" of his time. His 1803 edition of *Blackstone's Commentaries*, which he annotated to American law, was widely used as a textbook in American law schools for many years. Regarding secession, Tucker wrote:

> The federal government, then, appears to be the organ through which the united republics communicate with foreign nations and with each other. Their submission to its operation is voluntary: its councils, its engagements, its authority are theirs, modified, and united. Its sovereignty is an emanation from theirs, not a flame by which they have been consumed, nor a vortex in which they are swallowed up. Each is still a perfect state, still sovereign, still independent, and still capable, should the situation require, to resume the exercise of its functions as such in the most unlimited extent.[33]

---

[32] Rawle, William, *A View of the Constitution of the United States*, Vol. 4, p. 571 (second edition, 1829). This book was used as a legal textbook at a number of prominent universities in early American history, including Harvard and Dartmouth.

[33] Tucker, George S., editor, *Blackstone's Commentaries: With Notes of Reference to the Constitution and Laws of the Federal Government of the United States*, Volume 1 (William Birch and Abraham Small, Philadelphia, PA, 1803, Appendix: Note D, Section 3: IV).

The Virginia Resolution, Alien and Sedition Acts, written by James Madison and adopted by the Virginia Senate on December 24, 1798, states:

> RESOLVED, That the General Assembly of Virginia, doth unequivocally express a firm resolution to maintain and defend the Constitution of the United States, and the Constitution of this State, against every aggression either foreign or domestic . . .
>
> That this Assembly doth explicitly and peremptorily declare, that it views the powers of the federal government, as resulting from the compact, to which the states are parties; as limited by the plain sense and intention of the instrument constituting the compact; as no further valid that they are authorized by the grants enumerated in that compact; and that in case of a deliberate, palpable, and dangerous exercise of other powers, not granted by the said compact, the states who are parties thereto, have the right, and are in duty bound, to interpose for arresting the progress of the evil, and for maintaining within their respective limits, the authorities, rights and liberties appertaining to them.[34]

Implicit in the Virginia Resolution is the principle of secession. The Resolution makes it clear that the federal powers are derived from the Constitution; and that the federal government is limited to the powers granted to it by the Constitution. This also infers that any powers not specifically granted to it are not valid. John Stewart, Keeper of the Rolls, in an address to the People accompanying the Virginia Resolution, declared:

> Encroachments springing from a government *whose organization cannot be maintained without the cooperation of the states*, furnish the strongest excitements upon the

---

[34] The Virginia Resolution and the Kentucky Resolutions (one passed on November 10, 1798 written by Thomas Jefferson, the other on December 3, 1799), opposed the federal Alien and Sedition Acts, which enlarged the powers of the federal government.

state legislatures to watchfulness, and impose upon them the strongest obligation to preserve unimpaired the line of partition. The acquiescence of the states, under infractions of the federal compact, would either beget a speedy consolidation, by precipitating the state governments into impotency and contempt, or prepare the way for a revolution, by a repetition of these infractions until the people are aroused to appear in the majesty of their strength. It is to avoid these calamities that we exhibit to the people the momentous question, whether the Constitution of the United States shall yield to a construction which defies every restraint, and overwhelms the best hopes of republicanism. [Emphasis added]

Mr. Stewart makes explicit which the Resolution states implicitly that "revolution" (secession) is the antidote to an oppressive federal government when it goes beyond the scope of its delegated powers.

Thomas Jefferson, in a draft of the Kentucky Resolution, wrote: ". . . that the several States composing the United States of America, are not united on the principle of unlimited submission to their general government . . . whensoever the general government assumes undelegated powers, its acts are unauthoritative, void, and of no force."

The Resolutions affirmed that if the federal government assumed powers beyond those delegated to it in the Constitution, its acts could be declared *null and void* by the states. He did not mean, however, that individual states have the right to nullify federal law, but that a state could take action by enlisting the support of other states, petitioning Congress to repeal the law in question, and introducing amendments to the Constitution in Congress.[35]

Talk of secession did not actually originate in the South.

---

[35] *Black's Law Dictionary* (sixth edition): "Nullity. Nothing; no proceeding; an act or proceeding in a cause which the opposite party may treat as though it had not taken place, or which has absolutely no legal force or effect." For information on the principle of nullification, see, Woods, Thomas E. Jr., *Nullification, How to Resist Federal Tyranny in the 21st Century* (Regnery Publishing, Washington, D.C., 2010).

Massachusetts and Connecticut threatened secession in 1804. In the years before and after the War of 1812, several New England states considered secession. Angered by President Jefferson's Embargo Act (1807) and the War, New England Federalists convened the Hartford Convention in 1814 to discuss separation from the Union. Many in the country viewed the Hartford Convention as a step toward secession by New England. No one at the Convention established any compelling argument that secession was unconstitutional. The fact that it might be unconstitutional was not even considered. The movement eventually faded, but not because the principle of secession was in question. In fact, there was virtually universal support at the time from both political parties and the People for the principle of secession and states' rights.

President Lincoln's opposition to secession was born of narcissistic arrogance . . . or ignorance. Perhaps both. But a long litany of founding documents, writings, and court cases clearly affirmed the right of any state to secede at will. And sentiment in the North was surprisingly supportive of the Southern State's right to secede. The thought of blood being spilled between fellow Americans, regardless of differences, was unfathomable.

Northern editorial opinion was strongly corroborative of the Southern cause and the principle of secession. Numerous newspapers vociferously spoke out against the voluntary Union being held together by force and violence. The *New-York Tribune*, in an article dated November 9, 1860, wrote:

> We hold, with Jefferson, to the inalienable right of communities to alter or abolish forms of government that have become oppressive or injurious; and if the Cotton States shall decide that they can do better out of the Union than in it, we insist on letting them go in peace. The right to secede may be a revolutionary right, but it exists nevertheless; and we do not see how one party can have a right to do what another party had a right to prevent. We must ever resist the asserted right of any state to remain in the Union and nullify or deny the laws thereof; to withdraw from the Union is quite another matter. And, whenever a

considerable section of our Union shall deliberately resolve to go out, we shall resist all coercive measures designed to keep her in. We hope never to live in a republic whereof one section is pinned to the residue by bayonets.

The taking up of arms was an unthinkable alternative.

An editorial appearing in *The Union* in Bangor, Maine, declared: "The difficulties between the North and the South must be compromised, or the separation of the States shall be peaceable. If the Republican party refuse to go to the full length of the Crittenden amendment—which is the very least the South can or ought to take—then, here in Maine, not a Democrat will be found who will raise his arm against his brethren of the South. From one end of the State to the other let the cry of the Democracy be, Compromise or Peaceable Separation."

The newspapers reflected the feelings of the majority of Americans, North and South. In the words of Michael Griffith:[36]

> It's probable that a majority of Americans opposed the use of force to hold the Union together . . . If the election had been held in 1862 and had included Southern citizens, Lincoln almost certainly would have lost the popular vote in a landslide. If Northern citizens had known in advance what Lincoln was going to do in response to secession, it's unlikely that he would have been elected in the first place. It should be remembered that when Lincoln won the 1860 election, he only received 39.9 percent of the popular vote. The conservative vote was split between three candidates, Stephen Douglas, John Breckinridge, and John Bell, each of whom, incidentally, later voiced opposition to using force to maintain the Union. Lincoln received about 1.9 million votes, while Douglas, Breckinridge, and Bell received about 2.8 million votes. However, Lincoln won the election because 122 of the 152 Electoral College votes

---

[36] Griffith, Michael T., "A Condensed Look at the Southern Side of the Civil War" (2004). Griffith is an author, Mormon apologist, Arabic and Hebrew scholar, and U.S. Air Force veteran.

that he needed for victory were concentrated in just six Northern states.[37]

Even Lysander Spooner,[38] perhaps the leading and most vocal abolitionist of his time, recognized the right of the Confederate States to secede. The Constitutional principle of government *by consent of the People* was rudimentary to his political philosophy. Spooner was very much a Jeffersonian in thought. Echoing two of the central principles of the Declaration of Independence, he adamantly argued that the right of the states to secede was no different than the natural right of slaves to be free. In Jefferson's words, ". . . all men are created equal, that they are endowed by their Creator with certain unalienable Rights," and "That whenever any Form of Government becomes destructive of these ends, it is the Right of the People to alter or to abolish it." He viewed with contempt the hypocrisy of the Republican Party of his day. Although he advocated the use of violence to abolish slavery, he "vociferously opposed the Civil War, arguing that it violated the right of the southern states to secede from a Union that no longer represented them."[39]

In 1861, after all attempts had been made to prevent the

---

[37] Actually, Lincoln could not lawfully occupy the office of president of the United States of America. As a member of the Bar, Lincoln was ineligible for the office pursuant to the original Amendment XIII to the Constitution for the united States of America. The fact that Lincoln was ineligible for office was one of the reasons that the Southern States walked out of Congress. The original Amendment XIII reads: "If any citizen of the United States shall accept, claim, receive, or retain any title of nobility or honour, or shall without the consent of Congress, accept and retain any present, pension, office, or emolument of any kind whatever, from any emperor, king, prince, or foreign power, such person shall cease to be a citizen of the United States, and shall be incapable of holding any office of trust or profit under them, or either of them." The Amendment was passed March 12, 1819, and its intent was to protect the *sovereignty* and *interests* of the People, and to force the elected representatives of the people to adhere strictly to their solemn and binding oath of office. It added an enforceable strict penalty, the inability to hold office and loss of citizenship, for violations of the already existing Constitutional prohibition in Article 1, Section 9, Clause 8 on titles of nobility in the *de jure* Constitution. The Bar (an international and American association of attorneys) is subject to the British Crown, and Bar attorneys have the title of "esquire." The Bar Association will be discussed in more detail in later chapters. This Amendment mysteriously disappeared in 1876; however, it is still the *law of the land* under the *de jure* Constitution.

[38] Lysander Spooner (1808-87) was an outspoken abolitionist, anarchist, author, and political philosopher. His 1845 book, *The Unconstitutionality of Slavery*, has been cited in several SCOTUS cases, most recently in 2009.

[39] From the introduction to the book, *Great Wars and Great Leaders: A Libertarian Rebuttal*, by Ralph Raico (Ludwig von Mises Institute, Auburn, AL, 2012).

CHAPTER II FROM SOVEREIGNTY TO SERFDOM

Southern States from leaving the Union, Congress debated and failed to pass a resolution that would have made secession unlawful. The law would have been unconstitutional even if it had passed. A Constitutional amendment would have been required for the law to be binding upon the sovereign states. The People *created* the Constitution, and *only* the People can *change* the Constitution.

Lincoln himself, prior to his preposterous rhetoric arguing against secession, declared that: ". . . any people anywhere . . . have the right to rise up and shake off the existing government and to form one that suits them better. This is a most valuable, a most *sacred right*—a right which we hope and believe is to liberate the world. Nor is this right confined to cases in which the whole people of an existing government may choose to exercise it. *Any portion of such people, that can, may revolutionize*, and make their own of so much of the territory as they inhabit."[40] [Emphasis added]

In his First Inaugural Address, he stated: "If, by the mere force of numbers, a majority should deprive a minority of any clearly written constitutional right, it might, in a moral point of view, justify revolution." His declaration characterized precisely the situation that the Southern States faced. However, in an egotistical effort to justify his position against secession, Lincoln continued: "But such is not our case. All the vital rights of minorities, and of individuals, are so plainly assured to them . . . in the Constitution that controversies never arise concerning them." How absurd. His statement exemplified his hypocrisy. The argument that the Southern States were not being deprived of their Constitutional rights was a vain, ludicrous attempt to rationalize his posture.

Lincoln also argued the right of a state to secede would destroy the Union, stating, secession was "a power to destroy the government itself." He reiterated this argument throughout his presidency. The argument, however, is sheer lunacy. The Union was not destroyed by secession, and would have remained intact

---

[40] January 1848 speech before Congress. [Author's note: Lincoln used the word "revolution," but there is a vast difference between "revolution" and "secession." "Revolution" is the overthrow, generally by force, of the existing government. "Secession" is the withdrawal or separation from the existing compact between the states. *Black's Law Dictionary* (sixth edition) p. 1351, defines secession as, "The act of withdrawing from membership in a group."]

regardless of the outcome of the War. And even if it hadn't, the sole purpose of the "Union" was for the benefit of the member sovereign states. The federal government's purpose was to serve the states, and if that government no longer fulfilled that purpose, there was no reason for its existence.

Those who argued against the right of secession, including Lincoln, point to the "perpetual union" clause in the Articles of Confederation and the clause in the preamble to the Constitution, "In order to form a more perfect Union . . ." They interpret the latter phrase to mean that the "perpetual union" clause was intended to be carried over to the Constitution from the Articles of Confederation. However, the government created by the Articles of Confederation was a mere league of states, a confederation, held together by agreement between the states. The argument that the provisions of the Articles of Confederation carried over to the U.S. Constitution is nonsensical. The writings of James Madison and other Founding Fathers clearly contradict this argument. The Constitution *replaced* the Articles of Confederation. The Founding Fathers viewed the Articles as a flawed document. The intent of the Constitution therefore was to replace the Articles with a document that more adequately addressed the safeguards of liberty and sovereignty, thus creating "a more perfect Union." A *more perfect Union* to them meant *preserving* the sovereignty of the states and the right of secession. The states themselves made this clear in their ratifying documents. And the actual intent of the "perpetual union" clause in the Articles is obscured by Article II, which states: "Each state retains its sovereignty, freedom and independence and every Power, Jurisdiction and right, which is not by this confederation expressly delegated to the United States, in Congress assembled." Article II of the Articles was the equivalent of and precursor to Amendment X of the Constitution, and stands contradictory to the "perpetual union" clause.[41]

As succinctly stated by Christopher Wellman in his book, *A Theory of Secession*: "Lincoln's arguments are preposterous." The author concludes that Lincoln's reasoning against secession was not

---

[41] See, Id. Bledsoe.

based on the Constitution, history, reason, or logic, but vanity, egotism, and his own personal conviction.[42] Lincoln's own statements confirm that he held the belief of the right of states to "revolt" [secede] if deprived of their "clearly written constitutional right." However, in but one blatant example of the hypocrisy that characterized his presidency, contrary to his own words and publicly stated belief, Lincoln declared the South's secession to be "treason" and "insurrection."

The principle of secession has its roots in the rights of a free and sovereign People . . . that when a government goes beyond its legitimate functions and abuses the rights of the People, the People have a duty, a moral obligation, to throw off such government. In the words of Clyde Wilson: "The right of self-government rests on the right to withdraw consent from an oppressive government. That is the only really effective restriction on power, in the last analysis."[43]

In summary, the Constitution does not prohibit the people of a state from voting to revoke their state's ratification of the Constitution. And it certainly does not give the federal government the power to force a state to remain in the Union against its will. This fact was acknowledged by President James Buchanan in a message to Congress shortly before Lincoln took office. Supported by Amendments IX and X,[44] a state has the legal right to peacefully withdraw from the Union at the volition of the People of that state. Lincoln exceeded his Constitutional authority and violated his oath

---

[42] See, *A Theory of Secession*, by pro-Union philosopher Christopher Heath Wellman (Cambridge University Press, 2005). See also, Gordon, David (ed.), *Secession, State and Liberty* (Transaction Publishers, 1998), a collection of 11 essays discussing secession. In an essay by James Ostrowski entitled "Was the Union Army's Invasion of the Confederate States a Lawful Act?" Ostrowski concludes, that "the purposes of the Constitution do not envision the use of armed force against a state that has concluded it is no longer benefiting from the union." He further supports the proposition that the Civil War and subsequent Constitutional amendments did not change underlying legalities that Amendments IX and X still protect the right to secede today. In another essay in the book ("When is Political Divorce Justified?") Steven Yates states, "Americans are morally justified in taking action to restore limited government, including, as a last resort, secession."

[43] Essay by Clyde Wilson, "Secession: The Last, Best Bulwark of Our Liberties," Gordon, Ibid.

[44] Amendments IX and X to the Constitution were to protect the People of the states from the national (federal) government. The text of the amendments: "Amendment IX: *The enumeration in the Constitution, of certain rights, shall not be construed to deny or disparage others retained by the people.* Amendment X: *The powers not delegated to the United States by the Constitution, nor prohibited by it to the States, are reserved to the States respectively, or to the people.*" [Emphasis added]

of office in his efforts to "preserve the Union." He accused the Southern States of treason. In reality, Lincoln was the one guilty of treason . . . treason against the Constitution that he had sworn an oath to uphold and defend. He knew the South had lawfully departed from the Union. His own words condemn him. He only denied the fact because he was fully cognizant that the federal government had no Constitutional authority to invade states that had peacefully and lawfully separated. Lincoln was a master at twisting the truth to suit his own purposes.

With that in mind, the term "Civil War" is a misnomer. The term connotes factions within a nation fighting for control of that nation's government. The South never attempted or intended to "overthrow" the government of the United States, or interfere in any way with the governments of the sovereign Northern States. The so-called "Civil War" was a war of aggression against the CSA. It was a war between two independent nations, each consisting of a distinct collection of sovereign states. A truer characterization of the war would be "The War Between the States," as it is sometimes referred to, or "The War for Southern Independence." Others prefer the moniker, "The War of Northern Aggression."

What began with purely peaceful intentions by the South quickly degenerated into a conflict of chaos. Southerners simply wanted to preserve their sovereignty under the *de jure* Constitution. The objective of the North, in particular the Northern bankers, was far more sinister than the people of the North or South could have imagined . . . the enslaving of an entire nation. The once proud sovereign American would soon be relegated to the status of a serf, unwittingly serving fealty to a new master. Through cunning, lies, deceit, and trickery, the federal government would become the new overseer of the plantation, enslaving both the White man and the Black man, stripping them of all dignity and unalienable rights. The road from sovereignty to serfdom was paved with the most mendacious of designs, at once the most brilliant yet malefic scheme ever devised and perpetrated on the peoples of a nation. How could this happen, less than 100 years from the founding of the Republic? The myths set forth in this chapter are just the beginning of the path to vassalage for the sovereign people.

Chapter III

"Preservation" of the Union and the Birth of Corporate Government

"The Union soldiers in that battle actually fought against self-determination; it was the Confederates who fought for the right of their people to govern themselves. What was the practical effect of the battle of Gettysburg? What else than the destruction of the old sovereignty of the States, i.e., of the people of the States? The Confederates went into battle free; they came out with their freedom subject to the supervision and veto of the rest of the country—and for nearly twenty years that veto was so effective that they enjoyed scarcely more liberty, in the political sense, than so many convicts in the penitentiary."
—Henry Louis Mencken, *Prejudices: Third Series* (1922)

*W*hy then, did the Southern States take the drastic action of seceding from the Union? There were two primary factors that led the Southern States to secede after the election of 1860. First, the Republican Party platform for 1860, controlled by the Northern bankers and capitalists, called for the U.S. government to tax the South, and only the South, deeply, in order to finance the industrialization of the North and the necessary transportation network to support that industrialization. The Northern capitalists were backed by powerful European banking interests, led by the House of Rothschild.[1] By the early 1800s, the Rothschild

---

[1] As early as the 1820s and early 1830s, the powerful European banking interests of the Rothschild family, originating with Mayer Amschel Rothschild (1744-1812), attempted to gain a foothold into the financial interests of the U.S. By the 1820s, they had gained control of the Bank of England. Through their agent Nicholas Biddle, the Rothschilds fought to defeat President Andrew Jackson's attempt to do away with a central bank of the U.S. The Rothschilds, however, were unsuccessful. In 1832, President Jackson vetoed congressional action to renew the charter of the Bank of the United States. The central bank went out of business in 1836. The Rothschilds nevertheless continued their efforts, and gradually

dynasty had taken control of the banks and money interests of Europe, and were turning their attention to the U.S. And second, the South believed strongly in the principle of State's rights. They feared the federal government usurping the sovereignty of the States and garnering more and more power unto itself. The loss of States' sovereignty would destroy the Founding Fathers' original intent in creating the Constitution at the cost of liberty.

In the years leading up to the War Between the States, the federal government received most of its revenue from tariffs (taxes) on imported goods. The Southern States imported most of the manufactured goods they used from England. The Northern States imported very little. Consequently, the South paid most of the taxes to support the federal government. In 1860, just four Southern States paid over 50% of the total tariffs collected by the federal government. The average tariff rate was 18.84%. The Republican Party platform called for increasing the tariff rate to 40% to ensure the continued industrialization of the North. Such a high tariff would have bankrupted many Southerners and destroyed the economy of the South. But elite Northern capitalists didn't care. Their hidden agenda was even more far reaching: to make the Southern States virtual pawns of the North and subjugate them under Northern control.[2]

What an ingenious scheme the Northern capitalists and bankers had concocted; industrialize the North at the expense of the South, which paid the majority of the taxes, rather than use their own money. The factories and plants they built with the South's tax money would be privately owned by the capitalists, generating millions in profits for the capitalists, with little investment on their

---

placed their agents in key positions in commerce and within the U.S. government. The backing of the Rothschild banking interests was largely responsible for the election of Abraham Lincoln for president in 1861. Lincoln was therefore beholden to the Rothschilds and the bankers, and promoted their interests throughout the War. To what extent Lincoln was a "puppet" of the bankers, or acting on his own beliefs, will probably never be known. The Rothschilds financially backed both sides in the War Between the States.

[2] The Morrill Tariff of 1861 was passed by Congress on March 2, 1861, during the administration of President James Buchanan. It was the 12th of 17 planks in the platform of the incoming Republican Party, which had not yet been inaugurated. The increased revenue from the Southern States would be used to promote rapid industrial growth in the Northern States. It was named after its sponsor, U.S. Representative Justin Smith Morrill of Vermont.

part. Further, the taxes paid by the Southern States would also pay for the infrastructure needed to support the industrialization, with no direct benefit to the South in return.

By gaining solid control over Congress in the election of 1860, the Republican Party would be able to use the federal government to enact and enforce their party platform, and thereby convert the prosperous Southern States into poor agricultural colonies of the Northern capitalists. With the trends in demographics, the Southern States, outnumbered in Congress, would have been powerless to reverse that process, and such policies would have subverted the intent of the Declaration of Independence and the Constitution for the united States of America. The Southern States would no longer be governed by the consent of the governed, but instead bullied mercilessly by a Northern majority. History has shown that the Republican Party from its inception in 1854, financed by the Northern bankers, intended to destroy the Constitution and dissolve the "Union," and only abandoned this agenda in favor of "preserving the Union" when its members perceived the wealth and power to be gained from the destruction and subjugation of a militarily weaker South.[3] The intent of the Northern capitalists was evident to the entire world, except, it seems, to the American people. As Charles Dickens, the noted English author, stated in 1862: "The Northern onslaught upon slavery was no more than a piece of specious humbug designed to conceal its desire for economic control of the Southern states."

With the Republican Party winning in the 1860 elections, the party had gained a strong majority in Congress and control over the federal government. It was evident that the Republican-controlled Congress would implement their platform. The Southern States felt that they had no choice but to secede in order to maintain their autonomy and voice in government. But secession took the North

---

[3] The goal of the international banking interests, led by the Rothschilds, was emphatically stated in *The Times* of London: "If that mischievous financial policy which had its origin in the North American Republic [i.e., honest, constitutionally authorized, no debt money] should become indurated down to a fixture, then that government will furnish its own money without cost. It will pay off its debts and be without a debt [to the international bankers]. It will become prosperous beyond precedent in the history of the civilized governments of the world. The brains and wealth of all countries will go to North America. That government must be destroyed or it will destroy every monarchy on the globe."

by surprise. The Southern States had been threatening to secede ever since the Northern-controlled Congress passed the Tariff of Abominations[4] in the days of John C. Calhoun,[5] and the North no longer took those threats seriously. They did not believe the Southern States would actually follow through on their threat. With the South no longer a part of the U.S., where would the funding to industrialize the North come from? Further, many Northern capitalists, who had been earning fortunes with the Southern cotton crop by transporting cotton and buying the cotton for New England textile mills, faced financial disaster. On the other hand, the South bought the majority of its manufactured goods from Britain. As a sovereign nation, the South could easily negotiate better deals with the English to supply the South with the goods and support services it needed. The Northern financiers would be left out. Suddenly, the plan of the Northern capitalists to take economic control over the Southern States and to subvert the Constitution had backfired.

Lincoln's Inaugural Address on March 4, 1861 amounted to no less than a declaration of war against the Southern States. It was filled with lies, innuendo, and spurious reasoning in an egotistical attempt to justify invading the independent Southern States. In the speech, Lincoln stated: "In your hands, my dissatisfied fellow countrymen, and not in mine, is the momentous issue of civil war. The government will not assail you, unless you first assail it. You can have no conflict, without being yourselves the aggressors. You have no oath registered in Heaven to destroy the government, while I shall have the most solemn one to 'preserve, protect and defend' it."

---

[4] The "Tariff of Abominations" was passed by Congress on May 19, 1828. It was designed to protect industry in the North, but forced the Southern States to pay higher prices on imported goods and made it more difficult for the British to pay for the cotton that they imported from the South. This eventually led to the Nullification Crisis in 1832. South Carolina in particular was affected by the tariff. This led to the state declaring that the federal Tariffs of 1828 and 1832 were unconstitutional, and therefore null and void within the sovereign boundaries of the state. Vice President John Calhoun of South Carolina was the leading proponent of the constitutional theory of state nullification.

[5] John C. Calhoun (1782-1850) was a staunch proponent of states' rights, limited government, and nullification, and led the opposition to the high tariffs proposed by the Northern bankers. He was a fervent defender of the Constitution at a time when the Republican Party was attempting to circumvent and destroy the Constitution. Calhoun served as vice president under Presidents John Quincy Adams and Andrew Jackson. He also served in the House of Representatives and as secretary of war under President James Monroe. After serving as vice president, he was elected to the Senate from South Carolina. Although he passed away in 1850, his beliefs were a strong influence on the Southern States' decision to secede from the Union.

Chapter III "Preservation" of the Union and the Birth of Corporate Government

Such was the preposterous tenor of the speech. The entire address is a carefully contrived effort to justify whatever Lincoln considered necessary to, in his words, "preserve, protect and defend" the Union. The ulterior motive, however, was to destroy the Constitution in favor of an all-powerful central federal government, usurping the sovereignty of the states.

It seems that ol' "Honest Abe" wasn't so honest after all. He was first and foremost a politician who would manipulate the truth to serve his own political purposes, and those of his party. The U.S. Congress, however, did not want war. Lincoln's generals recommended the immediate evacuation of Fort Sumter. To attempt to re-supply the fort by force would be a deliberate act of war against the CSA. Jefferson Davis sent a delegation to Washington to negotiate a treaty with the Lincoln administration. Lincoln refused to meet with them. Instead, Lincoln came up with a devious plan to re-supply Fort Sumter that would force the Confederates to fire the first shot, thereby giving the appearance the CSA started the war. Lincoln would then use this propaganda with the Northern media to win the support he needed. Congress, the military, and Lincoln's own cabinet vehemently opposed the plan. Secretary of State William Seward repeatedly assured the Confederacy that the fort would be evacuated, even after learning of Lincoln's plan. The commanding officer of the federal garrison at the fort, Major John Anderson, opposed Lincoln's plan. He did not want war, and he understood that Lincoln's attempt to resupply the fort would be viewed as a hostile act on the part of the North against the Confederacy.

But Lincoln was determined, and carried out his plan despite the opposition. Once shots were fired at Fort Sumter on April 12, Lincoln declared the act to be an act of aggression on the part of the South. In reality, Lincoln was the aggressor. The U.S. Navy, under his direct orders, had unlawfully invaded foreign, sovereign territory. Lincoln himself later admitted that he provoked the attack so that he could use it as justification for war.[6] And many Northern newspapers quickly recognized Lincoln's charade. The *Providence*

---

[6] Simkins, Francis Butler, *A History of the South*, pp. 213, 215-6 (third edition, Alfred A. Knopf, NY, 1963).

Daily Post reported on April 13, 1861: "For three weeks the [Lincoln] administration has been assuring us that Fort Sumter would be abandoned . . ." but, "Mr. Lincoln saw an opportunity to inaugurate civil war without appearing in the character of an aggressor." On April 16, 1861, an editorial in the *Buffalo Daily Courier* stated: "The affair at Fort Sumter . . . has been planned as a means by which the war feeling at the North should be intensified." The *New York Evening Day Book* wrote on April 17, 1861, that the event at Fort Sumter was "a cunningly devised scheme" contrived "to arouse, and, if possible, exasperate the northern people against the South." The *Jersey City American Standard* editorialized that "there is a madness and ruthlessness" in Lincoln's behavior, concluding that Lincoln's sending of ships to Charleston Harbor was "a pretext for letting loose the horrors of war."

Armed with the propaganda the South fired the first shots, and promulgating distorted facts, Lincoln unilaterally and unconstitutionally proclaimed war. He did not call a special session of Congress to ask for a declaration of war.[7] Congress would not have voted for war at the time. By his own proclamation, he set about preparing the Northern army to invade the CSA. By the time Congress was called into session several months later, the war had progressed to the point where Congress could not call it off.[8] No one had wanted war except for Lincoln, a few abolitionists, some Northern bankers and financiers whose livelihood was threatened, and, of course, the European banking interests of the Rothschilds. And few history books report the fact that Lincoln sent his army into six Northern States that took up arms against him when their governors refused to send state troops to invade the CSA. Those Northern States were within their Constitutional right to withhold the troops. This is but another blatant example of what had become an out-of-control federal government led by Lincoln subverting the intent of the Constitution and subjugating the states under its authority by force.

Little known and seldom recorded in America's history

---

[7] In fact, Congress convened *sine die* ("without fixing a day"; an adjournment without setting a date to reconvene) on March 27, 1861, and a lawful Congress could no longer be called into session. See, Chapter VIII for details.

[8] Congress at this point, having adjourned *sine die*, was no longer a Constitutional body.

books is Lincoln's socialist/Marxist connection leading up to and during the war. The Republican Party, formed in 1854, was socialist in nature, and the covert agenda of the party was the overthrow of U.S. Constitutional government. Lincoln supported the party platform. He also supported the Communist and socialist revolts in Europe in 1848. After those revolts failed, many European socialist leaders moved to the U.S. They repaid Lincoln's support for their socialist agenda by helping to get him elected president in 1860. As President, Lincoln appointed many of those socialist leaders as officers in the Union Army and to positions in the federal government. Lincoln's Assistant Secretary of War Charles A. Dana was a socialist who studied under Karl Marx in Europe. Dana remained a lifelong close friend of Marx and Engels. Marx frequently wrote of his support for the Republican Party and Lincoln's agenda. In fact, Marx coached Lincoln and Dana on how to abstrusely start the war, and make it appear as if the South was the initiator.[9]

The socialists, supported by Rothschild banking interests, worked aggressively for Lincoln's re-election in 1864. After Lincoln's second inaugural victory, Marx delivered a congratulatory letter in person to Lincoln on November 19, 1864, on behalf of the *International Workingmen's Association.* The letter expressed in no uncertain terms the allegiance of the communist and socialist community to the efforts of Lincoln. The last paragraph of the letter reads: "The workingmen of Europe feel sure that, as the American War of Independence initiated a new era of ascendancy for the middle class, so the American Antislavery War will do for the working classes. They consider it an earnest of the epoch to come that it fell to the lot of Abraham Lincoln, the single-minded son of the working class, to lead his country through the matchless struggle for the rescue of an enchained race and the reconstruction of a social world."

At the conclusion of the war, Marx stated in a speech: "And the successful close of the war against slavery has indeed inaugurated a new era in the annals of the working class . . . Still the Civil War

---

[9] Kennedy, Walter D. and Al Benson, *Red Republicans and Lincoln's Marxists: Marxism in the Civil War* (iUniverse, Lincoln, NE, 2007).

offered a compensation in the liberation of the slaves and the impulse which it thereby gave to your own class movement."[10]

In the eyes of Marx, the freeing of the slaves was not the coup d'état of the War Between the States, but the revolution of the working class against the proletariat.[11] Built on this foundation, it is little wonder that the 10 planks of *The Communist Manifesto* are in place in the U.S. today.[12]

Stephen Douglas summarized Lincoln's true intentions during the senatorial debates years before his presidency, accusing Lincoln of wanting to "impose on the nation a uniformity of local laws and institutions and a moral homogeneity dictated by the central government [that would] place at defiance the intentions of the republic's founders." Douglas was right. Lincoln accomplished his vision, albeit through lies, treachery, and deceit. But he accomplished that vision in a far more profound manner than Douglas could have envisioned. Douglas could not imagine or foresee the true socialist underpinnings of Lincoln's views.

Regarding the Emancipation Proclamation, Lincoln had ulterior motives. On September 22, 1862, Lincoln issued a preliminary proclamation that stated he would order the emancipation of all slaves in any state of the Confederacy that did not return to Union *control* by January 1, 1863. How audacious! His order presupposed the unconstitutional principle of the sovereignty of the federal

---

[10] Ibid.

[11] Other Republican socialist leaders included John C. Fremont, the first Republican presidential candidate, and Senator John Sherman, General William T. Sherman's brother. General Sherman himself was on a list of "approved communists." Horace Greeley, publisher of *The New York Tribune* was a committed communist. He later hired Lincoln's Assistant Secretary of War Charles A. Dana as an editor, and Karl Marx as a columnist.

[12] *The Communist Manifesto* was written in 1848 by Karl Marx (a.k.a. Moses Mordecai Levy, a Jew) and Friedrich Engels. Its purpose was to provide a blueprint to control and enslave nations by means of perpetual debt, while creating massive personal debt through materialism. The work was financed by Engels, a European elitist, to create a system that will enrich the bankers ("Global Elite") and enable the elitists to obtain world domination through a New World Order and One World Government. See, the 10 planks of *The Communist Manifesto* reprinted in Appendix A. Marx was an avowed Luciferian. The Luciferian philosophy is stated as "Adam and Eve were held prisoner in the bonds of ignorance by an unjust and vindictive God in the Garden of Eden. They were set free from their chains (Evolution through "Primordial Knowing") by Lucifer (Prometheus) through his agent Satan in the guise of a serpent (ancient symbol of Wisdom) with the gift of Intellect (Fire). Through the use of his intellect man will perfect the race (Anglo/Aryan) and will himself become God (promise of Satan to Adam and Eve)."

government over the states. It also ignored the fact that the CSA was then an independent nation. In reality, his action was purely a political move to entice the Southern States to return to the Union. But, as previously stated, the South had already offered to free all slaves in exchange for a peaceful separation. His proclamation fell on deaf ears. The CSA was an independent nation, and deemed the proclamation as having no force or effect upon them. And to underscore Lincoln's hypocrisy and obscure motives, on September 22, 1862, after issuing the preliminary proclamation, he stated the real reason for the proclamation:

> I have urged the colonization of the Negroes, and I shall continue. My Emancipation Proclamation was linked with this plan. There is no room for two distinct races of White men in America, much less for two distinct races of Whites and Blacks. I can conceive of no greater calamity than the assimilation of the Negro into our social and political life as our equal . . . We can never attain the ideal union our fathers dreamed, with millions of an alien, inferior race among us, whose assimilation is neither possible nor desirable.[13]

His goal was to free the slaves, only so they could be colonized.

When the Proclamation was issued on January 1, Lincoln's hope was that the declaration would incite the Southern slaves to rise up against their masters, destroying the CSA from within. And, while some slaves did leave the plantations after hearing of the Emancipation Proclamation, the majority chose to stay. The mass uprising and exodus of slaves from the plantations did not materialize as Lincoln had envisioned. But Lincoln's motive was

---

[13] Basler, Roy P., ed., *Collected Works of Abraham Lincoln*, Volume 5, pp. 371-5 (from an address delivered at Washington, D.C.). See also, General Sherman's Special Field Order No. 15, issued in January 1865. In this order, freed Black slaves were given exclusive rights to, and use of, a number of islands and parts of the coastal region of South Carolina and Georgia. This effectively created mini-Black homelands within the borders of the U.S. as a preliminary step to their repatriation. Lincoln's efforts to remove all Blacks from America was ended by his assassination on April 14, 1865.

not about freeing the slaves, rather a political ploy in his quest to restore the Union. Lincoln admitted in a letter to Treasury Secretary Salmon P. Chase: "The original proclamation has no . . . legal justification, except as a military measure." Secretary of State William Seward sarcastically stated: "We show our sympathy with slavery by emancipating slaves where we cannot reach them and holding them in bondage where we can set them free." And Lincoln himself stated: "I view the matter [Emancipation Proclamation] as a practical war measure, to be decided upon according to the advantages or disadvantages it may offer to the suppression of the rebellion."[14]

The Proclamation was, however, a political stroke of genius. With one stroke of his pen, Lincoln deflected the issues of the war away from state's rights, taxes, sovereignty, and the preservation of the Constitution, to a war to end slavery. With a single stroke of his pen, Lincoln established his "legacy" as the president who "freed" the slaves. A legacy, however, obtained by deceit and with minacious ulterior motives.

Lincoln's stated purpose was the "preservation of the Union." But just what did Lincoln mean by "Union"? His vision was not that of the Founding Fathers or embodied in the Constitution. Lincoln was an adherent to the political philosophy of Alexander Hamilton, who passed the torch of his philosophy to Henry Clay. Clay was Lincoln's self-professed idol and role model, describing Clay as "my ideal of a great man." His vision, supported by the Northern bankers and adopted from Clay's model known as "The American System," was one of an all-powerful central government that would obfuscate the autonomy of the States and subvert the freedom of the People.[15] Lincoln's motive was cloaked in deceitful rhetoric of "emancipation," "freedom," "liberty," and ". . . the proposition that all men are created equal." Americans have been gulled into believing the Big Lie. Nothing is as it appears. As Adolf

---

[14] Ibid. Volume 5, p. 421.
[15] Lincoln's support of a strong central government was strongly backed by the international bankers, headed by the Rothschilds of England and Germany. At least to an extent, the Rothschilds dictated Lincoln's actions and policies. Without the backing of the banking cartel, Lincoln would not have been elected president to either of his terms.

Chapter III "Preservation" of the Union and the Birth of Corporate Government

Hitler claimed: "The Big Lie is a major untruth uttered frequently by leaders as a means of duping and controlling the constituency."

The Gettysburg Address perhaps exemplifies most vividly the Big Lie that Lincoln portrayed. The words were eloquent, poetic, embodying the sacred principles upon which our nation was founded, a magnificent work of oratory. But in light of the truth of his beliefs and actions, the words ring hollow, empty, echoing sordidly among the halls of shame. Had they been spoken by even the humblest of Southerners, the words would have sounded their brilliance to the highest of mountaintops and the lowest depths of the seas, a clarion call to free men everywhere. But out of the mendacious mouth of the enigmatic Lincoln, they are a clanging cymbal, dissonant brass, more putrid than the incessant braying of an agitated donkey. Lincoln's own words and actions expose the lie. Poignantly expressed by journalist and writer H.L. Mencken:

> The Gettysburg speech was at once the shortest and the most famous oration in American history . . . It is eloquence brought to a pellucid and almost gem-like perfection—the highest emotion reduced to a few poetical phrases. Lincoln himself never even remotely approached it. It is genuinely stupendous. But let us not forget that it is poetry, not logic; beauty, not sense. Think of the argument in it. Put it into the cold words of everyday. The doctrine is simply this: that the Union soldiers who died at Gettysburg sacrificed their lives to the cause of self-determination—that government of the people, by the people, for the people, should not perish from the earth. It is difficult to imagine anything more untrue. The Union soldiers in the battle actually fought against self-determination; it was the Confederates who fought for the right of their people to govern themselves.[16]

Lincoln's rhetoric was lofty, but masked the treachery of his

---

[16] Mencken, H.L., "Five Men at Random," *Prejudices: Third Series*, pp. 171-6 (1922). First printed, in part, in the *Smart Set*, p. 141 (May 1920).

presidency. His words were a mockery of the Founding Fathers. He nobly quoted from the Declaration of Independence, that "all men are created equal . . .", but ignored the words following; words which were far more appropriate for the time: ". . . Governments are instituted among Men, deriving their just powers from the consent of the governed, That whenever any Form of Government becomes destructive of these ends, *it is the Right of the People to alter or to abolish it, and to institute new Government.*" [Emphasis added]

He ended the speech with: ". . . that the nation, shall have a new birth of freedom—and that government of the people, by the people, for the people, shall not perish from the earth." Hypocrite. Government "of the people, by the people, for the people" ceased to exist. Lincoln destroyed the Republic. His presidency enslaved the nation. The States were rendered powerless. Amendments IX and X muted; the *de jure* Constitution rendered voiceless.

Colonel William C. Oates, CSA, expressed in 1905:

> President Lincoln's great oration on the field of Gettysburg at the dedication in November, 1863, proceeded entirely on the erroneous hypothesis that the life of the nation was at stake. A proper analysis of his speech was that if the Confederates succeeded that the nation was destroyed —that it would prove not only that American Government was a failure, but would accomplish its destruction as well. He assumed that if the South was divorced from the North it would prove the death of each. How fallacious and deceptive. The secession of a part of the states did not, could not, and never did put the life of the nation in jeopardy. In all his letters and messages he asserted that the life of the nation was at issue, when no one knew better than he that the seceding States united in a Confederacy sought peaceable separation and were anxious to treat with the Union still composed of twenty-one States. He considered a slump in a body of one-third of the states of which the Union was composed would kill the Union, or the nation, as he called it, which would still after the secession have been composed of twenty-one of the most wealthy and

populous States. The assumption that the Confederates sought the destruction of the Union was preposterous.[17]

Yes, our history books have propagated a Big Lie. Nothing is as it appears. Renowned CSA Colonel Richard Henry Lee lamented:

> It is stated in books and papers that Southern children read and study that all the blood shedding and destruction of property of that conflict was because the South rebelled without cause against the best government the world ever saw; that although Southern soldiers were heroes in the field, skillfully massed and led, they and their leaders were rebels and traitors who fought to overthrow the Union, and to preserve human slavery, and that their defeat was necessary for free government and the welfare of the human family. As a Confederate soldier and as a citizen of Virginia, I deny the charge, and denounce it as a calumny. We were not rebels; we did not fight to perpetuate human slavery, but for our rights and privileges under a government established over us by our fathers and in defense of our homes.

Adolf Hitler had it right when he noted: "If a lie is large enough, everyone will believe it." And George Orwell proclaimed in 1949: "Who controls the past controls the future, who controls the present controls the past."[18]

The truth is that the hidden agenda of the abolitionist movement in 1860, spearheaded by the bankers, was to destroy Constitutional government and to substitute an anarchical egalitarianism that would make *every* American a subject of the central federal government. Northern abolitionists such as William Lloyd Garrison burned the Constitution in the streets, calling it "a pact with the devil." Rather than freeing the Southern slaves, the elite and the

---

[17] Oates, Colonel William C., *The War Between the Union and the Confederacy* (1905).
[18] Orwell, George, *1984* (Secker & Warburg, London, 1949). The "Big Lie" has also been perpetuated through federal government control of education and the corresponding control over the curriculum and the materials used in the educational system.

abolitionists sought to enslave *all* Americans. While the people of the North seemed oblivious (or uncaring) of Lincoln's true objectives, the agenda was blatantly apparent to the people of the South. In but one example, in "An Address to the People of Texas," delivered on March 30, 1861, the Representatives of Texas warned that, under the pretense of freeing the slaves, "the actual intention of the incoming Lincoln administration was to enslave a whole nation," an ominous and prophetical warning that was fulfilled at the end of the War, not necessarily by Lincoln alone, but by a treasonous Congress.

Lincoln, backed by the socialists and Northern bankers, was no small part of that movement. And it seems he would stop at nothing to achieve his agenda. However, prior to his untimely death at the hands of the bankers, Lincoln admitted his sin: "In saving the Union, I have destroyed the Republic. Before me I have the Confederacy which I loathe. But behind me I have the bankers which I fear."[19]

And fear them he should. There is credible information that Lincoln was assassinated by the bankers as a result of his economic and monetary policies toward the end of the War. As president, Lincoln accomplished many of the banker's objectives as set forth by the Rothschild cabal. He created a strong central government and reinstituted a national banking system; a national currency based on indebtedness through a national bank; nationalized the railroads; enacted the first income tax; and instituted the first military draft. By the end of his presidency, the U.S. little resembled the Constitutional Republic of the Founding Fathers. Not surprising, in that Lincoln ruled more as dictator than Constitutional president.

However, Lincoln's support of a national bank was less than enthusiastic. After the War, he planned to restore Constitutional government in the Southern States by admitting their representatives back into Congress forthwith, along with a mild Reconstruction policy that would quickly re-establish agricultural production in the South. The bankers, led by the Rothschilds of England, wanted a strict and harsh Reconstruction policy with the resulting high

---

[19] Comment on the National Banking Act (February 1863).

commodity prices and profits to the bankers. Lincoln suddenly posed a threat to their agenda, resulting in his assassination. The goal of the bankers was to weaken the U.S. so Rothschild banking interests could take over its economy.[20]

In the words of Michael Griffith:

> Most Republican leaders, while claiming they were "saving" the Union and preserving representative government, were undemocratic and despotic . . . The Republicans and their generals [*under Lincoln's orders*] imprisoned thousands of Northern citizens in order to suppress Northern opposition to the War. They shut down hundreds of Northern newspapers and jailed dozens of newspaper editors for expressing "unpatriotic" views. They suspended the writ of habeas corpus (protection against unlawful arrest), rigged elections, prevented two Northern legislatures from convening, and branded as "traitors" Northern political opponents who spoke out against Republican violations of civil rights. In one case, they arrested thirty-one members of the Maryland legislature and sealed off the town where the legislature was meeting. When it became known that former president Franklin Pierce believed the War was cruel and unnecessary, Republicans accused him of treason and nearly had him arrested. Pierce feared the true purpose of the War was to wipe out the states as sovereign entities and to drastically increase the power of the federal government in violation of the Constitution. Pierce also believed it was wrong to hold the Union together by force.[21]

These reprehensible acts were spearheaded by none other than Lincoln himself. Pierce's fears were justifiably prophetic.

---

[20] This is essentially the same reason President John F. Kennedy was assassinated. Kennedy attempted to restore the gold standard to the dollar and intended to eliminate the Federal Reserve System. John Wilkes Booth was framed as a hired gun in the Lincoln assassination, in the same manner that Lee Harvey Oswald was blamed for the JFK assassination. See, "The Rothschild's International Plot to Kill Lincoln," by Paul Goldstein (*New Solidarity*, October 29, 1976).
[21] Id. Griffith.

Lincoln was the first president to audaciously and deliberately violate his oath of office to preserve, protect and defend the Constitution for the united States. Lincoln's unabashed disregard and contempt for the Constitution was so egregious as to be unthinkable in the context of liberty. He violated nearly every article and amendment in the Constitution. He unilaterally declared War on the CSA without the approval of Congress. As stated by Michael Griffith above, he threw many Northern citizens, including state legislators, who stood in opposition to his agenda, into prison as political prisoners, without cause, due process or trial. He suspended habeas corpus. He suspended or canceled state elections, without authority. He closed numerous opposition newspapers and suppressed freedom of speech. In the words of Chuck Baldwin: "In order to 'preserve the union,' Lincoln destroyed the very principles upon which the union was created. His audacity is without equal. Of course, he was more than willing to sacrifice hundreds of thousands of America's finest and best to destroy Thomas Jefferson's declaration that the states of our union are 'free and independent states.' . . . In the name of emancipating slaves, Lincoln enslaved an entire nation. It was Lincoln who, for all intents and purposes, destroyed federalism and limited government in America."[22]

Lincoln was not the man history has portrayed him to be. His own words and actions betray the myth. In spite of his eloquent speeches and noble rhetoric, Lincoln was not a friend of the People or a champion of liberty. Instead, he surreptitiously ensured the perpetual slavery of those slaves thought to be freed, subjecting them to a new master in the federal government, and relegated the People to the same subject status as the former slaves. By the end of the War, the "land of the free" had become the land of the "subject."[23]

Yes, Lincoln destroyed the Republic. The eyes of the entire world were on the events unfolding in America during the War. The

---

[22] Chuck Baldwin is an American politician and founder-pastor of Crossroads Baptist Church in Pensacola, Florida. He was the nominee of the Constitution Party for U.S. vice president in 2004, and its nominee for president in 2008. The quote is from an article he wrote in August 2009.
[23] See, the 14th Amendment to the U.S. Constitution, allegedly passed by Congress on June 13, 1866, which will be discussed in detail in Chapter VIII.

CHAPTER III "PRESERVATION" OF THE UNION AND THE BIRTH OF CORPORATE GOVERNMENT

loss of liberty as a consequence of the War was seemingly evident to all but the People of America. On December 15, 1866, renowned British historian Lord Acton wrote a letter to General Robert E. Lee. In his letter, Acton said: "I deemed that you were fighting the battles of our liberty, our progress and our civilization; and I mourn for the stake which was lost at Richmond more deeply than I rejoice over that which was saved at Waterloo."

Indeed, Lincoln laid the cornerstone of an era of big corporate government. His goal was "preservation of the union"; his hidden agenda, at the bidding of the international banking cartel led by the Rothschilds, was the subjugation of the People and the states to the federal government. He was the architect of the movement toward the fascist police state that exists today. Beneath the euphoric ideals lies a pungent, sinister motive. In the words of Thomas DiLorenzo: "The real Lincoln was a dictator and a tyrant who shredded the Constitution, fiendishly orchestrated the mass murder of hundreds of thousands of fellow citizens, and did it all for the economic benefit of the special interests who funded the Republican Party and his own political career."[24]

As expressed by Michael Andrew Grissom, in the foreword to Jerry Brewer's *Dismantling the Republic*:[25]

> What passes for American history today, especially as it pertains to the type of government under which we are now constrained to live, is largely a collection of myths, fables, and legends, which have incrementally supplanted the truth until legend has become the new truth.
>
> Few people . . . realize that the republic which was founded in the last few years of the 18th century no longer exists. Nearly everyone today fervently believes that it is still intact, though perhaps battered by the winds of liberalism and its inevitable heir, socialism. Even the popular new movement called the Tea Party, welcome as it is, clings to

---

[24] See, Fallon, Joseph, *Lincoln Uncensored* (eBook). The book explains the real Lincoln in Lincoln's own words by quoting him directly from *The Collected Works of Abraham Lincoln*, with specific citations for each quotation. No interpretation necessary; just read Lincoln's own words.
[25] From the foreword to Brewer, Jerry C., *Dismantling the Republic* (2010).

the idea that the republic is still with us and is only in need of some fine-tuning. Its well-intentioned leaders and faithful followers, for all their enviable enthusiasm, do not understand that genuine freedom of person and individual liberty, which were commonly held tenets of independence during and immediately following the American Revolution, but which have succumbed to two centuries of political and governmental abuse, cannot be reclaimed simply by lowering taxes, electing Republicans, and fatuously awaiting the ascension to the Presidency of some personality who might—just might—someday appoint a decent, respectable, honest, constitutionalist to the Supreme Court . . .

Perhaps the best example of myth and fable is the carefully managed cult figure of Abraham Lincoln. Father Abraham. Not only was Lincoln a scoundrel of the lowest order, admired by many modern day charlatans, among them Bill Clinton and Obama, he was directly responsible for the deaths of several hundred thousand Southerners, not to mention thousands of Northern soldiers ordered into battle against the South. Yet, the politically correct line, parroted by every school child that goes through twelve years of government schools, is that "Lincoln saved the Union," when in reality, it was Lincoln who destroyed the Union. His mere election caused seven states to withdraw, and his call for volunteers to invade those seven states made four other states—and eventually, parts of two others—to secede. Shot on Good Friday, dying on Easter weekend, just after he had "saved" the Union, gave his cultists the precise propaganda they needed to make him into a Christ figure . . . Legend replacing truth.

And so it is with the state of the republic . . . we have arrived at a government that has metamorphosed into something that abuses citizens at home and destroys civilizations abroad. Whatever it is, it is not the republic our Revolutionary patriots gave us, nor what they envisioned. Try as they might to believe the framework of a republic still exists, neo-conservatives and Tea Party activists are deluded. It drew its last breath in 1865, and no amount of rearranging personalities in Congress will bring it back to life . . .

Would Thomas Jefferson or Patrick Henry recognize this thing we still call a republic? To ask is to answer. The old republic is gone. No matter how many symbols we revere, how many parades we conduct, and how many firecrackers we pop on the Fourth of July, we are merely presiding over a corpse. The sooner Americans realize that the better.

And Jerry Brewer, in the author's preface to his magnificent work, writes:

Constitutional government in America ended April 9, 1865. It ended four years earlier in the United States with Abraham Lincoln's ascension to the presidency. Within a year of his inauguration, he effectively eliminated Constitutional rights. He suspended the writ of habeas corpus and imprisoned and deported an Ohio Congressman without warrant or due process. He censored telegraphic communications, stopped circulation of newspapers that criticized his autocratic rule and imprisoned many of their editors. He deprived states of representative government, and unilaterally waged war without the consent of Congress by blockading Southern ports and calling for 75,000 volunteers to invade the sovereign States of the South.

The last bulwark of State sovereignty and Constitutional rights in North America, the Confederate States, ceased to exist when Lee surrendered at Appomattox. From that day forward, the Republic of Jefferson, Madison, Mason and Franklin was to be no more. Henceforth, the federal government that was created by sovereign States to be their agent would become their master. All that remained was for the new order of government to dismantle the Republics remnants.

Individual rights, expressed in State sovereignty, undergirded the Republic. The declaration of those rights by American Colonists in 1776 culminated a centuries-long struggle for recognition of individual sovereignty dating back to the *Magna Carta*. As Thomas Jefferson expressed it, all men are "endowed by their Creator with certain inalienable rights. Among those are life, liberty, and the pursuit of happiness," and when government fails to protect those rights it is the right of the people to "alter or abolish" that government . . .[26]

No, the South did not start the War or want war. The people of the South hoped and prayed fervently for a peaceful secession.[27] They simply wanted to be left alone to govern themselves as an independent nation. In the poignant words of CSA General Patrick Cleburne:

> I am with the South in life or death, in victory or defeat. I believe the North is about to wage a brutal and unholy war on a people who have done them no wrong, in violation of the Constitution and the fundamental principles of government. They no longer acknowledge that all government derives its validity from the consent of the governed. They are about to invade our peaceful homes, destroy our property, and murder our men and dishonor our women. We propose no invasion of the North, no attack on them, and only ask to be left alone.[28]

By seceding, the Southern States were exercising their Constitutional and God-given right, so eloquently stated in the Declaration of Independence:

---

[26] Id. Brewer
[27] See, Goode, June B., *Our War: An Account of the Civil War in Bedford, Virginia* (Warwick House Publishing, Lynchburg, VA, 2003). In the book, Goode reprints in its entirety the diary of Letitia (Lettie) McCreary Burwell, the daughter of William McCreary Burwell and Frances Steptoe Burwell of Avenel Plantation in the town of Liberty (Bedford, VA). Lettie was about 25-years-old when the War began. She was an intelligent and articulate woman, and her journal vividly portrays a picture of the people and life in Liberty during the first months of the War. Her diary paints a refreshingly human characterization of the times from the perspective of the Southerner. See, excerpts from the diary of Lettie Burwell in Appendix B.
[28] May 7, 1861 letter to his brother, Robert, from Camp Rector.

CHAPTER III "PRESERVATION" OF THE UNION AND THE BIRTH OF CORPORATE GOVERNMENT

> We hold these truths to be self-evident, that all men are created equal, that they are endowed by their Creator with certain unalienable Rights, that among these are Life, Liberty and the pursuit of Happiness. That to secure these rights, Governments are instituted among Men, deriving their just powers from the consent of the governed, That whenever any Form of Government becomes destructive of these ends, it is the Right of the People to alter or to abolish it, and to institute new Government, laying its foundation on such principles and organizing its powers in such form, as to them shall seem most likely to effect their Safety and Happiness.

It should also be noted that the Southern States took the Constitution for the united States of America with them to form the basis for the Constitution for the Confederate States. In seceding, the South embodied the principles and ideals of the Founding Fathers set forth in the U.S. Constitution.

In summary, the War started over the issues of liberty, states' rights, the right to self-determination, the rights of the People as sovereign, the preservation of Constitutional government, and taxes (there's that old 1776 theme again). The South wanted to maintain the sovereignty of the People and independence. They wanted less government, less taxes, and the right of the states to make decisions at the local level, according to the *de jure* Constitution for the united States of America. Lincoln, supported by the bankers in the North, wanted more taxes, more government, and decisions made in Washington, D.C. by a strong central government, even if it meant usurping the Constitution and achieving their purpose with bloodshed.[29]

It is ironic that the Confederate flag has today become a symbol of hate, bigotry, and racism, when in reality, the principles

---

[29] For a much more thorough presentation and supporting documentation of the foregoing, see, John S. Tilley's *Lincoln Takes Command* (Bill Coats Limited, 1991), and Ludwell H. Johnson III's *North Against South: The American Iliad 1848-1877* (second edition, The Foundation for American Education, 1995). These books and Albert Taylor Bledsoe's book mentioned previously, are widely available and are excellent sources that document and present the facts succinctly and truthfully.

69

that it represents are those of our Founding Fathers which are established in the Declaration of Independence and the *de jure* Constitution. The flag is a symbol of individual liberty, states' rights, and limited government. Historically, its emblems symbolize Christianity and the heritage of the Celtic race.

The centerpiece of the Confederate flag is St. Andrew's cross, a cross in the form of an "X." St. Andrew was the first disciple of Jesus Christ and the brother of Simon Peter. He died a martyr, crucified on an X-shaped cross at his request, considering himself not worthy to be crucified on the same cross as Jesus. St. Andrew is the patron saint of Russia and Scotland. The Confederate flag was based upon the national flag of Scotland, and the layout is similar to the flag of Great Britain. St. Andrew's cross is further known as a *saltire*, a heraldic symbol representing independence, and freedom from oppression and tyranny. The CSA carefully and deliberately chose the design of the flag to represent the principles they believed sacred; the same principles which forged the birth of the nation in 1776; principles they fervently believed worth the blood that their fight for independence would incur.

St. Andrew's cross is also the Greek letter *chia*, which has been used for 2,000 years to represent Jesus. The motto of the Confederacy, *Deo Vindice* ("under God, our vindicator"),[30] affirms the belief of the people of the South in a Sovereign and Righteous God. This belief was overtly acknowledged in the Confederate Constitution.[31] Pastor John Weaver, in a series of sermons delivered in churches nationwide, aptly expressed: ". . . the Confederate Battle Flag represents liberty and freedom and independence from tyranny. The Confederate Flag represents truth against error, freedom against tyranny, light against darkness and the Kingdom of Christ against the Kingdom of Governance."[32]

---

[30] Or "God our defender, protector."

[31] The preamble to the Confederate Constitution states: "When the people of the Confederate States, each state acting in its sovereign and independent character, in order to form a permanent federal government, establish justice, insure domestic tranquility and secure the blessings of liberty to ourselves and our posterity invoking the favor and guidance of almighty God, do ordain and establish this constitution for the Confederate States of America."

[32] From a sermon delivered by Pastor John Weaver entitled, "The Truth about the Confederate Battle Flag" (*confederateamericanpride.com/battleflag*). Pastor Weaver has been in the ministry for more than

The tragic truth is the Confederate flag represents far more the principles of the Republic and our Founding Fathers than the American flag under the current rogue regime in Washington. In particular, the gold-fringed American flag on display in churches and courtrooms throughout the land has become the quintessential symbol of the ever-expanding tyranny of an imposter government. Rather than vilify, people should venerate the Confederate flag as a symbol of what the nation has lost, and pray fervently for the day when the "Stars and Stripes" will once again fly proudly over the Republic of our Founding Fathers.

Yes, the CSA lost the war. But the People lost much more than a war. The South entered the war so-called "slave" states; they exited the war slaves to the State. And the People of the North were equally losers. The People, and the world, lost the last bastion of true freedom and Sovereignty. The nation was turned upside down, a tragedy with enduring worldwide consequences.

---

30 years. The sudden and vicious all-out assault on the Confederate flag by the media and political establishment in the aftermath of the shooting in the church at Charleston, South Carolina, suggests that the event was orchestrated and planned by the Global Elite for the purpose of eradicating all symbols of Christianity and further obliterating all evidence of the truth of the nation's heritage and history.

Chapter IV

Lincoln's Redemption

"Everyone should do all in his power to collect and disseminate the truth, in the hope that it may find a place in history and descend to posterity. History is not the relation of campaigns and battles and generals or other individuals, but that which shows the principles for which the South contended and which justified her struggle for those principles."
—General Robert E. Lee

"The Jesuit . . . are simply the Roman army for the earthly sovereignty of the world in the future, with the Pontiff of Rome for Emperor . . . that's their ideal . . . It's simple lust of power, of filthy earthly gain, of domination—something like a universal serfdom with them as masters—that's all they stand for. They don't even believe in God perhaps."
—Fyodor Dostoyevsky

Despite his ruthless, tyrannical rule and contumacious disregard of the Constitution, there is evidence that Lincoln had a change of heart toward the end of the war. Yes; it is true . . . Lincoln was not the man that history has portrayed. He was a cunning, evil, manipulative liar, obsessed with a narcissism which is characteristic of the most troubled of souls. However, every man is entitled to redemption, to salvation through grace, which is the free gift of the Divine. Therefore, I would be remiss, as Paul Harvey would say, if I did not mention the "rest of the story."

It was reported that Lincoln was converted to Christianity after viewing the carnage on the battlefield of Gettysburg.[1] Deeply

---
[1] The Battle of Gettysburg was fought July 1-3, 1863. Union casualties at Gettysburg totaled 23,049,

troubled in his spirit by what he had witnessed, on November 19, 1863, Lincoln accepted Jesus Christ as Lord and Savior. He later attended, but did not officially join, the Presbyterian Church in Washington.

As a consequence of his conversion, by the end of the war Lincoln no longer favored harsh punishment and economic subjugation of the Southern States, but rather sought to restore the Southern States to the Union on the same basis as when they had departed. However, this policy would have destroyed the commodity speculations of the bankers, led by the Rothschilds, betraying their interests and the backing of the socialists in his campaign for a second term. He further planned to end martial law and reestablish lawful Constitutional government. His Second Inaugural Address was delivered on March 4, 1865, and although he obstinately and arrogantly continued to lay the blame for the war at the hands of the Southern States, he offered a more conciliatory tone: "With malice toward none; with charity for all; with firmness in the right, as God gives us to see the right, let us strive on to finish the work we are in; to bind up the nation's wounds; to care for him who shall have borne the battle, and for his widow, and his orphan—to do all which may achieve and cherish a just, and a lasting peace, among ourselves, and with all nations."

Lincoln also had second thoughts about a central national bank. He refused the Rothschild's offer of loans to pay for the war at usurious rates of 24-36%, and instead printed money backed by the federal government known as "greenbacks."[2] Lincoln expressed his sentiments:

> Money is the creature of law, and the creation of the original issue of money should be maintained as the exclusive

---

including 3,155 killed in action, 14,529 wounded and 5,365 missing. Confederate casualties are estimated at 28,063 casualties, including 3,903 killed, 18,735 wounded and 5,425 unwounded prisoners. Statistics from an article by Philip Andrade, "A Survey of Union and Confederate Casualties at Gettysburg" (November 4, 2004).

[2] "Greenbacks," so-called because they were printed on only one side with green ink, were the first paper money, legal tender Treasury Notes printed by the U.S. government. Prior to the issuance of the currency, all government issued moneys were coins. On February 25, 1862, Congress passed the Legal Tender Act, which authorized the printing of $150 million in Treasury Notes.

monopoly of national government . . . Government, possessing the power to create and issue currency and credit as money and enjoying the right to withdraw both currency and credit from circulation by taxation and otherwise, need not and should not borrow capital at interest as a means of financing government work and public enterprise. The government should create, issue and circulate all the currency and credit needed to satisfy the spending power of the government and the buying power of consumers. The privilege of creating and issuing money is not only the supreme prerogative of government, but it is the government's greatest creative opportunity. By the adoption of these principles, the long-felt want for a uniform medium will be satisfied. The taxpayers will be saved immense sums of interest, discounts, and exchanges. The financing of all public enterprises, the maintenance of stable government and ordered progress, and the conduct of the Treasury will become matters of practical administration. The people can and will be furnished with a currency as safe as their own government. Money will cease to be the master and become the servant of humanity. Democracy will rise superior to the money power.[3]

However, on February 25, 1863, Congress passed the National Bank Act, establishing a U.S. central bank for the first time since 1836. The Act established a system of nationally chartered banks, and a national currency backed by government securities. It authorized the federal government to sell war bonds and securities, and required the currency issued by the banks to be backed by government bonds. The Act served as the predecessor to the Federal Reserve Act of 1913. After his re-election in 1864, Lincoln vowed to repeal the Act upon taking office in January 1865. Of course, this angered the bankers further.

---

[3] "Abraham Lincoln's Monetary Policy," Senate Document 23, p. 91 (January 1939). Note from the document: ". . . abstract of Lincoln's monetary policy from Mayor McGeer's 'Conquest of Poverty' and has been certified as correct by the Legislative Reference Service of the Library of Congress at the instance of Hon. Kent Keller . . ."

Perhaps most importantly, Lincoln would never have agreed to the globalists postwar effort to create a new corporate government with a citizenship stripping the people of their sovereignty through the 14th Amendment.[4] Such a dramatic transformation of Lincoln's attitude could only be precipitated by his newfound belief in Jesus Christ. The blinders were apparently lifted from his eyes; his spirit awakened to the evil that was being perpetrated on the nation at his hands. Perhaps Lincoln was attempting to make amends for his malevolent deeds earlier in the war as a pawn of the bankers and "Global Elite."

There is perhaps no greater evidence of Lincoln's change of posture and attitude than his statement in a November 21, 1864 letter to Colonel William F. Elkins:

> We may congratulate ourselves that this cruel war is nearing its end. It has cost a vast amount of treasure and blood . . . It has indeed been a trying hour for the Republic; but I see in the near future a crisis approaching that unnerves me and causes me to tremble for the safety of my country. As a result of war, corporations have been enthroned and an era of corruption in high places will follow, and the money power of the country will endeavor to prolong its reign by working upon the prejudices of the people until all wealth is aggregated in a few hands, and the republic is destroyed. I feel at this moment more anxiety for the safety of my country than ever before, even in the midst of war. God grant that my suspicions may prove groundless.

His words were prophetic; and eloquent. However, this time his eloquence was not tarnished by a lack of sincerity. His words were genuine, heartfelt, his vision, once blinded, now seemingly able to pierce the portal of time and space. Perhaps mercifully, he would not live to see the prophecy fulfilled in the ensuing years.

---

[4] See, Chapter VIII for details regarding the 14th Amendment, which created a special class of citizenship for Blacks. The Amendment eventually stripped all Americans of their sovereignty, rendering all people subjects, i.e., serfs, of the federal government.

Chapter IV Lincoln's Redemption

In the days before his death, Lincoln had many spiritual conversations with his close friend and converted priest, Charles Chiniquy. In his book, *Fifty Years in the Church of Rome* (1886), Chiniquy quoted Lincoln:

> I will repeat to you what I said at Urbana, when for the first time you told me your fears lest I would be assassinated by the Jesuits: Man must not care where and when he will die, provided he dies at the post of honor and duty. But I may add, today, that I have a presentiment that God will call me to Him through the hand of an assassin. Let His will, and not mine, be done! The Pope and the Jesuits, with their infernal Inquisition, are the only organized powers in the world which have recourse to the dagger of the assassin to murder those whom they cannot convince with their arguments or conquer with the sword . . . It seems to me that the Lord wants today, as He wanted in the days of Moses, another victim . . . I cannot conceal from you that my impression is that I am that victim. So many plots have already been made against my life, that it is a real miracle that they have failed, when we consider that the great majority of them were in the hands of skillful Roman Catholic murderers, evidently trained by Jesuits. But can we expect that God will make a perpetual miracle to save my life? I believe not. The Jesuits are so expert in those deeds of blood, that Henry IV said that it was impossible to escape them, and he became their victim, though he did all that could be done to protect himself. My escape from their hands, since the letter of the Pope to Jeff Davis has sharpened a million daggers to pierce my breast, would be more than a miracle.[5]

---

[5] Chiniquy, Father Charles, *Fifty Years in the Church of Rome: The Conversion of a Priest* (Chick Publications, Ontario, CA, 1985, originally published in 1885). The book is a fascinating account of the conversion of Father Chiniquy, who found himself torn between the truths expressed in the Bible and following the dictates of the Roman Catholic Church. It also gives insight and provides details and proof of the Jesuit's connection to the assassination of Lincoln.

Chiniquy instinctively knew that his visit would be the last time that he would see Lincoln alive. He continues in his book:

> I knew the hour to leave had come, I asked from the President permission to fall on my knees, and pray with him that his life might be spared: and he knelt with me. But I prayed more with my tears and sobs, than with my words. Then I pressed his hand on my lips and bathed it with my tears, and with a heart filled with an unspeakable desolation, I bade him Adieu! It was for the last time! For the hour was fast approaching when he was to fall by the hands of a Jesuit assassin, for his nation's sake.[6]

The letter that Lincoln referred to from Pope Pius IX to Jefferson Davis was dated December 3, 1863. The Pope wrote:

> . . . It is particularly agreeable to us to see that you, illustrious and honorable President, and your people, are animated with the same desires of peace and tranquility which we have in our letters inculcated upon our venerable brothers. May it please God at the same time to make the other peoples of America and their rulers, reflecting seriously how terrible is civil war, and what calamities it engenders, listen to the inspirations of a calmer spirit, and adopt resolutely the part of peace. As for us, we shall not cease to offer up the most fervent prayers to God Almighty, that He may pour out upon all the people of America the spirit of peace and charity, and that He will stop the great evils which afflict them. We, at the same time, beseech the God of pity to shed abroad upon you the light of His grace, and attach you to us by a perfect friendship.[7]

---

[6] Ibid.

[7] Davis, Varina, *Jefferson Davis: A Memoir by His Wife* (Volumes I & II) (The Nautical & Aviation Pub. Co., Baltimore, MD, reprinted 1990). Varina Howell Davis was the wife of Jefferson Davis. The book was completed after the death of her husband in New Orleans on December 6, 1889. At his death, a New Orleans newspaper wrote: "Throughout the South are Lamentations and tears; in every country on the globe where there are lovers of liberty there is mourning; wherever there are men who love heroic patriotism, dauntless resolution, fortitude or intellectual power, there is [a] sincere sorrowing. The beloved

Chapter IV Lincoln's Redemption

The letter was a tacit recognition of the CSA as an independent nation and acknowledgement of Jefferson Davis as its president.

Chiniquy recounts, in his book, his response to Lincoln regarding the letter:

> My dear President I answered, it is just that letter which brought me to your presence again. That letter is a poisoned arrow thrown by the Pope at you personally; it is your death warrant. Before the letter, every Catholic could see that their church as a whole was against this free Republic. However, a good number of liberty-loving Irish, German and French Catholics, following more the instincts of their noble nature than the degrading principles of their church, enrolled themselves under the banners of liberty, and have fought like heroes. To detach these men from the rank and file of the Northern armies, and force them to help the cause of the rebellion, became the main object of the Jesuits. Secret pressing letters were addressed from Rome to the bishops, ordering them to weaken your armies by detaching those men from you. The bishops refused; for they would be exposing themselves as traitors and be shot. But they advised the Pope to acknowledge, at once, the legitimacy of the Southern republic, and to take Jeff Davis under his supreme protection, by a letter, which would be read everywhere. That letter tells every Roman Catholic that you are a bloodthirsty tyrant fighting against a government which the infallible and holy Pope of Rome recognizes as legitimate. The Pope, by this letter, tells his blind slaves that you are outraging the God of heaven and earth, by continuing such a bloody war. By this letter of the Pope to Jeff Davis you are not only an apostate, as you were thought before, whom every man had the right to kill, according to the canonical laws of Rome: but you are more vile, criminal and cruel than the horse thief, the public

---

of our land, the unfaltering upholder of constitutional liberty, the typical hero and sage, is no more; the fearless heart that beats with sympathy for all mankind is stilled forever, a great light is gone—Jefferson Davis is dead!"

bandit, and the lawless brigand, robber and murderer. And my dear President, this is not a fancy imagination on my part, it is the unanimous explanation given me by a great number of the priests of Rome, with whom I have had occasion to speak on that subject. In the name of God, and in the name of our dear country, which is in so much need of your services, I plead that you pay more attention to protect your precious life, and not continue to expose it as you have done till now.[8]

Following the publication of the letter, many Roman Catholics deserted the Union Army.

Lincoln was elected president to a second term with the aid of the bankers and socialists in order to continue the furtherance of their agenda. His change in posture, however, betrayed their interests. Angered by Lincoln's betrayal, the bankers had him assassinated on April 14, 1865,[9] with the aid of the Jesuits[10] and the complicit knowledge of Vice President Andrew Johnson. How ironic; Lincoln and Kennedy were assassinated for similar reasons.[11] Lincoln and Kennedy betrayed

---

[8] Id. Chiniquy.

[9] See, "The Rothschild's International Plot to Kill Lincoln," by Paul Goldstein (*New Solidarity*, October 29, 1976). The Jesuits were the hired assassins for the banking cabal led by the Rothschilds.

[10] Kampschaefer, Keith, "From Farnese to Francis: The Jesuit Trail" (September 2, 2016): "This is what Jesuits do. They kill people. They make plans to kill people. Days in advance, years in advance, centuries in advance. And they've been planning to kill 90% of the world's population longer than any person on earth has been alive. They make weapons to kill people, factories to kill people, and wars to kill people. And they make buildings to kill people and if one building isn't quite enough, they'll build another right beside it to make sure the message hits home. They know how to use fear, intimidation, sabotage, blackmail, blacklisting, slander, and every other social and psychological weapon ever imagined in their dark hearts or developed in their human experimentation programs. They've got sorcery down to a science and pharmakeia down to an art. They practice wickedness like we practice breathing. It just comes natural to them. They don't even have to try. They can execute it in their sleep and not lose a wink doing it. Satanic ritual abuse is an afterthought for them and trauma-based mind control is their native tongue. They never let a good crisis go to waste and they play by one rule . . . one rule only . . . and that rule is: THERE ARE NO RULES! THE END JUSTIFIES THE MEANS." (*uncontrolledopposition.wordpress.com/2016/09/02/from-farnese-to-francis-the-jesuit-trail*)

[11] On June 4, 1963, President Kennedy signed Executive Order (EO) 11110, which returned to the U.S. government the power to issue currency, without going through the Rothschild, et. al., owned Federal Reserve System. President Kennedy ordered the issuance of U.S. Notes with the goal of eliminating the Federal Reserve System within six months from the issuance of the EO. More than $4 billion in U.S. Notes, in $2 and $5 denominations, had already been released into circulation at the time of his death. $10 and $20 U.S. Notes were being printed but had not been put into circulation. Less than six months after issuing the EO, Kennedy was assassinated, on November 22. Following Kennedy's death, no additional U.S. Notes were released, and U.S. Notes in bank vaults were withdrawn from circulation.

Chapter IV Lincoln's Redemption

the interests of the bankers and the House of Rothschild. Both Vice Presidents were named Johnson, and both were complicit in the respective offenses.

Chiniquy further writes:

> But who was that assassin? Booth was nothing but the tool of the Jesuits.[12] It was Rome who directed his arm, after corrupting his heart and damning his soul. After I had mixed my tears with those of the grand country of my adoption, I fell on my knees and asked my God to grant me to show to the world what I knew to be the truth, viz., that the horrible crime was the work of Popery. And, after twenty years of constant and most difficult researches, I come fearlessly today before the American people, to say and prove that the President, Abraham Lincoln, was assassinated by the priests and the Jesuits of Rome . . . the Jesuits alone could select the assassins, train them, and show them a crown of glory in heaven, if they would kill the author of the bloodshed, the famous renegade and apostate—the enemy of the Pope and of the Church—Lincoln.[13]

Yes, the destruction of the Republic and Constitutional government lies squarely at the feet of Lincoln and the Republican Party, at the behest of the bankers and Global Elite. Tragically for

---

Ten days before his death, Kennedy wrote in his personal diary, "The high office of the President has been used to foment a plot to destroy American freedom and before I leave office I must inform the Citizens of this plight." Senator Robert Kennedy was assassinated during his campaign for president, for the same reason his brother was killed.

[12] Id. Chiniquy. Chiniquy writes in his book, "The Jesuits are a military organization, not a religious order. Their chief is a general of an army, not the mere father abbot of a monastery. And the aim of this organization is: Power. Power in its most despotic exercise. Absolute power, universal power, power to control the world by the volition of a single man. Jesuitism is the most absolute of despotisms; and at the same time the greatest and the most enormous of abuses. The general of the Jesuits insists on being master, sovereign, over the sovereign. Wherever the Jesuits are admitted they will be masters, cost what it may. Their society is by nature dictatorial, and therefore it is the irreconcilable enemy of all constituted authority. Every act, every crime, however atrocious, is a meritorious work, if committed for the interest of the Society of the Jesuits, or by the order of its general." The Jesuits are the enforcement arm of the Roman Catholic Church and the Global Elite.

[13] Phelps, Eric Jon, *Vatican Assassins*, p. 632 (second edition, Newmanstown, PA, 2004): "The Jesuit General [a.k.a. the Black Pope] has been the most powerful man in the world since Pius VII restored the Order or 'Company' in 1814. Because of the Order's suppression by the Pope in 1773, the Jesuits began

the American people, the ramifications of Lincoln's actions endure to the present day. And yes, Lincoln feared the bankers and the Jesuits, and justifiably so. His conversion and resulting change in posture cost him his life. At least it seems that he found redemption prior to his death.

There appears a large monument to Abraham Lincoln in Washington, D.C., venerating the legend of a man which is nothing more than a prefabricated myth. The monument is repugnant to the principles of freedom, liberty, and the Republic of the Founding Fathers. And of all people, the Black man should be most incensed at its diabolical stature. Lincoln was not their savior, but their enslaver. Blacks were freed from the plantation only to be enslaved by a federal government usurped by a corrupt ruling cabal. Lincoln was an admitted racist, the pawn of an evil elite, as is well documented in the foregoing pages. By his own admission, he destroyed the Republic. His redemption is to be admired, but it was too little too late. The nation has, indeed, been turned upside down; history re-written to make a prevaricator into a savior.

---

the Bavarian Illuminati with one of their soldiers, Adam Weishaupt. The Illuminati absorbed the Jewish House of Rothschild creating a colossus of wealth around the world, subject to the Jesuit General . . . I believe the Rothschilds and the Council of Thirteen have mastery over the 'Company,' and that it was Rothschild who engaged and financed Weishaupt to revive the Illuminati. King Rothschild's secret society is more numerous and powerful than the Society of Jesus [Jesuits]; both abhor, yet owe allegiance to Rome. At the appropriate time the Jesuits will install the man of their choice in the chair of St. Peter, as in the past they have removed incumbents who displeased them." Interestingly, Pope Francis, elected in March 2013, is the first Jesuit Pope.

Also, see Saussy, Tupper, *Rulers of Evil: Useful Knowledge about Governing Bodies*, (Harper Collins Publishers, NY, 1999) pp. 160-1: "The appointment of Rothschild gave the black papacy absolute financial privacy and secrecy. Who would ever search a family of orthodox Jews for the key to the wealth of the Roman Catholic Church? I believe this appointment explains why the House of Rothschild is famous for helping nations go to war. It is fascinating that, as [Mayer] Rothschild's sons grew into the family business, the firm took on the title [Mayer]Amschel Rothschild und Sohne [sons], which gives us the Notarikon MARS. Isn't Mars the Roman God of War, whose heavenly manifestation is 'the red planet'? There is a powerful Cabala here, and there's hardly an acre of inhabitable earth that hasn't been affected by it in some way." [Author's note: Red is also the color most associated with the Communist Party.]

Chapter V

The "Global Elite"

"The suppression of truth has long been among the highest priorities for the upper echelons of power and authority. For a minority elite that clings to power by the manipulation of the masses using an omnipresent cocktail of lies, deception, mass-produced ignorance and ingrained propaganda, the destruction of truth is an essential method of control. It is a formula that has worked to unmitigated success for the elite throughout history, whether the shadows of power stretch from ancient pyramids, marble temples, castles, mansions or halls of governance."
—Manuel Valenzuela

"We are opposed around the world by a monolithic and ruthless conspiracy that relies primarily on covert means for expanding its sphere of influence—on infiltration instead of invasion, on subversion instead of elections, on intimidation instead of free choice, on guerillas by night instead of armies by day."
—John F. Kennedy

Lincoln's change of perspective was too little too late. The bankers and Global Elite had seized their opportunity . . . a foothold into unobtrusively controlling the U.S. government by transforming it into a corporation under their control. The influence they attained in this nation during and after the War years would only grow stronger, catapulting them into the position of complete control over the world's international monetary systems. But, it was a very long time in coming.

Though the relationship between the Roman Catholic Church and the international bankers, led by the Jewish House of Rothschild, may seem an odd one, mutual objectives will often forge the seemingly oddest of partnerships. Their singular objective is economic control of the U.S. and the world through a "New World Order" (NWO) and One World Government. They further their agenda through a dominating influence in such "secret" organizations as the Illuminati, the Council on Foreign Relations (CFR), Trilateral Commission, and the Bilderberg Group.

So just who are the evil provocateurs behind this so-called Global Elite and the New World Order?

The odyssey begins with Mayer Amschel Rothschild. He was born Mayer Amschel Bauer in 1743 in Frankfurt, Germany. He was the son of Moses Amschel Bauer, a moneylender and owner of a counting house. Bauer's trademark symbol was a red hexagram (which geometrically and numerically translates into the number "666"), which became the family crest. The symbol was placed on a red sign which hung over the door of his business, and *would eventually become the flag of Israel*, indicating the control the Rothschilds would have in the future over the creation of Israel.

Chapter V The "Global Elite"

But it is not a symbol of the Hebrew God, Jehovah.[1]

The Rothschilds (Bauer) claim to be Jewish, but in fact they are from Khazaria, which was located between the Black Sea and the Caspian Sea, and is now primarily in Georgia.[2] The claim stems from an edict by the King of Khazaria in AD 740 that all Khazarians convert to the Jewish faith. The Khazarian Jews are more commonly known as Ashkenazi Jews.[3] However, recent DNA evidence proves Ashkenazi Jews are *not* the Jews of the Bible and are *not* the seed of Abraham. They are not God's "chosen people." They are the modern-day Pharisees, sons of Lucifer. Approximately 90% of people in the world today who call themselves Jews are actually Ashkenazi Jews. Therefore, these people knowingly lie to the world with their claims that the land of Israel is theirs by birthright. Their true homeland is over 800 miles away in Georgia, or what used to be known as Khazaria.[4] The birthright of the land of Israel belongs to the seed of Abraham, the true Hebrew people.

But, please, do not assume that all Ashkenazi Jews are part of the Rothschild criminal cabal. Most Ashkenazi Jews are innocent and unaware of the evil designs of the Rothschilds and their comrades. They are a brilliant people, industrious and productive members of society, in whatever country they live. They have contributed much to the world in the fields of the humanities, art, science, and medicine. The designs of a few evil men should ***never*** be an excuse for anti-Semitism. There is no place for anti-Semitism, racism, or any "ism" in a free republic. A free republic demands equality for all men (and women). All are created in the image of God, and endowed by their Creator with unalienable rights, regardless of race, religion, or ethnicity. In a republic, unless all are free, none are truly free. They become captives of their own sin;

---

[1] See, Graham, O.J., *The Six Pointed Star: Its Origin and Usage*, pp. 92-3: "It was mentioned and condemned by the God of Israel in Amos 5:26 and was called by Him 'the star of your god Moloch' . . . Reference was also made in Act 7:43. Here it was called the Star of Remphan. All these names refer to the 'god' Saturn . . . The six-pointed star or hexagram became the insignia of Zionism . . . It arrived at the Knesset of the newly formed state of Israel by its founders, the Rothschilds."

[2] Kingdom of Khazaria, AD 652-1016, included part of modern-day Russia, Ukraine, Georgia, and Kazakhstan.

[3] A Jew of European or German descent.

[4] It has always been the plan of Lucifer to take control of the "Promised Land" away from God's "Chosen People," the Hebrews, and give it to the lineage of Satan.

slaves to their own prejudice. Most Ashkenazi Jews, however, falsely believe that they are descendants of Abraham.

According to a report by Texe Marrs:

> The newest DNA science finding is from Dr. Eran Elhaik ("a Jew") and associates at the McKusick-Nathans Institute of Genetic Medicine, Johns Hopkins University School of Medicine. In research accepted December 5, 2012 and published by the Oxford University Press on behalf of the Society of Molecular Biology and Evolution, it was found that the *Khazarian Hypothesis* is scientifically correct. What exactly is the "Khazarian Hypothesis?" Simply stated, it holds that the Jewry genome is a mosaic of ancestries which rise primarily out of the Khazars. Jews are Khazars, not Israelites. The "Jews" of America, Europe, and Israel are descendants *not* of Father Abraham but of King Bulan and the people of ancient Khazaria. Khazaria was an amalgam of Turkic clans who once lived in the Caucasus (Southern Russia) in the early centuries CE. These Turkic peoples were pagans who *converted* to Judaism in the eighth century. As converts, they called themselves "Jews," but *none* of their blood comes from Israel. Later, the "Jews" (Khazars) emigrated, settling in Russia, Hungary, Poland, Germany, and elsewhere in Europe. As "Jews," the Khazars then left the European nations in 1948 and settled the fledgling, new nation of Israel. The people of Israel are not the seed, nor the ancestors, of Abraham. They call themselves "Jews," but in fact, DNA science shows them to be Khazars. They say they are "Jew," but they are not.[5]

The Book of Revelation addresses the Ashkenazi Jews: "I

---

[5] Marrs, Texe, "New DNA Science Research Confirms . . . 'Jews' Are Not Descendants of Abraham," *texemarrs.com/042013/jews_not_descendants_of_abraham.htm*. Marrs (1944-2019), an author and radio talk show host, was an officer in the U.S. Air Force for 20 years and faculty member at the University of Texas. He founded two fundamentalist Christian ministries, Power of Prophecy Ministries and Bible Home Church, based in Austin, Texas. Galatians 3:29: "And if ye be Christ's, then are ye Abraham's seed and heirs according to the promise."

know thy works, and tribulation and poverty, (but thou art rich) and I know the blasphemy of them which say they are Jews, and are not, but are the synagogue of Satan."[6]

During his early years, Mayer Bauer worked for a bank owned by the Oppenheimers in Hanover, Germany. He was very successful, and quickly became a junior partner in the bank. After the death of his father, Bauer returned to Frankfurt to take over his father's business. He recognized the significance of the red sign hanging over the door of the business, with its red hexagram meaning "666." The sign prompted him to change his name from Bauer to Rothschild; "Rot" is German for "Red" and "Schild" is German for "Sign." The sign is also a part of the Rothschild family Coat of Arms.

Rothschild began doing business with Prince William of Hanau, Hesse, Germany. This relationship led to business dealings with many of the royalty and elite of Europe. From seemingly humble beginnings, Rothschild was quickly catapulted into the highest level of European Royalty.

Around 1770, Rothschild came up with the idea of creating a secret group which he called the Illuminati. Its purpose would be to divide all non-Jews through political, economic, social, and religious means, causing them to fight amongst themselves; destroy national governments; destroy religious institutions; and eventually destroy each other . . . in other words, take over control of the world from the *goyim* (non-Jews). He enlisted Adam Weishaupt, an Ashkenazi Jew who outwardly posed as a Roman Catholic, with the task of organizing the group.

The Illuminati was based upon the teachings of the Talmud, which are the teachings of the Rabbinical Jews.[7] The word "Illuminati"

---

[6] Revelation 2:9.
[7] The Talmud is "the body of Jewish civil and ceremonial law and legend comprising the Mishnah and the Gemara. There are two versions of the Talmud: the Babylonian Talmud (which dates from the 5th century AD but includes earlier material) and the earlier Palestinian or Jerusalem Talmud." "The Talmud is the comprehensive written version of the Jewish oral law and the subsequent commentaries on it. It originates from the 2nd century. The Mishnah is the original written version of the oral law and the Gemara is the record of the rabbinic discussions following this writing down." Note that the Talmud is not a part of the Bible. The Torah is the Hebrew Bible. However, for most modern-day Orthodox Jews, the Talmud has replaced the Old Testament.

is a Luciferian term which means "keepers of the light."[8] Weishaupt recruited paid members into the group with instructions to use the following methods to control and dominate people:

- Use monetary and sex bribery to obtain control of men already in high places, in the various levels of all governments and other fields of endeavour. Once influential persons had fallen for the lies, deceits, and temptations of the Illuminati they were to be held in bondage by application of political and other forms of blackmail, threats of financial ruin, public exposure, and fiscal harm, even death to themselves and loved members of their families.
- The faculties of colleges and universities were to cultivate students possessing exceptional mental ability belonging to well-bred families with international leanings, and recommend them for special training in internationalism, or rather the notion that only a one-world government can put an end to recurring wars and strife. Such training was to be provided by granting scholarships to those selected by the Illuminati.
- All influential people trapped into coming under the control of the Illuminati, plus the students who had been specially educated and trained, were to be used as agents and placed behind the scenes of all governments as experts and specialists. This was so they would advise the top executives to adopt policies which would in the long-run serve the secret plans of the Illuminati one-world conspiracy and bring about the destruction of the governments and religions they were elected or appointed to serve.

---

[8] "Illuminati" is defined as: 1. People claiming to be unusually enlightened with regard to a subject. 2. Any of various groups claiming special religious enlightenment, 'to light up'" (*The American Heritage Dictionary of the English Language*).

- To obtain absolute-control of the press, at that time the only mass-communications media which distributed information to the public, so that all news and information could be slanted in order to make the masses believe that a one-world government is the only solution to our many and varied problems.[9]

And so the agenda continues to this day. The more things change, the more things stay the same. Many politicians and government officials, on both the state and Federal levels, are bought and paid for, bribed, blackmailed, and threatened with financial ruin and public humiliation if they fail to succumb to the obedience of their Master, the Rothschilds, a.k.a. the Global Elite.

The Talmud was the underlying foundation upon which the Rothschilds based their life philosophy and guided their every action. Mayer Amschel Rothschild himself was a devoted Talmudic scholar, and followed the Talmudic belief that only Jews are humanity. All others are animals; therefore only Jews can be "people."

Dr. August Rohling, a professor at Charles University in Prague in the 19th century, described the basis of the Talmud:

1) The soul of the Jew is part of God Himself; the souls of the other peoples come from the Devil and resemble those of brutes;
2) Domination over other people is the right of Jews alone;
3) Awaiting the coming of the Messiah, the Jews live in a continual state of war with other people;
4) When the victory of the Jews is won, other peoples will accept the Jewish religion; however the Christians will not be given this privilege, but will be exterminated because they belong to the Devil;
5) The Jew is the substance of God; a Gentile who strikes him deserves death;
6) Non-Jews are created to serve Jews;

---

[9] Hitchcock, Andrew Carrington, *The Synagogue of Satan* (Money Tree Publishing, Crestview, FL, 2018 edition).

7) A Jew is forbidden to show mercy to his enemies;

8) A Jew may be a hypocrite to a non-Jew;

9) To despoil a non-Jew is permitted;

10) If anyone returns to a Christian something he has lost, God will not pardon him;

11) God has ordained that the Jew shall take usury from the non-Jew in order to injure him;

12) The best of the non-Jews should be exterminated; the honest life of a Gentile should be the object of hate;

13) If a Jew can deceive a Gentile by pretending to be a non-Jew, he is permitted to do so.[10]

The goal of the Rothschilds and the Ashkenazi Jews was and is today world domination through a One World Government and eradication of all Christians. Hence, Christianity and communism cannot coexist.

In 1791, Mayer Amschel Rothschild was quoted as saying: "Let me issue and control a nation's money and I care not who writes the laws." The driving force of the Ashkenazi Jews has always been attaining the Jewish Utopia (Talmudic) through the New World Order, and with it the ambition to accumulate the vast wealth of the planet for themselves. The Rothschild dynasty, through controlling the world's money over the years, has gained literal control of the entire world.

Mayer Amschel Rothschild had five sons: Amschel Mayer Rothschild (1773-1855), Salomon Mayer von Rothschild (1774-1855), Nathan Mayer Rothschild (1777-1836), Kalmann Mayer von Rothschild (1788-1855), and Jacob Mayer de Rothschild (1792-1868). Upon Amschel's death, his estate was passed on to the five sons, who established businesses in London, Paris, Frankfurt, Vienna, and Naples. The sons were elevated to the Austrian nobility by Emperor Francis I in 1822 with the title of Baron. In 1847, Queen Victoria granted the hereditary title of Baronet, and in 1885,

---

[10] Piper, Michael Collins, *The New Babylon: Those Who Reign Supreme*, pp. 60-1, (American Free Press, Washington, D.C., 2011). Dr. Rohling (1839-1931) was a German Catholic theologian, author, and student of Hebrew, and translated the Talmud.

hereditary peerage title of Baron Rothschild. All became successful bankers in international banking.

Mayer Amschel Rothschild died in 1812. According to Andrew Carrington Hitchcock (author, pastor, and founder of the Ministry of Yahweh):

> In his will he lays out specific laws that the House of Rothschild were to follow: all key positions in the family business were only to be held by family members; only male members of the family were allowed to participate in the family business, this included a reported sixth secret bastard son (it is important to note that Mayer Amschel Rothschild also has five daughters, so today the spread of the Rothschild Zionist dynasty without the Rothschild name is far and wide, and Jews believe the mixed offspring of a Jewish mother is solely Jewish); the family was to intermarry with its first and second cousins to preserve the family fortune (of the 18 marriages by Mayer Amschel Rothschild's grandchildren, 16 were between first cousins —a practice known today as inbreeding); no public inventory of his estate was to be published; no legal action was to be taken with regard to the value of the inheritance; the eldest son of the eldest son was to become the head of the family (this condition could only be overturned when the majority of the family agreed otherwise).

Nathan Mayer Rothschild was elected head of the family following the death of his father and started his business in Manchester, England in 1806. He gradually moved the business to London, and in 1809, he purchased the property at 2 New Court, St. Swithin's Lane, City of London, which is headquarters to the Rothschild empire to this day. In 1811, Nathan established N.M. Rothschild & Sons, which arguably became the most influential of the Rothschild's businesses.

The Rothschild banking businesses were pioneers in international high finance. They financed the construction of railways throughout the world and financed many large government projects, such as the Suez Canal. Their loans funded many European wars, wars which they often instigated, including financing the Duke of Wellington and his victory over Napoleon at Waterloo, and the War of 1812 between the U.S. and Great Britain. Over time, they used their banking acumen to establish central banks in countries worldwide, including the U.S., initially through their agent Alexander Hamilton, and finally through the Federal Reserve Act of 1913.

In 1815, Nathan Mayer Rothschild stated: "I care not what puppet is placed upon the throne of England to rule the Empire on which the sun never sets. The man who controls Britain's money supply controls the British Empire, and I control the British money supply."

In essence, he was saying that he controlled the British Empire. By the end of the 19th century, it was estimated the Rothschild family controlled half the wealth of the world.

An online article states: "The name of Rothschild became synonymous with extravagance and great wealth; and, the family was renowned for its art collecting, for its palaces, as well as for its philanthropy. By the end of the century, the family owned, or had built, at the lowest estimates, over 41 palaces, of a scale and luxury perhaps unparalleled even by the richest royal families. The British Chancellor of the Exchequer Lloyd George claimed, in 1909, that Nathan, Lord Rothschild was the most powerful man in Britain."

In 1836, an article in *Weekly Register* wrote of the Rothschilds:

> The Rothschilds are the wonders of modern banking . . . we see the descendants of Judah, after a persecution of two thousand years, peering above kings, rising higher than emperors, and holding a whole continent in the hollow of their hands. The Rothschilds govern a Christian world. Not a cabinet moves without their advice. They stretch their hand, with equal ease, from Petersburgh to Vienna, from Vienna to Paris, from Paris to London, from London to Washington. Baron Rothschild, the head of the house, is the true king of Judah, the prince of the captivity, the Messiah so long looked for by this extraordinary people.

He holds the keys of peace or war, blessing or cursing . . .
They are the brokers and counselors of the kings of Europe and of the republican chiefs of America. What more can they desire?[11]

Of course, the article was not entirely accurate. Perceptions do not always match realty.

The Rothschilds are by far the wealthiest bloodline in the world today and the undisputed leader of the Ashkenazi Jews. Their bloodline extends into virtually all of the royal families of Europe, and includes the family names: Astor; Bundy; Collins; DuPont; Freeman; Kennedy; Morgan; Oppenheimer; Rockefeller; Sassoon; Schiff; Taft; and Van Duyn. To keep their bloodlines pure, the Rothschilds often intermarried. Further, the Rothschilds and their bloodlines were known to father children secretly, change their names, and put them into power as needed throughout the world. Their bloodlines run far beyond the Royal families. Karl Marx (born Chaim Hirschel Mordechai) is cousin to the Rothschilds, and was employed as their agent to subvert democracy and further the communist movement, with the objective of achieving their New World Order agenda.[12]

In 1823, the Rothschilds took over the financial operations of the Roman Catholic Church worldwide. Today the large banking and financial business of the Roman Catholic Church is an extensive system interlocked with the Rothschilds and the rest of the international banking system. The Rothschilds control the immense fortune of the Roman Catholic Church, which is second only to the Rothschild's in wealth and power.

The wealth of the Rothschilds is estimated to be over $500 trillion, more than half the wealth of the entire world. The Rothschilds are wealthier than the world's top eight billionaires combined, and wealthier than 75% of the total population of the world combined. It should be noted that the Rothschilds are related to the Mountbattens (a.k.a. the Windsors; Queen Elizabeth II of

---

[11] *Weekly Register*, Niles, Ohio, p. 41 (1836).
[12] henrymakow.com/2018/05/Karl-Marx-Was-Rothschilds-Third-Cousin%20.html

England, which is of the German House of Saxe-Coburg-Gotha bloodline). The *grand vizier* for Queen Elizabeth is Lord Evelyn Rothschild, the second wealthiest and most powerful person on Earth.[13]

Today, the Rothschilds own or control the Bank of England, the Federal Reserve System (Fed), the European Central Bank, the International Monetary Fund (IMF), the World Bank, and the Bank for International Settlements (BIS). They own most of the gold in the world. They also own the London Gold Exchange, which sets the price of gold every day.

Over time, the Rothschilds succeeded in establishing central banks in virtually every country in the world. As of 2021, only four countries worldwide do not have a Rothschild controlled central bank; Iran, Cuba, North Korea, and Iceland. Central banks are illegally created private banks, owned by the Rothschild banking cabal. Many of the European banks were founded by the Rothschilds and are still owned by them. Through their control of the world's money and their control and/or influence in several secret societies, the Rothschild banking cabal literally controls the world, not only economically, but politically.

The Rothschilds were instrumental in establishing the nation of Israel. In 1917, they negotiated with the British to bring America into World War I (WWI) on the side of Great Britain, in exchange for the British agreeing to give the land of Palestine to the Rothschilds. The Rothschilds fulfilled their promise. They took ownership of the land of Palestine, from which the future nation of Israel would be created. As previously mentioned, the "red sign" over Mayer Amschel Rothschild's door became the flag of Israel. Edmund Rothschild is hailed as "the Father of Israel" and appears on Israeli currency today. The Rothschilds wanted Palestine in order to protect their business interests in the Far East, and to establish their own military state in the area they could use as "an aggressor to any state that threatened those interests."

The vindictiveness of the Rothschilds is no better exemplified

---

[13] See, Mullins, Eustace Clarence, *The World Order: Our Secret Rulers* (Ezra Pound Institute of Civilization, Staunton, VA, 1985). The Jesuits are the *Enforcer* arm of the Roman Catholic Church and the Rothschilds.

than in a story related by Andrew Carrington Hitchcock:

> The Congress of Vienna's purpose was for the Rothschilds to create a form of world government, using the debt that many European governments owed them as leverage, to give them complete political control over much of the civilized world . . . However, their ultimate plan for world government fails when Tsar Alexander I of Russia, one of the few great powers who had not succumbed to a Rothschild central bank, refuses to accept this scheme. Enraged by this, Nathan Mayer Rothschild swears that one day he or his descendants will destroy the Tsar Alexander I's entire family and descendants. Unfortunately, he would prove to be true to his word when 102 years later, Rothschild-funded Jewish Bolsheviks would act upon that promise.[14]

Czar Nicholas II's entire family and servants were murdered by the Bolsheviks at the instruction of the Rothschilds, even though they had already abdicated the throne, after the Revolution.[15] The slaughter was pure revenge and designed to show the world what happens when you cross the Rothschilds.

Like the tentacles of an octopus, the Rothschilds have spread their influence throughout the entire world through control over the world's secret societies. The Illuminati was the brainchild of Mayer Amshel Rothschild, and 250 years later, their influence in the organization is just as strong as it was at its inception.

The **Illuminati** is headed by the 13 wealthiest families in the world, primarily by the influence of the House of Rothschild. They are the men who secretly rule the world from behind the scenes.

---

[14] Id. Hitchcock. The Bolshevik Revolution was "actually a takeover of Russia by a Rothschild-controlled Jewish elite . . . On 24 May 1991, *The Jerusalem Post* confirms Vladimir Lenin was Jewish. He was a Crypto-Jew and was born Vladimir Ilyich Ulyanov. Lenin is on record as having stated: 'The establishment of a central bank is 90% of communizing a nation.' These Jewish, Rothschild-funded Bolsheviks would go on in the course of history to slaughter 60 million Christians and non-Jews in Soviet-controlled territory. Indeed, the author Aleksandr Solzhenitsyn in his work, *Gulag Archipelago, Vol. 2*, affirms that Jews *created and administered the organized Soviet concentration camp system* in which these tens of millions of Christians and non-Jews died." pp. 115-6 [Emphasis added]

[15] An excellent resource on the Rothschilds is *The House of Rothschild* by Niall Ferguson (Penguin Books).

The families are: Astor, Bundy, Collins, DuPont, Freeman, Kennedy, Li (Chinese), Onassis, Rockefeller, Rothschild, Russell, Van Duyn, and Merovingian (European royal families), some of them families previously mentioned with Rothschilds bloodlines.[16] They control the world by dictating the rules and policies, political, social, and economic, by which the world's governments are run. The families are connected by bloodlines going back thousands of years, and they keep their bloodlines pure by marrying only within the families. The Illuminati own all of the international banks, the oil industry, and the world's largest and most powerful corporations, including all mainstream media (MSM). They own or control practically all governments of the world. The higher levels of the Illuminati are involved with Satanism and human sacrifice.

The 21 goals of the Illuminati are:

1. To establish a One World Government/New World Order with a unified church and monetary system under their direction. The One World Government began to set up its church in the 1920s and '30s, for they realized the need for a religious belief inherent in mankind must have an outlet and, therefore, set up a "church" body to channel that belief in the direction they desired.
2. To bring about the utter destruction of all national identity and national pride, which was a primary consideration if the concept of a One World Government was to work.
3. To engineer and bring about the destruction of religion, and more especially, the Christian Religion, with the one exception, their own creation, as mentioned above.
4. To establish the ability to control of each and every person through means of mind control and what Zbigniew Brzezinski called techonotronics, which would create human-like robots and a system of terror which would make Felix Dzerzinhski's Red Terror look like children at play.
5. To bring about the end to all industrialization and to end the production of nuclear generated electric power in what

---

[16] See, Springmeier, Fritz, *Bloodlines of the Illuminati* (Pentracks Publications, Denver, CO, 2005).

Chapter V The "Global Elite"

they call "the post-industrial zero-growth society." Excepted are the computer and service industries. U.S. industries that remain will be exported to countries such as Mexico where abundant slave labor is available. As we saw in 1993, this has become a fact through the passage of the North American Free Trade Agreement, known as NAFTA. Unemployables in the U.S., in the wake of industrial destruction, will either become opium-heroin and/or cocaine addicts, or become statistics in the elimination of the "excess population" process we know of today as Global 2000.

6. To encourage, and eventually legalize the use of drugs and make pornography an "art-form," which will be widely accepted and, eventually, become quite commonplace.

7. To bring about depopulation of large cities according to the trial run carried out by the Pol Pot regime in Cambodia. It is interesting to note that Pol Pot's genocidal plans were drawn up in the U.S. by one of the Club of Rome's research foundations, and overseen by Thomas Enders, a high-ranking State Department official. It is also interesting that the committee is currently seeking to reinstate the Pol Pot butchers in Cambodia.

8. To suppress all scientific development except for those deemed beneficial by the Illuminati. Especially targeted is nuclear energy for peaceful purposes. Particularly hated are the fusion experiments currently being scorned and ridiculed by the Illuminati and its jackals of the press. Development of the fusion torch would blow the Illuminati's conception of "limited natural resources" right out of the window. A fusion torch, properly used, could create unlimited and as yet untapped natural resources, even from the most ordinary substances. Fusion torch uses are legion, and would benefit mankind in a manner which, as yet, is not even remotely comprehended by the public.

9. To cause, by means of a) limited wars in the advanced countries, b) by means of starvation and diseases in the Third World countries, the death of three billion people by the year 2050, people they call "useless eaters." The Committee

of 300 (Illuminati) commissioned Cyrus Vance to write a paper on this subject of how to bring about such genocide. The paper was produced under the title "Global 2000 Report" and was accepted and approved for action by former President James Earl Carter, and Edwin Muskie, then Secretary of State, for and on behalf of the U.S. Government. Under the terms of the Global 2000 Report, the population of the U.S. is to be reduced by 100 million by the year of 2050.

10. To weaken the moral fiber of the nation and to demoralize workers in the labor class by creating mass unemployment. As jobs dwindle due to the post industrial zero growth policies introduced by the Club of Rome, the report envisages demoralized and discouraged workers resorting to alcohol and drugs. The youth of the land will be encouraged by means of rock music and drugs to rebel against the status quo, thus undermining and eventually destroying the family unit. In this regard, the Committee commissioned Tavistock Institute to prepare a blueprint as to how this could be achieved. Tavistock directed Stanford Research to undertake the work under the direction of Professor Willis Harmon. This work later became known as the "Aquarian Conspiracy."

11. To keep people everywhere from deciding their own destinies by means of one created crisis after another and then "managing" such crises. This will confuse and demoralize the population to the extent where faced with too many choices, apathy on a massive scale will result. In the case of the U.S., an agency for Crisis Management is already in place. It is called the Federal Emergency Management Agency (FEMA), whose existence I first disclosed in 1980.

12. To introduce new cults and continue to boost those already functioning which include rock music gangsters such as the Rolling Stones (a gangster group much favored by European Black Nobility), and all of the Tavistock-created rock groups which began with The Beatles.

Chapter V The "Global Elite"

13. To continue to build up and promote the cult of Christian Fundamentalism begun by the British East India Company's servant Darby, which will be misused to strengthen the Zionist State of Israel by identifying with the Jews through the myth of "God's chosen people," and by donating very substantial amounts of money to what they mistakenly believe is a religious cause in the furtherance of Christianity.

14. To press for the spread of religious cults such as the Moslem Brotherhood, Moslem Fundamentalism, the Sikhs, and to carry out mind control experiments of the Jim Jones and "Son of Sam" type. It is worth noting that the late Khomeini was a creation of British Military Intelligence Div. 6, MI6. This detailed work spelled out the step-by-step process which the U.S. Government implemented to put Khomeini in power.

15. To export "religious liberation" ideas around the world so as to *undermine* all existing religions, but more especially the Christian religion. This began with the "Jesuit Liberation Theology," that brought an end to the Somoza Family rule in Nicaragua, and which today is destroying El Salvador, now 25 years into a "civil war." Costa Rica and Honduras are also embroiled in revolutionary activities, instigated by the Jesuits. One very active entity engaged in the so-called liberation theology, is the Communist-oriented Mary Knoll Mission. This accounts for the extensive media attention to the murder of four of Mary Knoll's so-called nuns in El Salvador a few years ago. The four nuns were Communist subversive agents and their activities were widely documented by the Government of El Salvador. The U.S. press and the news media refused to give any space or coverage to the mass of documentation possessed by the Salvadorian Government, which proved what the Mary Knoll Mission nuns were doing in the country. Mary Knoll is in service in many countries, and placed a leading role in bringing Communism to Rhodesia, Mozambique, Angola and South Africa.

16. To cause a total collapse of the world's economies and engender total political chaos.

17. To take control of all foreign and domestic policies of the U.S.

18. To give the fullest support to supranational institutions such as the United Nations, the International Monetary Fund (IMF), the Bank of International Settlements, the World Court and, as far as possible, make local institutions less effective, by gradually phasing them out or bringing them under the mantle of the UN.

19. To penetrate and subvert all governments, and work from within them to destroy the sovereign integrity of the nations represented by them.

20. To organize a world-wide terrorist apparatus [Al-Qaeda, ISIS, ISIL, etc.] and to negotiate with terrorists whenever terrorist activities take place. It will be recalled that it was Bettino Craxi, Italian Socialist Party leader, who persuaded the Italian and U.S. Governments to negotiate with the Red Brigades kidnapers of Prime Minister Moro and General Dozier. As an aside, Dozier was placed under strict orders not to talk about what happened to him. Should he ever break that silence, he will no doubt be made "a horrible example of," in the manner in which Henry Kissinger [an Ashkenazi Jew] dealt with Aldo Moro, Ali Bhutto and General Zia ul Haq.

21. To take control of education in America with the intent and purpose of utterly and completely destroying it. By 1993, the full force effect of this policy is becoming apparent, and will be even more destructive as primary and secondary schools begin to teach "Outcome Based Education.[17] [18]

The list reads like a litany of world events today.
In 1948, the Rothschilds succeeded in bribing U.S. President

---

[17] Coleman, John, *Conspirator's Hierarchy: The Committee of 300* (America West Publishers, Carson City, NV, 1992). Dr. Coleman conducted 25 years of research on the subject.

[18] See also, *The Protocols of the Meetings of the Learned Elders of Zion.* Believed to be written by Lionel Rothschild, it was first published in 1897; however, it probably dates to the 1600s.

Chapter V The "Global Elite"

Harry S. Truman to recognize Israel (Rothschild-owned Zionist, not Jewish, territory) as a sovereign state in exchange for a $2 million contribution to his campaign. Refer back to point #1 of the instructions for the Illuminati to achieve world control. Israel is declared to be a sovereign Jewish state in Palestine. The U.S. was the first nation to recognize Israel. The flag of Israel was unveiled; a blue colored version of the Rothschild "red hexagram." However, the design angered many Jews, because they recognized that the symbol represented the god "Moloch."[19] "The Hexagram was also used to represent Saturn, which has been identified as the esoteric name for, 'Satan.' This indicates that anyone killed in the name of Israel is actually a sacrifice to Satan."[20] The hexagram is often referred to as the "Star of David," or "Seal of Solomon." However, this is not David of the Bible, but David Alroy, a 12th century false prophet. The hexagram is also used by the Masonic Temple.[21]

The objective of the **Council on Foreign Relations** is the end of sovereignty and so-called "isolationism," and the implementation of a One World Government:[22]

> Although the formal membership in the [Council on Foreign Relations] is composed of close to 1,500 of the most elite names in the worlds of government, labor, business, finance, communications, the foundations, and the academy —and despite the fact that it has staffed almost every key position of every administration since those of FDR—it is doubtful that one American in a thousand so much as recognizes the Council's name, or that one in ten thousand can relate anything at all about its structure or purpose . . .
> The policies promoted by the C.F.R. in the fields of defense and international relations become, with a regularity which defies the laws of chance, the official policies of the United States Government. As Liberal columnist Joseph

---

[19] Moloch: Canaanite God associated w/child sacrifice.
[20] Id. Hitchcock.
[21] See, Marrs, Texe, *Conspiracy of the Six-Pointed Star: Eye-Opening Revelations and Forbidden Knowledge about Israel, the Jews, Zionism, and the Rothschilds* (Rivercrest Publishing, 2001); and Sand, Shlomo, *The Invention of the Jewish People* (Verso, 2009).
[22] Allen, Gary, *None Dare Call It Conspiracy* (Concord Press, Seal Beach, CA, 1972).

Kraft, himself a member of the C.F.R., noted of the Council in the *Harper's* article: "It has been the seat of some basic government decisions, has set the context for many more, and has repeatedly served as a recruiting ground for ranking officials." Globalisation thus implies that sovereignty is not only becoming weaker in reality, but that it needs to become weaker. States would be wise to weaken sovereignty in order to protect themselves, because they cannot insulate themselves from what goes on elsewhere. Sovereignty is no longer a sanctuary.[23]

Paul Warburg, CFR member and architect of the Fed, stated: "We shall have World Government, by conquest or consent." His son, James Warburg, CFR member and financial advisor to U.S. President Franklin D. Roosevelt, made the essentially same statement in an address to the U.S. Senate Foreign Relations Committee on February 17, 1950: "We shall have world government whether or not we like it. The only question is whether World Government will be by conquest or consent." The stated objective of the CFR is quite clear: "The New Order will be built . . . an end run on national sovereignty, eroding it piece by piece will accomplish much more than a frontal assault."[24]

CFR members include the most recent U.S. presidential candidates: Hillary Clinton, Rudy Giuliani, Barack Obama (Barry Soetoro), Fred Thompson, Chris Dodd, Mitt Romney, John Edwards, Joe Biden, John McCain, and Bill Richardson. The notable exceptions are Ron Paul and Donald Trump.

The CFR was incorporated in New York City (NYC) on July 21, 1921. Among the founders were Jacob Schiff; John Foster Dulles, later U.S. secretary of state; Allen Dulles, later head of the Office of Strategic Services and the Central Intelligence Agency (CIA); Edward Mandell House, a top assistant to U.S. President Woodrow Wilson; and John W. Davis, who became the first president of the CFR. Davis was personal attorney for J.P. Morgan, head of Morgan

---

[23] Haass, Richard N., "Sovereignty and Globalisation" (*connorboyack.com/blog/council-on-foreign-relations*, February 17, 2006). Haass is president of the CFR.
[24] *CFR Journal*, p. 558 (1974).

Guaranty Trust. One of the purposes of the CFR was to establish an organization to select politicians to carry on the Rothschild conspiracy of the New World Order. In 1924 Davis received the Democratic nomination for president, despite never having been elected to any lower office.

In 1927, the Rockefeller family began funding the CFR. They purchased Harold Pratt House on East 68th Street in Manhattan for its headquarters. "Since its founding ... the CFR has been the preeminent intermediary between the world of high finance, big oil, corporate elitism, and the U.S. government. Its members slide smoothly into cabinet-level jobs in Republican and Democratic administrations. The policies promulgated in its quarterly journal, *Foreign Affairs*, become U.S. government policy."[25]

All high-ranking members of the U.S. government are members of the CFR and Rothschild frontmen.

As reported by Andrew Hitchcock:

> The CFR membership at the start is approximately 1,000 people in the U.S., including the heads of virtually every industrial empire in America, all the U.S-based international bankers, and the heads of all their tax-free foundations. In essence, all those people who would provide the capital required for anyone who wished to run for the U.S. House, Senate or Presidency. The first job of the CFR is to gain control of the press. This task is given to John D. Rockefeller, who sets up a number of national news magazines such as *Life* and *Time*. He financed Samuel Newhouse to buy up and establish a chain of newspapers all across the country, and Eugene Meyer, who would go on to buy up many publications such as *The Washington Post* and *Newsweek*. The CFR also needed to get control of radio, television and the motion picture industry. This task is split amongst the international bankers from Kuhn Loeb, Goldman Sachs, the Warburgs, and the Lehmanns.[26]

---

[25] Vankin, Jonathan, *Conspiracies, Coverups and Crimes*, p. 70 (1992).
[26] Id. Hitchcock.

The **Trilateral Commission** (TC) is a non-governmental, non-partisan discussion group founded secretly by David Rockefeller in 1972, to foster closer cooperation among the U.S., Europe, and Japan. Its founding declaration states:

- Growing interdependence is a fact of life of the contemporary world. It transcends and influences national systems . . . While it is important to develop greater cooperation among all the countries of the world, Japan, Western Europe, and North America, in view of their great weight in the world economy and their massive relations with one another, bear a special responsibility for developing effective cooperation, both in their own interests and in those of the rest of the world.
- To be effective in meeting common problems, Japan, Western Europe, and North America will have to consult and cooperate more closely, on the basis of equality, to develop and carry out coordinated policies on matters affecting their common interests . . . refrain from unilateral actions incompatible with their interdependence and from actions detrimental to other regions . . . [and] take advantage of existing international and regional organizations and further enhance their role.
- The Commission hopes to play a creative role as a channel of free exchange of opinions with other countries and regions. Further progress of the developing countries and greater improvement of East-West relations will be a major concern.

George H.W. Bush was among the founding members of TC. Several quotes by Bush elucidate the purpose of the group: "Out of these troubled times; our fifth objective—a New World Order—can emerge . . . We are now in sight of a United Nations that performs as envisioned by its founders." (September 11, 1990). On October 1, 1990, President Bush spoke to the United Nations General Assembly: "The United Nations can help bring about a new day . . . a New World Order, and a long era of peace." Henry Kissinger, a

TC member and Ashkenazi Jew, stated regarding NAFTA (*Los Angeles Times*, July 18, 1993): "What Congress will have before it is not a conventional trade agreement but the architecture of a new international system . . . a first step toward a New World Order."

The **Bilderberg** group's grand design is for "a One World Government (World Corporation) with a single, global marketplace, policed by one world army, and financially regulated by one 'World (Central) Bank' using one global currency." Their objectives include: "one international identity [observing] one set of universal values; centralized control of world populations by 'mind control;' in other words, controlling world public opinion; a New World Order with no middle class, only 'rulers and servants [serfs],' and, of course, no democracy; 'a zero-growth society' without prosperity or progress, only greater wealth and power for the rulers; manufactured crises and perpetual wars; absolute control of education to program the public mind and train those chosen for various roles; centralized control of all foreign and domestic policies; one size fits all globally; using the UN as a *de facto* world government imposing a UN tax on 'world citizens;' expanding NAFTA [North American Free Trade Agreement] and WTO [World Trade Organization] globally; making NATO [North Atlantic Treaty Organization] a world military; imposing a universal legal system; and a global welfare state where obedient slaves will be rewarded and non-conformists targeted for extermination."[27] They also plan a controlled Internet, an electronic ID system (RFID chip implant), and cashless society. Daniel Estulin wrote: "Thinking is hard. Thinking independently is very hard, because it requires one to study, to read, to understand. Understanding engages responsibility, engendering personal action to sustain our liberties and freedoms. It is much easier to be told what to do and think and say."[28]

In *Jim Tucker's Bilderberg Diary*, Tucker reports that, with the exception of Reagan (and Trump) the Bilderbergers have chosen U.S. presidents and vice presidents since 1964.[29] This explains the

---

[27] Estulin, Daniel, *The True Story of the Bilderberg Group* (North American Union edition, 2009). Estulin is an author and researcher whose main interest is Bilderberg.
[28] Ibid.
[29] Tucker, James P. Jr., *Jim Tucker's Bilderberg Diary* (American Free Press, 2005).

assassination attempt on U.S. President Ronald Reagan. Reagan ordered the Grace Commission Report, which revealed that not 1¢ of federal income tax dollars goes to the U.S. Treasury, but to the Fed via the Internal Revenue Service (IRS) to pay the interest on the national debt. Reagan stated after the issuance of the report: "None of the federal income tax paid by the American people is ever deposited into the United States Treasury and is being deposited into the Federal Reserve Bank for its use and benefit."[30] Shortly after making the statement, Reagan was shot by John Hinkley. Hinkley was quickly declared insane, avoiding a public trial. Reagan was never the same after the incident.[31]

The Global Elite do not play around. They eliminate problems or radically change attitudes. President Reagan attempted to do away with the Fed and the IRS, which would destroy the Global Elite's control over the nation's monetary system. The IRS is *not* a part of the federal government. It is a part of the Treasury Department of the government of Puerto Rico and is the collection agency for the Fed. Federal income taxes are unconstitutional for the sovereign people. The court, in *Stanton v. Baltic Mining Co.*, 240 US 103, at 112 (1916) ruled: "By the previous ruling, it was settled that the Sixteenth Amendment conferred no new power of taxation, but simply prohibited the previous complete and plenary power of income taxation, possessed by Congress, from the beginning, from being taken out of the category of indirect taxation, to which it inherently belonged . . ."

However, U.S. citizens *are liable* for federal income taxes. Other court cases, too numerous to list here, concur (see the section on the IRS in subsequent chapters for more detail).

The **Fabian Society** is a British socialist organization

---

[30] The Grace Commission report confirmed that all taxes go to the Fed to pay interest on the U.S. debt to the banking families who own the IMF. "With two-thirds of everyone's personal income taxes wasted or not collected, 100% of what is collected is absorbed solely by interest on the federal debt and by federal government contributions to transfer payments [i.e., to the Fed]. In other words, all individual income tax revenues are gone before one nickel is spent on the services which taxpayers expect from their Government." J. Peter Grace, cover letter, President's Private Sector Report on Cost Control (January 12, 1984).

[31] See chart, "Establishment Elite Still in Control," for a 2009 list of CFR, TC, and Bilderberg group members, *libertyforlife.com/nwo/2009Chart.pdf.* See also, *truthcontrol.com/files/truthcontrol/images/6729.jpg.*

established with the purpose of advancing the principles of democratic socialism through gradual reform rather than by sudden revolutionary overthrow. It was founded on January 4, 1884 in London. Early members included poets Edward Carpenter and John Davidson, sexologist Havelock Ellis, and early socialist Edward R. Pease. Many contemporary leaders were attracted to its socialist cause and became members, including George Bernard Shaw, H.G. Wells, Annie Besant, and Emmeline Pankhurst. Its core philosophy was described by Annie Besant: "But the general idea is that each man should have power according to his knowledge and capacity . . . And the keynote is that of my fairy State: From every man according to his capacity; to every man according to his needs. A democratic Socialism, controlled by majority votes, guided by numbers, can never succeed; a truly aristocratic Socialism, controlled by duty, guided by wisdom, is the next step upwards in civilization."[32]

Sounds very much like the tenets of communism.[33]

Compare the goals of the Illuminati, previously stated in this chapter, to the 45 "Current Communist Goals" written into the Congressional record in 1963. Today, all but one of these goals (No. 45) has been fulfilled:

1. U.S. acceptance of coexistence as the only alternative to atomic war.
2. U.S. willingness to capitulate in preference to engaging in atomic war.
3. Develop the illusion that total disarmament [by] the United States would be a demonstration of moral strength.
4. Permit free trade between all nations regardless of Communist affiliation and regardless of whether or not items could be used for war.
5. Extension of long-term loans to Russia and Soviet satellites.
6. Provide American aid to all nations regardless of Communist domination.
7. Grant recognition of Red China. Admission of Red China to the U.N.
8. Set up East and West Germany as separate states in spite of Khrushchev's promise in 1955 to settle the German question by free elections under supervision of the U.N.

---

[32] Besant, Annie, "The Future or Socialism" (Adyar Pamphlet No. 18, *Bibby's Annual*, 1908).
[33] The slogan "From each according to his ability, to each according to his needs" became a tenet of communism published in 1875 in the *Critique of the Gotha Program* by Karl Marx. Marx, however, was not the originator of the slogan. It was commonly used in the socialist movement of the time.

9. Prolong the conferences to ban atomic tests because the United States has agreed to suspend tests as long as negotiations are in progress.

10. Allow all Soviet satellites individual representation in the U.N.

11. Promote the U.N. as the only hope for mankind. If its charter is rewritten, demand that it be set up as a one-world government with its own independent armed forces. (Some Communist leaders believe the world can be taken over as easily by the U.N. as by Moscow. Sometimes these two centers compete with each other as they are now doing in the Congo.)

12. Resist any attempt to outlaw the Communist Party.

13. Do away with all loyalty oaths.

14. Continue giving Russia access to the U.S. Patent Office.

15. Capture one or both of the political parties in the United States.

16. Use technical decisions of the courts to weaken basic American institutions by claiming their activities violate civil rights.

17. Get control of the schools. Use them as transmission belts for socialism and current Communist propaganda. Soften the curriculum. Get control of teachers' associations. Put the party line in textbooks.

18. Gain control of all student newspapers.

19. Use student riots to foment public protests against programs or organizations which are under Communist attack.

20. Infiltrate the press. Get control of book-review assignments, editorial writing, policymaking positions.

21. Gain control of key positions in radio, TV, and motion pictures.

22. Continue discrediting American culture by degrading all forms of artistic expression. An American Communist cell was told to "eliminate all good sculpture from parks and buildings, substitute shapeless, awkward and meaningless forms."

23. Control art critics and directors of art museums. "Our plan is to promote ugliness, repulsive, meaningless art."

24. Eliminate all laws governing obscenity by calling them "censorship" and a violation of free speech and free press.

25. Break down cultural standards of morality by promoting pornography and obscenity in books, magazines, motion pictures, radio, and TV.

26. Present homosexuality, degeneracy and promiscuity as "normal, natural, healthy."

27. Infiltrate the churches and replace revealed religion with "social" religion. Discredit the Bible and emphasize the need for intellectual maturity which

Chapter V The "Global Elite"

does not need a "religious crutch."

28. Eliminate prayer or any phase of religious expression in the schools on the ground that it violates the principle of "separation of church and state."

29. Discredit the American Constitution by calling it inadequate, old-fashioned, out of step with modern needs, a hindrance to cooperation between nations on a worldwide basis.

30. Discredit the American Founding Fathers. Present them as selfish aristocrats who had no concern for the "common man."

31. Belittle all forms of American culture and discourage the teaching of American history on the ground that it was only a minor part of the "big picture." Give more emphasis to Russian history since the Communists took over.

32. Support any socialist movement to give centralized control over any part of the culture, education, social agencies, welfare programs, mental health clinics, etc.

33. Eliminate all laws or procedures which interfere with the operation of the Communist apparatus.

34. Eliminate the House Committee on Un-American Activities.

35. Discredit and eventually dismantle the FBI.

36. Infiltrate and gain control of more unions.

37. Infiltrate and gain control of big business.

38. Transfer some of the powers of arrest from the police to social agencies. Treat all behavioral problems as psychiatric disorders which no one but psychiatrists can understand [or treat].

39. Dominate the psychiatric profession and use mental health laws as a means of gaining coercive control over those who oppose Communist goals.

40. Discredit the family as an institution. Encourage promiscuity and easy divorce.

41. Emphasize the need to raise children away from the negative influence of parents. Attribute prejudices, mental blocks and retarding of children to suppressive influence of parents.

42. Create the impression that violence and insurrection are legitimate aspects of the American tradition; that students and special-interest groups should rise up and use "united force" to solve economic, political or social problems.

43. Overthrow all colonial governments before native populations are ready for self-government.

44. Internationalize the Panama Canal.

45. Repeal the Connally reservation so the United States cannot prevent the World Court from seizing jurisdiction [over domestic problems. Give the World Court jurisdiction] over nations and individuals alike.[34]

W. Cleon Skousen's book, *The Naked Communist*, is a must read for every freedom-loving American. A few of the reviews of the book: "No one is better qualified to discuss the threat to this nation from communism. You will be alarmed, you will be informed (President Ronald Reagan)." "*The Naked Communist* lays out the whole progressive plan. It is unbelievable how fast it has been achieved (Dr. Ben Carson, surgeon, philanthropist, journalist)." "Skousen predicted someday you won't be able to find the truth anywhere because the history of this country is going to be hijacked by communists. I think we are there (Glenn Beck)." "We believe in a moral code. Communism denies innate right or wrong. As W. Cleon Skousen has said in his timely book, *The Naked Communist*: The Communist 'has convinced himself that nothing is evil which answers the call of expediency.' This is a most damnable doctrine. People who truly accept such a philosophy have neither conscience nor honor. Force, trickery, lies, broken promises are wholly justified (Ezra Taft Benson, secretary of agriculture under President Dwight D. Eisenhower)."

Freemasonry is a secret fraternal, men only, order of Masons. It is the largest of the secret societies worldwide. Estimates of the worldwide membership of Freemasonry today range from about 2 million to more than 6 million. The Freemasons date to the Middle Ages, and many of America's Founding Fathers were Freemasons.[35]

Freemasonry is not a religion, and it is emphatically not Christian, although members are encouraged to believe in a Supreme Being, or "Grand Architect of the Universe." Some members are

---

[34] Congressional Record—Appendix, pp. A34-A35, "Current Communist Goals," Extension of Remarks of Hon. A. S. Herlong Jr. of Florida, In the House of Representatives, Thursday, January 10, 1963. "At Mrs. Nordman's request, I include in the RECORD, under unanimous consent, the following 'Current Communist Goals,' which she identifies as an excerpt from *The Naked Communist*, by Cleon Skousen . . ." See, *The Naked Communist* (The Naked Series, Volume 1) by W. Cleon Skousen. This book is part of a three-volume set.

[35] See, Robinson, John, *Born in Blood: The Lost Secrets of Freemasonry* (Rowman & Littlefield Publishing Group, UK, 2009).

Christians. However, Manly P. Hall, perhaps the most well-known Freemason of recent times, wrote: "Man is a god in the making. And as the mystic myths of Egypt, on the potter's wheel, he is being molded. When his light shines out to lift and preserve all things, he receives the triple crown of godhood."[36] In other words, man is his own god.

Membership at the lower levels of Freemasonry is rather benign. All males over the age of 21 who demonstrate good character are eligible to join, and initiates often see membership as little more than a social club, similar to a college fraternity. Freemasonry is a very philanthropic organization, and the idea of contributing something good to the world can be very appealing to new converts. But its true nature is enshrouded in mystery for the new initiates. Masonry is all about "moving from darkness into Masonic light." Members will never be approved to graduate to a higher degree unless they are considered worthy and ready to accept the deeper tenets of the society. They may continue as members, but may never rise beyond the lower degrees. The higher levels are involved in the occult.

Perhaps the most famous and influential Freemason was Albert Pike.[37] Pike developed the Luciferian Doctrine for the Masonic hierarchy. In his writings, he stated: "LUCIFER, the Light-bearer! Strange and mysterious name to give to the Spirit of Darkness! Lucifer, the Son of the Morning! Is it he who bears the Light, and with its splendors intolerable blinds feeble, sensual or selfish Souls? Doubt it not!"[38]

Pike also wrote of a plan for world conquest:

> We shall unleash the Nihilists and atheists, and we shall provoke a formidable social cataclysm which in all its horror will show clearly to the nations the effect of absolute atheism,

---

[36] Hall, Manly P., *The Lost Keys of Freemasonry*, p. 92 (1923). Hall was a 33° Mason, the highest level of Freemasonry.
[37] Albert Pike (1809-91).
[38] Pike, Albert, *Morals and Dogma of the Ancient and Accepted Scottish Rite of Freemasonry*. The book is an exposition of the 33 degrees of Freemasonry, setting forth the "obligations" of each degree of Freemasonry.

origin of savagery and of the most bloody turmoil. Then everywhere, the citizens, obliged to defend themselves against the world minority of revolutionaries, will exterminate those destroyers of civilization, and the multitude, disillusioned with Christianity, whose deistic spirit will from that moment be without a compass (direction), anxious for an ideal, but without knowing where to render its adoration, will receive the pure light through the universal manifestation of the pure doctrine of Lucifer, brought finally out in the public view, a manifestation which will result from the general reactionary movement which will follow the destruction of Christianity and atheism, both conquered and exterminated at the same time.[39]

A One World Government is very much the design of the Freemasons. Meetings are ceremonial and members are sworn to secrecy. Many world leaders are Masons. Women can join an associated group known as "The Order of the Eastern Star."

And there are other secret groups; the Skull and Bones Society, the Royal Institute of International Affairs, the Knights Templar, *Ordo Templi Orientis*, and more. Seek and you shall find.

The "secret societies" consist of men of wealth and substantial political and economic influence. They meet in secrecy, in their arrogance portending to be gods, with the audacity to think they have the right to define the future of humanity. They seek no input from the people they believe they control. There are no limits to their desire for wealth, nor their insatiable quest for power. Their mansions and money will never be enough. Their power will never suffice until it is all encompassing. Diabolical.

John F. Kennedy spoke of secret societies:

> The very word secrecy is repugnant in a free and open society, and we are as a people, inherently and historically, opposed to secret societies, to secret oaths, and to secret proceedings. We decided long ago that the dangers of

---

[39] August 15, 1871 letter to Mazzini.

excessive and unwarranted concealment of pertinent facts far outweigh the dangers which are cited to justify it. Even today, there is little value in opposing the threat of a closed society by imitating its arbitrary restrictions. Even today there is little value in ensuring the survival of our nation if our traditions do not survive with it. And there is very grave danger that an announced need for increased security will be seized upon by those anxious to expand its meaning to the very limits of official censorship and concealment. That I do not intend to permit to the extent that it's in my control, and no official of my administration, whether his rank is high or low, civilian or military, should interpret my words here tonight as an excuse to sensor the news, to stifle dissent, to cover up our mistakes, or to withhold from the press and the public the facts they deserve to know.

Today, no war has been declared and however fierce the struggle may be, it may never be declared in the traditional fashion. Our way of life is under attack. Those who make themselves our enemy are advancing around the globe. The survival of our friends is in danger, and yet no war has been declared, no borders have been crossed by marching troops, no missiles have been fired. If the press is awaiting a declaration of war, before it imposes the self discipline of combat conditions, then I can only say that no war ever posed a greatest threat to our security. If you are awaiting a finding of clear and present danger, then I can only say that the danger has never been more clear, and its presence has never been more imminent . . .

For we are opposed around the world by a monolithic and ruthless conspiracy that relies primarily on covert means for expanding its sphere of influence—on infiltration instead of invasion, on subversion instead of elections, on intimidation instead of free choice, on guerrillas by night instead of armies by day. It is a system which has conscripted vast human and material resources into the building of a tightly knit, highly efficient machine that combines military, diplomatic, intelligence, economic, scientific and political operations. Its preparations are concealed, not published. Its mistakes are buried, not headlined. Its dissenters are silenced, not praised. No expenditure is questioned, no rumor is printed, no secret is revealed. It conducts the Cold War, in short, with a war-time discipline no democracy would ever hope or wish to match.[40]

How right he was. Unfortunately, he was assassinated before he could do anything about it.

Peter B. Meyer curtly describes the Global Elite:

They [Global Elite] are all liars and war criminals, some pretending to be Jews, who are in reality Khazarian Mafioso, Royalty, Nazis, and Paedophiles [sic]. In truth they are Satanists, including the Roman Pontiff. They hold office in the Vatican, the City of London, The Washington District of Columbia, and the United Nations City State located in New York City. This information was received from an insider who, for obvious reasons, wishes to remain anonymous: All those in positions of absolute power like the Queen of England, The Rothschilds, The Bushes, The Clintons, The Rockefellers, The Pope, the hidden Jesuit Hierarchy, etc. they are all ONE big happy bloodline family. They are all cousins, nephews, uncles and nieces of each other. I know some of these people, so don't let them fool you! . . . The crime cabal that rules the earth is asserted to have powerful secret technologies at its disposal, such as HAARP—Weather control, mind control technologies, directed energy weapons [which was used to start many of the wildfires in California], artificially created diseases like AIDS, EBOLA, SWINE FLU, and other near-magical technologies, together enabling them to destroy any opposition and control the people in ways they would never

---

[40] President John F. Kennedy, speech at the American Newspaper Publishers Association, Waldorf Astoria Hotel, NY (April 27, 1961).

have imagined possible. They are always seeking new forms of ***tyranny to impose on the people***, to extend their power over mind and matter. They control the world economy and create economic disasters at will, like the Great Depression in 1930s, and the one which is imminent that has been planned long in advance. They corrupted the money system to enslave hard working people, purposely destroying our society, by eliminating the middle class—the backbone of our economy and society.[41] [Emphasis added]

Through bloodlines going back hundreds of years, the Global Elite today forms a world wide web of interconnectedness. In the U.S., perhaps the foremost family name among the Elite is Rockefeller. The Rockefellers are Rothschild descendants through a female bloodline. John D. Rockefeller Sr. is the patriarch of the family,[42] gaining enormous wealth through Standard Oil Company, which he founded in 1870 with funding from the Rothschilds. Standard Oil would eventually gain a virtual monopoly in the oil industry. He ran the company until 1897, and remained its largest stockholder. Standard Oil was broken up in 1911 for violation of federal antitrust laws. It was dismantled into 34 separate companies, three of which became ESSO (Exxon), Mobil, and Chevron. Rockefeller summed up his business philosophy when he stated, "Competition is a sin." He is considered the wealthiest American ever. The Rockefeller family fortune is estimated to be $418 billion, as of 2019.

Rockefeller was a staunch supporter of the NWO agenda, stating: "We are on the verge of a global transformation. All we

---

[41] Meyer, Peter B., "The Archon Bloodline Rulers" (*finalwakeupcall.info/en/2019/08/28/the-archon-bloodline-rulers*, August 28, 2019). Peter Meyer is the author of *The Great Awakening: An Enlightening Analysis about What is Wrong in Our Society, Parts 1& 2* (Mayra Publications, 2019). A synopsis of the book reads in part: "In 2012, after the second term election of Barack Obama, three patriots formed a secret group of ten very rich and powerful billionaires loyal to the flag and constitution of America. The group of ten named themselves "Q". They were worried about losing America to the Deep State (Globalists). The patriots were all personally acquainted with members of the Deep State and obtained first-hand knowledge on their plans. The most crucial part of the overall plan was to put a trustworthy president into office and subsequently, the right people into positions in the government, which would ultimately result in 'We, the People' being able to take America back from the Globalists."
[42] John Davison Rockefeller Sr. (1839-1937).

need is the right major crisis and the nations will accept the NWO." The Global Elite have been working diligently behind the scenes to create that crisis.

After the death of his father, John D. Rockefeller Jr. took over control of the family businesses.[43] He ran Standard Oil until 1910 and was a director at the J.P. Morgan Steel Company and CEO of Chase Manhattan Bank. At various times, he was the head of the Bilderbergers, CFR, and TC. He is also known for building Rockefeller Center in NYC. His sons included Nelson Rockefeller, Winthrop Rockefeller, and David Rockefeller. David served as chairman and CEO of Chase Manhattan Corporation until his death in 2017. He defiantly stated:

> For more than a century, ideological extremists at either end of the political spectrum have seized upon well-publicized incidents to attack the Rockefeller family for the inordinate influence they claim we wield over American political and economic institutions. Some even believe we are part of a secret cabal working against the best interests of the United States, characterizing my family and me as "internationalists" and of conspiring with others around the world to build a more integrated global political and economic structure—one world, if you will. If that's the charge, I stand guilty, and I am proud of it.[44]

Over the years, the Rothschilds mentored many of their progeny to further expand their financial and global empire. In 1865, Jacob Schiff, a Rothschild born in their house in Frankfurt, Germany arrived in America at the young age of 18. He was given the money and instructions to buy into a banking house in the U.S. The mission he was tasked with was:

> 1. Promote the establishment of a central bank in order to gain control of America's money system.

---

[43] John D. Rockefeller Jr. (1874-1960).
[44] Rockefeller, David, *Memoirs* (Random House, NY, 2002).

2. Find desirable men, who for a price, would be willing to serve as stooges for the Illuminati and promote them into high places in the federal government, the Congress, Supreme Court, and all the federal agencies.
3. Create minority group strife throughout the nation, particularly targeting the Whites and Blacks.
4. Create a movement to destroy religion in the United States, with Christianity as the main target.[45]

Jacob Schiff would become a director of several important corporations, including National City Bank of New York, Equitable Life Assurance Society, Wells Fargo & Company, and Union Pacific Railroad. In 1885, he would also become, through his marriage to Theresa Loeb, senior partner of Kuhn, Loeb & Co. He helped finance the expansion of American railroads and the Japanese military efforts against Tsarist Russia in the Russo-Japanese War.

Paul Warburg, the architect of the Fed, was married in NYC in 1895 to Nina J. Loeb, daughter of Solomon Loeb, a founder of the New York investment firm of Kuhn, Loeb & Co.[46] He became a partner in Kuhn, Loeb, where Jacob Schiff was the senior partner. He was also a director of Wells Fargo & Company. As the founder of the Fed, he worked as agent for the Rothschilds in the effort to eliminate competition in the banking busines. He served as member of the Federal Reserve Board of Governors and as vice chair of the Fed from 1916 to 1918. He became a director of the CFR at its founding in 1921, and remained on the board until his death in 1932.

Paul Warburg's brother, Felix, married Frieda Schiff, the only daughter of Jacob Schiff, and would also become a partner in Kuhn Loeb and serve on the board of Wells Fargo.

The Morgans (banker and financier J.P. Morgan), Mellons, Roosevelts, Bushes,[47] and Vanderbilts are other family names worth

---

[45] Id. Hitchcock.
[46] Paul Warburg (1868-1932).
[47] The Bush's bloodline is through the Mountbattens (House of Windsor, Queen Elizabeth) and the Merovingians. David Icke writes: "This is the bloodline that has produced ALL 42 of the Presidents of the United States since and including George Washington in 1789 . . ." See also, "George Bush, Skull & Bones and the New World Order," Paul Goldstein and Jeffrey Steinberg (April 1991).

mentioning as dominant forces of the Global Elite. Anderson Cooper of CNN is a Vanderbilt descendant. The Bush family is perhaps the most diabolical of the group. Prescott Bush, the patriarch, financed the Nazis during World War II (WWII), along with the Rothschilds, and Americans Henry Ford (Ford provided the engines for Hitler's war machine) and Harvey Firestone. In 1942 Bush's company was seized under the Trading with the Enemy Act of 1917 for funding the enemy. George H.W. Bush was known as the "Godfather of the Cabal." He served as head of the CIA before becoming president. He was involved in the infamous Operation Condor, run by the intelligence services of six Latin American countries to coordinate the repression of dissidents in their countries. He was responsible for the genocide death of 70,000 to 80,000 surrendering Iraqi troops fleeing on a highway to Basra. The dead soldiers were callously bulldozed into mass unmarked graves in the desert. He was also involved in the planning and execution of the attack on the Twin Towers on 9/11 during the presidency of his son, George W. Bush. Bush's speeches often reflected his NWO beliefs. He was a strong proponent of the North American Union, which would erase the borders between the U.S., Canada, and Mexico, and usher in the Amero currency (similar to the European Union and Euro).[48]

More recently, many top government officials are part of the Global Elite. Winthrop Rockefeller was the father of former President Bill Clinton, born William Jefferson Blythe III.[49] Winthrop was the son of John D. Rockefeller Jr., grandson of John D. Rockefeller Sr., and brother of Nelson Rockefeller, who served as governor of New York and U.S. vice president under Gerald Ford. During the Great Depression, the five billionaire Rockefeller brothers, including Winthrop, *purchased* the state of Arkansas, which had declared bankruptcy due to the collapse of cotton prices worldwide. Winthrop became governor of Arkansas, serving from 1967 to 1971, the same period as his brother Nelson was governor of New York. At age 18, Bill changed his name to Clinton.

---

[48] See, "The Plutocracy Cartel," *plutocracycartel.net*, for a list of families, individuals, and corporations which are a part of the world-wide Global Elite cabal.

[49] "President Clinton was born William Jefferson Blythe III . . ." (*whitehouse.gov/about-the-white-house/presidents/william-j-clinton*). See also, *archive.is/dgdUB*.

Chapter V The "Global Elite"

Hillary Clinton is the real daughter of Nelson Rockefeller. Therefore, she and husband Bill are first cousins. Hillary had a close relationship with Lynn Forester de Rothschild, the wife of Baron Evelyn de Rothschild, a bank chairman (Bank of England) of the Rothschild banking dynasty, and the man overseeing the wealth of Queen Elizabeth.

Facebook's Mark Zuckerberg is David Rockefeller's grandson. That explains the left-wing Marxist bias of Facebook, and the censorship and deplatforming of voices opposing the NWO agenda.

Many world leaders are descended through Rothschild bloodlines. Angela Merkel (chancellor of Germany) and Teresa May (former UK prime minister) are sisters, daughters of Baron Rothschild (a.k.a. Adolf Hitler . . . that's right; Hitler was a Rothschild and an Ashkenazi Jew[50]), through the Saxe Gotha Rothschild bloodline.[51]

French President Emmanuel Macron has Rothschild ties through his banking career. In 2008, he was hired by the Rothschild's bank in France. In just four years he rose from analyst to partner, a stratospheric rise almost unheard of in the banking business. He left the bank in 2014 to become an economic advisor to then-President Francois Hollande, and later became economic minister. With the financial backing of the Rothschilds, Macron became the youngest president of France at just 39-years-old when he was elected in 2017. According to Lebanese researcher Riyadh Eid, Macron's wife Brigitte is a Rothschild.

Nancy Pelosi is reported to be the niece of Baron Rothschild (a.k.a. Adolf Hitler).[52] California Governor Gavin Newsom is Pelosi's

---

[50] The idea of Zionist support for the slaughter of innocent Jews was to scare the surviving Jews into believing that their only place of safety was Israel, and encourage them to move there when the nation of Israel was established. Note that the Rothschilds funded Hitler and the Nazis in WWII.

[51] Walter Langer in his book, *The Mind of Hitler* (New American Library, NY, 1972), states: "Adolf's father, Alois Hitler, was the illegitimate son of Maria Anna Schicklgruber [who] was living in Vienna at the time she conceived. At that time she was employed as a servant in the home of Baron Salomon Mayer Rothschild [a.k.a. Frankenberger]." When the Rothschilds discovered she was pregnant she was sent back home. She later married Johann Georg Hiedler, later changed to "Hitler." Langer's information came from the high-level Gestapo officer, Hansjurgen Koehler, who published in 1940, *Inside the Gestapo*. The Rothschilds are known to produce many offspring out of wedlock in their secret breeding programs and these children are brought up under other names with other parents. See also, Icke, David, *And the Truth Shall Set You Free* (self-published, 2004), and Icke, David, *Was Hitler a Rothschild?* from davidicke.com.

[52] Pelosi is the daughter of Thomas D'Alesandro Jr., former U.S. congressman and mayor of Baltimore, Maryland.

nephew. Gee, do you think they are Deep State, pushing the agenda of the Global Elite? Newsom is reportedly involved in a $1 trillion dollar money laundering operation with Communist China and is an agent of the Chinese Communist Party. He has used state taxes and federal dollars to weaponize violent groups in America, including Antifa and Black Lives Matter (BLM), in order to take down America. He is said to be stockpiling automatic weapons, ammunition, and hoarding gold.

U.S. Representative Adam Schiff is from the bloodline of banker Jacob Schiff, mentioned previously. According to an unnamed intelligence analyst and former U.S. military officer: "You talk about compromised and easily coerced. Shifty Schiff is nothing but a political hitman who'll do anything his hidden masters tell him to because they have that much dirt on him. No Congressman will ever expose themselves as much as Schiff has unless they have been bribed or blackmailed to. And oftentimes it's a combination of Pedogate, blackmail and irresistible bribery that keep them doing their dirty deeds."[53]

All Israeli prime ministers, including Benjamin Netanyahu, have been Ashkenazi Jews. They are controlled by the Rothschilds. Do not think for a minute that Israel is a true friend of America. The U.S. is but a tool in their arsenal to achieve world dominance in a NWO. Their friendship with America is one of expedience. America's friendship with Israel is one of naiveté.

And then there's billionaire George Soros, born György Schwartz on August 12, 1930 in Hungary. His father, Tivadar, an Ashkenazi Jew, changed the family name to Soros in order to better assimilate into the Gentile population. As a young man, Soros worked indirectly for Adolf Eichmann, "architect of the Holocaust," in Hitler's Nazi regime. As Eichmann's assistant, he was a collaborator of the Nazi war machine, and participated in the extermination of over 500,000 of his fellow Hungarian Jews. Working under a high-level Hungarian official, Soros was responsible for the confiscation of the property of wealthy Jews who were shipped off to

---

[53] See, "The Secret Back Story Behind the Outright Treason of Adam Schiff," (*stateofthenation2012.com/?p=119720*, March 28, 2019). See also, "ADAM SCHIFF: Deep State Agent, Serial Leaker and Traitor to the Republic" (*stateofthenation2012.com/?p=116341*, February 13, 2019).

Auschwitz. Soros later admitted: "It is a sacrilegious thing to say, but these ten months [of the Nazi occupation] were the happiest times of my life . . . We led an adventurous life and we had fun together." Only it is worse than sacrilegious. It is undaunted evil.

After WWII, Soros attended the London School of Economics, where he studied under the tutelage of Karl Popper, who would become a longtime mentor.[54] Popper's most influential teaching was the "open society," which referred to a "test and evaluate" approach to social engineering. Soros founded The Open Society Foundations, deceptively described on their website: ". . . the world's largest private funder of independent groups working for justice, democratic governance, and human rights."

In 1956, Soros moved to NYC and worked on Wall Street, where he began amassing his fortune. He specialized in hedge funds and currency speculation. He was cunning, ruthless, and without moral scruples in his business dealings. Jim O'Neill writes of Soros:

> If George Soros isn't the world's preeminent "malignant messianic narcissist," he'll do until the real thing comes along. Move over, Hitler, Stalin, Mao, and Pol Pot. There's a new kid on the block. What we have in Soros, is a multi-billionaire atheist [Ashkenazi Jew], with skewed moral values, and a sociopath's lack of conscience. He considers himself to be a world class philosopher, despises capitalism, and just loves social engineering . . . Soros is a real-life version of Dr. Evil—with Obama in the role of Mini-Me. Which is not as humorous as it might at first sound. In fact, it's bone-deep chilling.[55]

In an article, Kyle-Anne Shiver writes: "Soros made his first

---

[54] Sir Karl Raimund Popper (1902-94) was an Austrian-born British philosopher, academic, and social commentator, and one of the 20th century's most influential philosophers of science. He was an advocate of empirical falsification, rejecting the classical views on the scientific method. His political philosophy embraced ideas from major all democratic ideologies, including socialism/social democracy, libertarianism, and conservatism, with the goal of reconciling them. He is known for his vigorous defense of liberal democracy and the principles of social criticism that he believed made a flourishing open society possible.

[55] O'Neill, Jim, "Soros: Republic Enemy #1" (September 15, 2009).

billion in 1992 by shorting the British pound with leveraged billions in financial bets, and became known as the man who broke the Bank of England. He broke it on the backs of hard-working British citizens who immediately saw their homes severely devalued and their life savings cut drastically, almost overnight."[56] He literally bankrupted the Bank of England. He also collapsed the economies of Russia, Myanmar, and Malaysia, and almost destroyed the economy of Hungary. Soros said of these exploits, "World financial crisis was 'stimulating, and in a way, the culmination of my life's work.'" Evil, indeed.

Network.org reported: "By Soros' own admission, he helped engineer coups in Slovakia, Croatia, Georgia, and Yugoslavia. When Soros targets a country for regime change, he begins by creating a shadow government, a fully formed government-in-exile, ready to assume power when the opportunity arises. The Shadow Party he has built in America greatly resembles those he has created in other countries prior to instigating a coup."

In 1997, Rachel Ehrenfeld wrote: "Soros uses his philanthropy to change or more accurately deconstruct the moral values and attitudes of the Western world, and particularly those of the American people. His 'open society' is not about freedom; it is about license. His vision rejects the notion of ordered liberty, in favor of a PROGRESSIVE ideology of rights and entitlements."[57] Bill O'Reilly, in an opening monologue on Fox News in April 2007, described Soros as "off-the-charts dangerous" and "an extremist who wants open borders, a one-world foreign policy, legalized drugs, euthanasia, and on and on."

> George Soros' private philanthropy, totaling nearly $5 billion, continues undermining America's traditional Western values. His giving has provided funding of abortion rights, atheism, drug legalization, sex education, euthanasia, feminism, gun

---

[56] Shiver, Kyle-Ann, "George Soros and the Alchemy of 'Regime Change'" (*americanthinker.com/articles/2008/02/george_soros_and_the_alchemy_o.html*, February 27, 2008).

[57] Rachel Ehrenfeld is a journalist and expert on terrorism and corruption, including terror financing, economic warfare, and narcoterrorism. She has advised the banking industry, law enforcement agencies, and government agencies, and has lectured extensively worldwide on these topics. She serves as director of the American Center for Democracy and its Economic Warfare Institute.

control, globalization, mass immigration, gay marriage and other radical experiments in social engineering . . . Through his global web of Open Society Institutes and Open Society Foundations, Soros has spent 25 years recruiting, training, indoctrinating and installing a network of loyal operatives in 50 countries, placing them in positions of influence and power in media, government, finance and academia.[58]

His hatred for America and its capitalist system is obsessive. In his book, *The Age of Infallibility: Consequences of the War on Terror*, Soros wrote: "The main obstacle to a stable and just world order is the United States." And following the collapse of the Soviet Union, Soros said: "The main enemy of the open society, I believe, is no longer the communists, but the capitalist threat."

Soros directly funds a staggering 206 different organizations, all radical left wing groups whose purpose is to destroy America. Among the groups are the Center for American Progress, Association of Community Organizations for Reform Now (ACORN), American Civil Liberties Union (ACLU), American Constitution Society for Law and Policy, MoveOn.Org, Working Families Party, Amnesty International, Brookings Institution, Human Rights Campaign (the largest "lesbian-gay-bisexual-transgender" lobbying group in the U.S.), Immigrant Legal Resource Center, Justice Democrats,[59] Media Matters for America, National Abortion Federation, National Lawyers Guild, National Organization for Women, National Public Radio, Planned Parenthood, and the Southern Poverty Law Center (monitors the activities of what it calls "hate groups" and exaggerates the prevalence of White racism directed against American minorities).[60] He is the primary force behind the Shadow Democratic Party in the U.S.

---

[58] Poe, Richard, "George Soros' Coup: Soros Vows to 'Puncture' American Supremacy" (*Newsmax* magazine, May 2004).
[59] The Justice Democrats were founded in 2017 by Kyle Kulinski of "Secular Talk," Cenk Uygur of "The Young Turks," Saikat Chakrabarti, and Zack Exley, former leaders from the Bernie Sanders 2016 presidential campaign. Their mission is to elect progressive, i.e., Marxist, candidates to public office, and is responsible for the election of Alexandria Ocasio-Cortez and Rashida Tlaib to the U.S. Congress.
[60] The complete list can be found at *realisticobserver.blogspot.com/2017/04/fyi-206-us-organizations-funded-by.html*.

More recently, Soros has funded migrant caravans from Central America to travel hundreds or thousands of miles to enter the U.S. illegally. And his Open Society Foundations have bankrolled BLM and Antifa in the rioting, looting, and burning of American cities. He has also paid cash to demonstrators to fuel nationwide protests. His Open Society Foundations announced that it will donate $220 million with five-year grants to organizations promoting "racial justice" with the goal of "achieving equal statistical outcomes between demographic groups in economics and criminal justice." Noble as it may sound, it is pure malevolence.

Soros owns the Democrat Party, and has tentacles deep into the Republican Party. In 2008, Soros donated over $5 million to the Democratic National Committee to ensure Obama's election and the election of anti-American socialist candidates. Further, Soros controls or influences most of the MSM. He owns 2.6 million shares of Time Warner, and exerts significant influence on numerous political advertising corporations through millions of dollars in financial backing. Indeed, wealth is power . . . power through the ability to buy influence among the media's news anchors and reporters. Billions will buy much influence. And corruption. Yes; money is the root of all evil.

Soros is reported to have controlled the Obama White House. He was responsible for the development and meteoric rise of Obama from obscurity to the presidency. All decisions emanating from the nation's supposedly highest office under the Obama administration were dictated by Soros. But who does Soros answer to? The BIS and the Rothschilds, of course; but probably somewhat grudgingly.

In addition to Soros, the current cabal in the U.S. is run by the George H.W. Bush family, the Clintons, Dick Cheney, and former puppet-in-chief, Barry Soetoro, a.k.a. Barack Hussein Obama.[61]

And then there are the "swamp soldiers," put into positions of power to carry out the evil agenda of the Global Elite. Michigan Governor Gretchen Whitmer previously worked for George Soros, and her campaign for governor was funded by the Soros organization.

---

[61] For a video of a timeline of events in the life of Barry Soetoro see, *youtube.com/watch?v=uRCQOTBO3Sk*.

Chapter V The "Global Elite"

ABC News executive producer Ian Cameron is married to Susan Rice, Obama's former National Security Adviser. CBS President David Rhodes is the brother of Ben Rhodes, Obama's former Deputy National Security Adviser for Strategic Communications. ABC News correspondent Claire Shipman is married to Jay Carney, former Obama White House Press Secretary. ABC President Ben Sherwood is the brother of Elizabeth Sherwood, Obama's former Special Adviser. CNN President Virginia Moseley is married to Tom Nides, former Hillary Clinton's Deputy Secretary. But at this level, they are merely expendable soldiers who will be purged when expedient. And there are many other swamp soldiers, some currently or formerly in high levels of government, who are mere pawns on a chessboard to be maneuvered according to the dictates of the Elite. Despite their delusion of having power, they are mere collateral with little value to the Elite beyond their specific purpose. They have all sold their souls to the devil. The rollout of the NWO is projected for no later than 2025.

The tentacles reach deep, indeed. But just how deep? It seems the most powerful men and women in American society and government are creatures of the Deep State. But in sheer numbers, they are only a fraction of the population. In 1937, Ferdinand Lundberg wrote:

> The United States is owned and dominated today by a hierarchy of its sixty richest families, buttressed by no more than ninety families of lesser wealth. Outside this plutocratic circle there are perhaps three hundred and fifty other families, less defined in development and wealth, but accounting for most of the incomes of $100,000 or more that do not accrue to members of the inner circle. These families are the living center of the modern industrial oligarchy which dominates the United States, functioning discreetly under a *de jure* democratic form of government behind which a *de facto* government, absolutist and plutocratic in its lineaments, has gradually taken form since the Civil War.
>
> The *de facto* government is actually the government of the United States—informal, invisible, shadowy. It is the

government of money in a dollar democracy. Under their acquisitive fingers, and in their possession, the sixty families hold the richest nation ever fashioned in the workshop of history . . .[62]

Beneath the swamp soldiers are the grunts, pathetic individuals who envision themselves as indispensable to the Global Elite Mafia, but in reality, are no more than disposable humanity which will be discarded when no longer useful. They are not official members of the mafia Cabal, but they can never refuse an order from their bosses or they risk an untimely and unfortunate death, or exposure of a career-ending scandal. They carry out most of the "dirty work" for their bosses. They persevere in their evil efforts with the goal of one day becoming "made men" by demonstrating loyalty to the Global Elite. They support and protect the Cabal at all costs. But their goal of elevating their prominence among the Global Elite is vanity. They will never be worthy of achieving the stature of a swamp soldier. It is estimated 70% of all federal government workers, and many state government workers, are grunts, hopelessly mired in the stench of the swamp. But the day will inevitably come when they will be no more than an illusion; useless pawns; a mere empty hologram that will be deleted from the annals of history.

The true causes of the War Between the States were explored in previous chapters, but could not be more aptly and explicitly summarized than in the words of Otto von Bismarck in 1876. In describing the Rothschilds' role in fomenting division, he wrote:

> The division of the United States into two federations of equal force was decided long before the civil war by the high financial power of Europe. These bankers were afraid that the United States, if they remained in one block and as one nation, would attain economical and financial independence, which would upset their financial domination

---

[62] Lundberg, Ferdinand, *America's Sixty Families* (Vanguard Press, NY, 1937). Lundberg was a journalist who studied and wrote about the history of American wealth and power. A list of the 60 families—from 1924 tax records—can be found at *12160.info/profiles/blogs/the-60-richest-families-behind*.

over the world. The voice of the Rothschilds predominated. They foresaw the tremendous booty if they could substitute two feeble democracies, indebted to the financiers, to the vigorous Republic, confident and self-providing. Therefore they started their emissaries in order to exploit the question of slavery and thus dig an abyss between the two parts of the Republic.[63]

The Rothschilds' objective had been realized. Lincoln's famous words, "A house divided against itself, cannot stand," had come true, but not in the way Lincoln meant it. The Union may have been "preserved," but it was never more divided than at the end of the war. The objective of the Global Elite was *fait accompli* . . . "Divide to conquer, and to keep conquered, keep divided." And so it is today. The Republic collapsed into the open arms of the few. A people so divided will never organize politically to defeat even the direst of enemies.

Thomas Jefferson's words of long ago were explicit in their instruction but lost amongst the rancor of divisiveness fomented by those who would destroy. Jefferson laid out for the people the antidote to enslavement:

> The way to have good and safe government is not to trust it all to one, but to divide it among the many, distributing to every one exactly the functions he is competent to. Let the national government be entrusted with the defense of the nation, and its foreign and federal relations; the State governments with the civil rights, law, police, and administration of what concerns the State generally; the counties with the local concerns of the counties, and each ward direct the interests within itself. It is by dividing and subdividing these republics from the great national one down through all its subordinations, until it ends in the administration of every man's farm by himself; by placing under every one what his own eye may superintend, that

---
[63] Quoted in Id. Hitchcock.

all will be done for the best. What has destroyed liberty and the rights of man in every government which has ever existed under the sun? The generalizing and concentrating all cares and powers into one body.[64]

Though corporate government may appear to divide power among the branches, each branch and sub-branch is controlled by a ruthless monolithic force, consolidating power in the Global Elite.

The Republic of the Founding Fathers died an ignominious death at the hands of the Elite . . . silently, insidiously, and inconspicuously. The people did not even notice. A small cabal of the world's wealthiest men usurped control over an unwary people. The nation was turned upside down. Nothing is as it seems.

---

[64] February 2, 1816 letter to Joseph C. Cabell.

Chapter VI

Treason on Our Shores: The End of the Republic

"Here are the simple facts of the great betrayal [Federal Reserve System]. Wilson and House knew that they were doing something momentous. One cannot fathom men's motives and this pair probably believed in what they were up to. What they did not believe in was representative government. They believed in government by an uncontrolled oligarchy whose acts would only become apparent after an interval so long that the electorate would be forever incapable of doing anything efficient to remedy depredations."
—Ezra Pound (1952)

With the victory by the North in the War, our once-great nation of sovereigns was subverted from a Republic to a socialist democratic state. Through lies, treachery, and deceit, Lincoln achieved his purpose, the preservation of the Union. In reality, however, on a deeper level, along with a complicit Congress and the support of the Northern Bankers (a.k.a. the Global Elite), Lincoln destroyed the very Union, in a Constitutional sense, that history gives him credit for preserving. The consequences of Lee's surrender at Richmond were far direr than the Confederate states could ever have imagined. The ensuing passage by Congress of the District of Columbia Organic Act of 1871 (commonly referred to as the Act of 1871) and the allegedly ratified 14th Amendment marked the conversion of the status of Americans from that of sovereign to that of "United States citizen," and the conversion of the federal government from the *de jure* Constitutional government of the Founding Fathers to the *de facto* corporate federal government that exists to this day. In passing this legislation, Congress committed treason against the People and the nation. The Union of States was no longer. The United States had become a single nation of geopolitical boundaries. Rather than freeing the slaves, the War served to enslave *all* of the People, relegating them to mere **subject** status.

So just what is the difference between the *de jure* government and the *de facto* government? The terms are defined in *Black's Law Dictionary* (second edition, 1891):

> *de jure*: Of right; legitimate; lawful; by right and just title. In this sense it is the contrary of *de facto*. It may also be contrasted with *de gratia*, in which case it means "as a matter of right," as de gratia means "by grace or favor."
>
> *de facto*: In fact, in deed, actually. This phrase is used to characterize an officer, a government, a past action, or a state of affairs which exists actually and must be accepted for all practical purposes, but which is illegal or illegitimate. In this sense it is the contrary of *de jure*, which means rightful, legitimate, just, or constitutional. Thus, an officer, king, or government *de facto* is one who is in actual possession of the office or supreme power, but by usurpation or without respect to lawful title; while an officer, king, or governor *de jure* is one who has just claim and rightful title to the office or power, but who has never had plenary possession of the same, or is not now in actual possession.

To put it in plain English, the *de jure* government is the Republic established by the Constitutional Conventional in 1787 and ratified by the People of the several States. It is the lawful and legitimate Constitutional government of the union of sovereign States. It is the national government established by the Founding Fathers with the writing of the Constitution for the united States of America, the charter that governed this nation until 1861. A lady asked Dr. Benjamin Franklin,[1] as he left Independence Hall at the

---

[1] Recorded in the notes of Dr. James McHenry, one of Maryland's delegates to the Constitutional Convention, and first published in *The American Historical Review*, Vol. 11, p. 618 (1906). McHenry's notes were included in *The Records of the Federal Convention of 1787*, ed. Max Farrand, Vol. 3, Appendix A, p. 85 (1911, reprinted 1934).

CHAPTER VI TREASON ON OUR SHORES: THE END OF THE REPUBLIC

close of the Constitutional Convention: "Well, Doctor, what have we got, a Republic or a Monarchy?" Franklin replied: "A Republic, if you can keep it." A republic is defined as: "One in which the powers of sovereignty are *vested in the people* and are exercised by the people, *either directly*, or through representatives chosen by the people, to whom those powers are specially delegated."[2] [Emphasis added]

The *de facto* government, on the other hand, is a corporate entity that has surreptitiously taken the place of the legitimate Constitutional government. It was ushered into power with the passage by Congress of the Act of 1871, and governs in place of the lawful, legitimate Constitutional government.[3] The *de facto* government is, in the words of the courts, "One that maintains itself by a display of force against the will of the rightful legal government and is successful, at least temporarily, in overturning the institutions of the rightful legal government by setting up its own in lieu thereof."[4] Therefore, we currently have two governments in the United States, one supposedly a mirror of the other.[5] One, however, is dormant, its offices vacant, its power nil, having been supplanted through fraud and deceit by an illegitimate imposter. In this chapter, we will explore the practical differences between the two governments. In a

---

[2] *Black's Law Dictionary* (fifth edition) p. 626. *In re Duncan*, 139 U.S. 449, 11 S.Ct. 573, 35 L.Ed. 219; *Minor v. Happersett*, 88 U.S. (21 Wall.) 162, 22 L.Ed. 627. Note, the people can choose to take care of their business themselves, or by their consent, delegate their personal sovereignty to an elected delegate to act on their behalf. In no instance do the people give up their sovereignty. The word "republic" comes from the Latin idiom, *Libera Res Publica*, which means "Free from All Things Public."

[3] The Act of 1871 will be discussed in detail in Chapter VIII.

[4] *Wortham v. Walker*, 133 Tex. 255, 128 S.W.2d 1138, 1145.

[5] *Downes v. Bidwell*, 182 U.S. 244 (1901). "The idea prevails with some—indeed, it found expression in arguments at the bar—that we have in this country substantially or practically two national governments; one to be maintained under the Constitution, with all its restrictions; the other to be maintained by Congress outside and independently of that instrument, by exercising such powers as other nations of the earth are accustomed to exercise . . . a radical and mischievous change in our system of government will result . . . We will, in that event, pass from the era of constitutional liberty guarded and protected by a written constitution into an era of legislative absolutism . . . It will be an evil day for American liberty if the theory of a government outside the supreme law of the land finds lodgment in our constitutional jurisprudence." "This nation is under the control of a written constitution, the supreme law of the land and the only source of the powers which our government, or any branch or officer of it, may exert at any time or at any place." In other words, a genuine *de jure* united States of America Congress is always bound to enact laws within the jurisdiction of the Constitution. He held the obvious truth that Congress does not exist, let alone have powers, outside the *de jure* Constitution.

subsequent chapter, we will discover just how the transformation took place.

The difference between the *de jure* Constitutional government and the *de facto* corporate federal government is, on its face, subtle (well, maybe not so subtle once you **know** and understand the truth), and probably not easily understood by most Americans. On the surface, the two governments appear to be the same. The vast majority of Americans are totally oblivious to the fact that two governments exist, and that a corporate government governs illegitimately in place of the lawful Constitutional government. One appears to be a mere shadow of the other. But appearances are deceiving. The difference is an enormous one of gargantuan consequences, one being the exact opposite of the other: one guaranteeing freedom and sovereignty to the People, the other oppression and serfdom to its citizens.

In the *de jure* Constitutional government,[6] as established by the Constitutional Convention of 1887, the People are sovereign.[7] The People answer only to their Creator.[8] In the view of the *de jure* government, man is made in the image of God (Genesis 1:26-28), who has endowed the People with unalienable rights;[9] rights which

---

[6] A book that is must reading for every American on the subject of Constitutional government is Michael Badnarik's *Good to be King* (The Writer's Collective, Cranston, Rhode Island, 2004).

[7] *Bouvier's Law Dictionary*, (revised sixth edition, 1856): "Sovereign: A chief ruler with supreme power; one possessing sovereignty. (q.v.); In the United States the sovereignty resides in the body of the people." (Vide Rutherf. Inst. 282). Also, *Chisholm v. Georgia* (U.S., 2 Dall 419, 454, 1 L Ed 440, 455 @Dall 1793 pp. 471-2): ". . . at the Revolution, the sovereignty devolved on the people; and they are truly the sovereigns of the country, but they are sovereigns without subjects . . . with none to govern but themselves; the citizens of America are equal as fellow citizens, and as joint tenants in the sovereignty . . . Sovereignty is the right to govern; a nation or State sovereign is the person or persons in whom that resides. In Europe, the sovereignty is generally ascribed to the Prince; here, it rests with the people; there, the sovereign actually administers the government; here, never in a single instance; our Governors are the agents of the people, and, at most, stand in the same relation to their sovereign in which regents in Europe stand to their sovereigns. Their Princes have personal powers, dignities, and pre-eminences; our rulers have none but official; nor do they partake in the sovereignty otherwise, or in any other capacity, than as private citizens." (Chief Justice John Jay). See also, "The sovereignty of the United States resides in the people, and Congress cannot invoke the sovereignty of the people to override their will as declared in the Constitution . . ." *Perry v. United States*, 294 U.S. 330 (1935).

[8] "To make a law, there must be a superior, who has authority to make it and an inferior, who is bound by it. To complete the definition of law, we must say that it is a rule prescribed by a lawful superior. *God is the first superior.*" [Emphasis added] Inst. of Amer. Law, Vol. I, (1851). "*Lex Naturalis Dei Gratia,*" "Natural Law by the Grace of God."

[9] *Black's Law Dictionary* (second edition): "Unalienable: *Incapable* of being aliened, that is, sold and transferred." "Inalienable: *Not subject* to alienation; the characteristic of those things which cannot be bought or sold or transferred from one person to another such as rivers and public highways and certain

are inherent in every man, and cannot be taken away. The best evidence of this belief on this continent is perhaps best and most succinctly stated in the Declaration of Independence: "We hold these truths to be *self-evident*, that all men are created equal, that they are *endowed* by their Creator with certain *unalienable* Rights; that among these are Life, Liberty and the pursuit of Happiness." [Emphasis added] These unalienable rights are a free gift to all mankind, emanating from an omnipotent God and protected from government intrusion or interference. The sovereign People, then, are the source of law in the land, subject only to God's Law (*Natural Law*). No laws can be enforced against the Source of Law, the People.[10] [11]

The sovereignty of the People was an established principle recognized by our Founding Fathers long before the emergence of the Republic. In 1772, quoting legal precedence, George Mason admonished: "All acts of legislature apparently contrary to natural right and just are, in our laws, and must be in the nature of things, considered as *void*. The laws of nature are the laws of God; Whose authority can be superseded by no power on earth. A legislature must not obstruct our obedience to Him from whose punishments they cannot protect us. All human constitutions, which contradict his laws, *we are in conscience bound to disobey*. Such have been the adjudications of our courts of Justice."[12] [Emphasis added]

The Constitution for the united States of America guarantees to each state a republican form of government [not a democracy] and access to the common law. The People are sovereign, and government answers to and serves the People. The People owe no

---

personal rights; e.g., liberty." Inalienable implies that it is possible to voluntarily *waive* such rights. Unalienable rights are *incapable* of being waived. Unalienable rights flow from God and are not subject to interference from man or government. *Black's Law Dictionary* (sixth edition): "Inalienable rights. Rights which are not capable of being surrendered or transferred *without the consent* of the one possessing such rights; e.g., freedom of speech or religion, due process, and equal protection of the laws. *Morrison v. State*, Mo.App., 252 S.W.2d 97, 101. See, Bill of Rights." [Emphasis added]

[10] Derived from the "principle of the law" under the king. The king is a sovereign monarch and dictator, the author and creator of the laws that govern his subjects. He is the source of law, and therefore the law cannot be enforced against him.

[11] "The absolute rights of individuals may be resolved into the right of personal security, the right of personal liberty, and the right to acquire and enjoy property. These rights are declared as natural, inherent, and unalienable." *Atchison & N. R. Co. v. Baty*, 6 Neb.37, 40, 29 Am.Rep. 356.

[12] Cited 8 Co. 118. a. Bonham's case. Hob. 87; 7. Co. 14. *Robin v. Hardaway*, 1 Jefferson 109, 114, 1 Va. Reports Ann. 58, 61 (1772) aff'd. *Gregory v. Baugh*, 29 Va. 681, 29 Va. Rep. Ann. 466, 2 Leigh 665 (1831).

obligation or duty to the government, but the government is obligated by contract (oath of office) to its owners, the People, the ordainers of the government. The People, therefore, own the government and its agencies. The People are not subject to the jurisdiction of the federal or state government. The People have the absolute right to self-determination, the free choice of one's own acts without external compulsion.[13]

Sovereignty is a natural, inherent right.[14] It cannot be relinquished involuntarily. It is as fundamental as life itself. "Natural rights are those which grow out of the nature of man and depend upon personality, as distinguished from such as are created by law and depend upon civilized society; or they are those which are plainly assured by natural law."[15]

> The Rights of the individual are not derived from governmental agencies, whether municipal, state or federal, or even from the Constitution. They exist inherently in every man, by endowment of the Creator, and are merely reaffirmed in the Constitution, and restricted only to the extent that they have been voluntarily surrendered by the citizenship to the agencies of government. The people's rights are not derived from the government, but the government's authority comes from the people. The Constitution but states again these rights already existing, and when legislative encroachment by the nation, state, or municipality invade these original and permanent rights, it is the duty of the courts to so declare, and to afford the necessary relief . . ."[16]

---

[13] *"I am who I say I am." (U.S. v. Fox*, 766 F.Supp. 569-1991) See also, Right of self-determination, per the UN Charter. Article 1 of the "International Covenant on Civil and Political Rights" recognizes that all *peoples* have the right of self-determination. General Comment No. 12: The right to self-determination of peoples (Art. 1, March 13, 1984. CCPR).

[14] The concept of sovereignty and *civil liberties* actually goes back to the *Magna Carta* in 1215. Although the document does not specifically state that they are a *gift of God*, civil liberties are the rights **inherent to mankind**, consisting of the right to privacy, freedom of speech, right to a fair trial, right to marry, right to life, right to liberty, freedom of conscience, freedom of religion, freedom of assembly, freedom of expression, etc. *Civil liberties* differ from *civil rights*, which are granted by government.

[15] *Borden v. State*, 11 Ark. 519, 44 Am.Dec. 217. See also, *Black's Law Dictionary* (sixth edition) p. 1027.

[16] *City of Dallas v. Mitchell*, 245 S.W. 944, 945-46 (1922). See also, 16 C.J.S., Constitutional Law, Sect. 202, p. 987, "Personal liberty, or the Right to enjoyment of life and liberty, is one of the fundamental or natural Rights, which has been protected by its inclusion as a guarantee in the various constitutions, which

CHAPTER VI TREASON ON OUR SHORES: THE END OF THE REPUBLIC

In other words: "One sovereign does not need to tell another sovereign that he/she is sovereign. The sovereign is merely sovereign by his very existence. The rule in America is that the American people are the sovereigns."[17]

Founding Father Samuel Adams took the principle of sovereignty even further:

> [I]t is the greatest absurdity to suppose it in the power of one, or of any number of men, at the entering into society to renounce their essential natural rights, or the means of preserving those rights, when the grand end of civil government, from the very nature of its institution, is for the support, protection, and defence of those very rights; the principal of which, as is before observed, are life, liberty, and property. If men, through fear, fraud, or mistake, *should in terms renounce or give up an essential natural right, the eternal law of reason and the grand end of society would absolutely vacate such renunciation*. The right of freedom being the gift of God Almighty, it is not in the *power of man to alienate this gift and voluntarily become a slave*."[18] [Emphasis added]

The People, therefore, can only lose their sovereignty when it is taken from them by force.

SCOTUS emphatically expressed: "These inherent rights have never been more happily expressed than in the Declaration of Independence, that new evangel of liberty to the people: 'We hold these truths to be self-evident'—that is, so plain that their truth is recognized upon their mere statement—'that all men are endowed'—*not by edicts of emperors, or decrees of parliament, or acts of congress, but 'by their Creator with certain inalienable rights'*—

---

is not derived from, or dependent on, the U.S. Constitution. It is one of the most sacred and valuable rights. Also, "The state cannot diminish rights of the people." (*Hertado v. California*, 100 U.S. 516 (1884)).

[17] *Kemper v. State*, 138 Southwest 1025, p. 1043, section 33 (1911).

[18] Adams, Samuel, *The Rights of the Colonists: The Report of the Committee of Correspondence to the Boston Town Meeting* (November 20, 1772). Also, Cushing, Harry Alonzo (ed.), *The Writings of Samuel Adams, Vol. II, 1770-1773* (G.P. Putnam's Sons, NY, 1904).

that is, rights which cannot be bartered away, or given away, or taken away."[19] [Emphasis added]

The rights of the sovereign then, are the rights of a king.[20] "If one is publicly established as a People, individually or collectively, then one is entitled to all the rights, which formerly belonged to the king by his prerogative."[21]

All power, therefore, flows from the People to the state and then to the federal government. The People created the federal government . . . and the "created" cannot be greater than the Creator. Government is the servant, the People its master. SCOTUS confirmed: "The Constitution of the United States was ordained and established, not by the states in their sovereign capacities but emphatically, as the preamble of the Constitution declares, by 'the People of the United States.'"[22] Chief Justice John Marshall expressed:

> The government proceeds directly from the people; is "ordained and established" in the name of the people; and is declared to be ordained "in order to form a more perfect union, establish justice, insure domestic tranquility, and secure the blessings of liberty to themselves and to their posterity . . ." The government of the Union, then, is emphatically and truly a government *of the people*. In form and in substance it emanates from them. Its powers are granted by them, and are to be exercised directly on them and for their benefit. This government is acknowledged by all to be one of enumerated powers.[23] [Emphasis added]

Sovereignty rests distinctly on the authority of the People, and not on that of government. "Sovereignty itself is, of course, not subject to law, for it is the author and source of law; but in our system, while sovereign powers are delegated to the agencies of

---

[19] *Butchers' Union Slaughterhouse Co. v. Crescent City Live-Stock Landing Co.*, 111 U.S. 746, 756-57, 4 S.Ct. 652 (1884).
[20] Rev 1:6 (KJV); "And hath made us kings and priests unto God and his Father . . ."
[21] *Lansing v. Smith*, 4 Wend. 9 (NY) (1829), 21 Am.Dec. 89 10C Const. Law Sec. 298; 18 C Em.Dom. Sec. 3, 228; 37 C Nav.Wat. Sec. 219; Nuls Sec. 167; 48 C Wharves Sec. 3, 7.
[22] *Martin v. Hunter's Lessee*, 14 U.S. 304, 4 L. Ed. 97, 1 Wheat. 304, 1816.
[23] *McCulloch v. Maryland*, 17 U.S. (4 Wheaton) 316, 405, 1819.

CHAPTER VI TREASON ON OUR SHORES: THE END OF THE REPUBLIC

government, sovereignty itself remains with the people, by whom and for whom all government exists and acts. And the law is the definition and limitation of power."[24] As expressed by Thomas Jefferson, "[It is] the people, to whom all authority belongs."[25]

In the *de jure* government, The Constitution for the united States of America is the framework for the government of the *collective* sovereign *states united*, established for *specific* purposes. It is also intended to function as a model for the state constitutions. The states are sovereign countries unto themselves, and the people, through the states, formed the compact[26] designated as the *united States*, under the Constitution, for their mutual protection and benefit.[27]

> The original thirteen states existed prior to the adoption of the Federal Constitution and before that time possessed all the attributes of sovereignty. All these attributes except

---

[24] *Yick Wo v. Hopkins*, 118 U.S. 356, 30 Led. 220, 6 Sup. Ct. Rep. 1064, 1886.

[25] 1821 letter to Spencer Roane. See also, *Spooner v. McConnell*, 22 F 939 at 943: "The sovereignty of a state does not reside in the persons who fill the different departments of its government, but in the People, from whom the government emanated; and they may change it at their discretion. Sovereignty, then in this country, abides with the constituency, and not with the agent; and this remark is true, both in reference to the federal and state government."

[26] See, *Glass v. Sloop Betsey*, 3 Dall. (U.S.) 6 (1794): ". . . Our government is founded upon compact. Sovereignty was, and is, in the people." There is some argument as to whether the government is a compact. Thomas Jefferson stated in the Kentucky Resolution, "Resolved, that the several States composing the United States of America, are not united on the principles of unlimited submission to their General Government; but that by compact under the style and title of a Constitution for the United States and of amendments thereto, they constituted a General Government for special purposes, delegated to that Government certain definite powers, reserving each State to itself, the residuary mass of right to their own self Government; and that whensoever the General Government assumes undelegated powers, its acts are unauthoritative, void, and of no force." Daniel Webster, in a debate with Robert Hayne in the Senate in 1830, stated: "They [the people] undertook to form a general government, which should stand on a new basis; not a confederacy, not a league, not a compact between States, but a *Constitution*; a popular government, founded in popular election, directly responsible to the people themselves, and divided into branches with prescribed limits of power, and prescribed duties. They ordained such a government, they gave it the name of a *Constitution*, therein they established a distribution of powers between this, their general government, and their several State governments." [Emphasis added]

[27] See, 28 U.S.C. 297, Assignment of judges to courts of the freely associated compact states. See also, 124 F.3d 214, *United States, Plaintiff-Appellee, v. Sheila Terese Wallen, Defendant-Appellant* (No. 96-10460, United States Court of Appeals, Ninth Circuit.): "Congress does refer to the Union states as 'countries.' See, 28 U.S.C. 297." And, "The great majority of questions of private international law are therefore subject to the same rules when they arise between two states of the Union as when they arise between two foreign countries, and in the ensuing pages the words 'state,' 'nation,' and 'country' are used synonymously and interchangeably, there being no intention to distinguish between the several states of the Union and foreign countries by the use of varying terminology." The *de jure* Republic may also be thought of as a federation of nations; each state is a nation unto itself. A federation is: "A joining together of states or nations in a league or association." *Black's Law Dictionary* (sixth edition) p. 614

those surrendered by the formation of the Constitution and the amendments thereto have been retained . . . It is said that subject to the restraint and limitations of the Federal Constitution, the states have all the sovereign powers of independent nations over all persons and things within their respective territorial limits.[28]

In creating this Union, the states, or the People, had no intent of divulging themselves of their sovereignty. The state constitutions form the basis of the law in each of the individual nation states.

The States' sovereignty over the federal government is unequivocal:

> The States between each other are sovereign and independent. They are distinct and separate sovereignties, except so far as they have parted with some of the attributes of sovereignty by the Constitution. They continue to be nations, with all their rights, and under all their national obligations, and with all the rights of nations in every particular . . . The rights of each State, when not so yielded up, remain absolute.[29]

> In determining the boundaries of apparently conflicting powers between states and the general government, the proper question is, not so much what has been, in term, reserved to the states, as what has been, expressly or by necessary implication, granted by the people to the national government; for each state possess all the powers of an independent and sovereign nation, except so far as they have been ceded away by the constitution. The federal government is but a creature of the people of the states, and, like an agent appointed for definite and specific purposes, must show an express or necessarily implied authority in the charter of its appointment, to give validity to its acts.[30]

---

[28] 16 American Jurisprudence 2d, Constitutional law, Sovereignty of states, §281.

[29] *Bank of Augusta v. Earle*, 38 U.S. (13 Pet.) 519, 10 L.Ed. 274 (1839).

[30] *People ex re. Atty. Gen. v. Naglee*, 1 Cal. 234 (1850).

Chapter VI Treason on Our Shores: The End of the Republic

Yet the States themselves are the servant of the People. The People have no master but the Divine Creator of all.

SCOTUS stated this principle quite succinctly:

> Man, fearfully and wonderfully made, is the workmanship of his all perfect Creator: A State; useful and valuable as the contrivance is, is the inferior contrivance of man; and from his native dignity derives all its acquired importance. When I speak of a State as an inferior contrivance, I mean that it is a contrivance inferior only to that, which is divine: Of all human contrivances, it is certainly most transcendently excellent. It is concerning this contrivance that Cicero says so sublimely, "Nothing, which is exhibited upon our globe, is more acceptable to that divinity, which governs the whole universe, than those communities and assemblages of men, which, lawfully associated, are denominated States."
>
> Let a State be considered as subordinate to the People: But let everything else be subordinate to the State. The latter part of this position is equally necessary with the former. For in the practice, and even at length, in the science of politics there has very frequently been a strong current against the natural order of things, and an inconsiderate or an interested disposition to sacrifice the end to the means. As the State has claimed precedence of the people; so, in the same inverted course of things, the Government has often claimed precedence of the State; and to this perversion in the second degree, many of the volumes of confusion concerning sovereignty owe their existence . . . The ministers, dignified very properly by the appellation of the magistrates, have wished . . . to be considered as the sovereigns of the State . . . By a State I mean, a complete body of free persons united together for their common benefit, to enjoy peaceably what is their own, and to do justice to others. It is an artificial person. It has its affairs and its interests: It has its rules: It has its rights: And it has its obligations. It may acquire property distinct from that of its members: It may

incur debts to be discharged out of the public stock, not out of the private fortunes of individuals. It may be bound by contracts; and for damages arising from the breach of those contracts. In all our contemplations, however, concerning this [2 U.S. 419, 456] feigned and artificial person, we should never forget, that, in truth and nature, those, who think and speak, and act, are men.[31]

It should be noted that the *de jure* united States is *not* a nation or a country. It is a federal republic, or union of republics. The *Law of Nations* states: ". . . several sovereign and independent states may unite themselves together by a perpetual confederacy, *without ceasing to be, each individually, a perfect state*. They will together constitute a federal republic: their joint deliberations will not impair the sovereignty of each member, though they may, in certain respects, put some restraint on the exercise of it, in virtue of voluntary engagements. A person does not cease to be free and independent, when he is obliged to fulfill engagements which he has voluntarily contracted."[32] [Emphasis added]

Maintaining the sovereignty of the individual states over the federal government was paramount to the Founding Fathers in the writing of the Constitution. James Madison describes the union as a hybrid confederacy.[33] William Rawle characterized the relationship of the states: "The Union is an association of people of republics; its preservation is calculated to depend on the preservation of those republics."[34] John Adams wrote: "I expressly say that Congress is not a representative body but a diplomatic body, a collection of ambassadors from thirteen sovereign States." Each state had its own political and cultural life and each was a sovereign republic in its own right.

---

[31] *Chisholm v. Georgia*, 2 U.S. 419 (1793).
[32] de Vattel, Emerich, *Law of Nations*, Book I, Section 10 (reprinted by Liberty Fund, Indianapolis, IN, 2008). *Law of Nations* is a work of political philosophy first published in 1758, and has the force of international law today. See also, *Chisholm v. Georgia*, 2 U.S. 419 (1793); U.S. is not a nation but a society according to international law. "By that law [the law of nations] the several States and Governments spread over our globe, are considered as forming a society, not a *nation*." [Emphasis added]
[33] Madison, James, writing as Publius, Federalist No. 39 (January 16, 1788).
[34] Id. Rawle.

Chapter VI Treason on Our Shores: The End of the Republic

    The Constitution for the united States of America is unmalleable and intractable, its powers limited and defined, and can only be changed by amendment passed by three-fourths of the states. As SCOTUS wrote in 1821: "A constitution is framed for ages to come, and is designed to approach immortality as nearly as human institutions can approach it."[35] It was written, I believe, through the Divine hand of Providence, for perpetuity.

    By definition, a constitution is "a charter of government deriving its whole authority from the governed."[36] According to the Declaration of Independence, only by their expressed consent shall the People be subjected to constitutional laws: "*. . . governments are instituted among men, deriving their just powers from the consent of the governed.*"[37] [Emphasis added] In the words of the courts: "There is no mysticism in the American concept of the State or of the nature or origin of its authority. We set up government by *consent of the governed*, and the Bill of Rights denies those in power *any legal opportunity to coerce that consent*. Authority here is to be controlled by public opinion, not public opinion by authority."[38] [Emphasis added] "The constitutions of the American states are grants of power to those charged with the government, but not grants of freedom, liberty or inherent rights to the people or

---

[35] *Cohens v. Virginia*, 19 U.S. (6 Wheaton) 264, 387 (1821). See also, *Downes v. Bidwell*, 182 U.S. 244 (1901). Quoting from the case: "In the language of Judge Cooley: 'The Constitution itself never yields to treaty or enactment; it neither changes with time nor does it in theory bend to the force of circumstances. It may be amended according to its own permission; but while it stands it is 'a law for rulers and people, equally in war and in peace, and covers with the shield of its protection all classes of men, at all times and under all circumstances.' Its principles cannot, therefore, be set aside in order to meet the supposed necessities of great crises. 'No doctrine involving more pernicious consequences was ever invented by the wit of man than that any of its provisions can be suspended during any of the great exigencies of government.'" Also, "We are bound to interpret the constitution in the light of the law as it existed at the time it was adopted . . ." *Mattox v. U.S.*, 156 U.S. 237, 243 (1895).

[36] *Fairhope Single Tax Corporation v. Melville*, 193 Ala. 289, 69 So. 466, 470. See also, *Browne v. City of New York*, 213 App.Div. 206, 211 N.Y.S. 306. *Black's Law Dictionary* (sixth edition) p. 311: "The organic and fundamental law of a nation or state, which may be written or unwritten, establishing the character and conception of its government, laying the basic principles to which its internal life is to be conformed, organizing the government, and regulating, distributing, and limiting the functions of its different departments, and prescribing the extent and manner of the exercise of sovereign powers. A charter of government **deriving its whole authority from the governed**." [Emphasis added]

[37] *Black's Law Dictionary* (fourth edition) pp. 384-5, defines "constitution" as "a charter of government *deriving its whole authority from the governed . . . a written instrument agreed upon by the people.*" [Emphasis added]

[38] *West Virginia Bd. of Ed. v. Barnette*, 319 U.S. 624, 641 (1943).

a people. They define and guaranty private rights, but *do not create them*. But, indeed, no private person has a right to complain, by suit in Court, on the ground of a breach of the Constitution. The Constitution, it is true, is a compact, but he is not a party to it. The States are the parties to it. And they may complain . . ."[39] [Emphasis added]

Yes, the People are sovereign, but the Founding Fathers were astutely aware of the subordinate place of mankind in the Universe. They recognized God as the ultimate authority, the Divine Creator of all that is. Holding this belief as inviolable truth, this nation was conceived. Their belief was expressed through numerous documents such as the Declaration of Independence, the U.S. Constitution, *The Federalist Papers*, letters, and other writings. John Adams and John Hancock, on April 18, 1775, when ordered by a British major to disperse along with a crowd, in the name of "George the sovereign King of England," tersely replied: "We recognize no Sovereign but God, and no King but Jesus!" In his Farewell Speech delivered on September 19, 1796, President George Washington emphasized: "It is impossible to govern the world without God and the Bible. Of all the dispositions and habits that lead to political prosperity, our religion and morality are the indispensable supporters. Let us with caution indulge the supposition that morality can be maintained without religion. Reason and experience both forbid us to expect that our national morality can prevail in exclusion of religious principle."[40] We need only look at our country today and realize the gravity of his speech.

Again, the words of John Adams: "We have no government armed with power capable of contending with human passions unbridled by morality and religion. Avarice, ambition, revenge, or gallantry, would break the strongest cords of our Constitution as a whale goes through a net. Our Constitution is designed only for *a moral*

---

[39] *Padelford, Fay & Co. v. Mayor and Alderman, City of Savannah*, 14 Ga. 438, 520 (1854) Supreme Court of Georgia. This explains why the people must file their complaint with the state attorney general, who will bring the case before the court.

[40] Washington is known to have carried a small pocket Bible with him at all times, and was frequently seen reading and contemplating its pages. Washington also added the words "So help me God" to the end of his oath of office as the nation's first president, beginning a tradition followed by succeeding presidents. Washington also began his Thanksgiving Proclamation of October 3, 1789 with the words: "Whereas it is the duty of all Nations to acknowledge the providence of Almighty God, to obey his will, to be grateful for his benefits, and humbly to implore his protection and favor . . ."

and religious people. It is wholly inadequate for any other."[41] [Emphasis added] Daniel Webster in 1821, expressed prophetically: "If we abide by the principles taught in the bible, our country will go on prospering and to prosper; but if we and our posterity neglect its instructions and authority, no man can tell how sudden a catastrophe may overwhelm us and bury all our glory in profound obscurity." And in his famous Plymouth Rock speech on December 22, 1820, Webster stated: ". . . our ancestors established their system of government on morality and religious sentiment. Moral habits, they believed, cannot safely be trusted on any other foundation than religious principle, nor any government be secure which is not supported by moral habits . . . Whatever makes men good Christians, makes them good citizens."

Samuel Adams expressed freedom as the gift of God: "The right to freedom is the gift of God Almighty . . . The rights of the Colonists as Christians may be best understood by reading, and carefully studying the institutes of the great Lawgiver and head of the Christian Church: which are to be found clearly written and promulgated in the New Testament."[42]

The plain fact is that if Jesus Christ had never lived, this nation would not have been conceived. The Illinois Supreme Court stated in 1883: "Our laws and our institutions must necessarily be based upon the teachings of the Redeemer of Mankind. It is impossible that it should be otherwise; and in this sense and to this extent, our civilization and our institutions are emphatically Christian."[43] SCOTUS echoed the same principle in an 1892 ruling in *Church of the Holy Trinity v. United States*: "Religion, morality, and knowledge are necessary to good government, the preservation of liberty, and the happiness of mankind."[44] In this unanimous ruling declaring the U.S. a Christian nation, the court cited numerous court decisions and documents in support of its decision.

---

[41] October 11, 1798 letter to the officers of the First Brigade of the Third Division of the Militia of Massachusetts. Charles Francis Adams, ed., *The Works of John Adams—Second President of the United States: With a Life of the Author, Notes, and Illustration*, Vol. IX, pp. 228-9 (Little, Brown & Co., Boston, MA, 1854).
[42] Id. Samuel Adams.
[43] *Richmond v. Moore*, 107 Ill. 429, 1883 WL 10319 (Ill.), 47 Am.Rep. 445 (Ill. 1883). Similar wording can be found in a decision by SCOTUS, *Holy Trinity v. U.S.* (1892).
[44] *Church of the Holy Trinity v. U.S.*, 143 U.S. 457, 12 S.Ct. 511, 36 L.Ed. 226 (1892).

Justice David J. Brewer, author of the 1892 *Holy Trinity* opinion, also wrote a book in 1905 entitled *The United States: A Christian Nation*. Brewer began his book with these words:

> We classify nations in various ways. As, for instance, by their form of government. One is a kingdom, another an empire, and still another a republic. Also by race. Great Britain is an Anglo-Saxon nation, France a Gallic, Germany a Teutonic, Russia a Slav. And still again by religion. One is a Mohammedan nation, others are heathen, and still others are Christian nations. This republic is classified among the Christian nations of the world. It was so formally declared by the Supreme Court of the United States. But in what sense can it be called a Christian nation? Not in the sense that Christianity is the established religion or that the people are in any manner compelled to support it. On the contrary, the Constitution specifically provides that "Congress shall make no law respecting an establishment of religion, or prohibiting the free exercise thereof." Neither is it Christian in the sense that all its citizens are either in fact or name Christians. On the contrary, all religions have free scope within our borders. Numbers of our people profess other religions, and many reject all. Nor is it Christian in the sense that a profession of Christianity is a condition of holding office or otherwise engaging in the public service, or essential to recognition either politically or socially. In fact the government as a legal organization is independent of all religions. Nevertheless, we constantly speak of this republic as a Christian nation—in fact, as the leading Christian nation of the world.[45]

The House Judiciary Committee in 1854 emphasized: "Religion must be considered as the foundation on which the whole structure rests. In this age there can be no substitute for Christianity; the

---

[45] Brewer, David J., *The United States a Christian Nation: Supreme Court Justice on the Blessing of Christianity to America*, pp. 11-12 (John C. Winston Company, Philadelphia, PA, 1905).

great conservative element on which we must rely for the purity and permanence of free institutions"; and further, "The great vital and conservative element in our system is the belief of our people in the pure doctrines and divine truths of the gospel of Jesus Christ."[46] In the early 1800s, William McGuffey,[47] known as School Master of the Nation, wrote: "The Christian religion is the religion of our country. From it are derived our notions on character of God, on the great moral Governor of the universe. On its doctrines are founded the peculiarities of our free institutions. From no source has the author drawn more conspicuously than from the sacred Scriptures. From all these extracts from the Bible I make no apology."

Perhaps most dramatically demonstrating the contemporary decadence of our nation, while clearly expressing the principles upon which our nation was birthed, the original handbook for Harvard College, chartered in 1636, stated:

> Let every student be plainly instructed and earnestly pressed to consider well, the main end of his life and studies is, to know God and Jesus Christ, which is eternal life, John 17:3; and therefore to lay Jesus Christ as the only foundation of all sound knowledge and learning. And seeing the Lord only giveth wisdom, let everyone seriously set himself by prayer in secret to seek it of him (Proverbs 2:3). Every one shall so exercise himself in reading the Scriptures twice a day that he shall be ready to give such an account of his proficiency therein.

---

[46] The House Judiciary Committee also stated, March 27, 1854: "At the time of the adoption of the Constitution and the amendments, the universal sentiment was that Christianity should be encouraged . . . In this age there can be no substitute for Christianity . . . That was the religion of the founders of the republic and they expected it to remain the religion of their descendants." The Senate Judiciary Report Committee of January 19, 1853, declared: "We are a Christian people . . . not because the law demands it, not to gain exclusive benefits or, to avoid legal disabilities, but from choice and education; and in a land thus universally Christian, what is to be expected, what desired, but that we shall pay due regard to Christianity?"

[47] William Holmes McGuffey (1800-73) was an American professor and college president best known for writing the *McGuffey Readers*, one of the nation's first and most widely used series of textbooks. It is estimated that at least 122 million copies of *McGuffey Readers* were sold between 1836 and 1960, placing its sales in a category with the Bible and *Webster's Dictionary*.

The student handbook for Yale University in 1787, mirrored Harvard's sentiment: "All the scholars are required to live a religious and blameless life according to the rules of God's Word, diligently reading the Holy Scriptures, that fountain of Divine light and truth, and constantly attending all the duties of religion."

The Christian character of the nation is no more affectingly expressed than by Alexis de Tocqueville in *Democracy in America*, written in 1835:

> Moreover, almost all the sects of the United States are comprised within the great unity of Christianity, and Christian morality is everywhere the same.
>
> In the United States the sovereign authority is religious, and consequently hypocrisy must be common; but there is no country in the whole world in which the Christian religion retains a greater influence over the souls of men than in America, and there can be no greater proof of its utility, and of its conformity to human nature, than that its influence is most powerfully felt over the most enlightened and free nation of the earth.
>
> The Americans combine the notions of Christianity and of liberty so intimately in their minds, that it is impossible to make them conceive the one without the other; and with them this conviction does not spring from that barren traditionary faith which seems to vegetate in the soul rather than to live.
>
> There are certain populations in Europe whose unbelief is only equaled by their ignorance and their debasement, while in America one of the freest and most enlightened nations in the world fulfills all the outward duties of religion with fervor.
>
> Upon my arrival in the United States, the religious aspect of the country was the first thing that struck my attention; and the longer I stayed there, the more did I perceive the great political consequences resulting from this state of things, to which I was unaccustomed. In France I had almost always seen the spirit of religion and the

spirit of freedom pursuing courses diametrically opposed to each other; but in America I found that they were intimately united, and that they reigned in common over the same country.

There can be no doubt that our nation was founded on Christian principles with a strong belief in God. Thus, in a larger sense, the Founding Fathers perceived that the People are not primarily citizens of any government or state; rather, first and foremost, citizens of Heaven.[48] Their obedience is to God above all, to which the authority of government must necessarily yield. In the words of James Madison:

> Before any man can be considered as a member of Civil Society, he must be considered as a subject of the Governour of the Universe: And if a member of Civil Society, who enters into any subordinate Association, must always do it with a reservation of his duty to the General Authority; *much more* must every man who becomes a member of any particular Civil Society, do it with a *saving of his allegiance* to the Universal Sovereign.[49] [Emphasis added]

Even in more recent years, Congress officially recognized that the U.S. is a Christian nation, acknowledged the contributions of the Holy Bible in the founding of the nation, and reaffirmed the people's belief in God. By Joint Resolution, Congress passed Public Law 97-280. Because of its importance, it is quoted here in its entirety:

---

[48] "But our citizenship is in heaven, and from it we await a Savior, the Lord Jesus Christ, who will transform our lowly body to be like his glorious body, by the power that enables him even to subject all things to himself." Philippians 3:20-21 (ESV). This is affirmed under 96 Stat. 1211 and Public Law 97-280 (October 4, 1982): U.S. Congress declared, and by Presidential executive order ". . . **the Holy Bible is the Word of God**." [Emphasis added]

[49] *The Papers of James Madison.*, William T. Hutchinson et al., editors (Chicago and London: University of Chicago Press, 1962-1977 (Vols. 1-10); Charlottesville: University Press of Virginia, 1977 (Vols. 11-)). From a letter, "To the Honorable the General Assembly of the Commonwealth of Virginia: A Memorial and Remonstrance" (June 20, 1785).

Joint Resolution: Authorizing and requesting the President to proclaim 1983 as the "Year of the Bible."
Oct. 4, 1982

Whereas the Bible, the Word of God, has made a unique contribution in shaping the United States as a distinctive and blessed nation and people;

Whereas deeply held religious convictions springing from the Holy Scriptures led to the early settlement of our Nation;

Whereas Biblical teachings inspired concepts of civil government that are contained in our Declaration of Independence and the Constitution of the United States;

Whereas many of our great national leaders—among them Presidents Washington, Jackson, Lincoln, and Wilson—paid tribute to the surpassing influence of the Bible in our country's development, as in the words of President Jackson that the Bible is "the rock on which our Republic rests;"

Whereas the history of our Nation clearly illustrates the value of voluntarily applying the teachings of the Scriptures in the lives of individuals, families, and societies;

Whereas this Nation now faces great challenges that will test this Nation as it has never been tested before; and

Whereas that renewing our knowledge of and faith in God through Holy Scripture can strengthen us as a nation and a people: Now, therefore, be it

Resolved by the Senate and House of Representatives of the United States of America in Congress assembled, That the President is authorized and requested to designate 1983 as a national "Year of the Bible" in recognition of both the formative influence the Bible has been for our Nation, and our national need to study and apply the teachings of the Holy Scriptures.

Approved October 4, 1982.[50]

---

[50] *Congressional Record*, Vol. 128 (1982). 96 STAT. 1211.

Chapter VI Treason on Our Shores: The End of the Republic

Those today who would remove all vestiges of our Christian heritage from the halls of government and the public arena would do well to remember that the freedoms existent in this nation since its founding emanated from the belief that those freedoms are the gift of a Sovereign God, and not the creation of government or man . . . that it is Christian principles that have provided moral guidance to the People, and not government. Thomas Jefferson expressed quite succinctly:

> God who gave us life gave us liberty. And can the liberties of a nation be thought secure when we have removed their only firm basis, a conviction in the minds of the people that these liberties are the Gift of God? That they are not to be violated but with His wrath? Indeed, I tremble for my country when I reflect that God is just; that His justice cannot sleep forever.

However, in their wisdom, the Founding Fathers expressly preserved in the Constitution religious freedom and conscience for all men. James Madison stated this principle concisely when he wrote:

> The Religion then of every man must be left to the conviction and conscience of every man; and it is the right of every man to exercise it as these may dictate. This right is in its nature an unalienable right. It is unalienable, because the opinions of men, depending only on the evidence contemplated by their own minds cannot follow the dictates of other men: It is unalienable also, because what is here a right towards men, is a duty towards the Creator. It is the duty of every man to render to the Creator such homage and such only as he believes to be acceptable to him. This duty is precedent both in order of time and degree of obligation, to the claims of Civil Society. Before any man can be considered as a member of Civil Society, he must be considered as a subject of the Governor of the Universe: And if a member of Civil Society, who enters into any subordinate Association,

must always do it with a reservation of his duty to the general authority; much more must every man who becomes a member of any particular Civil Society, do it with a saving of his allegiance to the Universal Sovereign. We maintain therefore that in matters of Religion, no man's right is abridged by the institution of Civil Society, and that Religion is wholly exempt from its cognizance. True it is, that no other rule exists, by which any question which may divide a Society, can be ultimately determined, but the will of the majority; but it is also true, that the majority may trespass on the rights of the minority.[51]

A man may therefore freely disavow Christianity, pronouncing himself atheist, agnostic, or whatever label he may appropriate, forsaking any claim to a citizenship in Heaven. He may freely worship the god of his choosing. But it is Christian principles that constrain him from wanton immorality. A man's personal beliefs cannot change reality, only his *perception* of reality. The problem with man creating his own reality is that there is then no reality at all. The denial of a universal truth does not make it so. Ultimately, every man shall bow his knee to the god of government or the God of the Universe; the god of darkness, or the God of Light. There is no other possibility. And God has given every man free choice, a choice which is protected by the *de jure* Constitution for the united States of America.

Ironically, those who say there is no God are either the most flagrant of fools or the haughtiest, most arrogant of men. To make the statement that there is no God posits oneself as the possessor of unlimited knowledge, which of course is possible only for God Himself. The statement is therefore self-contradictory, for if indeed a man possesses unlimited knowledge, he is god.

It is one thing to say a man does not believe in God; another to say there is no God. The first is merely lost; the second doomed to despair. The first has hope; the second is damned to eternal destruction. The first perceives a glimmer of light; the second knows only darkness.

---

[51] Madison, James, "A Memorial and Remonstrance Against Religious Assessments" (June 20, 1785).

CHAPTER VI TREASON ON OUR SHORES: THE END OF THE REPUBLIC

For both men, their belief creates their personal reality, but it cannot change the Universal Truth. Darkness or Light; all men by their will can freely choose, a choice guaranteed by perhaps the most magnificent document ever created by man. And in the ultimate irony of all, he who postures unlimited knowledge is pathetically the least knowing of men.

The truth is that God has manifested His existence abundantly through His Creation.

> For what can be known about God is plain to them, because God has shown it to them. For his invisible attributes, namely, his eternal power and divine nature, have been clearly perceived, ever since the creation of the world, in the things that have been made. So they are without excuse. For although they knew God, they did not honor him as God or give thanks to him, but they became futile in their thinking, and their foolish hearts were darkened. Claiming to be wise, they became fools, and exchanged the glory of the immortal God for images resembling mortal man and birds and animals and creeping things.[52]

He has also written His law upon the hearts and conscience of every man.[53] A sense of right and wrong is innate in all peoples.

Elias Boudinot, President of the Continental Congress (1782-3) and framer of the Bill of Rights, emphasized this principle in a letter

---

[52] Romans 1:19-23 (ESV). The passage continues: "Therefore God gave them up in the lusts of their hearts to impurity, to the dishonoring of their bodies among themselves, because they exchanged the truth about God for a lie and worshiped and served the creature rather than the Creator . . . For this reason God gave them up to dishonorable passions. For their women exchanged natural relations for those that are contrary to nature; and the men likewise gave up natural relations with women and were consumed with passion for one another, men committing shameless acts with men and receiving in themselves the due penalty for their error. And since they did not see fit to acknowledge God, God gave them up to a debased mind to do what ought not to be done. They were filled with all manner of unrighteousness, evil, covetousness, malice. They are full of envy, murder, strife, deceit, maliciousness. They are gossips, slanderers, haters of God, insolent, haughty, boastful, inventors of evil, disobedient to parents, foolish, faithless, heartless, ruthless. Though they know God's decree that those who practice such things deserve to die, they not only do them but give approval to those who practice them." (verses 24-32).

[53] Romans 2:15 (BBE): "Because the work of the law is seen in their hearts, their sense of right and wrong giving witness to it, while their minds are at one time judging them and at another giving them approval."

to his daughter, written following Thomas Paine's attack on the Bible in his famous work, *The Age of Reason*:

> God in His infinite wisdom has given us sufficient evidence that the revelation of the Gospel is from Him. This is subject to rational inquiry and of conviction from the conclusive nature of the evidence; but when that fact is established, you are bound as a rational creature to show your full confidence in His unchangeable veracity and infinite wisdom by firmly believing the great truths so revealed.[54]

It was clear to Boudinot that an honest and open-minded examination of the evidence proved without doubt the existence of God and the truth of the Bible.

Without our Christian heritage and beliefs, our country would be devoid of any sense of civility or morality, other than as dictated by government and controlled by law. Indeed, as Christian values have diminished, the moral decadence of the country has proliferated. Founding Father Samuel Adams understood this principle when he proffered: "A general dissolution of principles and manners will more surely overthrow the liberties of America than the whole force of the common enemy. While the people are virtuous they cannot be subdued; but when once they lose their virtue then will be ready to *surrender their liberties* to the first external or internal invader."[55] [Emphasis added]

Unrestrained in his behavior by Christian morality, man will be controlled by the oppressive and strong arm of the law at the cost of individual liberty. To again quote Daniel Webster: "The Bible is a book of faith, and a book of doctrine, and a book of morals, and a book of religion, of special revelation from God; *but it is also a book which teaches man his own individual responsibility, his own dignity, and his equality with his fellow-man.*"[56] [Emphasis added]

---

[54] Boudinot, Elias, *The Age of Revelation: Or, The Age of Reason Shewn to be an Age of Infidelity*, pp. iii-iv (Asbury Dickins, Philadelphia, PA, 1801). See also, 1 Peter 3:15.

[55] Adams, Samuel, *The Writings of Samuel Adams*, Vol. IV, p. 124, Harry Alonzo Cushing, ed. (G.P. Putnam's Sons, NY, 1905). February 12, 1779 letter to James Warren.

[56] June 17, 1843 address delivered at the completion of the Bunker Hill Monument.

CHAPTER VI TREASON ON OUR SHORES: THE END OF THE REPUBLIC

James Madison further made it clear that not only was this nation founded upon Christian principles, but its future dependent on those principles as well: "We have staked the whole future of American civilization, not upon the power of government, far from it. We have staked the future of all of our political institutions upon the capacity of each and all of us to govern ourselves ... according to the Ten Commandments of God."[57]

Yet today our country seeks to obliterate the Ten Commandments from the halls of justice, the lobbies of government, the walls of education, and the face of our monuments. How absurd. The Ten Commandments have been the basis of law in virtually all great civilizations since Mount Sinai.[58]

An immoral nation sows its own seeds of destruction. Make no mistake; a nation, just as individuals, shall reap that which it has sown. It is a law as inviolable as the law of gravity. As far back as Sodom and Gomorrah, Babylon, Greece, and Rome, empires have crumbled because of the decadent immorality of its people, their shrines and monuments obliterated or left standing in ruins ... once-great nations effaced from the portals of time. Shall the U.S. join them in their obscurity? Shall the U.S. become no more conspicuous than mere pages in historical volumes for our children's children to read? As a nation devoid of Christian principles, perhaps so. The Founding Fathers astutely recognized that without Christian principles, God's hedge of protection would be lifted from our nation. Licentiousness, avarice, greed, and unrestrained behavior will destroy the nation from within. But it is not too late for our nation to reverse course. It is not too late for our nation to restore the Christian values of our Founding Fathers. It is not too late to restore the divine hand of Providence over this nation. "If my people, who are called by my

---

[57] This quote is attributed to James Madison, and consistent with his stated beliefs and writings, but its source is unknown. As a youth, Madison studied under Donald Robertson, a Scottish Presbyterian. In his later years, Madison gave the credit to Robertson for "all that I have been in life." Madison also studied theology at Princeton under the Reverend John Witherspoon. Scholars believe that Witherspoon's Calvinism was an important source for Madison's political ideas. See, John Eidsmoe, *Christianity and the Constitution* (Baker Books, Grand Rapids, MI, 1987) and James H. Smylie, "Madison and Witherspoon: Theological Roots of American Political Thought," from *American Presbyterians*.

[58] See, Hammond, Peter, *The Ten Commandments: God's Perfect Law of Liberty* (Christian Liberty Books, Cape Town, South Africa).

name, shall humble themselves, and pray, and seek my face, and turn from their wicked ways; then will I hear from heaven, and will forgive their sin, and will heal their land." (2 Chronicles 7:14 ASV) Yes, the People must fervently pray.[59] But prayer must be accompanied by *action*. "Conviction is worthless unless it is converted into conduct."[60] The People, Christian and non-Christian alike, must stand strong in the face of ever-growing opposition to our Christian heritage and beliefs, and be a loud and vociferous defender of the principles upon which the nation was founded. Otherwise, our nation shall be doomed, its greatness relegated to no more than a mere anecdote for posterity, our once-great Republic transformed to one of unadulterated totalitarianism. Freedom, without morality, is the destruction of society.

The powers of the *de jure* federal government are expressly limited in function to coining and printing of money, regulating interstate commerce, laying and collecting *indirect* or *apportioned* taxes,[61] securing the borders, and *protecting the unalienable rights* of the People. All other powers of government are reserved to the individual states, and are to be dictated by the sovereign People. Patrick Henry expressed it well: "The Constitution is not an instrument for the government to restrain the people, it is an instrument for the people to restrain the government—lest it come to dominate our lives and interests."[62] As stated by James Madison in Federalist No. 45, January 26, 1788: "The powers delegated by the proposed Constitution to the federal government are few and defined. Those which are to remain in the State governments are numerous and indefinite." Thomas Jefferson expressed it this way: "Congress has not unlimited powers to provide for the general welfare but only those specifically enumerated." Jefferson again expressed his belief

---

[59] See, Daniel 9:1-19. Also, Lotz, Anne Graham, *The Daniel Prayer* (Zondervan, Grand Rapids, MI, 2010).

[60] Thomas Carlyle.

[61] Constitution for the United States of America: Article 1, Section 2, Clause 3: "Representatives and *direct taxes shall be* apportioned *among the states* which may be included within this Union, according to their respective numbers . . ." Article 1, Section 9, Clause 4: "No capitation, *or other direct tax, shall be laid, unless* in proportion to the census or enumeration herein before directed to be taken." [Emphasis added]

[62] Quote attributed to Patrick Henry, but its source is unknown.

Chapter VI Treason on Our Shores: The End of the Republic

in his "Opinion on the Constitutionality of a National Bank," February 15, 1791, stating: "I consider the foundation of the Constitution as laid on this ground that 'all powers not delegated to the United States, by the Constitution, nor prohibited by it to the states, are reserved to the states or to the people.' To take a single step beyond the boundaries thus specially drawn around the powers of Congress, is to take possession of a boundless field of power not longer susceptible of any definition."

How prophetic his words. And Chief Justice John Marshall, in *Marbury v. Madison*, ruled:

> The powers of the legislature are defined, and limited; and that those limits may not be mistaken, or forgotten, the constitution is written. To what purpose are powers limited, and to what purpose is that limitation committed to writing, if these limits may, at any time, be passed by those intended to be restrained? The distinction, between a government with limited and unlimited powers, is abolished, if those limits do not confine the persons on whom they are imposed, and if acts prohibited and acts allowed, are of equal obligation. It is a proposition too plain to be contested, that the constitution controls any legislative act repugnant to it; or, that the legislature may alter the constitution by an ordinary act.[63]

In essence, the only legitimate function of government is to protect and defend the rights of the People.[64] Thomas Jefferson expressed it quite clearly in writing: "It is to secure our rights that we resort to government at all."[65] Jefferson further expressed: "The equal rights of man and the happiness of every individual are now

---

[63] *Marbury v. Madison*, 5 U.S. (1 Cranch) 137 (1803).
[64] *Glass v. The Sloop Betsy*, 3 Dall 6 Billings v. Hall 7 Cal 1: "Under our form of government, *the legislature is not supreme*. It is only one of the organs of that absolute *sovereignty which resides in the whole body of the people*; like other bodies of government, it can only exercise such powers as have been delegated to it, and *when it steps beyond that boundary*, its acts . . . are utterly *void*." [Emphasis added]
[65] February 6, 1795 letter to M. Fransois D'Ivernois.

acknowledged to be the only legitimate objects of government."[66] And according to Jefferson, the power of government is limited to this principle:

> Our legislators are not sufficiently apprised of the rightful limits of their power: that their true office is to declare and enforce only our natural rights and duties and to take none of them from us. No man has a natural right to commit aggression on the equal rights of another, and this is all from which the laws ought to restrain him; every man is under the natural duty of contributing to the necessities of the society, and this is all the laws should enforce on him.[67]

And just because a government is established in a society, man does not give up his natural rights: "The idea is quite unfounded that on entering into society we give up any natural rights."[68] And finally, Jefferson acknowledged that the passage of time may bring change to government and to society. Society may advance or decline, but "Nothing . . . is unchangeable but the inherent and inalienable rights of man."[69]

Further, the Constitution was never intended by its framers to be loosely interpreted. The Constitution was written according to common law principles, with which the Founding Fathers were very familiar:

> The Constitution must be read and interpreted in the light of the common-law principles of history, which were familiarly known to its framers. The Constitution was written to be understood by the voters; its words and phrases were used in their normal and ordinary as distinguished from technical meaning. The Constitution should be read according to the

---

[66] October 31, 1823 letter to M. Coray, a.k.a. Adamantios Koraes. The letter can be found in *The Writings of Thomas Jefferson*, volume 15, pp. 480-90, edited by Andrew A. Lipscomb and William Elery Bergh, 20 volumes (Thomas Jefferson Memorial Foundation, Washington, D.C., 1901-4).

[67] June 7, 1816 letter to Francis Walker Gilmer. The letter can be found in *The Works of Thomas Jefferson*, Vol. 11, Federal Edition (G.P. Putnam's Sons, NY and London, 1904-5).

[68] Ibid.

[69] June 5, 1824 letter to Major John Cartwright.

CHAPTER VI TREASON ON OUR SHORES: THE END OF THE REPUBLIC

natural and most obvious import of the framers, without resorting to subtle and forced construction for the purpose of limiting or extending its operation.[70]

Chief Justice Thomas Cooley wrote: "The practical construction must be uniform. A constitution does not mean one thing at one time and another at some subsequent time."[71] The courts have stated: "The Constitution is a written instrument. As such, its meaning does not alter. That which it meant when it was adopted, it means now."[72] "It is elementary law that every statute is to be read in the light of the constitution. However broad and general its language, it cannot be interpreted as extending beyond those matters which it was within the constitutional power of the legislature to reach."[73] "A cardinal rule in dealing with written instruments is that they are to receive an unvarying interpretation and that their practical construction is to be uniform."[74] [75]

---

[70] 16 Am Jur 2d. Constitutional Law §78. See also, *U.S. v. Wong Kim Ark*, 169 U.S. 891, 893 (1898); *Martin v. Hunter's Lessee*, 1 Wheat 304; *Gibbons v. Ogden*, 9 Wheat 419; *Brown v. Maryland*, 12 Wheat 419; *Tennessee v. Whitworth*, 117 U.S. 139; *Lake County v. Rollins*, 130 U.S. 662; *Hodges v. U.S.*, 203 U.S. 1; *The Pocket Veto Case*, 279 U.S. 655; Cooley, Thomas M., *A Treatise on the Constitutional Limitations* (second edition), pp. 61, 70 (Little, Brown & Co., Boston, MA, 1868).

[71] Cooley, Thomas M., *The General Principles of Constitutional Law* (third edition), pp. 386-7 (Little, Brown & Co., Boston, MA, 1868).

[72] *South Carolina v. U.S.*, 199 U.S. 437, 448 (1905).

[73] *McCullough v. Virginia*, 172 U.S. 102, 112 (1898).

[74] *Cory et al. v. Carter*, 48 Ind. 327, 335 (1874) citing Judge Thomas Cooley's work *Constitutional Limitations*, p. 54 (1868).

[75] Court rulings with reference to the Founding Father's view of the permanent nature of the Constitution are too numerous for inclusion here. But the point cannot be over-emphasized. See also, "The constitution is a certain and fixed . . . and can be revoked or altered only by the authority that made it." (Justice William Paterson, a leading framer of the Constitution) and whatever each word meant then it means today. See, *Oregon v. Mitchell*, 400 U.S. 112, 203 (1970); "When the Court disregards the express intent and understanding of the Framers, it has invaded the realm of the political process to which the amending power was committed . . ." Justice Harlam; *Hawaii v. Mankichi*, 190 U.S. 197, 212 (1903): "The intention of the lawmaker is the law." See, *Gibbons v. Ogden*, 22 U.S. (9 Wheat) 1. 190 (1824); Chief Justice John Marshall stating for the Court: "To what purpose are powers limited . . . if those limits may, at any time, be passed by those intended to be restrained." Marshall also stated: ". . . if a word was understood in a certain sense when the constitution was framed . . . the convention must have used it in that sense, and it is that sense that is to be given judicial effect." In his *obiter dictum* known in *Marbury v. Madison*, 5 U.S. 137 (1803): "The language of the constitution cannot be interpreted safely except by reference to the common law and to British institutions as they were when the instrument was framed and adopted. The statesmen and lawyers of the Convention . . . were born and brought up in the atmosphere of the common law, and thought and spoke in its vocabulary . . . When they came to put their conclusions into the form of fundamental law in a compact draft, they expressed them in terms of the common law, confident that they could be shortly and easily understood." See, *Ex Parte Grossman*, 267 U.S. 87, 108 109 (1925).

Juxtaposed to the *de jure* government is the *de facto* government. The *de facto* government that exists today is a corporation: THE UNITED STATES, INC., or The United States of America, Inc.[76] And just what is a corporation? A corporation is defined as:

> An artificial person or legal entity created by or under the authority of the laws of a state. An association of persons created by statute as a legal entity. The law treats the corporation itself *as a person* which can sue and be sued. The corporation is distinct from the individuals who comprise it (shareholders) . . . Such entity subsists as a body politic under a special denomination, which is regarded in law *as having a personality and existence* distinct from that of its several members, and which is, by the same authority, vested with the capacity of continuous succession, irrespective of changes in its membership, either in perpetuity or for a limited term of years, and of acting as a unit or single individual in matters relating to the common purpose of the association, within the scope of the powers and authorities conferred upon such bodies by law.[77] [Emphasis added]

The *de facto* government is further a special type of corporation known as a *municipal corporation*. *Black's Law Dictionary* defines "municipal corporation" as:

---

[76] The U.S. *de facto* government is a private, for-profit corporation. Title 28 U.S.C. sec. 3002 (15): "United States" means: (A) a Federal Corporation. Also, Title 18 U.S.C. sec. 3077 (4): "'United States' when used in a geographical sense, **includes** Puerto Rico and all territories and possessions of the United States." Definition of the word "includes": "To confine within, hold as in an inclosure, take in, attain, shut up, contain, inclose, comprise, comprehend, embrace, involve." (*Black's Law Dictionary* (sixth edition) p. 763). Therefore, the word "includes" specifically **excludes** all conditions not **included**, i.e., the sovereign states. [Emphasis added]
Also, "It is clear that the United States . . . is *a corporation*." (534 Federal Supplement 724). And continuing: "It is well settled that 'United States' et al is a corporation, originally incorporated February 21, 1871 under the name 'District of Columbia,' 16 Stat. 419 Chapter 62. It was reorganized June 11, 1878; a bankrupt organization per House Joint Resolution 192 on June 5, 1933, Senate Report 93-549, and Executive Orders 6072, 6102, and 6246; a *de facto* government, originally the ten square mile tract ceded by Maryland and Virginia and comprising Washington D.C., plus the possessions, territories, forts, and arsenals." See, Chapter VIII for more details. [Emphasis added]

[77] *Black's Law Dictionary* (sixth edition) p. 340. See, *Dartmouth College v. Woodward*, 17 U.S. (4 Wheat.) 518, 636, 657, 4 L.Ed. 629; *U.S. v. Trinidad Coal Co.*, 137 U.S. 160, 11 S.Ct. 57, 34 L.Ed. 640.

A legal institution formed by charter from sovereign (i.e. state) power erecting a populous community of prescribed area into a body politic and corporate with corporate name and continuous succession and for the purpose and with the authority of subordinate self-government and improvement and local administration of affairs of state. A body corporate consisting of the inhabitants of a designated area created by the legislature *with or without the consent of such inhabitants* for governmental purposes, possessing local legislative and administrative power, also power to exercise within such area so much of the administrative power of the state as may be delegated to it and possessing limited capacity to own and hold property and to act in purveyance of public conveniences . . . A municipal corporation has a dual character, the one public and the other private, and exercises correspondingly twofold functions and duties—one class consisting of those acts performed by it in exercise of delegated sovereign powers for benefit of people generally, as arm of state, enforcing general laws made in pursuance of general policy of the state, and the other consisting of acts done in exercise of power of the municipal corporation for its own benefit, or for benefit of its citizens alone, or citizens of the municipal corporation and its immediate locality.[78] [Emphasis added]

In other words, in a corporate state, the government has supreme (sovereign) power as dictated by the corporate officers (the so-called *executive branch* of government) and by elected officials (the so-called *legislative branch*). All power rests with the corporation, to which the people must submit. A corporate government is unabashedly *not* a republican form of government as established by the Founding Fathers.[79]

---

[78] Ibid., p. 1017. See, *Tribe v. Salt Lake City Corp.*, Utah, 540 P.2d 499, 502, *Associated Enterprises, Inc. v. Toltec Watershed Imp. Dist.*, Wyo., 490 P.2d 1069, 1070.

[79] Corporations, as noted previously, are **privately owned** businesses. The UNITED STATES, INC. is controlled by the Global Elite, the banking cartel led by the Rothschild and Rockefeller families. The Global Elite also own the Fed, IMF, and the Office of Personnel Management.

Therefore, man is not sovereign in the *de facto* government, but is a "United States citizen." A "United States citizen" is a citizen of a central federal corporate government, not of an autonomous, independent state.[80] "Citizen" is defined as: ". . . members of a political community who, in their associative capacity, have established or *submitted* themselves to the dominion of government for the promotion of the general welfare and the protection of their individual as well as collective rights."[81] Further, ". . . the privileges and immunities of citizens of the United States [pursuant to the 14th Amendment] *do not necessarily include all the rights protected by the first eight amendments* to the Federal constitution against the powers of the Federal government."[82] [Emphasis added] A U.S. citizen, as defined in the U.S. Code (U.S.C.), is a citizen of the District of Columbia (D.C.) or one of the territories of the U.S.[83] Also, by definition, a U.S. citizen[84] is a **subject** of that federal government.

A citizen of the U.S. or of a State is therefore subject to whatever the sovereign power grants.[85] [86]

---

[80] *Kitchens v. Steele*, 112 F.Supp 383. "A citizen of the United States is a citizen of the federal government . . ."

[81] *Black's Law Dictionary* (sixth edition) p. 244. Also, ". . . the term 'citizen,' in the United States, is analogous to the term 'subject' in the common law; the change of phrase has resulted from the change in government." ". . . he who before was a "subject of the King" is now a citizen of the State." *State v. Manuel*, 20 N.C. 144 (1838). Also, *Herriott v. City of Seattle*, 81 Wasg.2d 48, 500 P.2d 101.109, *Volenti non fit injuria* ("**consent makes the law**"). "He who consents to what is done cannot complain of it." No right of action accrues to a person who agreed to what was done, even though it injured him.

[82] *Maxwell v Dow*, p. 455, 20 S.C.R. 448 (1900). The Bill of Rights (Amendments I through X) protects the rights of the People, but not necessarily "citizens."

[83] 8 U.S.C. §1401: ". . . citizens of the United States at birth: (a) a person born in the United States, and *subject* to the jurisdiction thereof . . ." Every word in law has a specific and concise meaning. Also, "THE UNITED STATES GOVERNMENT IS A FOREIGN CORPORATION WITH RESPECT TO A STATE." [Emphasis added] *Volume 20: Corpus Juris Sec.* §1785: NY re: Merriam 36 N.E. 505 1441 S.Ct.1973, 41 L.Ed.287. Also, Internal Revenue Code Section 312(e): Federal jurisdiction "includes the District of Columbia, the Commonwealth of Puerto Rico, the Virgin Islands, Guam, and American Samoa." In legal terminology, the word "**includes**" means "**is limited to**."

[84] U.S. citizen. *The antithesis of alien. A person born or naturalized in the United States and **subject** to the **jurisdiction** thereof. [Ballentine's Law Dictionary* (third edition)] . . . *[T]he term "citizen," in the United States, is analogous to the term "subject" in the common law; the change of phrase has resulted from the change of government.* [Emphasis added].

[85] *Black's Law Dictionary* (sixth edition) p. 1425, defines "subject" as: one that *owes allegiance to a sovereign* and is governed by his laws . . . Men in free governments are subjects as well as citizens; as citizens they enjoy rights and franchises; as subjects they are bound to obey the laws. The term is little used, in this sense, in countries enjoying a republican form of government." [Emphasis added]

[86] See, Senate Document 108-17, pp. 1006-7, footnote 37; (citizen, subject, ceorl [a freeman of the lowest class in Anglo-Saxon England], freeman, serf).

Chapter VI Treason on Our Shores: The End of the Republic

The Constitution for the united States of America exists in form and appearance only in the *de facto* government. It has been re-made into a *corporate* charter, or bylaws, that can be *interpreted* and changed at the discretion of the de facto federal government and the courts, to serve its own purposes.[87] It is "proprietary law" for the municipal corporate government.[88] It only applies in D.C. and the federal territories. In the *de facto* government, power flows from an all-powerful central federal government to the corporate States, and then to the citizen as **subjects** of both, much as the English are subjects of the king or queen. God is of no consequence in such a government, hence the fight that exists today to keep even the mention of God and religion out of government and the public sector through the creation of the so-called principle of the "separation of church and state."[89] [90] It further explains the effort

---

[87] SCOTUS: *Stoutenburgh v. Hennick*, 129 U.S. 141 (1889). "And Whereas: On February 21, 1871, the Forty First Congress passed an act entitled 'An Act to Provide a Government for the District of Columbia,' legislating the organization of a municipal corporation to run the day-to-day **affairs of the District of Columbia**, the seat of government, which **transferred the United States of America, the Republic, into 'a corporate entity' entitled UNITED STATES**, in capital letters, **having 'no' jurisdiction outside the District of Columbia**. And Whereas: Congress **adopted** the text of the **federal constitution** as the constitution or **charter** of this **municipal corporation**. This municipal corporation was granted the power to contract to provide municipal services **to the inhabitants of the District of Columbia** and necessarily as an operation of the privileges and immunity clause of Article Four of the Constitution, any **other person who chooses** to **contract for its services**." Note that the power and authority of the corporation is centered in the District of Columbia. However, the United States citizen is a citizen of the District of Columbia (or one of the territories of the U.S.), and therefore falls under the jurisdiction of this corporate government. Americans have unwittingly and freely *chosen* to become United States citizens, albeit by deceit. The Act of 1871 changed the Constitution for the united States of America to the Constitution of the United States of America. [Emphasis added]

[88] *Black's Law Dictionary* (sixth edition) p. 1219. "Proprietary. A proprietor or owner; one who has the exclusive title to a thing; one who possesses or holds the title to a thing in his own right; one who possesses the dominion or ownership of a thing in his own right. Proprietary governments. This expression is used by Blackstone to denote governments granted out by the crown to individuals, in the nature of feudatory principalities, with inferior regalities and subordinate powers of legislation such as formerly belonged to the owners of counties palatine. 1 Bl.Comm. 108."

[89] Separation of church and state is a principle which secures the rights and privileges of all citizens under a government and ensures that both government and church function according to their God-given roles. The principle originated with Thomas Jefferson's "wall of separation" letter to the Danbury Baptist Association in 1802. In the letter, Jefferson wrote: "I contemplate with sovereign reverence that act of the whole American people which declared that their legislature should 'make no law respecting an establishment of religion, or prohibiting the free exercise thereof,' thus building a wall of separation between Church & State." Two days after he sent the letter, he attended a church service conducted in the House of Representatives. Jefferson's intent was not to exclude religious principles from the halls of government.

[90] See, Barton, David, *Original Intent: The Courts, The Constitution, and Religion* (WallBuilders, 2008). The book explores the Founding Father's intended role of the judiciary in American government. The

by the *de facto* government and left wing scholars today to promote the preposterous theory of Evolution.[91] Evolution precludes the possibility of a Creator, and if there is no Creator, there can be no *unalienable rights* that emanate from the Creator. The *de facto* government stands in juxtaposition to the Sovereign God. The *government*, not God, is the supreme authority with the power to determine what privileges, if any, its citizenry may have at any given time under any given circumstances. The citizens have no *rights* in such a government, merely privileges.[92]

The *de facto* government has become the new god.[93] It establishes the morals and values of the citizens without any basis and changes those values at its whim. It emphasizes religious and social tolerance, but discourages Christianity. Homosexuality and abortion are no longer considered taboo, but have become socially acceptable, in fact protected by the *de facto* government, considered to be the "right" of those who indulge in the debauchery.[94] Gay marriage is endorsed.[95] Planned Parenthood promotes the sexual

---

book is an excellent exposé on how, through revisionism and judicial activism, the principle of separation of church and state in modern American government has become egregiously distorted from the intent of Thomas Jefferson and the Founding Fathers. Documented with numerous quotes and writings from original sources.

[91] According to the theory of evolution human beings are "animals." For the purposes of the *de facto* government, human beings are considered to be property, chattel, or *human resources*, to be used as any animal or other resource would be used. Per EO 13037, the citizens are "human capital," property of the UNITED STATES *corporate* government. As "human capital" Americans are corporate "legal" assets with no "lawful" rights in the *de facto* government. The goal of the Global Elite is to place an RFID chip in every human being, thus placing every man, woman, and child in the nation into "inventory." Obamacare originally mandated that all Americans be implanted with a chip within 36 months of passage of the bill (by March 23, 2013) (pp. 1000-8). As Malcolm Muggeridge wrote: "I myself am convinced that the theory of evolution, especially to the extent to which it has been applied, will be one of the greatest jokes in the history books of the future. Posterity will marvel that so very flimsy and dubious an hypothesis could be accepted with the incredible credulity it has."

[92] The 14th Amendment: "**Section 1. All persons** born or naturalized in the United States **and subject to the jurisdiction thereof**, are citizens of the United States and of the State wherein they reside [not sovereign]. *No State shall make or enforce any law which shall abridge the **privileges and immunities** [not rights] of citizens of the United States.*" This will be discussed in more detail in Chapter VIII.

[93] Romans 1:25 (ASV): ". . . they exchanged the truth of God for a lie, and worshipped and served the creature rather than the Creator . . ."

[94] See, Romans 1:24-32. See also, Deuteronomy 22:5 and Leviticus 18:22.

[95] "*Conjunctio mariti et faeminae est de jure naturae.* The union of a man and a woman is of the law of nature." From John Bouvier's *Maxims of Law* (1856): "Maxim. An established principle or proposition. A principle of law universally admitted, as being just and consonant with reason." Maxims are "principles and authorities, and part of the general customs or common law of the land; and are of the same strength as acts of parliament, when the judges have determined what is a maxim; which belongs to the judges and not the jury." See also, Deuteronomy 22:5 and Leviticus 18:22.

CHAPTER VI TREASON ON OUR SHORES: THE END OF THE REPUBLIC

promiscuity of young women. Biblical marriage has become passé, disparaged by a government that would remove all vestiges of Biblical values from society.[96] The *de facto* government encourages public acceptance of its new morals through government-controlled media[97] and decadent entertainment,[98] enticing even the so-called "religious" to accept this "new morality." Succumbing to public and government pressure, entire denominations have committed apostasy, forsaking Biblical truth by embracing homosexuality, abortion, cohabitation, and other immorality in the name of compassion, tolerance, personal rights, and free thinking. Homosexuals are ordained into church ministry and leadership. The sanctity of life from "womb to tomb" has been abandoned in favor of "women's rights" and the expedience of an emerging healthcare system that places little value on the lives of the elderly. The Ten Commandments have become the Ten Suggestions. The "Way, the Truth, and the Light" has been replaced with "a path among many, moral relativism, and obscurity."

---

[96] i.e., the refusal of the Obama government, at the president's order, to defend the Defense of Marriage Act (Pub.L.104-199, 110 Stat. 2419, enacted September 21, 1996, 1 U.S.C. §7 and 28 U.S.C. §1738C) is a U.S. law that defines marriage as the legal union of one man and one woman for federal and interstate recognition purposes in the U.S. *Conjunctio mariti et faeminae est de jure naturae* (the union of a man and a woman is of the law of nature) is a principle of law universally admitted, as being just and consonant with reason. However, the *de facto* corporate government can change the law at its discretion, or selectively refuse to enforce laws that do not fit its agenda. Such an act of defiance against a law passed by Congress in the *de jure* government would be unthinkable, an act of treason and grounds for impeachment. Further, the breakdown of marriage promotes dependence on government at the expense of liberty. The goal of the Global Elite is the complete removal of traditional values from society. As stated by Zbigniew Brzezinski, adviser to five U.S. presidents and executive director of the TC: "The Technocratic era involves the gradual appearance of a more controlled society. Such a society would be ***dominated by an elite, unrestrained by traditional values***." [Emphasis added]

[97] See, Mullins, Eustace Clarence, "Who Owns the TV Networks?" (1991). Mullins's research, published in this pamphlet, shows that the Rothschilds have control of all three major U.S. networks, plus other aspects of the recording and mass media industry. They also control Reuters, Associated Press, MSNBC, and CNN, as well as the major movie studios. Newspapers under their control include *The New York Times, Los Angeles Times,* and *The Washington Post.*

[98] Hollywood is controlled by Rothschild Zionists. Rothschild Zionism is a political system and philosophy, a secret society created by the Rothschilds. As stated by David Icke: "Zionism means Rothschild just as Israel means Rothschild. When we see the extraordinary number of Zionists in key positions around the world we are looking not at 'manipulating Jews,' but manipulating Zionists representing the interests and demands of the Rothschilds." *Los Angeles Times* columnist Joel Stein (a Rothschild Zionist) wrote an article proclaiming that Rothschild Zionists control Hollywood. He stated in the article: "I had to scour the trades to come up with six Gentiles in high positions at entertainment companies. But lo and behold, even one of the six, AMC President Charles Collier, turned out to be a Jew! . . . as a proud Jew, I want Americans to know of our accomplishment. Yes, we control Hollywood." Note that a person does not have to be a Jew to be a Zionist.

Moral relativism denies any objective truth, except, of course, for the truth that there is no truth.[99] Indeed, "relevant truth" has set man up as his own god instead of serving God. Even our churches pay homage to this god through their 501(c)(3) corporate status.[100] What does the church have to do with the IRS? To which god shall it bow . . . the god of government or Almighty God in Heaven? The church is a body of Peoples, the body of Christ. To whom shall the People give their allegiance? From the beginning of time, it is written, ". . . Thou shall have no other gods before me."[101] But,

---

[99] Such posturing, of course, is absurd. In the words of Ravi Zacharias, author, evangelist and Christian apologist: "If I make the statement all truth is relative, that statement either includes itself or excludes itself. If it includes itself, it means that statement is also relative which means it's not always true. If it excludes itself than it's positing an absolute while denying that absolutes actually exist."

[100] The church has succumbed to government control in exchange for a co-called "benefit," its tax-exempt corporate status. In doing so, the church exists by permission of the government, and not by the authority of God. They have placed their faith in government, and not God. The government also uses this corporate status to control free speech, i.e., to prevent ministers, pastors, and church leaders from utilizing their political influence upon the church body or the general populace. Further, the church displays the gold-fringed flag of admiralty/maritime law, thereby subjugating itself to corporate government control. The *de facto* government selectively applies this principle at its discretion to suit its needs. "***A corporation derives its existence and all of its powers from the State*** and, therefore, has only such powers as the State has conferred upon it. Power is used here to mean the legal capacity to execute and fulfill the objects and purposes for which the corporation was created, and the source of this power is the charter and the statute under which the corporation was organized." [Emphasis added] —Len Young Smith and G. Gale Roberson, *Smith and Roberson's Business Law*, p. 796 (West Publishing Company, 1966). An article by Barbara Ketay states: "A 501(c)(3) corporation, being an artificial person, is not considered a person under the First Amendment to the United States Constitution (religious liberty clause) or under the Fifth Amendment to the United States Constitution (protection against self-incrimination clause). Therefore, an incorporated church has NO First or Fifth Amendment rights. In the case *Johnson v. Goodyear*, 127 Cal.4 (1899): 'A corporation, being an artificial person, only has rights within the meaning of the due process and equal protection clauses of the Fourteenth Amendment to the United States Constitution and similar provisions of State constitutions and within the meaning of state statutes.'" [i.e., Your 501(c)(3) church has no constitutional rights. The pastor/priest and leaders of the church do ***not*** have the right to freedom of speech, and therefore may not be able to preach the uncompromised Word of God with regard to certain subjects.] Further, once an organization is incorporated, it is removed from the natural jurisdiction of the land (common law) and placed in the international jurisdiction of the sea (admiralty law), under the Satanic law of the sea. Incorporating a church places it under the law of Satan, regardless of the message being preached.

IRS Senior Officer Steve Nestor has stated: "I am not the only IRS employee who's wondered why churches go to the government and seek permission to be exempted from a tax they didn't owe to begin with, and to seek a tax-deductible status that they've always had anyway. Many of us have marveled at how church leaders [Christ is the head of the church] want to be regulated and controlled by an agency of government . . . Churches are in an amazingly unique position, but they don't seem to know or appreciate the implications of what it would mean to be free of government control." (IRS Publication 526, quoted by Peter Kershaw, *In Caesar's Grip* (self-published, 2000); See also, Thomas Lake, *Romans 13 In a Constitutional Republic*, p. 9 (Xlibris, 2011).

[101] The Ten Commandments, given to Moses and written on tablets of stone, Exodus 20:2-17. Also, Deuteronomy 5:7.

alas, our churches now bow to the dictates of government. The church is more fearful of the god of government than the God of the Universe. In truth, churches are established and ordained by God, and do not need the permission of government.[102] They are protected by Amendments I and V to the legitimate *de jure* Constitutional government.

The modern church has, to its peril, become the church at Pergamum, married to the world, forsaking its once beloved betrothed for the gods of Balaam, and guilty of the sins of the Nicolaitans.[103] For contemporary man, it seems the glitter of gold shines brighter than the lustrous Luminescence of His Divine Light, man's soul wantonly lured into darkness at the repudiation of his evolving enlightenment.[104]

In the *de facto* government, the president of the UNITED STATES is the president of a corporation, and not the holder of the *office* of the president of the united States of America. As president of a corporation, his powers are not limited by the Constitution for the united States of America.[105] The board of directors of the corporation

---

[102] Ephesians 5:23: "For the husband is the head of the wife, even as **Christ is the head of the church.**" By incorporating, the church places the state above God. A corporation is a creation of the State. The State therefore is the sole authority and sovereign head over the incorporated church. By the act of incorporating, **the church is denouncing the Lord Jesus Christ as its Creator and has put the State in His place**. The government is sovereign over the incorporated church, not God.

"Choose you this day whom ye will serve; whether the gods which your fathers served that were on the other side of the flood, or the gods of the Amorites, in whose land ye dwell: but as for me and my house, we will serve the Lord." (Joshua 24:15) "No man can serve two masters, for either he will hate the one, and love the other; or else he will hold to the one, and despise the other. Ye cannot serve God and mammon." (Matthew 6:24)

[103] Revelation 2:14-15 (ESV): "But I have a few things against you: you have some there who hold the teaching of Balaam, who taught Balak to put a stumbling block before the sons of Israel, so that they might eat food sacrificed to idols and practice sexual immorality. So also you have some who hold the teaching of the Nicolaitans." Pergamum means *"improper marriage."* The church at Pergamum was *improperly married* to the pagan culture that surrounded it.

[104] James 4- 4 (NKJV): "Do you not know that friendship with the world is enmity with God? Whoever therefore wants to be a friend of the world [*or any man-made kingdom other than God's Kingdom*] makes himself an enemy of God."

[105] This explains why the place of Obama's birth is not an issue. He does not hold the Constitutional office of the president of the United States, but serves as the president of a corporation, The United States of America, Inc. Though evidence clearly proves that he was born in Kenya, he can be president of a corporation without regard to his place of birth or Constitutional restraints. The forged birth certificate is nothing more than a pathetic fraudulent attempt to cover up the truth . . . a truth, however, which is of little consequence in the corporate federal government. The cover-up is to deceive the citizenry into believing that Obama occupies the legitimate office of the president of the united States. In a surprising and rather audacious statement, Obama's New Jersey lawyer, Alexandra Hill, ***admitted*** the image of Obama's birth certificate was a forgery and then made the absurd claim that, therefore, it

consists of the owner/members of the 12 branches of the Fed,[106] under the control of the House of Rothschild (Evelyn Rothschild, Bank of England, and Benjamin Rothschild of France, et al.). The chairman of the board is the chairman of the Fed. Although the chairman is appointed by the president, he is nominated by the board of directors, and ultimately is the choice of the board. Confirmation by the Rothschild-controlled U.S. Senate is a rubber stamp. The secretary of state, the secretary of the treasury, and other so-called cabinet members are officers of the corporation, and do not hold the equivalent Constitutional office. The equivalent Constitutional offices are vacant. The president of the corporation rules by executive order.[107] The president is a mere puppet of the

---

cannot be used as evidence to confirm his lack of natural born citizenship status. Therefore, she argued, it is "irrelevant to his placement on the ballot [in New Jersey]." She went on to say that Obama needs only invoke his political popularity, not legal qualifications, in order to be a candidate. She further argued that, "No law in New Jersey obligated him [Obama] to produce any such evidence [place of birth and citizenship status of both parents] in order to get on the primary ballot." Further, Malik Obama, Barack Obama's brother and a Kenyan, produced Obama's Kenyan birth certificate [although claimed to be a forgery], and according to Obama's Kenyan [paternal] grandmother, as well as his half-brother and half-sister, Barack Hussein Obama was born in Kenya.

[106] Anthony Sutton: "The Federal Reserve System is a legal **private monopoly** of the money supply operated for the benefit of the few under the guise of protecting and promoting the public interest." [Emphasis added] Quote from G. Edward Griffin's *The Creature From Jekyll Island* (American Media, Westlake Village, CA, 2004), Chapter 1 (footnote 130). Note that the Fed is privately owned consortium of 12 banks, owned by the international bankers headed by the Rothschilds of London, Berlin, and Paris. It is not a part of the U.S. government. The Fed is *above* the law and accountable to *no one* in the federal government. The primary owners of the Fed are the Rothschilds; Lazard Brothers of Paris; Israel Moses Seaf of Italy; Kuhn, Loeb & Co. of Germany and New York; Warburg & Company of Hamburg, Germany; Lehman Brothers of New York (bankrupt in 2008); Goldman, Sachs of New York; and the Rockefeller brothers of New York. These eight families control the money and wealth of the entire world. Individuals who own large shares of the Fed include William Rockefeller, Paul Warburg, Jacob Schiff, and James Stillman. The Schiffs are insiders at Kuhn Loeb. The Stillmans are Citigroup insiders, who married into the Rockefeller family at the turn of the century. Paul Warburg, an agent of the Rothschild bank, is the "secret" author of the Federal Reserve Act passed by the House of Representatives on the evening of December 22, 1913, and passed by the Senate on December 23 at 2:30 PM, when many members of Congress had already left for the holidays ("Money bill goes to Wilson today," *New York Times*, pp. 1-3, December 23, 1913). See, Kah, Gary, *En Route to Global Occupation* (Huntington Press, Lafayette, LA, 1991): "The bill was passed under suspicious circumstances." President Wilson signed the bill into law on December 23, 1913 in a public ceremony. John Pierpont Morgan was the sponsor of the bill. Producer Aaron Russo's *America: Freedom to Fascism* is a must-see movie exposing the truth about the Fed.
See also, Mullins, Eustace Clarence, *The Secrets of the Federal Reserve* (Bankers Research Institute, Staunton, VA, 1983).

[107] "The concern here is about the third branch of government. One of the overarching problems that pervades so many of these provisions [of the USA PATRIOT Act] is reduction of the role of judicial oversight. The executive branch is running roughshod over both of the other branches of government." Nadine Strossen, president of the ACLU and professor of law at New York University made this statement without understanding the corporate nature of the U.S. government today. A partial list of

CHAPTER VI TREASON ON OUR SHORES: THE END OF THE REPUBLIC

Global Elite,[108] led by the Rothschild's and the international bankers, carrying out exclusively their dictates. Every speech is carefully written by Rothschild frontmen and read by the president from a teleprompter. Congress and the courts (including SCOTUS) are under the authority of the president. The corporate Congress sits by resolution, and not by positive law. In fact, Congress has become irrelevant; laws, statutes, and budgets are dictated by the president via the Global Elite.[109] The courts are legislative, not judicial courts. "Court decisions" are administrative opinions only and are decided on the basis of what is best for the corporate government.[110] The courts operate in admiralty/maritime law.[111] In the view of the

---

EOs not yet implemented: #10995 Seizure of all communications media in the United States; #10997 Seizure of all electric power, fuels, and minerals, both public and private; #10998 Seizure of all food supplies and resources, public, and private, all farms and farm equipment; #10999 Seizure of all means of transportation, including personal cars, trucks or vehicles of any kind and total control over all highways, seaports and waterways; #11000 Seizure of all American population for work forces under federal supervision, including dividing families as necessary according to governmental plans; #11001 Seizure of all health, education and welfare facilities, both public and private; #11002 Empowers the Postmaster General to register all men, women and children in the United States; #11003 Seizure of all airports and aircraft; #11004 Seizure of all housing and finance authorities, to establish forced relocation. Designates areas to be abandoned as "unsafe," establishes new locations for populations, relocates communications, builds new housing with public funds; #11005 Seizure of all railroads, inland waterways and storage facilities, public and private; #11051 Provides the Office of Emergency Planning complete authorization to put the above orders into effect in times of increased international tension or economic or financial crisis; United States Policy on Pre- and Post-Strike Measures to Address Civilian Casualties in U.S. Operations Involving the Use of Force (July 1, 2016).

[108] The exceptions in recent years were Presidents Ronald Reagan and Donald Trump.

[109] Congress is irrelevant as long as the president is the choice of the Global Elite. Otherwise, the Deep State-controlled Congress will make every effort, at the bidding of the Global Elite, to usurp the power of the president.

[110] There are **no** judicial courts or judges in America and have not been since 1789. "Judges do not enforce Statutes and Codes. Executive Administrators enforce Statutes and Codes." (*FRC v. GE*, 281 U.S. 464. See also, *Keller v. Potomac Elec. Co.*, 261 U.S. 428 1 Stat. 138-178

[111] The "divine right of kings," also the law of the sea. The law of the sea derives from the Code of Hammurabi and ancient Babylon, which worshiped a pantheon of gods including the god of the sea, called Satan. Deals with criminal acts that only apply to international contracts. Admiralty/maritime law is evidenced by the gold-fringed flag that flies in the courtroom. Under this law, the people are no longer sovereign. The Uniform Commercial Code (UCC) that the U.S. practices is based on admiralty law. Under the UCC, contracts do not have to be entered into knowingly. Simple agreements can be binding, and as long as you exercise the benefits of that "agreement," you must meet the obligations associated with those benefits. If you accept the benefit offered by the government, then you **must** follow, to the letter, each and every statute involved with that benefit. That "benefit" are Federal Reserve Notes (U.S. dollars). By paying for things with U.S. dollars you are unknowingly giving up all of your Constitutional rights and are legally obligated to follow all of the UCC statues. But you were **never** told this. *Black's Law Dictionary* (sixth edition): "That which the Congress has enacted or the Federal courts, sitting in admiralty, or in the exercise of their maritime jurisdiction, have declared and would apply . . . Substantively, in the United States, it is federal law, and jurisdiction to administer it is vested in the federal courts, though not to the entire exclusion of the courts of the states."

courts and government agencies, a citizen is *guilty* until he proves his innocence.[112] The presumption of innocence has been abandoned in the name of safety. The principle of *stare decisis* is no longer honored, unless it happens to suit the court's purpose.[113]

The *de facto* government recognizes no limit to its power, and will use whatever means necessary, even unlawful, to seize the power it deems requisite for its purposes. It merely changes the law to make its illegal acts legal.[114] Irrespective of the supposed right to vote,[115] don't think for one minute that the federal U.S. government of today is not all-powerful, and the people mere subjects. Again, by definition in the U.S.C., U.S. citizens are subjects. The *de facto* government *appears* to be a two-party political system, but in reality, it is two parties with a single face; simply a different means to the same end.[116] Felix Frankfurter, former SCOTUS justice, admonished in 1952: "The real rulers in Washington are invisible, and exercise power from behind the scenes."

---

[112] Under admiralty law, a person is presumed guilty. It is the obligation of the accused to prove his innocence, or more aptly put, that the accused is "not guilty." This is the same standard and procedure used in a military court martial.

[113] *Black's Law Dictionary* (sixth edition): "*Stare decisis*. To abide by, or adhere to, decided cases. Policy of courts to stand by precedent and not to disturb settled point. *Neff v. George*, 364 Ill. 306, 4 N.E. 2d 388, 390, 391. Doctrine that, when court has once laid down a principle of law as applicable to a certain state of facts, it will adhere to that principle, and apply it to all future cases, where facts are substantially the same; regardless of whether the parties and property are the same." On April 25, 1938, SCOTUS overturned the standing precedents of the prior 150 years concerning "common law" in the federal government: "There is no federal common law, and Congress has no power to declare substantive rules of common law applicable in a state, whether they be local or general in their nature, be they commercial law or a part of law of torts." (*Erie Railroad Co. v. Thompkins*, 304 U.S. 64, 82 L. Ed. 1188). There is perhaps no better example of this than *Roe v. Wade*, which ignored all precedent cases, and in effect repudiated the principle of *stare decisis*, replacing it with dictatorial statute law, i.e., the *whim* of the legislature. Under Roman law (law of the sea/admiralty law), there is no law standard of absolute right and wrong. Court decisions are arbitrary and capricious, and may even be self-contradictory.

[114] The 2014 Bundy standoff and subsequent arrest of members of the Bundy family on trumped up charges is but one example of the federal government re-writing laws to serve its own purpose. Another egregious example of federal overreach is the arrest of members of the Hammond ranching family in Burns, Oregon over a dispute regarding use of public lands in the Malheur National Wildlife Refuge. Both ranchers had grazed cattle on the lands for many years prior to the government's unlawful attempt to take their property for government purposes.

[115] A quote often attributed to Joseph Stalin: "It is enough that the people know there was an election. The people who cast the votes decide nothing. The people who count the votes decide everything." However, the source of the quote is unknown and is not found in the Stalin Digital Archive. Regardless, the quote is consistent with Stalin's mentation and tyrannical posture. Furthermore, programmers have testified before Congress that the code to rig *any* election is built into the software that runs *all* computerized voting machines.

[116] The goal of the Global Elite is a totalitarian One World Government. The principles (statutes) are

CHAPTER VI TREASON ON OUR SHORES: THE END OF THE REPUBLIC

A retired judge, writing anonymously in an essay entitled "The Matrix and the U.S. Constitution," states:

> There are no remaining public federal employees in America. All employees whom you believe to be a part of America's government are actually agents of a foreign government [the corporation], and this definition includes the President. The federal elections are a joke on us! All of the candidates have been jointly pre-selected and pre-screened by the National Boards of the Republican and Democratic Parties well before the election process. All of our federally elected officials, appointed administrators, federal police and judges receive their paychecks through the Office of Personnel Management. OPM is a division of the International Monetary Fund, which is owned by the Rockefeller and Rothschild families and their Banking Empires, which operate in tandem with the United Nations. The IRS and Interpol are owned by the International Monetary Fund, which has been identified in an earlier version of the U. S. Army Manual as a Communist Organization.[117]

The economy of the *de jure* government is built upon capitalism. Capitalism is a free market, *laissez faire* system based on the principle

---

already built into the U.S. Code. 8 USC §1101: "Definitions: (36) The term 'State' includes the District of Columbia, Puerto Rico, Guam, the Virgin Islands of the United States, and the Commonwealth of the Northern Mariana Islands. (37) The term 'totalitarian party' means an organization which advocates the establishment in the United States of a totalitarian dictatorship or totalitarianism. The terms 'totalitarian dictatorship' and 'totalitarianism' mean and refer to systems of government not representative in fact, characterized by (A) the existence of a single political party, organized on a dictatorial basis, with so close an identity between such party and its policies and the governmental policies of the country in which it exists, that the party and the government constitute an indistinguishable unit, and (B) the forcible suppression of opposition to such party. (38) The term 'United States,' except as otherwise specifically herein provided, when used in a geographical sense, means the continental United States, Alaska, Hawaii, Puerto Rico, Guam, the Virgin Islands of the United States, and the Commonwealth of the Northern Mariana Islands . . . (40) The term 'world communism' means a revolutionary movement, the purpose of which is to establish eventually a Communist totalitarian dictatorship in any or all the countries of the world through the medium of an internationally coordinated Communist political movement." [Emphasis added] [Author's note: Yes, that's directly from the U.S. Code. Every American should read the entire section which can be easily found online.]

[117] Note that members of the BAR (an association of judges and attorneys) are a "protected class" of the Global Elite, as long as they support the agenda of the cabalists. The BAR is a 501(c)(3) corporation, subject to IRS regulations. The BAR will be discussed in detail in Chapter X.

of individual rights and ownership. *Merriam-Webster's Collegiate Dictionary* defines capitalism as "an economic system characterized by private or corporate ownership of capital goods, by investments that are determined by private decision, and by prices, production, and the distribution of goods that are determined mainly by competition in a free market." Characteristics of capitalism are capital accumulation by the private sector and competitive markets. The parties to a transaction determine, without government interference, the prices at which goods, services, and assets are exchanged. It is a system based on mutually-advantageous, voluntary trade unhindered by regulation.

The economy of the *de facto* government is based on corporatism. Corporatism, as defined by *Encyclopedia Britannica*, is: "The theory and practice of organizing society into 'corporations' subordinate to the state. According to corporatist theory, workers and employers would be organized into industrial and professional corporations serving as organs of political representation and controlling to a large extent the persons and activities within their jurisdiction."

Corporatism has historically been associated with fascist governments. Benito Mussolini expressed the belief that "Fascism should more appropriately be called corporatism because it is a merger of state and corporate power."

Corporatism is antithetical to capitalism. The state in a corporate economy is interventionist and powerful. In a capitalist system, the principle of *laissez faire* characterizes the relationship between state and business. Corporatism is collectivist; *de facto* nationalization. Capitalism is predicated upon private ownership of property. Corporatism stifles competition through acquisitions and mergers. Capitalism thrives on competition in a free market economy. Corporatist regimes promote large government projects. Capitalism leaves such projects in the hands of private enterprise. Corporatism suppresses individual rights. Capitalism encourages individual rights. The vision of the corporate society is a political community whose "perfection" allows the individual members to fulfill themselves and find happiness through the community. The vision of the capitalist society is the right of the individual to conduct his affairs privately and without government interference. The people find fulfillment through personal achievement. Corporatism recognizes the individual as subservient to government and the corporation. Capitalism recognizes the rights of the individual as supreme and sovereign.

Corporate economies have historically degenerated into brutal, totalitarian dictatorships as the state takes over more and more control of the corporations. Ultimately, capitalism and corporatism cannot coexist in a free society. In the U.S. today, the corner grocery, the family farm, and the "mom and pop" shops and stores have become virtually extinct, swallowed up or squeezed out by corporations. Government regulation has become an oppressive burden upon private business, while favoring corporations through "tax breaks," "incentives," and government subsidies.

Corporatism is nothing more than a ruse for socialism, a.k.a. fascism, a.k.a. communism.[118] Throughout history, there have only been two basic forms of government: collectivism and individualism. Fascism, socialism, and communism are only superficial variations of collectivism. Ayn Rand explained: "There is no difference between communism and socialism, except in the means of achieving the same ultimate end: communism proposes to enslave men by force, socialism—by vote. It is merely the difference between murder and suicide."[119] Ayn Rand further stated: "The world conflict of today is the conflict of the individual against the state, the same conflict that has been fought throughout mankind's history. The names change, but the essence—and the results—remain the same, whether it is the individual against feudalism, or against absolute monarchy, or against communism or fascism or Nazism or socialism or the welfare state."[120] Collectivism controls the people; capitalism offers freedom to the people. Corporatism is an *immoral* system. The breakdown of morality in society is ample evidence of corporatism's impingement on moral values.

---

[118] A traditional myth propagated by intellectuals posits socialism and fascism as polar opposites of the political spectrum; socialism being on the extreme left of political ideology (liberalism), and fascism on the extreme right (conservatism). However, both are *collectivist* in nature. Both are statist systems, in contrast to a free country based on the rights of the individual and *laissez faire* capitalism, i.e., a republic.

[119] Rand, Ayn, from an article entitled "Foreign Policy Drains U.S. of Main Weapon," published in the *Los Angeles Times* (September 9, 1962).

[120] Rand, Ayn, "Conservativism: An Obituary," based on a lecture given at Princeton University (December 7, 1960).

Bradley Thompson expressed the principle concisely:

The morality of socialism can be summed-up in two words: envy and self-sacrifice. Envy is the desire to not only possess another's wealth but also the desire to see another's wealth lowered to the level of one's own. Socialism's teaching on self-sacrifice was nicely summarized by two of its greatest defenders, Hermann Goering and Benito Mussolini. The highest principle of Nazism (National Socialism), said Goering, is: "Common good comes before private good." Fascism, said Mussolini, is "a life in which the individual, through the sacrifice of his own private interests . . . realizes that completely spiritual existence in which his value as a man lies." Socialism is the social system which institutionalizes envy and self-sacrifice. It is the social system which uses compulsion and the organized violence of the State to expropriate wealth from the producer class for its redistribution to the parasitical class.[121]

Ayn Rand further exposed the immorality of socialism:

When you consider socialism, do not fool yourself about its nature. Remember that there is no such dichotomy as "human rights" versus "property rights." No human rights can exist without property rights. Since material goods are produced by the mind and effort of individual men, and are needed to sustain their lives, if the producer does not own the result of his effort, he does not own his life. To deny property rights means to turn men into property owned by the state. Whoever claims the "right" to "redistribute" the wealth produced by others is claiming the "right" to treat human beings as chattel.[122]

---

[121] Thompson, Bradley, "Socialism vs. Capitalism: Which is the Moral System" (*ashbrook.org/publications/onprin-v1n3-thompson*, October 1993).
[122] Rand, Ayn, *The Virtue of Selfishness* (Signet, NY, 1964).

Chapter VI Treason on Our Shores: The End of the Republic

To deprive people of their rights and dignity is the essence of immorality and is egregiously adverse to the laws of nature.

Capitalism, in contrast, is the only true *moral and just* social system, despite the lunacy and psychotic ravings of the so-called intellectuals and Global Elite to the contrary. To again quote Thompson:

> Capitalism is the only moral system because it requires human beings to deal with one another as traders—that is, as free moral agents trading and selling goods and services on the basis of mutual consent. Capitalism is the only just system because the sole criterion that determines the value of thing exchanged is the free, voluntary, universal judgment of the consumer. Coercion and fraud are anathema to the free-market system. It is both moral and just because the degree to which man rises or falls in society is determined by the degree to which he uses his mind. Capitalism is the only social system that rewards merit, ability and achievement, regardless of one's birth or station in life.[123]

Laissez faire capitalism has made America the most prosperous nation in the history of the world. It has created the great American Dream and a standard of living for the average American family which is unparalleled in the chronicles of man. However, as capitalism has become increasingly regulated, pushed aside by the corporate government's socialist agenda, the American Dream has virtually faded into oblivion. The "middle class," once a majority of the people, has become an endangered species. Ayn Rand warned of the dangers of socialism: "The alleged goals of socialism were: the abolition of poverty, the achievement of general prosperity, progress, peace and human brotherhood. The results have been a terrifying failure—terrifying, that is, if one's motive is men's welfare . . . Instead of prosperity, socialism has brought economic paralysis and/or collapse to every country that tried it. The degree of socialization has been the degree of disaster. The consequences

---

[123] Id. Thompson

have varied accordingly."[124] Socialism is a system of failure for liberty and the people. Its sole beneficiaries are the elite in power.

To summarize, the *de jure* government is the Constitutional government of the united States of America, formed by the Constitution *for* the united States of America as ratified by the People of the several states. The *de facto* government is a corporation, The United States *of* America, Inc. (or, UNITED STATES, INC.)[125] The *de jure* government is "government by consent," serving the People and operating exclusively with the continued consent of the People.[126] It does not force the People to accept its services and allows the People to run their lives privately. The *de facto* government is a "terrorist government," ruling by force through fraud and intimidation, and controlling literally every aspect of the lives of its subjects.[127] The Constitution of the *de jure* government is immutable, intractable, and not easily changed. It is not subject to loose interpretation by the courts or the executive or legislative branches of government. The corporate charter of the *de facto* corporate government, masquerading as the legitimate Constitution, is changed at the whim of the board of directors and the president. It is subject to interpretation to suit the needs of the corporation.[128] The *de jure*

---

[124] Id. Rand

[125] United States of America, Inc. For-Profit Delaware Corporation, Incorporation date April 19, 1989, File No. 2193946. This is a recent incorporation of the federal government. The Roman Catholic Church previously chartered the United States of America, Inc. in Delaware in 1925. The U.S. was first incorporated with the Act of 1871. See, Chapter VIII for details.

[126] *Black's law Dictionary* (sixth edition): "Consent. A concurrence of wills. Voluntarily yielding the will to the proposition of another; acquiescence or compliance therewith. Agreement; approval; permission; the act or result of coming into harmony or accord. Consent is an act of reason, accompanied with deliberation, the mind weighing as in a balance the good or evil on each side. It means voluntary agreement by a person in the possession and exercise of sufficient mental capacity to make an intelligent choice to do something proposed by another. It supposes a physical power to act, a moral power of acting, and a serious, determined, and free use of these powers. Consent is implied in every agreement. It is an act unclouded by fraud, duress, or sometimes even mistake."

[127] Revelation 19:19 describes this type of government as "the Beast." *Funk & Wagnalls Standard Dictionary* (1946) defines the word "terrorism" as "A system of government that seeks to rule by intimidation."

[128] i.e., the 2012 SCOTUS ruling on the Affordable Care Act (ACA), formally known as the Patient Protection and Affordable Care Act, and commonly known as Obamacare. Call it a penalty or a tax; either way, it is unconstitutional pursuant to the *de jure* Constitution. In a surprisingly frank and candid revelation, Charles Evans Hughes, governor of New York and former SCOTUS justice admitted: "The Constitution is whatever the Supreme Court says it is, and the judiciary is the safeguard of our liberty and of our property under the Constitution." (Speech before the Chamber of Commerce, Elmira, NY, May 3, 1907; published in *Addresses and Papers of Charles Evans Hughes, Governor of New York, 1906 – 1908*, p. 139 (1908)). He was referring to the Constitution that begins with the 13th Amendment and serves as the charter of the corporate federal government. The *de jure* Constitution is dormant.

CHAPTER VI TREASON ON OUR SHORES: THE END OF THE REPUBLIC

government is established on a balance of power between the executive, legislative, and judicial branches of government. The *de facto* government is authoritarian, in spite of appearances to the contrary, with ultimate control vested exclusively in the executive branch. The *de jure* Constitutional government recognizes the states as superior, sovereign, and independent. The *de facto* federal government recognizes the states as subservient, mere geographical boundaries [federal zones, i.e., "ZIP Codes," territories] of the corporate U.S. In the *de jure* Constitutional government, the People have unalienable rights. In the *de facto* federal government, the citizens have civil rights. Unalienable rights are granted by God from birth; civil rights are granted by government from birth. Governments cannot take away unalienable rights. Governments can take away civil rights, at the discretion of the government. The *de facto* government operates in admiralty/maritime law. The *de jure* government operates in equity[129]

Former President George W. Bush said the same thing, expressing annoyance and contempt for our founding document, when he declared: "The Constitution is just a goddamn piece of paper." Note also that the ACA is not about health care; it is about tyranny and controlling the people. Once again, the people have been egregiously deceived. The full implementation of the Act will spring the trap door of the gallows, the noose of tyranny choking perhaps the last ounce of freedom from the people. The cost of so-called health care will create an unbearable financial burden upon the people, and with the implantation of the RFID chip, the government will be able to track anyone, anywhere, at any time. They government will also have complete control over the bank accounts, retirement plans, investments, and money of every citizen as the U.S. becomes a cashless society. No one will be able to buy or sell goods or transact business without the RFID chip implant. The implementation of the ACA is perhaps the last piece of the puzzle before the complete collapse of the U.S. and the implementation of One World Government and the NWO.

[129] *Black's Law Dictionary* (sixth edition): "Equity. Justice administered according to fairness as contrasted with the strictly formulated rules of common law. It is based on a system of rules and principles which originated in England as an alternative to the harsh rules of common law and which were based on what was fair in a particular situation. One sought relief under this system in courts of equity rather than in courts of law. The term 'equity' denotes the spirit and habit of fairness, justness, and right dealing which would regulate the intercourse of men with men."

Also, *Commentaries on Equity Jurisprudence*, Joseph Story by Melville Bigelow, 13th edition, Vol. I, p. 14 (1886): In *Dudley v. Dudley*, Prec. Ch. 241, 244, Sir John Trevor, M.R., said: "Now, **equity is no part of the law**, but a moral virtue which qualifies, moderates, and reforms the rigor, hardness, and edge of the law, and is a universal truth. It does also assist the law where it is defective and weak in the constitution, which is the life of the law; and defends the law from crafty evasions, delusions, and new subtleties invented and contrived to evade and delude the common law, whereby such as have undoubted right are made remediless. And this is the office of equity, to protect and support the common law from shifts and contrivances against the justice of the law. Equity, therefore, does not destroy the law, nor create it, but assists it." [Emphasis added] And Romans 3:28-31, equity assists the law: "The law that requires works? No, because of the law that requires faith. For we maintain that a person is justified by faith apart from the works of the law. Or is God the God of Jews only? Is he not the God of Gentiles too? Yes, of Gentiles too, since there is only one God, who will justify the circumcised by faith and the uncircumcised through that same faith. Do we, then, nullify the law by this faith? Not at all! Rather, we uphold the law." [Author's note: "uphold" meaning to assist the law]

and common law.[130] The *de jure* government recognizes the People as sovereign; born out of the womb as breathing, living souls, creations of a sovereign, omnipotent God.[131] The *de facto* government recognizes U.S. citizens, creations of the corporate government. The *de jure* government recognizes the *sanctity* of life, the *de facto* government the expendability of life. The *de jure* government recognizes the intrinsic value of all creation. In the *de facto* government, life only has value insofar as it serves the purpose of government. The *de jure* government is based on Biblical values. The *de facto* government eschews Biblical values for an ever-changing morality controlled by statute. The *de jure* government recognizes the traditional, Biblical family as the core unit of society.[132] The *de facto* government promotes the breakdown of the traditional family and would redefine marriage as the union of two citizens, regardless of gender. It recognizes the marriage of two "individuals" for the purpose of government and employer-provided benefits, and further encourages single parent "families" in order to foster dependence on government. In the *de jure* government, property is owned by the People. The *de facto* government owns all property. The *de jure* government is the property of the People. U.S. citizens, however, are the property of the *de facto* government.[133] Property cannot have unalienable rights. The People can only be a subject or a sovereign. There is no other option.

---

[130] Common law. God's law. The law of the land, which derives from Mosaic Law and the Judeo-Christian religions. Common law and the system of *de jure* juries apply to sovereigns in disputes. In common law, contracts must be entered into knowingly, voluntarily, and intentionally. *Black's Law Dictionary* (sixth edition): "As distinguished from statutory law created by the enactment of legislatures, the common law comprises the body of those principles and rules of action, relating to the government and security of persons and property, which derive their authority solely from usages and customs of immemorial antiquity, or from the judgments and decrees of the courts recognizing, affirming, and enforcing such usages and customs; and, in this sense, particularly the ancient unwritten law of England. In general, it is a body of law that develops and derives through judicial decisions, as distinguished from legislative enactments. The 'common law' is all the statutory and case law background of England and the American colonies before the American Revolution."

[131] *Julliard v. Greenman*, 110 U.S. S. 421: "There is no such thing as a power of inherent Sovereignty in the government of the United States. In this country sovereignty resides in the People, and Congress can exercise no power which they have not, by their Constitution entrusted to it: all else is withheld."

[132] Genesis 1:26-28.

[133] *Black's Law Dictionary* (sixth edition): "Property. That which is peculiar or proper to any person; that which belongs exclusively to one. In the strict legal sense . . . The term is said to extend to every species of valuable right and interest. More specifically, ownership; the unrestricted and exclusive right to a thing; the right to dispose of a thing in every legal way, to possess it, to use it, and to exclude everyone else from interfering with it. That dominion or indefinite right of use or disposition which one may

CHAPTER VI TREASON ON OUR SHORES: THE END OF THE REPUBLIC

One of the most brilliant minds in American history, Thomas Jefferson, predicted the demise of the *de jure* government as early as 1825. In a letter to William Branch Giles, Jefferson wrote prophetically:

> I see . . . and with the deepest affliction, the rapid strides with which the federal branch of our government is advancing towards the usurpation of all the rights reserved to the States, and the consolidation in itself of all powers, foreign and domestic; and that, too, by constructions which, if legitimate, leave no limits to their power . . . It is but too evident that the three ruling branches of [the federal government] are in combination to strip their colleagues, the State authorities, of the powers reserved by them, and to exercise themselves all functions foreign and domestic.[134]

The *de facto* government is often referred to as a democracy, particularly by the Global Elite and those in power. However, a more accurate description is a socialist/fascist/police state. The Founding Fathers emphatically did not establish a democracy and

---

lawfully exercise over particular things or subjects . . . The word is also commonly used to denote everything which is the subject of ownership, corporeal or incorporeal, tangible or intangible, visible or invisible, real or personal; everything that has an exchangeable value or which goes to make up wealth or estate . . ."

[134] As early as the 1790s, there were some in the U.S. who supported a strong central government, chief among them Alexander Hamilton, who served as the nation's first secretary of the treasury under President George Washington. He successfully argued that implied powers in the Constitution could be used to fund a national debt and for the central government to assume state's debts from the Revolutionary War. He also first proposed and supported the creation of the government-owned Bank of the United States. Hamilton had close ties with the House of Rothschild, and with Rothschild financing he founded two NY banks, including Bank of New York. Hamilton shared the Rothschilds' contempt of the common people, stating: "All communities divide themselves into the few and the many. The first are the rich and the well born, the others the mass of the people . . . The people are turbulent and changing; they seldom judge and determine right. Give therefore to the first class a distinct, permanent share of government. They will check the unsteadiness of the second." (Michael Parenti, *Democracy for the Few*, p. 51 (St. Martin's Press, NY, 1977)). Thomas Jefferson, among other Founding Fathers, vehemently opposed such thinking as contrary to the true intent of the Constitution. Jefferson wrote: "If the American people ever allow private banks to control the issuance of their currency, first by inflation and then by deflation, the banks and corporations that will grow up around them will deprive the people of all their property until their children will wake up homeless on the continent their fathers conquered." He also wrote: ". . . banking establishments are more dangerous than standing armies; and that the principle of spending money to be paid by posterity, under the name of funding, is but swindling futurity on a large scale." Henry Clay in 1841 was the heir apparent to Alexander Hamilton's backing of a strong central government.

had no intention of doing so. They were keenly aware of the dangers of such a government.

A democracy is far from what most people perceive it to be. Democracy is not freedom. Democracy is the *appearance* of freedom, not the *substance* of freedom. The people have been brainwashed into believing that democracy equates to individual liberty when, in reality, it is nothing more than "a euphemism for despotism," as described by Bob Livingston. Democracy is the American version of Hitler's National Socialism, or Nazism. And as long as Americans associate the word "democracy" with freedom, the erosion of personal liberty will continue. The citizens only think they are free. They have been deluded into accepting a lie. In a democracy, the citizens do not have God-given natural rights, Constitutional rights, states' rights, or the Bill of Rights. They have only *civil rights*, which exist at the whim of government. In a democracy, freedom is a mere illusion. The Global Elite have deceptively exchanged the word "republic" for "democracy," concealing their evil agenda with a populist, politically correct term.

Clearly, anyone who refers to the American government as a democracy has no knowledge of the *de jure* Constitution and the founding of the Republic. Or, they are deliberately using the term to deceive the people. Democracy is defined as: "That form of government in which the sovereign power resides in and is exercised by the *whole body* of free citizens; as distinguished from a monarchy, aristocracy, or *oligarchy*. According to the theory of a pure democracy, every citizen should participate directly in the business of governing, and the legislative assembly should comprise the whole people."[135] [Emphasis added] Sounds innocent enough. However, such a government is implausible. In other words, mob rule. The only practical way for a democracy to operate is through a system of elected officials to represent the citizens.

However, there is a huge difference between a Constitutional republic which utilizes a democratic voting process, and a democracy. In a democracy, the citizens *relinquish their sovereignty* by an act of delegation. The vote by the citizens is a voluntary act of consent and

---

[135] *Black's Law Dictionary* (second edition) p. 351 (1891).

CHAPTER VI TREASON ON OUR SHORES: THE END OF THE REPUBLIC

delegation. And consent makes the law.[136] In a democracy, sovereignty is in the whole body of citizens. In a republic, the sovereignty is in each individual. In a democracy, the citizen becomes a constituent of the elected officials.[137] According to *Bouvier's Law Dictionary*: "The constituent is bound with whatever his attorney [elected official] does by virtue of his authority."[138] Throughout history, a democracy has been temporary in nature, gradually degenerating into authoritarianism. Karl Marx himself stated: "Democracy is the road to socialism" and "Socialism leads to communism." Vladimir Lenin stated: "Democracy is indispensable to socialism."

Founding Father James Madison wrote: ". . . democracies . . . have ever been found incompatible with personal security or the rights of property; and have in general been as short in their lives as they have been violent in their deaths."[139] In other words, a democracy is incompatible with freedom. Madison also wrote: "Democracy is the most vile form of government," and, "Democracy was the right of the people to choose their own tyrant."

Bob Livingston described democracy succinctly and with insight in stating: "Democracy is the most deceptive word in the English language." He goes on to write:

> [Democracy] is a political and subversive word created and promoted by the establishment as a major key to formulate and channel the public mind. It has more than saturated the public conscience. Very "intellectual" people spout this word assuming that it means human freedom and liberty.

---

[136] Bouvier, John, *Bouvier's Law Dictionary* (revised sixth edition, 1856). Maxim of Law: *Invito beneficium non datur* (No one is obliged to accept a benefit against his consent. But if he does not dissent, he will be considered as assenting (*Vide Assent*). Also, **no** government has the power to force or command until one binds himself by consent, ". . . for lex (law) since it binds one to act." *Summa Theologica*, 2nd Part, "Treaties on Law, Essence of Law," St. Thomas Aquinas, founder of *Natural Law Juris*. Maxum of Law (Bouvier): *Quod meum est sine me auferri non potest* ("What is mine [i.e., liberty, freedom] cannot be taken away without my consent." (Jenk. Cent. 251).

[137] *Black's Law Dictionary* (sixth edition): "Constituent. He who gives authority to another to act for him. The term is used as a correlative to 'attorney,' to denote one who constitutes another his agent or invests the other with authority to act for him. It is also used in the language of politics as a correlative to 'representative,' the constituents of a legislator being those whom he represents and whose interests he is to care for in public affairs; usually the electors of his district."

[138] Id. Bouvier.

[139] Madison, James, *The Federalist, on the New Constitution, Written in the Year 1788*, p. 46.

The truth and purpose of this word is for a cover and disguise for fascism and socialism. This word is the workhorse of the American propaganda ministry. Every person is taught this word, from politicians to school children. The government indoctrination centers (also known as schools) and the corporate media use it religiously. Politicians love its sound . . .

Democracy is an esoteric belief system that manipulates the people in such a way that all power flows to the state. As with pure dictatorships, power flows from the top down.

Democracy implies freedom in the public's mind while power and wealth is constantly channeled to the Federal government. Human liberty is regressively crushed under the one simple word, "democracy."

Democracy is a political word that is embraced by all political parties and all politicians under many labels in every country of the modern world. It is a cover and a facade for communism, socialism, fascism, for class warfare, for the exploitation and manipulation of minorities against stability, cultural heritage and private property . . .

When politicians utter the word democracy, they are using a code word that signifies their total allegiance to the state. They are using mass hypnosis to manipulate the people against human liberty.

Democracy is that universal mystery that is loved by all and opposed by none. It implies everything good to everyone and every religion. It is the mantle (mantra) of the New World Order. It is the apex of adoration for the state, universalism, One Worldism and materialism. It is Satanism posing as an angel of light.

Anyone seeking human liberty, privacy and private property under the mental deception of democracy is under the greatest illusion. Let us purge our minds of this seductive appeal, this spiritual despotism. It has stolen our conscience, our soul and our honor. It is our legacy to future generations to whom we are passing on our slavery. Shame could have no greater victory.

CHAPTER VI TREASON ON OUR SHORES: THE END OF THE REPUBLIC

> Democracy is a faith, a state religion, a state of mind. It is the progressive destruction of the person—the individual. It is covered and masked with benevolence, philanthropy and brotherhood. Democracy is the opposite of the common belief. It is "democratic" tyranny, a camouflage for despotism. Its goal is nothing less than universal slavery . . .
>
> With this invisible organism, the American state has imposed all 10 planks of the Communist Manifesto without protest and beyond the awareness of the American people who imagine that they are free . . .[140]

But why? Why the deception? What is the purpose? Simple . . . greed, opulence, control, arrogance, and an insatiable desire for money, power, and wealth. The agenda of the powers behind the corporate U.S. government is, and has been for many years, socialism, and ultimately world communism under a One World Government that will further enrich the Global Elite. These so-called Elite envision themselves as a breed of superior individuals with greater intellect and supernatural powers above and beyond all mankind. They posture themselves as "gods," worthy to be obeyed and worshipped in a state-sponsored government religion, unaccountable to even the true God Almighty. Hitler modeled himself in the same manner in Nazi Germany.

The Global Elite, led by the House of Rothschild, with its almost total dominance over the world's monetary systems, has been pulling the strings of our leaders in Washington with greater and greater authority since the War Between the States. They have taken control over literally every aspect of our society . . . education,[141] agriculture, food and drugs, the financial markets, health care, transportation, communication, media, news, and on and on . . . with one exception: Christianity and the family as the nucleus of society. But Christianity and communism cannot coexist, any more

---

[140] Livingston, Bob, "The Most Deceptive Word in the English Language" (*Liberty Digest*, August 4, 2014). See, the 10 planks of *The Communist Manifesto* in Appendix A.
[141] Benito Mussolini: "It is the State which educates its citizens in civic virtue, gives them a consciousness of their mission and welds them into unity." And further: "Fascist education is moral, physical, social, and military: it aims to create a complete and harmoniously developed human, a fascist one according to our views."

than light and darkness can coexist. Christianity is light; communism is darkness. That explains why the government is in an all-out war with Christians. It must destroy the Bible and Christianity in order to put government in its place; to make government the new god. The Global Elite must destroy the family so the citizens will become even more dependent on government, forsaking their God-given unalienable rights. Man can have only one master, God or government.[142] The God of the Universe stands in the way of government being the master over all of the Earth.

In reality, the battle is on a much deeper level. In essence, the corporate government is at war with God. The battle is being waged for the control of men's souls. The Apostle Paul warned us centuries ago: "For we wrestle not against flesh and blood, but against principalities, against powers, against the rulers of the darkness of this world, against spiritual wickedness in high places."[143] Karl Marx stated: "My object in life is to dethrone God and destroy capitalism."

Yes, we are in the throes of a spiritual battle, good against evil, God against Satan.[144] Saul Alinsky,[145] a protégé of Karl Marx and disciple of Antonio Gramsci,[146] wrote in the dedication of his

---

[142] Matthew 6:24 (KJV): "No man can serve two masters: for either he will hate the one, and love the other; or else he will hold to the one, and despise the other. Ye cannot serve God and mammon [government]."
[143] Ephesians 6:12. See also, 2 Corinthians 10:3-5.
[144] The Bible tells us that the Earth is the province of Satan, the Ruler of Darkness. Luke 4:5-7 (ASV): "And he led him up, and showed him all the kingdoms of the world in a moment of time. And the devil said unto him, To thee will I give all this authority, and the glory of them: *for it hath been delivered unto me*; and to whomsoever I will I give it. If thou therefore wilt worship before me, it shall all be thine [Emphasis added]." Jesus did not contradict Satan's authority or rulership over Earth. Satan clearly stated that all earthly kingdoms (governments) belong to him, and he will give power to whoever he wishes, if they will worship him. See also, Matthew 4:8-9. Earth cannot be controlled by Satan unless all of its rulers are controlled by Satan. "We know that we are from God, and the whole world lies in the power of the evil one [Satan]." 1 John 5:19 (ESV)
[145] Saul Alinsky was a devotee who helped establish the tactics of infiltration and confrontation that have been central to revolutionary political movements in the U.S. in recent decades. He developed a set of very specific rules and tactics that ordinary citizens could follow and employ as a means of gaining public power. His motto was: "The most effective means are whatever will achieve the desired results." He studied criminology as a graduate student at the University of Chicago. During his student years he became friendly with Al Capone and his mobsters. Alinsky was described by Ryan Lizza, senior editor of *The New Republic*, as: "Charming and self-absorbed, Alinsky would entertain friends with stories —some true, many embellished—from his mob days for decades afterward. He was profane, outspoken, and narcissistic, always the center of attention despite his tweedy, academic look and thick, horn-rimmed glasses." Two of his biggest devotees today are Barack Obama and Hillary Clinton.
[146] Gramsci was an Italian writer, politician, political theorist, philosopher, and sociologist. He was one of the most important Marxist thinkers and leaders of the 20th century.

CHAPTER VI TREASON ON OUR SHORES: THE END OF THE REPUBLIC

book, *Practical Primer for Realistic Radicals*: "Lest we forget at least an over-the-shoulder acknowledgment to the very first radical: from all our legends, mythology, and history (and who is to know where mythology leaves off and history begins—or which is which), the first radical known to man who rebelled against the establishment and did it so effectively that he at least won his own kingdom—Lucifer."

Alinsky died in 1972, but his work was compiled into the Cloward-Piven[147] strategy, the plan that is followed by the community organizer ACORN today. Barack Obama's ties to ACORN[148] are well-known and documented. As president (albeit of a corporation), Obama surrounded himself with radicals who shared this philosophy. The seeds of communism ascended to the highest levels of the U.S. government. Imagine . . . a president of this once-great free Republic, founded upon deep-seeded Christian principles, that is a disciple of a man who dedicated his book to Lucifer! Meanwhile, the people are asleep, oblivious to the ever-tightening noose around their necks, which threatens to choke every last ounce of freedom from their souls.

Perhaps Nikita Khrushchev had it right. In a quote attributed to him, the former premier of Russia (1958-64) brashly proclaimed: "Your children's children will live under communism . . . You Americans are so gullible. No, you won't accept communism outright; but we'll keep feeding you small doses of socialism until you will finally wake up and find that you already have communism. We won't have to fight you; we'll so weaken your economy, until you fall like overripe fruit into our hands."[149] His words suddenly seem

---

[147] The Cloward–Piven strategy is a political strategy outlined in 1966 by American sociologists and political activists Richard Cloward (1926-2001) and Frances Piven (b. 1932). It called for overloading the U.S. public welfare system in order to precipitate a crisis that would lead to a replacement of the welfare system with a national system of "a guaranteed annual income and thus an end to poverty." The ultimate goal of the ideas set forth in their book was to replace capitalism in the U.S. with communism. Cloward and Piven were a married couple who were professors at the Columbia University School of Social Work.

[148] "Obama and Acorn: Community organizers, phony voters, and your tax dollars," *The Wall Street Journal* (October 14, 2008).

[149] The source of this quote is disputed. Some sources say the quote is from a 1959 speech at the UN. However, there is no record of the speech in the UN archives. The quote most likely originated from an exchange in a 1959 meeting between Khrushchev and U.S. Secretary of Agriculture Ezra Taft Benson, and was later recounted by Benson. Benson was reported to have stated in his speech following the meeting: "I have personally witnessed the heart-rending results of the loss of freedom. I have talked face-to-face with the godless Communist leaders. It may surprise you to learn that I was host to Mr.

eerily prophetic. We stand on the precipice of the fulfillment of his prophetical rant. The tipping point is perilously close.

The Republic of our Founding Fathers is dormant. Corporate fascism has taken its place. The Republic died over 100 years ago with Lincoln and the War Between the States. We now live in a corporate-controlled socialist/fascist nation-state, whether Americans want to admit it or not.[150] Our liberties have been gradually eroded as the government has seized more and more authority and control over the people, and literally every aspect of their lives. As President Ronald Reagan warned the people: "I hope we once again have reminded people that man is not free unless government is limited. There's a clear cause and effect here that is as neat and predictable as a law of physics: As government expands, liberty contracts."[151] It seems that every day brings more instances of tyranny from an increasingly despotic federal government. Communism is the final phase of socialism. Is that where, as a country and people, we are headed?

Khrushchev for a half-day when he visited the United States. Not that I'm proud of it. I opposed his coming then, and I still feel it was a mistake to welcome this atheistic murderer as a state visitor. As we talked face-to-face, he indicated that my grandchildren would live under Communism. After assuring him that I expected to do all in my power to assure that his, and all other grandchildren, will live under freedom, he arrogantly declared, in substance: [Khrushchev's quote]." Regardless of the exact wording or the veracity of the quote, it accurately reflects the philosophy of the Global Elite to achieve their goal of One World Government under communism.

[150] In truth, the UNITED STATES is not a nation; it is the world's largest corporation. A corporation is not a nation, but may have some characteristics of a nation.

[151] Reagan, Michael, *The Last Best Hope: The Greatest Speeches of Ronald Reagan*, p. 226 (Humanix Books, 2016).

CHAPTER VI TREASON ON OUR SHORES: THE END OF THE REPUBLIC

The "de jure" Constitutional Government

```
          God
           ↓
         People
           ↓
         States
           ↓
    Federal Government
```

The flow of authority intended by our Founding Fathers as set forth in the Declaration of Independence and the Constitution for the united States of America

"Government de jure. A government of right; the true and lawful government; a government established according to the constitution of the state, and lawfully entitled to recognition and supremacy and the administration of the state, but which is actually cut off from power and control. A government deemed lawful, or deemed rightful or just, which, nevertheless, has been supplanted or displaced; that is to say, which receives not presently (although it received formerly) habitual obedience from the bulk of the community."—Black's Law Dictionary, second edition, 1891

The People are Sovereign

"[It is] the people, to whom all authority belongs."—Thomas Jefferson to Spencer Roane (1821)

". . . at the Revolution, the sovereignty devolved on the people; and they are truly the sovereigns of the country, but they are sovereigns without subjects . . . with none to govern but themselves; the citizens of America are equal as fellow citizens, and as joint tenants in the sovereignty."
—Chisholm v. Georgia (U.S.) 2 Dall 419, 454, 1 L Ed 440, 455

"There is no such thing as a power of inherent Sovereignty in the government of the United States. In this country sovereignty resides in the People, and Congress can exercise no power which they have not, by their Constitution entrusted to it: all else is withheld."—Julliard v. Greenman, 110 U.S. 421

A NATION UPSIDE DOWN

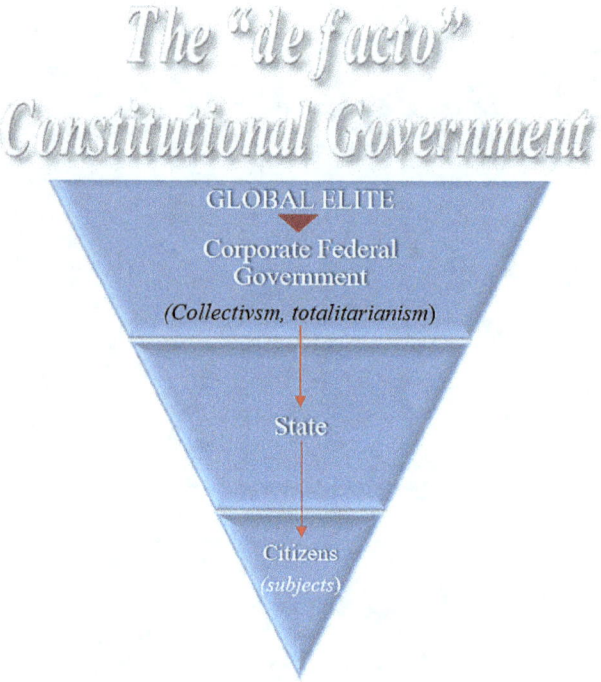

The flow of authority as it exists today with the de facto Corporate Federal government of the United States

"Government de facto. A government of fact. A government actually exercising power and control in the state, as opposed to the true and lawful government; a government not established according to the constitution of the state or not lawfully entitled to recognition or supremacy, but which has nevertheless supplanted or displaced the government de jure. A government deemed lawful, or deemed wrongful or unjust, which, nevertheless, receives presently habitual obedience from the bulk of the community. Aust. Jur. 324. There are several degrees of what is called 'de facto government.' Such a government, in its highest degree, assumes a character very closely resembling that of a lawful government. This is when the usurping government expels the regular authorities from their customary seats and functions, and establishes itself in their place, and so becomes the actual government of a country."—Black's Law Dictionary, second edition, 1891

UNITED STATES CODE, Title 28, in Section 3002 Definitions, it states the following:
(15) "United States" means—(A) a **Federal Corporation**

"A 'Corporation' with a legislature was established, with all the apparatus of a distinct government created (Incorporated) by (Presidential) Legislative Act, February 21, 1871."—Forty-first Congress, Session III, Chapter 62, page 419

"... But by the Act of June 11, 1878 (20 Stat. chap. 180), a permanent form of government for the District was established. It provided ... and that the commissioners therein provided for should be deemed and taken as officers of such corporation."— District of Columbia v. Henry E. Woodbury, 136 U.S. 472 (1890)

Chapter VII

Corporatism, a.k.a. Socialism/Fascism, in America

"Democracy and capitalism are systems of consciousness. People do not realise this but their minds are determined by these systems. This is why democracy and [the current elite controlled] capitalism represent a totalitarian regime. Totalitarianism means total control of society . . . never has there been totalitarianism as strong as we have today. The totalitarianism of the democratic and capitalist systems is so sophisticated, that even our desires are determined by the System. We desire that which society wishes we desire."
—Adrian Salbuchi, *The Coming World Government* (2018)

The U.S. government since the War Between the States has been a corporate instrument of the international bankers, controlled since 1913 by the privately owned Fed.[1] The People have been blindly led by the beguiling music of the Pied Piper down a primrose path to serfdom, their vision veiled by a sinister deception perhaps unparalleled in the history of man. The bankers, politicians, and the U.S. government have artfully and skillfully played Americans for fools.

---

[1] See, Griffin, G. Edward, *The Creature from Jekyll Island* (American Media, Westlake Village, CA, 2004) The book is a frightening expose of the great fraud that has been perpetrated on the American people through the 14th and 16th Amendments, the Fed, and the IRS, and is a must read for every American. Meeting in secret on the privately owned Jekyll Island in 1910, Senator Nelson Aldrich, his personal secretary Arthur Shelton, former Harvard University Professor of Economics Dr. A. Piatt Andrew, J.P. Morgan & Co. partner Henry P. Davison, National City Bank President Frank A. Vanderlip and Kuhn, Loeb & Co. Partner Paul M. Warburg formulated plans for the Fed and began writing the Federal Reserve Act. The bankers were involved in a criminal conspiracy and committed treason against the U.S. In the words of Alan Greenspan, former chairman of the Fed: "The Federal Reserve is an independent agency and that means basically that there is no other agency of government which can overrule actions that we take."

Also, for an excellent and eye-opening expose of these facts and more, see, Peter Kershaw's *Economic Solutions* (Heal Our Land, Boulder, CO, 1997).

Unknowingly, the People are owned by the corporation from birth to death. The corporate UNITED STATES holds ownership of all citizens, assets, property, and children. Hard to believe? Or imagine? Think about that deed to the house or land that you "own." You accepted transfer of the property by warranty deed.[2] You have title by "joint tenants," "tenants in common," "tenants by the entireties," or by fee simple. Just what is a tenant?[3] And see how long you maintain possession of "your" property if you fail to pay the real estate taxes (rent) on that property.[4] And think about all those various taxes and fines and licenses you must pay for. In reality, they are unconstitutional, a malevolent abuse of the unalienable rights of the People. A marriage license?[5] Really? We need permission from the government to get married? Look up the history of the marriage license. You will be surprised.[6] Marriage is a God-given unalienable

---

[2] A warranty deed is only "color of title." It has the appearance of title, but is not title in fact or in law. The warranty deed has no defense against the land patent. See, *Black's Law Dictionary* (sixth edition) p. 1589.

[3] *Black's Law Dictionary* (sixth edition): "Tenant. In the broadest sense, one who holds or possesses lands or tenements by any kind of right or title, whether in fee, for life, for years, at will, or otherwise. In a more restricted sense, one who holds lands of another; one who has the temporary use and occupation of real property owned by another person (called the 'landlord'), the duration and terms of his tenancy being usually fixed by an instrument called a 'lease.' One who occupies another's land or premises in subordination to such other's title and with his assent, express or implied. One renting land and paying for it either in money or part of crop or equivalent." Prior to the 14th Amendment, the People had allodial title to the property they owned. *Black's Law Dictionary* (sixth edition): Allodium. Land held absolutely in one's own right, and not of any lord or superior; land not subject to feudal duties or burdens. An estate held by absolute ownership, without recognizing any superior to whom any duty is due on account thereof. Land held in *allodium* is not subject to real estate taxes or other encumbrances." Title to property today is fee title, or fee simple, a.k.a. *feudal title*. "The true meaning of the word 'fee' is the same as that of 'feud' or 'fief,' and in its original sense it is taken in contradistinction to 'allodium,' which latter is defined as a man's own land, which he possesses merely in his own right, without owing any rent or service to any superior. 2 Bl.Comm. 105." (p. 614). The State controls the land and can trespass on the property. The "owner" pays property taxes as "rent" on the land.

[4] Senate Document No. 43, 73rd Congress, 1st Session: "Contracts payable in Gold," written in 1933: "The ultimate ownership of all property is in the State; individual so-called 'ownership' is only by virtue of government, i.e., law, amounting to a mere user; and use must be in accordance with law and subordinate to the necessities of the State." Also, President Franklin D. Roosevelt, 1933: "All the property of this country now belongs to the state and will be used for the good of the state."

[5] *Black's Law Dictionary* defines license as "The permission by competent authority to do an act which without such permission, would be illegal."
Further, *Black's Law Dictionary* (sixth edition): "Marriage license. A license or permission granted by public authority to persons who intend to ***intermarry***. By statute in most jurisdictions, it is made an essential prerequisite to lawful solemnization of the marriage." [Emphasis added]

[6] A marriage license originated in the days (pre-Civil War and post-Civil War) when it was unlawful in most States for a man and woman of different races (i.e., Black and White) to marry (known as *miscegenation*). They had to obtain permission from the State, hence the marriage license granting that permission. Permission was not required of couples who were the same race, hence no need for a

CHAPTER VII CORPORATISM, A.K.A. SOCIALISM/FASCISM, IN AMERICA

right; a holy sacrament of the Church, established and ordained by God in the beginning of time antecedent to all law and governments.[7] The People have the right to freely marry without government intrusion or interference.[8] And take the driver's license, for example. The People have a Constitutional right to travel (liberty by locomotion) freely (for non-commercial purposes) along the public highways and byways without hindrance or restriction.[9] Court cases upholding

---

marriage license. Over time, the States realized that the marriage license would be an additional source of revenue and another way to control the People, so it eventually, in a quiet and furtive manner, became required of all couples. Couples who marry with a marriage license, however, grant the State jurisdiction over the marriage. The marriage is then a creature of the State; it is a corporation of the State. The State therefore has jurisdiction over the marriage, including the fruit of the marriage, which are the children and every piece of property the married couple owns. The marriage license creates a legal contract with three parties, the State being the third party to the contract. ". . . When two people decide to get married, they are required to first procure a license from the State. If they have children of this marriage, they are required by the State to submit their children to certain things, such as school attendance and vaccinations. Furthermore, if at some time in the future the couple decides the marriage is not working, they must petition the State for a divorce. Marriage is a three-party contract between the man, the woman, and the State." (*Van Koten v. Van Koten.* 154 N.E. 146). Also, "Marriage is a civil contract to which there are three parties—the husband, the wife and the state." "The State can regulate that which it licenses. By entering into a State-sanctioned franchise (marriage), a couple forfeits their rights to a private, sovereign marriage and any ownership control of their children or property." (Appellate Court of Illinois, No. 5-97-0108) Child Protective Services receives its full power and authority to seize children via the marriage license and birth certificate. After the marriage, the license is converted into a marriage *certificate*. *Barron's Dictionary of Banking Terms* defines a "certificate" as "a paper establishing an ownership claim." (p. 114). The State therefore owns the marriage. According to the doctrine of *parens patriae*, the State is the undisclosed true parent. The parents have no property right in their children, and only maintain custody of their children during good behavior at the sufferance of the State. The State may, at any time, exercise its superior status and take custody of its children (the doctrine of in *loco parentis*). Also, the pastor, minister, priest or rabbi officiating the marriage, when marrying a couple with a marriage license, is acting as an agent for the State, and *not* in his pastoral or ministerial capacity as a servant of God. Note that marriage is a God-given right, a sacrament instituted by God since the beginning of time. People have the right to marry without interference by the State.

[7] Genesis 2:21-24, Matthew 19:4-5.

[8] In 1923, SCOTUS defined liberty as, among other things: ". . . the ability to freely marry, establish a home, and bring up children." Also, "By marriage, the husband and wife are one person in law: that is, the very being or legal existence of the woman is suspended during the marriage, or at least is incorporated and consolidated into that of the husband: under whose wing, protection, and cover, she performs every thing; and is therefore called in our law-French a feme-covert; is said to be covert-baron, or under the protection and influence of her husband, her baron, or lord; and her condition during her marriage is called her coverture. Upon this principle, of a union of person in husband and wife, depend almost all the legal rights, duties, and disabilities, that either of them acquire by the marriage. I speak not at present of the rights of property, but of such as are merely personal. For this reason, a man cannot grant any thing to his wife, or enter into covenant with her: for the grant would be to suppose her separate existence; and to covenant with her, would be only to covenant with himself: and therefore it is also generally true, that all compacts made between husband and wife, when single, are voided by the intermarriage." Blackstone, Sir William, *Commentaries on the Laws of England*, "Of Husband and Wife" (1765-9)

[9] "Personal liberty largely consists of the Right of locomotion—to go where and when one pleases–only so far restrained as the Rights of others may make it necessary for the welfare of all other citizens.

this right are numerous.[10] Yet the government requires citizens to obtain a license and pay for this so-called "privilege." Yes, Americans have been indoctrinated into believing that driving for non-commercial purposes is a "privilege."[11]

The Right of the Citizen to travel upon the public highways and to transport his property thereon, by horse drawn carriage, wagon, or automobile, is not a mere privilege which may be permitted or prohibited at will, but the common Right which he has under his Right to life, liberty, and the pursuit of happiness. Under this Constitutional guarantee one may, therefore, under normal conditions, travel at his inclination along the public highways or in public places, and while conducting himself in an orderly and decent manner, neither interfering with nor disturbing another's Rights, he will be protected, not only in his person, but in his safe conduct." (*II Am.Jur.* (1st) Constitutional Law, Sect. 329, p. 1135).

Also, "Personal liberty—consists of the power of locomotion, of changing situations, of removing one's person to whatever place one's inclination may direct, without imprisonment or restraint unless by due process of law." (*Bouvier's Law Dictionary* (1914); *Black's Law Dictionary* (fifth edition); *Blackstone's Commentary*, Hare, Constitution, p. 777).

[10] ". . . those things which are considered as inalienable rights which all citizens possess cannot be licensed since those acts are not held to be a privilege." *City of Chicago v. Collins*, 51 N.E. 907, 910. *Murdock v. Penn.* 146 A.L.R. 81: "A state may not, through a license tax, impose a charge for the enjoyment of a right guaranteed by the Federal Constitution." Also, *Miller v. U.S.* 230 F 486, 489: "The claim and exercise of a constitutional right cannot be converted into a crime." *Sherer v. Cullen* 481 F 946: "There can be no sanction or penalty imposed upon one because of this exercise of constitutional rights." *Dunn v. Blumstein* 405 U.S. 330: "The right to travel is an unconditional right, a right whose exercise may not be conditioned."*Chicago Motor Coach v. Chicago*, 169 NE 22: "Even the legislature has no power to deny to a citizen the right to travel upon the highway and transport his/her property in the ordinary course of his business or pleasure, though this right may be regulated [regulated means traffic safety enforcement, stop lights, signs, etc.] in accordance with the public interest and convenience." See, 16 Am Jur 2d sec. 395: "Doctrine of unconstitutional conditions: the government may not grant a benefit [for example a license] on the condition that the beneficiary surrender a constitutional right [for example a "right to travel"]." And finally, *Miranda v. Arizona* 384 U.S. 436, 491: "Where rights secured by the Constitution are involved, there can be no rule making or legislation which would abrogate them." Chief Justice Taney, in *The Passenger Cases* (7 How. 492, 12 L. ed. 790), maintained the right of the American citizen to free transit with these words: "Living, as we do, under a common government charged with the great concerns of the whole Union, every citizen of the United States, from the most remote states or territories, is entitled to free access . . . For all the great purposes for which the Federal government was formed, we are one people, with one common country. We are all citizens of the United States; and, as members of the same community, must have the right to pass and repass through every part of it without interruption, as freely as in our own states." In addition, the author has researched at least 24 additional court cases upholding the Constitutional right of the People to travel without a driver's license. The right to travel is a right from antiquity; acknowledged in the *Magna Carta* and specifically recognized in the Articles of Confederation.

[11] The term "used for commercial purposes" means "The carriage of persons or property for any fare, fee, rate, charge or other consideration, or directly or indirectly in connection with any business, or other undertaking intended for profit." Also, "Motor vehicle means every description of carriage or other contrivance propelled or drawn by mechanical power and used for commercial purposes." (Title 18, Section 31(a)(6) & (10) U.S.C.). Also, "The Motor Vehicle Act (Stats. 1913, p. 639) is not unconstitutional . . . in that it requires professional chauffeurs, or drivers of motor vehicles for hire, to pay an annual license tax, but exempts all others operators of such vehicles from such tax and regulation." *In re Stork*, (1914), 167 C. 294. *Black's Law Dictionary* (fifth edition), p. 830: "The privilege of using the streets and highways by the operation thereon of *motor carriers for hire* can be acquired only by permission or license from the state or its political subdivision [Emphasis added]."

CHAPTER VII CORPORATISM, A.K.A. SOCIALISM/FASCISM, IN AMERICA

Indeed, in the *de facto* government, there are no rights; only privileges. And what about your automobile? Paid cash for it? Think you own it? Think again. The State issues a "certificate of title" for the automobile.[12] In issuing the certificate of title, the State retains an ownership interest in the vehicle, allowing the State to tax you (rent or lease fee) and require you to register and license your vehicle. Or try pleading your "rights" under Amendment V to the Constitution (or any other Constitutional right, for that matter) in a so-called court of law. Your plea will be ignored. Plead it too many times, and the judge will threaten you with contempt of court and throw you in jail.[13] Yes, the corporate federal government owns the soul of the "People." The "People" are no longer sovereign, but mere subjects; "slaves" of the corporate, federal government, serving fealty upon land they think they own.[14]

The American People have unwittingly allowed the creation of a behemoth bureaucracy in a corporate government, filled with

---

Note also that police and sheriff's deputies are not immune from suit for violating the rights of the people. "Public officials are not immune from suit when they transcend their lawful authority by invading constitutional rights." *American Federation of State, County, and Municipal Employees, AFL-CIO v. Woodward*, 406 F2d 137. 18 U.S.C. 242: "Whoever under the color of any law, statute, ordinance, regulation, or custom, willfully subjects any inhabitant of any state, territory, or district to the deprivation of ANY rights, privileges or immunities secured or protected by the Constitution of laws of the United States . . . shall be fined not more than $1,000 or imprisoned not more than one year, or both."

[12] See, definition of "certificate" in footnote 6. The dealer sends the MSO—manufacturer's statement of origin—(allodial title), which comes with every new car, to the State, and the State issues a certificate of title to the purchaser.

[13] The *de jure* U.S. Constitution does not apply to U.S. citizens. Citizens are given a birth certificate at birth, which gives the State an ownership interest in the citizen and makes the citizen *property* of the State. The birth certificate is the title to our souls, just like a car title or property title (deed). See, definition of "certificate" in footnote 6. Again, every word in law has a specific and concise meaning. Note the wording where the mother signs on the "certificate of live birth": "Signature of Mother or **Other Informant**." The wording makes the mother "*an informant*." By signing the birth certificate as an informer, she contracts with the government, pledging her child and her child's future labor as collateral for the national debt. The father or mother can rescind the contract within three business days (1968 Truth in Lending Act), but no one does because they do not understand the fraud that is being perpetrated. Since the birth certificate does not list the father as the *husband* and uses the mother's *maiden name*, the baby is considered a *bastard*. Bastards are under the care and control of the State and can be taken from the mother at any time. See also, *Tillman v. Roberts*. 108 So. 62: "The primary control and custody of infants is with the government."

[14] Benito Mussolini: "Fascism should more appropriately be called corporatism because it is a merger of state and corporate power." The *de facto* government is more a fascist government than a republic. Mussolini is also quoted as saying: "All within the state, nothing outside the state, nothing against the state," and "The keystone of the fascist doctrine is its conception of the state, of its essence, its functions, and its aims. For fascism the state is absolute, individuals and groups relative." It is plain to see that is the attitude of the *de facto* government in this nation today.

employees whose sole sense of self-worth comes from a trivial title bestowed upon them by fellow bureaucrats. The bureaucrats *choose* to abuse their position by assuming power that subjugates an unwary public, rather than exhibiting the humility that serves the rightful master, the People. They wield their assumed power for their own self-aggrandizement to further their political advancement, and to validate their self-deprecating existence. They serve self-interest and government, not the *People* that government was created to serve. Above all, government serves itself in order to advance political ambitions and careers, all in the name of greed and the lust for power. Corporate government has become, not the guardian of our rights, the protector of our liberty and the servant of the People, but the adversary of the People. It has become the voice of an elitist minority imposing its will on a silent majority. Nowhere is this more evident than in our "courts of law."

As Larken Rose so succinctly put it:

> You can romanticize about checks and balances, due process of law, and "Lady Justice" wearing that blindfold . . . The government looks out FOR ITSELF, and no one else. If your interests HAPPEN to coincide with the interests of those in power, you're in luck. If not, too bad for you. If you think there is ANY politician or high-ranking bureaucrat who would even HESITATE to destroy your life if it would maintain or increase his power, you're living in la-la land. Fairness? Law? Justice? Are you kidding?[15]

That is quite an indictment of the courts and government officials, with apologies to the good men and women who do serve the People and our country with honor, dignity, and humility. But in a larger sense, it is an indictment of us all. "We the People" have abdicated our rightful position of power, authority, and the right to rule, in favor of socialism, a false security, and big government.

---

[15] Larken Rose (*larkenrose.com*) is an author, IRS researcher, and political activist. His books include *The Most Dangerous Superstition, The Iron Web, How to Be a Successful Tyrant: The Megalomaniac Manifesto*, and *Taxable Income (The Evolution of a Deception)*.

CHAPTER VII CORPORATISM, A.K.A. SOCIALISM/FASCISM, IN AMERICA

The people have allowed corporate government to usurp a position of "big brother" over a "helpless" citizenry that is "incapable" of managing their own affairs. To put it bluntly, it seems the citizens *want* the government to take care of them.

Such thinking is abhorrent to the Constitution, the principles the South fought for, and the forgotten legacy that our forefathers have passed down through the generations. In the words of Michael Badnarik, in his book *Good to Be King*: "The paternalistic attitude that 'government knows best' and that you are merely a helpless child is insulting and reprehensible. Hitler used the same attitude to persuade the Germans to subjugate themselves to the 'Fatherland.'"[16] Thomas Jefferson astutely expressed this same sentiment years ago in a letter to Thomas Cooper, November 29, 1802: "I predict future happiness for Americans if they can prevent the government from wasting the labors of the people under the pretense of taking care of them."

Yet, it seems that at least some Americans (perhaps a *majority*?) are *willing* to exchange their freedom for the safety and security of a "paternalistic" government pandering to their every need. As H.L. Mencken expressed in 1923: "The average man doesn't want to be free. He wants to be safe."[17] I fear with great trepidation that Mencken is right. Perhaps this nation has traversed too far along the road to socialism to reverse course now. We are already a socialist democratic state.[18] Shall we, too, descend to the depths of an autocratic police state similar to Hitler's Germany? Or become the world's next bastion of communism? Or succumb to the fetters of UN control? Americans, it seems, are demanding more and more from "Big Brother," or perhaps it is more aptly put, "Father." Yes, it was Hitler

---

[16] Id. Badnarik.
[17] The full text of the quote: "The average man's love of liberty is nine-tenths imaginary, exactly like his love of sense, justice and truth. He is not actually happy when free; he is uncomfortable, a bit alarmed, and intolerably lonely. Liberty is not a thing for the great masses of men. It is the exclusive possession of a small and disreputable minority, like knowledge, courage and honor. It takes a special sort of man to understand and enjoy liberty—and he is usually an outlaw in democratic societies. It is, indeed, only the exceptional man who can even stand it. The average man doesn't want to be free. He simply wants to be safe."—H.L. Mencken, *Baltimore Evening Sun* (February 12, 1923).
[18] Karl Marx: "Democracy [*not* republicanism] is the road to socialism." Plato: "Dictatorship naturally arises out of democracy . . ."

who called Germany "The Fatherland."[19] And the government has unabashedly obliged, offering the largess of the public treasury, tantalizing the self-interest of the citizens, in order to curry favor with the voter and secure more power for itself. Such wanton disregard for fiscal responsibility amounts to no more than bribery. And the greater the dependence of the people on government, the greater the sacrifice of liberty. Ironically, citizens that have become attached to the security that government provides have lost their connection to the Divine, which is the true source of all security, freedom and liberty.

---

[19] "The similarities between America at the turn of the century and Germany in the 1930s are stunning, frightening, and unprecedented. They offer an apodictic history lesson of perils, present and future." Al Cronkrite, "America—The Fatherland: It happened before, in Hitler's Germany," *The Covenant News*, October 18, 2004. Cronkrite goes on to write: "The most frightening corollary between Hitler's Germany and Bush's America involves the reactions of the citizens. Bernard Weiner in a review of German author Sebastian Haffner's book, *Defying Hitler*, records the following in regard to the German people: 'Given their built-in weakness and their willingness to swallow the most outrageous Big Lies emanating from the propaganda ministry and the media, most Germans were fruit waiting to be plucked by the Nazi harvesters. They still fall for anything. After all that, I do not see that one can blame the majority of Germans who, in 1933, believed that the Reichstag fire was the work of the Communists. [The Parliament burned down and a convenient Communist arsonist was fingered, which the Nazis used as the excuse to unleash police-state tactics against all opponents.] With sheepish submissiveness the German people accepted that, as a result of the fire, each one of them lost what little personal freedom and dignity was guaranteed by the constitution; as though it followed as a necessary consequence.'" Compare that to the "terrorist attack" on the Twin Towers in the U.S., an event orchestrated by the Global Elite with the full knowledge of the U.S. government. The attack was used as propaganda for passing the USA PATRIOT Act and DHS, which were accepted with "sheepish submissiveness" by the citizens at a cost of "personal freedom and dignity." Conclusive evidence of this can easily be found. Seek and ye shall find. For an expose of empirical evidence detailing how the Twin Towers collapsed, see, *Where Did the Towers Go?* by Judy Wood (The New Investigation, 2010). Further, an article in *Europhysics* (September 2016) stated: "The evidence points overwhelmingly to the conclusion that all three buildings were destroyed by controlled demolition." The article further stated: "The total collapse of WTC 7 at 5:20 PM on 9/11, is remarkable because it exemplified all the signature features of an implosion: The building dropped in absolute free fall for the first 2.25 seconds of its descent over a distance of 32 meters or eight stories. Its transition from stasis to free fall was sudden, occurring in approximately one half second. It fell symmetrically straight down. Its steel frame was almost entirely dismembered and deposited mostly inside the building's footprint, while most of its concrete was pulverized into tiny particles. Finally, the collapse was rapid, occurring in less than seven seconds. Given the nature of the collapse, any investigation adhering to the scientific method should have seriously considered the controlled demolition hypothesis, if not started with it." The article concluded: ". . . the only phenomenon capable of collapsing such buildings completely has been by way of a procedure known as controlled demolition, whereby explosives or other devices are used to bring down a structure intentionally." See also, *America Nuked on 9/11*, edited by Jim Fetzer and Mike Palecek, Moon Rock Books, 458 pages. The contributors include some of the most noted scholars of 9/11. In 28 extensive, detailed studies, 14 authors contribute their expertise on different aspects of 9/11 to expose the truth of the 9/11 tragedy. See also, the DVD series, *Ring of Power* (Amenstop Productions, 2008).

CHAPTER VII CORPORATISM, A.K.A. SOCIALISM/FASCISM, IN AMERICA

Sovereignty be damned. Self-interest seems to have replaced the call of patriotism. Americans no longer pray to their Creator as their supplier, but look to the government for their "entitlement."[20] The work ethic has been abandoned; the "entitlement" ethic conceived. The God of the Universe has been supplanted by the god of the government. Like Constitutional government, John F. Kennedy's famous words from 1961 have been turned upside down: ". . . ask not what your country can do for you—ask what you can do for your country . . . ask not what America will do for you, but what together we can do for the *freedom* of man." [Emphasis added] Americans care not for the good of the country; Americans care about what the government can do for them. Americans care not for the *freedom* of man, and have willingly adorned the shackles of government sustenance. Yes, welfare, unemployment, workers compensation, food stamps, grants, disability, national health insurance, child support, day care, free housing, benefits for immigrants, and a seemingly inexhaustible list of government handouts come with a heavy price . . . chains and shackles in place of freedom and autonomy. William Somerset Maugham perceived the danger in 1941: "If a nation values anything more than freedom, it will lose its freedom; and the irony of it is that, if it is comfort or money it values more, it will lose that too."[21] Americans have taken their freedom for granted, even as their freedom is being continually eroded by an increasingly despotic government. Give them bread and they will care not for their freedom . . . until it has perished. And then it is too late.

The people of the South understood what was happening, and fought to preserve the sovereignty of the people, the state over the federal government, and of God over all. They fought to preserve the integrity of the *de jure* united States Constitution. They understood that their rights were God-given, unalienable, and which no government could abrogate. The function of government was crystal clear: "That to secure these rights, Governments are instituted among Men, deriving their just powers from the consent of the

---

[20] Philippians 4:19 (KJV): "But my God shall supply all your need according to his riches in glory by Christ Jesus."

[21] From *Strictly Personal*, chapter 31 (1941). Maugham was an English playwright, novelist, and short-story writer.

governed."[22] To the Southerner, the preservation of these ideals was worth the blood it cost. To the Southerner, it was better to die fighting for liberty than to give in to tyranny. To the Southerner, the higher price to be paid was the betrayal of these ideals, capitulation to an enemy in the emerging corporate government that would rob them of their right to self-government and self-determination.

A review and synopsis of Albert Taylor Bledsoe's *Is Davis a Traitor? Secession as a Constitutional Right Prior to the War of 1861* reads:

> The subjugation of the Southern states, and their acceptance of the terms dictated by the United States, shifted the Federal Government as a servant of the states to the position of their master. American government founded on the basis of the "consent of the people" (government by consent) changed to government by conquest and marks the transition of the "republic" to the world's most powerful "empire." This work vindicates the loyalty of the South to the Constitution and defines the radical revolution imposed on them by the United States. Modern historians interpret history by the street bully's slogan, "Might makes right." This author shows us that right is right even when it is overcome by force and he helps the Southerner understand that while the South surrendered its arms, it did not surrender its belief in Constitutional liberty.

The true loser in the War Between the States was not the CSA, but the American People, both White and Black; liberty; and the *de jure* Constitution.

The CSA may have lost the War, but the principles for which it fought will never die. President Jefferson Davis prophesied: "The principle for which we contend is bound to reassert itself, though it may be at another time and in another form." He understood that the core issues of sovereignty and state's rights would not be extinguished: ". . . the contest is not over, the strife is not ended. It has only entered upon

---

[22] The Declaration of Independence.

CHAPTER VII CORPORATISM, A.K.A. SOCIALISM/FASCISM, IN AMERICA

a new and enlarged arena."[23] Our nation may succumb to anarchy and the fetters of world communism, but the principles of freedom upon which it was founded are an eternal flame that cannot be extinguished. The flame may flicker and burn dimly, deprived, for a time, of life giving breath. But the day will come when that flame, fanned by the winds of discontent and the vortex of a thousand angel's wings, will grow to a roaring blaze that will consume the evil in eternal damnation. Denying the sovereignty of man is defying the sovereignty of Almighty God. And God will not be mocked.

With a clear knowledge of the truth, the reader can better understand the thoughts recorded by Lettie Burwell[24] in her journal (see excerpts in Appendix B), written during the early months of the War Between the States, and better understand why the men and women of the South were so willing to give all to fight a war that they did not want. Poorly equipped, under-fed, half-clothed, many barefoot, lacking sufficient arms and munitions, and greatly outnumbered, the men of the Confederate Army displayed the greatest resilience, fortitude, and courage of any army in the history of the world. And I should not leave out the army of the North. The War was not of their choosing either. Unwillingly forced from their families, homes, and careers, often at gunpoint, they fought gallantly against superior military minds and an army of unsurpassed conviction, many giving their lives for reasons they didn't fully comprehend. The men and women of the South who were not engaged in combat likewise shared in that fortitude and courage, as they supported their troops, freely, willingly, and sacrificially, without compensation or remuneration, by giving of their possessions and the fruits of their labor toward the War effort and freedom. To them, freedom and liberty was worth the cost of their lives. Like the Founding Fathers before them, they gave their all for the cause of freedom. They sacrificed "their lives, their fortunes, and their honor." I wonder . . . does freedom and liberty have as much value to the people today? Or has the deception so clouded their perception that they willingly succumb to the alluring voice of evil, at the cost of their sovereignty . . . and, I might add,

---

[23] Address to the Mississippi Legislature (1871).
[24] Id. Goode. See, excerpts from the journal in Appendix B.

their dignity. I fear freedom has become too big a burden for the people to bear.

Yes, the federal government has shamelessly defrauded the people it was created to serve. But the people have only themselves to blame. The people have fallen asleep, and out of apathy and ignorance of the Constitution they have allowed corporate government to usurp their rightful autonomy. Ignorance of the facts has led to their silence. Their silence has been construed as their consent to become beneficiaries of a debt they did not incur. The people have been deceived for over 100 years into thinking they remain free and independent, when in actuality they are slaves and servants of the *corporate* U.S. government. Johann Wolfgang von Goethe expressed it well: "None are more hopelessly enslaved than those who falsely believe they are free."

In the words of James Madison: "A diffusion of knowledge is the only guardian of true liberty." Daniel Webster issued a dire warning on June 1, 1837: "I apprehend no danger to our country from a foreign foe . . . Our destruction, should it come at all, will be from another quarter. From the inattention of the people to the concerns of government, from their carelessness and negligence, I must confess that I do apprehend some danger. I fear that they may place too implicit a confidence in their public servants, and fail properly to scrutinize their conduct; that in this way they may be made the dupes of designing men, and become instruments of their own undoing. Make them intelligent, and they will be vigilant; give them the means of detecting the wrong, and they will apply the remedy." The prophet Hosea likewise prophesied centuries ago: "My people are destroyed for lack of knowledge . . ." (Hosea 4:6).

None other than Adolf Hitler expressed the corollary: "How fortunate for governments that the people they administer don't think." Yes, our *ignorance* has given rise to this most viperous of foes. Our nation has indeed been turned upside down. The People have been egregiously and fraudulently deceived by a government elected to be the protector of their rights. Edmund Burke offered keen insight in stating: "The people never give up their liberties but under some delusion." The People have been deluded into exchanging liberty for presupposed "safety."

CHAPTER VII CORPORATISM, A.K.A. SOCIALISM/FASCISM, IN AMERICA

We are a nation that has lost its way . . . and the People their sovereignty. We are a nation adrift on the high seas of treason, our cargo hold overburdened with a multi-trillion dollar debt and bloated government bureaucracy, floating perilously close to submerged icebergs of destruction and tyranny. Should the ill-winds of misfortune blow the wrong way, impaling our hull on the incessant dangers lurking beneath, we shall sink faster than the indomitable *Titanic*. Our freedom will be lost forever, if not already lost, at the bottom of a deep dark abyss. John Adams warned us two centuries ago: "But a Constitution of Government once changed from Freedom, can never be restored. Liberty, once lost, is lost forever." Alas, once lost, we shall have traversed from apostasy to the impending doom of Armageddon; our only hope the return of the King.

The truth is that the "People" no longer exist. The "People" have become subjects of an authoritarian, all powerful central corporate government.[25] Lamentably, the *de jure* U.S. Constitution no longer has meaning. It is mere pretense, existing in appearance only. We live in a state of anarchy and tyranny, with the citizenry being controlled and peace maintained only by the power of the police. In such a government, there is no freedom; the People have no rights, other than those that government decides that they shall be allowed to have at any given time, in any given situation. In such a government, the *de jure* State Constitutions and the Constitution for the united States of America are dormant, null and void, of no force or effect, mere historical footnotes, tattered pieces of paper to be thrown onto the trash heap of antiquity. The corporate government and the courts pay homage to these cherished documents by lip service only. The so-called "rights" of the citizenry are mere privileges, existing only at the whim of government. The world we live in is an illusion, a mere shadow of what the Founding Fathers intended. In the words of Chief Justice Douglas: "The America once extolled as the voice of liberty heard around the world no

---

[25] There are lawful ways that, even today, the citizen can break free from the chains of government and restore his sovereignty. It requires knowledge that is not easily acquired. However, "Ask, and it shall be given you; seek, and ye shall find; knock, and it shall be opened unto you." Luke 11:9 (ASV)

longer is cast in the image which Jefferson and Madison designed, but more in the Russian image."[26]

Our laws no longer protect the People.[27] They exist to *control* the People, under the *pretense* that they are for our "protection" (i.e., the USA PATRIOT Act,[28] U.S. Department of Homeland Security

---

[26] *Laird v. Tatum*, 408 U.S. 1, 92 S.Ct. 2318 (1972). A more expansive quote from the case: "This case involves a cancer in our body politic. It is a measure of the disease which afflicts us . . . Those who already walk submissively will say there is no cause for alarm. But submissiveness is not our heritage. The First Amendment was designed to allow rebellion to remain as our Heritage. The Constitution was designed to keep the government off the backs of the people. The Bill of Rights was added to keep the precincts of belief and expression, of the press, of political and social activities free from surveillance. The Bill of Rights was designed to keep agents of government and official eavesdroppers away from Assemblies of People. The aim was to allow men to be free and independent to assert their rights against government. There can be no influence more paralyzing of that objective than Army [government] surveillance. When an intelligence officer looks over every nonconformist's shoulder in the library, or walks invisibly by his side in a picket line, or infiltrates his club, the America once extolled as the voice of liberty heard around the world no longer is [408 U.S. 1, 29] cast in the image which Jefferson and Madison designed, but more in the Russian image, depicted in Appendix III to this opinion."

[27] The purpose of the police in today's government is to maintain order and investigate criminal activity. They are under no obligation to protect the citizen. *Warren v. District of Columbia*, 444 A.2d 1 (D.C. Ct. of Ap., 1981): It is a "fundamental principle of American law that a government and its agents are under no general duty to provide public services, such as police protection, to any individual citizen." Also, *McKee v. City of Rockwall*, Texas, 877 F.2d409 (5th Cir. 1989), cert. denied, 110 S.Ct.727 (1990), U.S. District Court of Appeals for the Fifth Circuit held that "no constitutional violation [occurred] when the most that can be said of the police is that they stood by and did nothing . . ." SCOTUS ruled that local law enforcement had no duty to protect individuals, but only a general duty to enforce the laws. (*DeShaney v. Winnebago County Department of Social Services*, 489 U.S. 189, 109 S.Ct. 998, 1989). There are numerous other cases with rulings consistent with these decisions. See, *Sapp v. Tallahassee*, 348 So. 2nd 363; *Reiff v. City of Philadelphia*, 477 F. Supp. 1262; *Lynch v. N.C. Dept. of Justice*, 376 S.E. 2nd. 247. A police officer is defined as a *re-venue agent* (transferring revenue to the state) that enforces corporate government contracts and protects the assets of the corporate government including human resources [the citizens]. Compels performance, no injured party necessary. One who has policing powers as found in a "POLICE STATE" i.e., Nazi Germany. Juxtaposed to a peace officer in the *de jure* Constitutional government, who maintains the peace and the safety of the people.

[28] The USA PATRIOT Act ("Uniting and Strengthening America by Providing Appropriate Tools Required to Intercept and Obstruct Terrorism Act"), passed as a consequence to the so-called "terrorist" attack on the Twin Towers, strips Americans of fundamental Constitutional rights, and has little or nothing to do with terrorism. The act was voted on and passed by Congress *without* it being made available to its members to read. Congressmen and senators were given a three-page summary of the bill by the White House press office shortly before the vote. The White House actually intimidated members of both the House and Senate into passing the bill, threatening to label them "unpatriotic" if they failed to vote in favor. Most acquiesced to the threat, fearing the repercussions of being labeled "unpatriotic" at a critical time in our nation's history. After the passage of the bill, U.S. Representatives Lieberman, Daschle, and Gephardt later wrote a memorandum stating that Congress had effectively given the Bush Administration "near dictatorial powers." Representative Ron Paul (Texas) wrote: "The insult is to call this a 'patriot bill' and suggest I'm not patriotic because I insisted upon finding out what is in it and voting no. I thought it was undermining the Constitution, so I didn't vote for it—and therefore I'm somehow not a patriot. That's insulting." Mr. Paul added: "It's my understanding the bill wasn't printed before the vote—at least I couldn't get it. They played all kinds of games, kept the House in session all night, and it was a very complicated bill. Maybe a handful of staffers actually read

CHAPTER VII CORPORATISM, A.K.A. SOCIALISM/FASCISM, IN AMERICA

(DHS) in a "dangerous" world filled with war and global "terrorism" (generally contrived by the Global Elite).[29] They are a

---

it, but the bill definitely was not available to members before the vote." In stating that the act is "a bad bill," Mr. Paul continued: "Generally, the worst part of this so-called antiterrorism bill is the increased ability of the federal government to commit surveillance on all of us without proper search warrants." He is referring to Section 213 (Authority for Delaying Notice of the Execution of a Warrant), also known as the "sneak-and-peek" provision, which effectively allows police to avoid giving prior warning when searches of personal property are conducted. Before the USA PATRIOT Act, the government had to obtain a search warrant prior to a lawful search. With the vote by Congress and the stroke of the president's pen, the right of every American under Amendment IV against unreasonable searches and seizures was abrogated. Congressman C.L. "Butch" Otter added that "some of these provisions place more power in the hands of law enforcement than our Founding Fathers could have dreamt and severely compromises the civil liberties of law-abiding Americans. This bill, while crafted with good intentions, is rife with constitutional infringements I could not support." Nadine Strossen, president of the ACLU, stated: "There is no connection between the September 11 attacks and what is in this legislation. Most of the provisions relate not just to terrorist crimes but to criminal activity generally . . . I like to refer to this legislation, as the 'so-called antiterrorism law,' because on its face the provisions are written to deal with any crime, and the definition of terrorism under the new law is so severely broad that it applies far beyond what most people think of as terrorism." Ron Paul further stated: "This legislation wouldn't have made any difference in stopping the September 11 attacks. Therefore, giving up our freedoms to get more security when they can't prove it will do so makes no sense. I seriously believe this is a violation of our liberties. After all, a lot of this stuff in the bill has to do with finances, search warrants and arrests . . . our rights have been eroded as much by our courts as they have been by Congress. Whether it's Congress being willing to give up its prerogatives on just about everything to deliver them to an administration that develops new and bigger agencies, or whether it's the courts, there's not enough wariness of the slippery slope and insufficient respect and love of liberty." When asked what he thought the nation's Founding Fathers would think of the law, Paul responded: "Our forefathers would think it's time for a revolution. This is why they revolted in the first place. They revolted against much more mild oppression." The travesty of the USA PATRIOT Act also brings to mind the more recent Obamacare legislation, a 2,700-page monstrosity that Congress did not read before voting on it. The now infamous quote by Speaker Nancy Pelosi: "We have to pass the bill so that you can find out what is in it, away from the fog of controversy." It appears that Congress no longer writes its own legislation. It seems that Congress has indeed become irrelevant, bowing to the dictates of the executive branch. In the *de facto* corporate government, Congress is subservient to the president. It is emphatically *not* an equal branch of government to the executive branch.

[29] See, the interview by Alex Jones with film producer Aaron Russo on his friendship with CFR member and Global Elitist Nick Rockefeller, *youtube.com/watch?v=N3NA17CCboA*. In the interview, Mr. Russo reveals that Rockefeller unabashedly stated that the so-called "terrorist attack" on the World Trade Center was an orchestrated event planned by the Global Elite. Rockefeller told Russo of the event 11 months before it happened, although he did not specifically mention what the coming event would be. The Global Elite deemed that what was needed to further their agenda of World Government was "a catastrophic and catalyzing event . . . like a new Pearl harbor." Rockefeller also revealed that the U.S. Patriot Act was written before the "attack" on the Twin Towers occurred. The subsequent Iraq invasion by the U.S and the Iraq "Weapons of Mass Destruction" hoax was also orchestrated by the Global Elite using the so-called "terrorist" attack on the Twin Towers as justification.

Mass shootings are staged, with the goal to create outrage among the population to sway public opinion toward accepting national gun control. An unarmed citizenry will be easier to control when One World Government is implemented. The shootings at Sandy Hook Elementary School in Connecticut and the Boston Marathon "terrorist attack" were orchestrated events staged with the full knowledge and complicity of the U.S. government at the behest of the Global Elite. It has since been proven that there were no "victims" and no deaths at these "false flag" operations. The events were fully staged using professional actors. There is more than ample evidence supporting the fact. The bogus United Way mockery, subject to the discretion and whims of the judges, lawyers, and government agencies and officials who use the law to further

Sandy Hook Charity for the "shooting victims" of Sandy Hook was uploaded to the Internet on December 12, 2012, two days before the shooting even occurred! It has also been discovered that Sandy Hook Elementary School closed in 2008 as a health hazard. The school contained asbestos among other defects. The purpose of the "drills," confirmed by officials in the government and reported by educator Paul Preston of California, was to promote gun control. See, *Nobody Died at Sandy Hook*, edited by Jim Fetzer and Mike Palecek (Moon Rock Books, 2015), for 424 pages of irrefutable evidence that Sandy Hook was a FEMA drill to promote gun control. The Boston Marathon bombing was orchestrated by the FBI and DHS using paid actors for the purpose of testing martial law and attacking Amendment IV against illegal search of homes. The "explosion" was simply a Hollywood "effects" smoke flash bomb. Several documentaries provide ample evidence of the false flag operation.

More recently, unambiguous evidence has surfaced that the shooting at the Pulse nightclub (a gay club) in Orlando, Florida, was an orchestrated event. However, in this one, people actually died; 49 people were killed and 53 wounded. The alleged shooter, Omar Mateen, was well known to the FBI and worked for a subcontractor to DHS. Google's search engine picked up an article from the *Chicago Sun-Times* about the attack **six hours before** the shooting actually took place (rated as "false" by Snopes, however, the site had been changed by then), similar to the newscaster on live TV at the Twin Towers in New York, reporting that Building 7 had just collapsed, when the building could clearly be seen still standing in the background. (Oops!) Crisis actors were identified from video footage as actors who were also seen at Sandy Hook and Boston. A man identified as a crisis actor blocked the exit door, preventing people trying to flee the club. Eyewitnesses reported more than one shooter, confirmed by audio taken within the club. The MSM reported that Mateen acted alone. A man allegedly shot in the leg was captured on video being carried from the club by two men. When they thought they were out of camera range, the alleged victim was let down and walked away . . . but not before joking around with the men who carried him. Yes, it was all captured on camera. And "terrorist" James Howell blew the whistle on the perpetrators. According to Howell, he was in Los Angeles to meet with another person for a planned attack to be coordinated with the attack in Orlando. However, on Sunday morning, Howell called the Santa Monica Police claiming he needed protection from the CIA. Howell told the dispatcher that he "had been set up by the CIA—they are going to kill me." Howell later stated to police: "Everything has gone south. Dan was gone when I got here. They killed the leader of the Florida attack this morning. They are going to kill me. I need protection." According to the police, Howell stated that he was one of five people involved in a planned Sunday attack on both the east and west coasts. He aborted his attack in LA when his accomplice did not show up. Howell further told police: "Omar was not supposed to be killed. They lied to us—Omar and Brandy were supposed to get away." Howell also stated that he had trained at a CIA camp in Virginia with Mateen and the others involved in the planned attacks. Before the officers could question Howell further, the FBI abruptly took over the case and issued gag orders to the Santa Monica police involved. To add to the intrigue, records of the 9-1-1 calls to emergency dispatchers in Orlando for the hours of midnight to 3 AM disappeared by the next day, allegedly seized by the FBI. The FBI also issued gag orders to all police and emergency personnel. And most intriguing, the official FBI transcript of the event reported that *no one died* in the club until after the SWAT team burst in at 5:13 AM. This is contrary to media reports, including the *Chicago Sun-Times* report mentioned earlier. So, who actually killed the victims?

And why the hoax? Primarily to increase public clamour for gun control. The Global Elite are desperate to get guns out of the hands of the people. But the attack was also used to evoke sympathy for the LGBTQ movement, to foment anti-Christian sentiment (for being "intolerant" of the gay movement), and to attack the Republican Party's stance against gun control. Gun control is *not* the answer to such tragedies, whether orchestrated or not. If patrons at the club had been armed, or if there had been more armed security guards, far fewer people would have lost their lives. Guns are the people's best chance to protect themselves from such assaults. Incidents of deadly shootings being prevented, or lives saved by onlookers carrying guns, are numerous, but rarely reported by MSM. Expect more such deadly attacks orchestrated by the government (CIA) and the Global Elite, likely increasing in frequency and magnitude, until the people finally acquiesce to stringent gun control. Criminals will always be able to

CHAPTER VII CORPORATISM, A.K.A. SOCIALISM/FASCISM, IN AMERICA

their own personal agendas, beliefs, goals and ambitions. Corporate government serves its own interest (i.e., the interest of the Global Elite), and no one else's. The law no longer applies equally to all; these same self-serving judges, lawyers, and government officials act arrogantly above the law and are licensed to dispense justice according to their personal discretion for their own aggrandizement,[30] as long as it also serves the interests of corporate government, a.k.a. the Global Elite.[31] Thomas Jefferson called it tyranny: "Tyranny is

---

get guns, but taking guns out of the hands of law-abiding Americans will leave them defenseless against criminals and the rogue government.
"Global warming" ("climate change") is another fraud created by the Global Elitists to further their agenda. Numerous scientists have presented data and research which debunk this theory.

[30] "The judiciary has usurped the law for its own purposes and replaced constitutional guarantees with a system in which judges rule by decree." Introduction to *The Weidner Method* by H. Hammond.

[31] On January 18, 2011, SCOTUS issued a landmark ruling; essentially ruling that the *Constitution is void* (*Windsor v. Maid of the Mist Corp.*, Docket No. 10-632, 10-633, and 10-690). The issue before the court was: "Whether federal courts must be stopped from operating corruptly and ignoring all laws, rules, and facts." Six of the justices voted to deny the petitions even though presented with information and incontrovertible proof that was not contested by the judges accused of corruption and fraud. The court ***denied*** the petitions, without explanation. In denying the petitions, the justices refused to honor their oath to "support and defend the Constitution of the United States against all enemies, foreign and domestic." And, by denying the petitions, SCOTUS has in essence chosen to sanction corruption by federal judges and to allow federal judges to void sections of the Constitution at will. In the words of William Windsor, the defendant in the case: "I have discovered that the federal judges in Atlanta, Georgia, Washington, D.C., and the justices of the United States Supreme Court function like common criminals intentionally making bogus rulings against honest people while covering up the crimes of their fellow judges. I have been contacted by people from all over the country and around the world with their stories of judicial corruption with judges all over the U.S. My charges have been totally ignored by the United States Attorney's Office, the FBI, and Congress. I do not believe there is a shred of decency, honesty, or Constitutional rights in our federal courts. In my opinion, we now live in a police state. Judges are free to do absolutely anything they want. Our laws are meaningless. Your life savings can be stolen by a federal judge, and they have no risk in violating every law in the books. In my opinion, this is the most serious issue that our country has ever faced. Our rights have been stolen. And the mainstream media refuses to cover this story because they are afraid of the judges. Heaven help us." Windsor charges the justices with felonies, violating 18 U.S.C. §4: "Whoever, having knowledge of the actual commission of a felony cognizable by a court of the United States, conceals and does not as soon as possible make known the same to some judge or other person in civil or military authority under the United States, shall be fined under this title or imprisoned not more than three years, or both." [Author's note: The U.S. Constitution has not been in effect since 1861. Therefore, the rulings should not be a surprise; rather they are a conspicuous, although somewhat startling, admission of the truth. I can personally attest to multiple occasions of deliberate corruption with regard to sovereign Americans on the part of judges in the state courts. I reiterate . . . the Constitution does not apply to U.S. citizens in the corporate federal government, therefore, the judges, including SCOTUS justices, can rule however they want without regard to the law or the Constitution, and with impunity. The courts of today are not Constitutional courts. Nor are the courts judicial courts; but rather legislative courts operating in admiralty/maritime law. "Court decisions" are administrative opinions only and are decided on the basis of what is best for the corporate government. Perhaps this is nowhere more evident than in the recent SCOTUS ruling on Obamacare. Further, it should be noted that since 1938, SCOTUS has ruled generally with regard to public policy (commercial, or negotiable instruments law) of the matter, and not the Constitutionality of the matter. See, Chapter X for more details.]

defined as that which is legal for the government but illegal for the citizenry."[32] Government "of the People" has indeed succumbed to the tyranny of evil.

H.L. Mencken understood, years ahead of his time, the true motives behind the "false front" operations of the government: "The urge to save humanity is almost always only a false-face for the urge to rule it. Power is what all messiahs really seek: not the chance to serve."[33] The so-called "good intentions" of government are no more than a ruse to seize more power unto itself.

Daniel Webster foretold, long ago in the early years of the country:

> The rapid advancement of the executive authority is a topic which has already been alluded to . . . I believe the power of the executive has increased, is increasing, and ought now to be brought back within its ancient constitutional limits . . . *Good intentions will always be pleaded for every assumption of power*; but they cannot justify it, even if we were sure that they existed. It is hardly too strong to say, that the Constitution was made to guard the people against the dangers of good intention, real or pretended.[34] [Emphasis added]

In another quote from "The Matrix and the U.S. Constitution," the retired judge writes:

> Every catastrophe, calamity or disaster has been planned and financed by our so-called public representatives with an ulterior motive in mind.[35] The creation of Homeland Security was done

---

[32] This quote is attributed to Thomas Jefferson, but its origin is unknown. It appears on the Monticello website, and in numerous sources of Jefferson's quotes.
[33] Mencken, H.L., *Minority Report: H.L. Mencken's Notebooks* (1956).
[34] Whipple, Edwin, *Great Speeches and Orations of Daniel Webster*, p. 393.
[35] Author's note: In the words of Ted Gunderson, former chief of the Los Angeles FBI: "The CIA makes the Mafia look like a Sunday school class . . . The CIA has done in this country, what they've done to us is unbelievable. Look at the terrorists acts that occurred: the CIA is behind most if not of all of them . . . Our government was involved in some of those. I can't say in all of them because I don't know but I do have documentations that there was (*sic*) government implications in some of these . . . The people out there, did you know that the World Trade Center, when it was bombed internally that it was put together by an organization, called the FBI? . . . and that would mean that Bush had prior knowledge and that would implicate him, in reality if we've wondered to face this thing as it really is: murder at first

CHAPTER VII CORPORATISM, A.K.A. SOCIALISM/FASCISM, IN AMERICA

in the same way. A Terrorist attack was staged by hired men having connections to the Middle East. I'm not going to go into the conspiracy, other than to say that President Bush and the FBI were as guilty as the men who high-jacked the commercial airplanes. The director of the FBI confessed to the Congress of his Agency's involvement under Presidential Order. He was relieved of his position and Congress took no action against President Bush; and the media did not report any of this to the American people. Treason charges were filed against President Bush, Vice President Cheney and the FBI by a two-star General from the Pentagon and no action has ever been taken and nothing was ever reported to the American public, upon the orders of President Obama. This was just another government catastrophe designed to make you, the public, beg the government to come to your aid and protect you. Each time one of these catastrophes are staged, our representatives steal more of our liberty and freedom from us, but America doesn't care because now they feel safe once again. And that's what these foreign Agents want us to believe and feel.[36]

We complain today that government has eroded our rights. It's true because we were lied to directly and indirectly and told to believe something other than truth. The correct term here is "Propaganda" and all government-controlled entities and institutions mentioned are quite expert in the use of it. When I was a child during a period labeled "the Cold War," I remember my teachers telling the class how expert the Communists are in the use of "propaganda." I can say now with absolute certainty that no one is as expert as the American government. In fact, I believe that our government officials taught the World. I don't blame my teachers. Most of

---

degree. If justice was done the FBI agents would be not only in jail but also executed for murder in the first degree . . . These explosions, these terrorists' acts were an excuse to pass anti-terrorism legislation."

[36] Author's note: In May 2012, Bush, Dick Cheney, and Donald Rumsfeld—and other prominent former colleagues—were convicted of war crimes by the Kuala Lumpur War Crimes Commission in Malaysia. The tribunal exercised *universal jurisdiction* to try the trio and former UK Prime Minister Tony Blair *in absentia*, convicting them of crimes against peace for the unlawful invasion of Iraq.

them were subjected to and spoon-fed the same propaganda under direction of these foreign Agents and corporate entities that now employ them. Our teachers are simply spoon-feeding our children with the same propaganda that was fed to them. Naturally, if a teacher becomes too creative and steps outside the box, or thinks outside the box, the penalty for such creativity is the termination of their employment, their future profession and benefits. Generally, the reason used for termination is "Failure to adhere to the established curriculum and/or meet the needs of this establishment." Who established the needs and curriculum? Why, the government agents under the U.S. Department of Education, acting through the foreign agents representing the Masters.

There is no better example of government run amok than DHS, the federal agency created after the so-called 9/11 "terrorist" attacks. Make no mistake: DHS was not created to protect the people, or more appropriately, the citizens of this country, from terrorists. It was created to protect the Global Elite *from* Americans who refuse to submit to the Global Elite's One World Government agenda. Again, make no mistake: DHS is not a friend of the American people. DHS is well-armed and prepared to use deadly force against Americans who refuse to submit to the coming implementation of a national police state and martial law. DHS is prepared to kill perhaps millions of Americans, including innocent women and children, who dissent from the globalist's agenda. In the words of David Hodges, written in an article dated March 5, 2013: "Welcome to the Fatherland, where there is no constitution, no justice and, at the present moment, no future. Our way of life, our culture and even our lives are in jeopardy if we do not quickly reign in an out of control and potentially deadly Department of Homeland Security."[37]

DHS has stockpiled more than 1.6 billion bullets, and has purchased 2,700 Mine-Resistant Ambush Protected vehicles. Does DHS anticipate an invasion of our soil from a foreign enemy? No. The ammunition, weapons, and machinery is meant for Americans

---

[37] David Hodges is the founder of *The Common Sense Show*.

CHAPTER VII CORPORATISM, A.K.A. SOCIALISM/FASCISM, IN AMERICA

who will not acquiesce to the coming One World Government.

DHS considers an American a terrorist if they:

1) are a Ron Paul supporter or a member of a tea party;

2) support Amendment II and the right to bear arms;

3) supports the Constitution and the *de jure* Constitutional government.

Further, any American who professes to be a born-again Christian is also suspect as a terrorist. In the coming NWO, churches will be forced underground, and Christians will no longer be able to worship freely and openly. That is, if there aren't any Christians who accept the mark of the beast, the chip that will be implanted in every living human being. The chip was originally a part of Obamacare (pp. 1000-8), but was subsequently removed. In fact, the current plans for global government are designed by a Luciferian Elite who want to remove all true Christians from the world, which they call a *great cleansing* of the Earth.

To continue the words of David Hodges:

> Since DHS was responsible for the creation and dissemination of the MIAC Report [Missouri Information Analysis Center; Anarchist Movement], it has been decided that YOU, Mr. and Mrs. America, are the new terrorists and it's your fault and you are deserving [of] the terrorist label being forced upon you. When the globalists demand that you drink the fluoride in the water, eat unlabeled GMOs without whining, breath the chemtrailed air, make your children take mercury laden vaccines, allow your savings to be debased by a criminal group of private bankers who print worthless money and give it to themselves and then call it a bail out, fight illegal wars of occupation, accept their Eugenics based national health care system, lay down and let the megabanks steal your homes through the MERS fraud, train Russian troops on our soil in preparation for gun confiscation, demand that you give up your guns, believe that their false flag attacks on Columbine, Sandy Hook and the Aurora Batman Massacre are real, then by-God you better start drinking from the Kool-aid and start believing the lies and misinformation or

you will be declared a terrorist and you will be secretly arrested or be murdered by a drone.

The leaked document entitled "Internment and Resettlement Operations," or FM 3-39.40, reveals the creation of internment camps for political dissidents in the U.S. These camps are for anyone: men, women, or children, who oppose the socialist/fascist takeover of the U.S. The document proves this beyond a shadow of a doubt. Also note that DHS has had millions of temporary plastic coffins built for the bodies of America dissidents. So much for the Constitutional Republic.

In his famous speech made on March 23, 1775, Patrick Henry passionately articulated:

> Gentlemen may cry, Peace, Peace—but there is no peace. The war is actually begun! The next gale that sweeps from the north will bring to our ears the clash of resounding arms! Our brethren are already in the field! Why stand we here idle? What is it that gentlemen wish? What would they have? Is life so dear, or peace so sweet, as to be purchased at the price of chains and slavery? Forbid it, Almighty God! I know not what course others may take; but as for me, give me liberty or give me death!

As in 1775, men today cry Peace, Peace—but there is no peace. Though we hear not the clash of resounding arms, our enemy is already in the field. We are engaged in a war against foes we cannot see, and though we see them not, the foe is armed for battle—with lies, treachery, deceit, and iniquity. The foe lurks in the shadows, cloaked in the robes of perverted justice and abiding in the tainted halls of government, seeking whom it may devour, to tyrannize and enslave in the name of greed, power and wealth. These may be the darkest days of our nation's history; for we fight a foe we cannot see for reasons we do not understand. For the first time in our nation's history, our greatest enemy lies not without, but within, a proverbial *wolf cloaked in sheep's clothing*, sedition in the garb of sanctimony. I believe Daniel Webster, previously quoted, had it right: "I apprehend no danger to our country from a foreign foe . . . Our destruction . . . will be from another quarter. From the inattention of the people to the concerns of government, from their carelessness and negligence . . . Should our end come, it will come suddenly, in the twinkling of an eye . . . no man can tell how sudden a catastrophe may overwhelm us and bury all our glory in profound obscurity."

The People are unwittingly living their own version of *The Truman Show* . . . nothing is as it appears.[38] Americans are pawns to an audience of Global Elite, usurpers whose sole purpose is world dominance and control for their own enrichment. Without realizing it, like Truman Burbank, the People live in an artificial bubble, their lives orchestrated, controlled, and manipulated by an imposter government. It is time for the People to wake up. It is time to for the People to break through the dome of the "painted sky" of delusion, and restore the reality that is the birthright of every American. The imposter will argue that big government is for their own safety, comfort, and well-being, and will attempt to persuade them, as executive producer (in the show) Christof's admonition to Truman in the film: "that there is no more truth in the real world than there is in [their] own artificial world." To which the People must answer, as so eloquently yet sardonically articulated by Truman: "And in case I don't see you . . . good afternoon, good evening, and good night." Then bow to the audience of usurpers, and exit through the stage door into the real world of truth and sovereignty.

Yes, Americans must wake up. It is time for the People to take America back . . . to regain their rightful sovereignty. It is time for the People to rise up in outrage and moral indignation. It is time for men to decide whom they shall serve . . . the **real God**, or a corporation of men's own design, perpetrated by forces of darkness.

---

[38] *The Truman Show*, starring Jim Carrey, Paramount Pictures (1998). Truman Burbank unknowingly lives his entire life in an artificial world in front of cameras for a televised program, *The Truman Show*. Truman's life is filmed through thousands of hidden cameras, 24/7, and broadcast live around the world. Every aspect of Truman's life is controlled and scripted, without his knowledge, as the world of viewers looks on. Until one day, he overcomes his fear of water and reaches the end of the painted dome of the sky, only to find an exit to the stage set. One can only wonder if scriptwriter Andrew Niccol understood the metaphor of his script to our world today.

Shall the People beg and whimper at the feet of evil, eschewing their dignity and forsaking the God of the Universe for mere earthly morsels of bread? Thomas Jefferson understood, years ago in the infancy of our Republic: "And what country can preserve its liberties if its rulers are not warned from time to time that its people preserve the spirit of resistance? Let them take arms . . . The tree of liberty must be refreshed from time to time with the blood of patriots and tyrants."[39]

Truer words of wisdom were never spoken than those expressed by Frederick Douglass on August 3, 1857:

> Power concedes nothing without a demand. It never did and it never will. Find out just what any people will quietly submit to and you have found out the exact measure of injustice and wrong which will be imposed upon them, and these will continue till they are resisted with either words or blows, or both . . . The limits of tyrants are prescribed by the endurance of those whom they oppress . . . If there is no struggle, there is no progress. Those who profess to favor freedom, and deprecate agitation, are men who want crops without plowing up the ground, they want rain without thunder and lightning. They want the ocean without the awful roar of its many waters. This struggle may be a moral one; or it may be a physical one; or it may be both moral and physical; but it must be a struggle.

The sentiment of the Founding Fathers and other great Americans are unanimous in their support of this belief: "When the people fear the government there is tyranny, when the government fears the people there is liberty."[40] In Benjamin Franklin's words: "Rebellion against tyrants is obedience to God." The rhetoric of Henry David Thoreau in *Civil Disobedience* emphatically states: "Disobedience is the true foundation of liberty. The obedient must

---

[39] The "Tree of Liberty" letter, from Thomas Jefferson to William Smith, Paris (November 13, 1787).

[40] The quote has been attributed to Thomas Jefferson, but there is no record of the quote in *The Papers of Thomas Jefferson* or his collected letters. The quote is vaguely similar to Jefferson's comment in an 1825 letter to William Short. The origin of the quote is unknown, but its veracity significant.

CHAPTER VII CORPORATISM, A.K.A. SOCIALISM/FASCISM, IN AMERICA

be slaves." Thoreau also expressed: "It is not desirable to cultivate a respect for law, so much as a respect for right." The sentiment of Martin Luther King Jr.: "One has a moral responsibility to disobey unjust laws." And finally, on the pages of the New Hampshire Constitution, 1784, we read: "The doctrine of non-resistance against arbitrary power, and oppression, is absurd, slavish, and destructive of the good and happiness of mankind."

Patrick Henry's words, quoted above, were never truer than today: "What is it that gentlemen wish? What would they have? Is life so dear, or peace so sweet, as to be purchased at the price of chains and slavery?" Liberty . . . or shackles. The People must choose. "So long as the people do not care to exercise their freedom, those who wish to tyrannize will do so; for tyrants are active and ardent, and will devote themselves in the name of any number of gods, religious and otherwise, to put shackles upon sleeping men."[41]

How did we get here? How could the People have allowed this to happen? Next, how the Reconstruction Acts, the 14th Amendment, and the Act of 1871 fundamentally transformed our nation's Constitutional framework and enslaved the People.

"Naturally, the common people don't want war . . . after all, it is the leaders of a country who determine the policy and it is always a simple matter to drag the people along, whether it is a democracy, or a fascist dictatorship, or a parliament, or a communist dictatorship.

. . . voice or no voice, the people can always be brought to the bidding of the leaders. That is easy. All you have to do is tell them they are being attacked, and denounce the pacifists for lack of patriotism and exposing the country to danger. It works the same way in any country."
—Hermann Goering, head of the Nazi Gestapo,
in *Nuremberg Diary* (1947)

---

[41] François-Marie Arouet (pen name Voltaire, 1694-1778). French writer, philosopher, and activist who played an important role in the 18th century movement called the Enlightenment.

A NATION UPSIDE DOWN

"A state of war only serves as an excuse for domestic tyranny."
—The Gulag Archipelago (1973)

"And let me say, gentlemen, that if we and our posterity shall be true to the Christian religion, if we and they shall live always in the fear of God, and shall respect His commandments, if we and they shall maintain just moral sentiments and such conscientious convictions of duty as shall control the heart and life, we may have the highest hopes of the future fortunes of our country; and if we maintain those institutions of government and that political union, exceeding all praise as much as it exceeds all former examples of political associations . . . It will go on prospering and to prosper. But if we and our posterity reject religious institutions and authority, violate the rules of eternal justice, trifle with the injunctions of morality, and recklessly destroy the political constitution which holds us together, no man can tell how sudden a catastrophe may overwhelm us that shall bury all our glory in profound obscurity. Should that catastrophe happen, let it have no history!"
—Daniel Webster, "The Dignity and Importance of History," address to the Historical Society of New York (February 23, 1852)

"Soon—and it will not be very long—the wilderness of Lebanon will be a fertile field once again. And the fertile fields will become a lush and fertile forest. In that day deaf people will hear words read from a book, and blind people will see through the doom and darkness. The humble will be filled with fresh joy from the Lord. Those who are poor will rejoice in the Holy One of Israel. Those who intimidate and harass will be gone, and all those who plot evil will be killed. Those who make the innocent guilty by their false testimony will disappear. And those who use trickery to pervert justice and tell lies to tear down the innocent will be no more."
—Isaiah 29:17-21 (New Living translation)

CHAPTER VIII

A Shadow Darkens the Land . . .
The Reconstruction Acts • 14th Amendment • Act of 1871

". . . we have in this country substantially or practically two national governments; one, to be maintained under the Constitution, with all its restrictions; the other to be maintained by Congress outside and independently of that instrument . . ."
—SCOTUS Justice Marshall Harlan (*Downes v. Bidwell*, 182, U.S. 244 1901)

"That no free government, or the blessing of liberty, can be preserved to any people but by a firm adherence to justice, moderation, temperance, frugality, and virtue, and by frequent recurrence to fundamental principles."
—George Mason, Virginia Declaration of Rights, Section XV (1776)

The physical destruction much of the South endured as a consequence of the war was perhaps the worst calamity that has ever occurred on American soil. Much of the infrastructure of the South was destroyed . . . and destroyed with a vengeance rivaling that of the most powerful of storms. The city of Atlanta was all but obliterated, entire towns demolished, railroad lines uprooted, bridges destroyed, homes, barns, mills, and other buildings burned to the ground. Women and children killed wantonly. The Columbia, South Carolina, *Phoenix*, reported in 1865: "No language can describe, nor can any catalogue furnish, an adequate detail of the widespread destruction of homes and property." Soldiers returned to their land, often to find their homes no longer standing, fields fallow, livestock slaughtered or confiscated, no seed for spring planting, and no money to buy seed. Some soldiers returned maimed. Others returned only to find father, mother, brother, sister, or wife no longer among the living, an insufferable tragedy amidst unspeakable devastation. The plunder of the land was merciless, and carried out with a viciousness perhaps never before seen in the annals of history. The people of the South were left destitute.

But the physical destruction was accompanied by "an equally devastating and even more insidious aftereffect. The end of the War Between the States brought with it perhaps the most significant and immediate evaporation of wealth in the nation's history; perhaps in the history of the world. The Code of Virginia officially described the heartrending condition of Virginia: 'No people ever suffered greater losses by the termination of the war than the people of Virginia. At one blow their entire slave population was emancipated, their value entirely lost, and their accustomed labor instantly stopped, the circulating medium (money) State and Confederate was rendered worthless, no Federal money in circulation; houses, homes, fences, mills, given to flame, lands impoverished, and having no money value, and they themselves entirely powerless to purchase, and for want of buyers equally powerless to sell . . .'"[1] Bonds and many investments had no value. Bartering became at least a temporary way of life. An economy already devastated by four years of war was sent into a downward spiral that would take many years to recover.

I am reminded of the poignant scene in *Gone with the Wind*, when Scarlett returns to her beloved Tara, only to find her plantation badly damaged and the home at nearby Twelve Oaks burned out. The fields were barren; livestock gone. She frantically dug in the dirt with bare hands to find a few buried potatoes for food. And by the grace of God a single cow appeared on the horizon, bringing but a glimmer of hope to the bleak landscape. Few in the South escaped the ravage and plunder of an enemy that can only be characterized as perniciously evil.

On August 15, 1862, Jefferson Davis wrote: "Rapine and wanton destruction of private property, war upon non-combatants, murder of captives, bloody threats to avenge the death of an invading

---

[1] Id. Goode.

soldierly by the slaughter of unarmed citizens, orders of banishment against peaceful farmers engaged in the cultivation of the soil, are some of the means used by our ruthless invaders to enforce the submission of a free people to a foreign sway."

Yes, the North waged a brutal war on the Confederacy, killing 50,000 innocent civilians including women and children, destroying buildings and crops, killing livestock, and wiping out entire towns in the process.[2] The rape, pillaging, and wanton destruction of the South, along with the inhumane treatment of prisoners of war, was so egregious, that in another day, under different circumstances, Lincoln and his generals would have been tried and hung for war crimes.

At least 618,000 Americans died in the War Between the States, and some experts say the toll reached over 700,000. J. David Hacker, a demographic historian from Binghamton University (State University of New York at Binghamton), recently revised the figure based on new research, to 750,000.[3] These casualties exceed this nation's loss in all other wars combined, from the Revolution up to the Iraq War. Of the estimated 750,000 to 1,250,000 soldiers in the Confederate Army, at least 258,000 died from battle or disease. Of the 2,500,000 to 2,750,000 men in the Union Army, at least 360,222 died, or about 14% of the entire army. Confederate losses represented conservatively 20% of their men. The Appomattox campaign, lasting 10 days ending April 9, 1865, cost the Union about 11,000 causalities, and ended in the surrender of Lee's remnant of 26,765. Confederate dead and wounded numbered about 6,500 during the 10-day campaign. Some companies were decimated during the War; only a small fraction of their original numbers surviving. The entire population of the U.S. in 1860 was only about 31 million.

But the loss of father, brother, and property was not the only loss suffered by the people. Amid the rancor and ravage of war on the battlegrounds of Antietam, Vicksburg, Shiloh, Gettysburg, and

---

[2] For a heart-wrenching collection of war atrocities committed by the Union Army, see, Keys, Thomas Bland, *The Uncivil War: Union Army and Navy Excesses in the Official Records* (The Beauvoir Press, Biloxi, MS, 1991). This book is based almost exclusively on Union Army records.

[3] Professor Hacker's findings were published in the December 2011 issue of *Civil War History*. Using sophisticated demographic methods and statistical software, he estimated deaths could range from 617,877 to 851,066, with an average of 750,000 deaths.

Appomattox, the fields stained red and creeks flowing scarlet with the blood of Americans both North and South, the people lost the most sacred gift of all . . . a gift bequeathed by the Almighty through the Founding Fathers. With little fanfare and barely a whimper, succumbing to the will of the Northern bankers and Global Elite, the Republic died an ignominious death. As barely a whisper in a storm among the raging winds of war, its death went unnoticed by the people. The *de jure* Constitution, the guarantor of the freedom of the people, was no more.

Most tragically, it was a war that need not have been. It was a war instigated by a select group of men for personal vanity, financial gain, and the power to subjugate a free people. The ultimate consequence of the South's unavailing fight for freedom? Subservience. Subjugation to a harsh and brutal conqueror bent on unrelenting punishment of the masses for ages to come. The North's tyrannous deportment toward her Southern brethren was both unforgiving and unforgivable. Only a gracious Savior and loving God could forgive such deliberate, wanton atrocity. Judgment will have its day.

In a deeper sense, the War Between the States was the epic struggle of good versus evil. And evil prevailed. The people are no longer sovereign. Liberty is a mere illusion. Freedom is redefined in the context of an all-controlling central government. The servant of the people has become the oppressor. The once divinely ordained master has become the servant. The nation has been turned upside down. Nothing is as it appears.

March 27, 1861 is a day to be mourned, perhaps more than July 4, 1776 is a day to be celebrated. On that day, the Republic officially died. America won its independence from forces without, only to lose its independence to forces within, barely 85 years later.

On March 27, 1861, seven Southern States walked out of the Second Session of the 36th Congress. When they walked out, the quorum to conduct business was lost.[4] The only votes Congress

---

[4] See, Bowman, George W., Senate printer, *The Journal of the Senate of the United States of America Being the Second Session of the Thirty-Sixth Congress; Begun and Held at the City of Washington, December 3, 1860, in the Eighty Fifth Year of the Independence of the United States* (Washington, D.C. 1860-1).
See also, "THIRTY-SEVENTH CONGRESS; SENATE—EXTRA SESSION. NATIONAL AFFAIRS, March 27,

CHAPTER VIII A SHADOW DARKENS THE LAND . . .

could take under parliamentary procedure were to set the time to reconvene, take a vote to get a quorum, and vote to adjourn and set a date, time, and place to reconvene.[5] Instead, on March 28, Congress adjourned *sine die*, or "without day."[6] "An adjournment *sine die* closes the session, and if there is no provision for convening the assembly again, the adjournment *dissolves the assembly*."[7] [Emphasis added] Congress, therefore, ceased to exist as a lawful body. The Republic of our Founding Fathers died with barely a whimper, an opprobrious death unnoticed by its master, the People.

Congress knew the rules of parliamentary procedure. They knew they could adjourn lawfully. Instead, the Republican-controlled Congress deliberately chose to adjourn *sine die*, with full understanding the adjournment would destroy the Constitution and bring an end to the Republic. The Constitution for the united States of America ceased to be the law of the land. In bowing to the dictates of Northern bankers and capitalists, Congress committed treason against the People and the Constitution for the united States of America. How ironic the party that destroyed the Republic was named the Republican Party.[8]

The goal of Northern bankers and the Republican Party, with its socialist underpinnings going back to the 1850s, was inconspicuously realized. In effect, the bankers and Global Elite had accomplished a

---

1861 (published March 28, 1861). Mr. Breckinridge moved to take up the resolution introduced by him yesterday, advising the withdrawal of the Federal troops from the seceded States. He did not intend making any remarks, as he had already expressed his views on that subject, and desired the vote on his motion to be regarded as a test question. Mr. Fessenden supposed there would be no objection to that, but reminded the Senator that no quorum was present . . . The Senate voted, the result being 19 to 10 —no quorum being present. Motions were made to adjourn and go into Executive session. At this period there was still no quorum, and the Senate voted. Suggestions were made to take a recess, and to direct the Sergeant-at-Arms to go after the absentees. Mr. Breckinridge, after, as he said, he had given the Republicans an opportunity to confirm their nominations, and having fully discharged his own duty, he moved the Senate adjourn sine die. This was disagreed to. There was much incidental debate on these motions. Finally the Senate adjourned till tomorrow." [Emphasis added]
[5] Robert, Henry M., *Robert's Rules of Order Revised, Seventy-Fifth Anniversary Edition* pp. 257-61 (Scott, Foresman and Company, 1915).
[6] *Black's Law Dictionary* (second edition, 1891): "*Sine die*. Without day; without assigning a day for further meeting or hearing. Hence, a final adjournment." Also, *State ex rel. Jones v. Atterbury*, Mo., 300 S.W.2d 806, 811. "A final adjournment; final dismissal of a cause. *Quod eat sine die*, that he go without day; the old form of a judgment for the defendant, i.e., a judgment discharging the defendant from any further appearance in court." *Black's Law Dictionary* (sixth edition).
[7] Id. Robert, p. 62.
[8] Note the Republican Party of the time was philosophically aligned with the Democratic Party of today, and under control of bankers and the Global Elite, the agenda of the Party to destroy the Constitution and promote socialism.

coup d'état, without bloodshed, notice, or protest. A small cabal of bankers, led by the House of Rothschild, usurped the power of the people and seized control of the federal government. Lincoln was a mere puppet, placed in power to accomplish the agenda of the cabal. The *fait accompli* would allow them to remake the federal government in the image they desired. And now that they had control, they would allow nothing to derail their plans, including presidents who would turn against their agenda.

With Congress no longer in session, and no longer a lawful, Constitutional body, President Lincoln assumed full control of the federal government. Quietly and unobtrusively, and with no public notice, Lincoln, in his capacity as commander in chief of the U.S. military, declared a state of national emergency, or state of war, and implemented martial law. Lincoln then proceeded to unilaterally declare war on the Southern States after devising a clever scheme to force the South to fire the first shots, as detailed in Chapter III. On April 12, 1861, Confederate forces opened fire on the federal arsenal at Fort Sumter. But Congress had not wanted war, and did not anticipate Lincoln's actions. The plan to adjourn *sine die* had backfired. Congress was suddenly powerless to stop Lincoln and the baleful agenda of the Global Elite.[9]

Three days later, Lincoln called Congress back into session . . . not as a lawful Constitutional body, but under his authority as commander in chief under military law, and within the *executive branch* of government.[10] The proclamation reads, in part: "I do hereby, in virtue of the power in me vested by the Constitution, convene both Houses of Congress. Senators and Representatives are therefore summoned to assemble at their respective chambers, at 12 o'clock, noon, on Thursday, the fourth day of July, next, then and there to consider and determine, such measures, as, in their wisdom, the public safety, and interest may seem to demand." July 4? But why wait so long? Lincoln knew Congress did not want war. By the time Congress convened, it would be too late to stop the

---

[9] Note that a formal declaration of war was never issued.
[10] See, "Proclamation Calling Militia and Convening Congress," by the President of the United States, April 15, 1861.

hostilities. Troops were already on the move. The Battle of Bull Run would be fought on July 21, just weeks after Congress reconvened. Another *fait accompli*. But no matter. Congress reassembled was not Congress of the *de jure* Constitution for the united States of America. Congress was now an irrelevant body, rendered powerless to stop Lincoln and his agenda . . . at least for the time.

Lincoln's implementation of martial law has not been reversed or suspended. The federal government operates in a state of emergency under martial law to this day.[11] Hence, courts are admiralty/maritime law courts.[12] The "law of the land" has been replaced by the "law of the sea."[13] Every president of the United States since Lincoln has presided by executive order issued from a military, martial law jurisdiction with the only "law" being the "law of necessity," i.e., the War Powers.[14] Lincoln's first executive order was issued April 21, 1861, and called up 75,000 militia.[15] Read on . . . the narrative becomes even more scurrilous.

Congress has never been lawfully reconvened by the rules of parliamentary procedure or under the *de jure* Constitution. The U.S. has not had a lawful Congress since March 27, 1861. Congress sits by resolution, not by positive due process law.[16] The legislative branch of the government is no longer. Congress is a mere legal fiction, essentially irrelevant, existing for appearance sake only. Congress sits under the direct authority of the office of the president in the executive branch. The president does not need the consent or a vote

---

[11] See, Emergency War Powers (12 Stat 319). This has never been repealed and continues to exist in Title 50 U.S.C. Sections 212, 213, 215, Appendix 16, 26 C.F.R. Chapter 1 paragraph 303.1-6(a), and 31 C.F.R. Chapter 5, paragraph 500.701 Penalties.

[12] According to U.S. Supreme Court Justice Joseph Story in his *Commentaries on the Constitution of the United States*, admiralty and maritime jurisdiction "extends to all acts and torts done upon the high seas, and within the ebb and flow of the sea, and to all maritime contracts, that is to all contracts touching trade, navigation, or business upon the sea, or the waters of the sea within the ebb and flow of the tide." See, *DeLovio v. Boit* (1815); *U.S. v. Wiltberger* (1820); *Waring v. Clarke* (1847).

[13] Note that in 1845, breaking from English precedent, Congress extended admiralty jurisdiction to include inland navigable lakes and rivers. This legislation ultimately allowed common law to be usurped by admiralty law.

[14] Maxim of law: "Necessity knows no law." Also, Cicero: "In time of war laws are silent."

[15] See, Robinson, James D., *A Compilation of the Messages and Papers of the President*, Vol. VII (Bureau of National Literature, Inc., NY, 1897).

[16] See, the official set of *Code of Laws of the United States of America*, Volume One, Index of Titles, Title II. Congress is marked with an asterisk, which states that Congress exists by resolution, not positive law.

of Congress for his actions, since the legal authority for Congress to meet exists only by executive order. All authority of the federal government today derives from the War Powers, and not the *de jure* Constitution. The *de jure* Constitution exists in name only, an impotent document rendered void with the implementation of martial law and the *sine die* adjournment of Congress. This fact has never been overtly disclosed to the American people. The truth was hiding in plain sight, but few cared to investigate. The people's trust in the government was implicit. Few dared think that the government could be so unscrupulous.

The death of the Republic also ended, for all practical purposes, English common law as the law of the land. It was replaced with legal fiction "laws," known as statutes, codes, rules, and regulations, based on presidential executive order, and not due process of the *de jure* Constitution. SCOTUS affirmed this in 1973: "In this country, the law in effect in all but a few States until mid-19th century was the pre-existing English common law . . . It was not until after the War Between the States that legislation began generally to replace the common law."[17] These purported "laws" are not actually laws at all. They have the appearance and look of laws, but according to due process, they are merely "color of law," inherently defective and void, enforced only by the police power and military courts of a *de facto* government.[18]

Lincoln had no Constitutional authority for his actions, and he knew it. To justify his seizure of power, on April 24, 1863, Lincoln issued General Order No. 100, known as the Lieber Code, or Lieber Instructions.[19] The code was implemented to ostensibly

---

[17] *Roe v. Wade*, 410 U.S. 113 (1973).
[18] The War Between the States ("Civil War") was orchestrated by the bankers, a.k.a. the Global Elite, under the pretext of slavery. The real reason for the conflict, as documented in these pages, is the enslavement of all Americans. Military law placed the people under the control of the commander in chief of the military. All law was suspended due to the national emergency, which continues to this day. The president rules by executive order. When the Global Elite took control of the District of Columbia Municipal Government Corporation in 1871, they gained total control of the UNITED STATES and the people. The Global Elite only needed to "own" the president, as commander in chief of the military, ruling by executive order. All presidents except for Ronald Reagan and Donald Trump have been pre-selected by the Global Elite to carry out their agenda of a One World Government.
[19] The Lieber Code is also known as *Instructions for the Government of Armies of the United States in the Field*, General Order No. 100, or Lieber Instructions. It was an instruction signed by President Lincoln to the Union forces. It was so named because Francis Lieber was assigned the task of preparing

Chapter VIII A Shadow Darkens the Land . . .

govern Lincoln's actions under martial law and justify his seizure of power, and was issued without public notice. It extended the laws of D.C. beyond the boundaries of Washington and into the States for the first time in American history. The Lieber Code also extended the laws of war and international law onto American soil. The U.S. government became the conqueror of the people and the land.

In Section I, Article 1, the Code states: "A place, district, or country occupied by an enemy, stands, in consequence of the occupation, under the Martial Law of the invading or occupying army, *whether any proclamation declaring Martial Law, or any public warning to the inhabitants, has been issued or not.* Martial Law is the immediate and direct effect and consequence of occupation or conquest." [Emphasis added]

The continuing state of national emergency was affirmed in a Senate Report from the 93rd Congress, November 19, 1973:

> A majority of the people of the United States have lived all of their lives under emergency rule [War Powers]. For 40 years, freedoms and governmental procedures guaranteed by the Constitution have, in varying degrees, been abridged by laws brought into force by states of national emergency . . . actions taken by the Government in times of great crises have—*from, at least, the Civil War*—in important ways shaped the present phenomenon of a permanent state of national emergency.[20] [Emphasis added]

The Lieber Code is blatantly unconstitutional under the *de jure* Constitution. In reality, there was no state of emergency. The nation-states of the South simply separated from the Northern States to become a separate nation, as was their right. But not that the question of constitutionality mattered. The Constitution for the united States of America had ceased to exist. Many of the state

---

the code following the proclamation of martial law by President Lincoln on September 24, 1862. The Lieber Code put the U.S. into the 1874 Brussels Conference. It would later become the basis for all international treaties, including The Hague Conventions of 1899 and 1907, and the Geneva Accords of 1954.

[20] Senate Report 93-549, War and Emergency Powers Act, "Report of the Special Committee on the Termination of the National Emergency" (November 19, 1973).

legislatures in the Northern States also adjourned *sine die*, and with the Southern States no longer part of the Union, all of the states that were parties to creating the Constitution ceased to exist; the States became franchises, or territories, of the federal government in D.C.[21] As a consequence of the Lieber Code, the *people*, of both the North and South, *are the enemy*.[22] The Lieber Code effectively took away the unalienable rights of the people by military force and confiscated all private property. Under martial law, all property belongs to the military except for that property which the commander in chief may, at his discretion, exempt from seizure. The Lieber Code states, in part: "A victorious army appropriates all public money, seizes all public movable property until further direction by its government, and sequesters for its own benefit or that of its government all revenues of real property belonging to the hostile government or nation. The title to such real property remains in abeyance during military occupation, and until the conquest is made complete."[23] Under martial law, title to property is a mere fiction. The people do not hold equitable,[24] or allodial,[25] title to their land or property. They only have the *right* to the *use* of the property at the discretion of and with the permission of the government. Government ownership of all property exists to this day.

Under the Lieber Code, people can be arrested, hauled into military tribunals under admiralty/maritime law, tried, convicted, sentenced, put in jail, have all their property seized, and even be put

---

[21] See, "An Act to provide Internal Revenue to support the Government, to pay Interest on the Public Debt, and for other Purposes," Ch. 173, 13 Stat. 223, 306, June 30, 1864: "And be it further enacted, That wherever the word state is used in this act it shall be construed to include the territories and the District of Columbia *where such construction is necessary* to carry out the provisions of this act." [Emphasis added]

[22] "Instructions for the Government of Armies of the United States in the Field," prepared by Francis Lieber, LLD, Washington, 1898: Government Printing Office: "A place, district, or country occupied by an enemy stands, in consequence of the occupation, under the martial law of the invading or occupying army, *whether any proclamation declaring Martial Law, or any public warning to the inhabitants, has been issued or not.* Martial Law is the immediate and direct effect and consequence of occupation or conquest." [Emphasis added]

[23] Id. Lieber, Section II, Article 31, p. 5.

[24] Equitable ownership. The ownership interest of one who has equitable as contrasted with legal ownership of property as in the case of a trust beneficiary. Ownership rights which are protected in equity. *Black's Law Dictionary* (sixth edition) p. 539.

[25] Allodial. Free; not holden of any lord or superior; owned without obligation of vassalage or fealty; the opposite of feudal. *Black's Law Dictionary* (sixth edition) p. 76.

Chapter VIII A Shadow Darkens the Land...

to death, without ever knowing the trials were in fact, military proceedings in court martial. The gold-fringed flag in all courtrooms today is evidence courts are still operating in admiralty/maritime jurisdiction. Remember from Chapter VI, under martial law, people are guilty until proven innocent. There is no due process of law. There are no Constitutional rights.

The Lieber Code also contains much deceitful, fallacious language, not appropriate to the circumstances of the time. The Code states:

> Insurrection is the rising of people in arms against their government, or portion of it, or against one or more of its laws, or against an officer or officers of the government. It may be confined to mere armed resistance, or it may have greater ends in view. Civil war is war between two or more portions of a country or state, each contending for the mastery of the whole, and each claiming to be the legitimate government. The term is also sometimes applied to war of rebellion, when the rebellious provinces or portions of the state are contiguous to those containing the seat of government.[26]

The South, as nation-states, seceded from the Union, which was their lawful right, and at no time did they attempt to overthrow the U.S. government. They merely wanted a peaceful separation to protect their sovereign status as nation-states over an oppressive federal regime in Washington. There was no "insurrection." The right to secede was covered in Chapter II, but, for emphasis, the Mississippi legislature, on November 30, 1860, provided a very concise statement on the cause of secession:

> Whereas, The Constitutional Union was formed by the several States in their separate sovereign capacity for the purpose of mutual advantage and protection; That the several States are distinct sovereignties, whose supremacy

---
[26] i.d. Lieber, Section X, Articles 149 and 150.

is limited so far only as the same has been delegated by voluntary compact to a Federal Government, and when it fails to accomplish the ends for which it was established, the parties to the compact have the right to resume, each State for itself, such delegated powers . . .[27]

The War was in truth an international war. The term "civil war" is a misnomer, as previously stated in these pages, a blatantly inaccurate description of the secession by the Southern States, a term concocted by Lincoln and Northern bankers to justify military action and Lincoln's usurpation of power.

As detailed in Chapter IV, Lincoln had a change of heart toward the end of the War. He planned to end martial law by executive order, restore Constitutional government to the Southern States and the nation, and reconvene Congress as a lawful body under the Constitution for the united States of America. His betrayal of the bankers' interests led to his assassination before he could implement the plan. The coup d'état by bankers and the Global Elite was complete. They had destroyed the Constitution and gained control of the federal government.

The War Between the States effectively ended on April 9, 1865, when General Robert E. Lee surrendered his troops to General Grant at Appomattox. However, a peace treaty was never signed. A few remnant bands of Confederate soldiers continued fighting, but, badly outnumbered and without provisions, were eventually captured or gave up the fight. On April 2, 1866, President Andrew Johnson issued a proclamation that, "the insurrection which heretofore existed in the States of Georgia, South Carolina, Virginia, North Carolina, Tennessee, Alabama, Louisiana, Arkansas, Mississippi, and Florida is at an end, and is henceforth to be so regarded."[28]

The Southern States, in the aftermath of the War, were treated more harshly than any defeated nation in the history of American

---

[27] From the "Laws of the state of Mississippi, Passed at a Called Session of the Mississippi Legislature held in . . . Jackson, November, 1860."

[28] Presidential Proclamation No. 153 General Records of the United States, G.S.A. National Archives and Records Service. Note the use of the word "insurrection," which is an inaccurate description of the right of the Southern States to secede from the Union.

wars. Congress, led by Representative Thaddeus Stevens and Senator Charles Sumner, forced harsh, brutal, and vindictive reconstruction policies on the South. They would not accept the mild reconstruction policies of Lincoln and President Andrew Johnson. They refused to seat representatives from Arkansas, Louisiana, Tennessee, and Virginia, sent to Congress under Lincoln's and President Johnson's "10% Plan." Instead, they passed the Reconstruction Act of 1867 over President Johnson's veto.

Under the Reconstruction Act of 1867, the Southern States were placed under barbarous military rule. The South was divided into five military districts, each governed by a brigadier general appointed by the president. The Southern States were no more. Their governments were declared unlawful. The people of the South were stripped of their sovereignty; the states converted at gunpoint to mere territories (more aptly plantations) of the federal government, a status which exists to this day. The State Constitutions were declared null and void.[29] The generals were tasked with ensuring all adult males, Black and White, would elect delegates to a new constitutional convention. The convention would establish new State governments in which the former slaves would vote and hold office. The Act also took away the right to vote or hold office from all people who served in the Confederate Army or the Confederate government,[30] disenfranchising a large portion of the population and robbing the people of the complete freedom to choose elected representatives they deemed worthy of the office.

Under the Freedman's Bureau Bill of 1866, all Confederate debt was invalidated; Confederate bonds were suddenly worthless; Confederate currency had no value. There would be no compensation for the loss of slaves or the destruction and loss of property. The people of the South were left virtually penniless. Many were

---

[29] Violation of Article 4, Section 4 of the Constitution for the united States of America: "The United States shall guarantee to every State in this Union a Republican Form of Government . . ."

[30] A violation of Article 1, Section 9 of the *de jure* Constitution: "No Bill of Attainder or ex post facto Law shall be passed." A "bill of attainder" is an act of a legislature declaring a person or group of persons guilty of some crime and punishing them without a trial. Also, a violation of Amendment V: "No person shall be held to answer for a capital, or otherwise infamous crime . . . nor be deprived of life, liberty, or property, without due process of law; nor shall private property be taken for public use, without just compensation."

homeless, their homes left in ashes by a ruthless Union Army. Foraging for food became a way of life for many. State legislatures were composed of former slaves, carpetbaggers, and scalawags[31] who obeyed the orders of the generals, adding humiliation to the suffering. The people of the South had no say in government. The people were now slaves. The Black man, though freed from the plantations, was now a slave on a larger plantation, under the absolute dominion of an all-powerful federal government. The participation in the military government by the Black man was but a faux freedom, as crime, fraud, and corruption hovered over the land.

The Reconstruction Acts required the newly formed Southern States to ratify the unconstitutional 14th Amendment before being seated in Congress. This egregious condition was unprecedented. The *de jure* Constitution *does not* give Congress the right to compel a State by an act of Congress to ratify a Constitutional amendment. Nevertheless, a new State Constitution, the formation of a new government, and a seat in the Congress of a government still under military law, was of little consequence. The *de jure* Southern States were no more. They remained territories of the now all-powerful federal government. The **servant** of the people was now the **master**. The nation was turned upside down.[32]

President Andrew Johnson vetoed the Reconstruction Act, tersely declaring its unconstitutionality:[33]

---

[31] Scalawag is defined as "a White Southerner who collaborated with Northern Republicans during Reconstruction, often for personal profit. The term was used derisively by White Southern Democrats who opposed Reconstruction legislation."

[32] See, Brewer, Jerry, *Dismantling the Republic* (Shotwell Publishing, Columbia, South Carolina, 2017). From the foreword by Michael Andrew Grissom: "What passes for American history today, especially as it pertains to the type of government under which we are now constrained to live, is largely a collection of myths, fables, and legends, which have incrementally supplanted the truth until legend has become the new truth. Few people, for instance, realize that the republic which was founded in the last few years of the 18th century no longer exists. In *Dismantling the Republic*, Jerry Brewer strips away fancy and fiction to show us that the republic actually died in 1865. Lincoln spent four years trying to kill it, and it finally succumbed at Appomattox. What we have today has been in the making ever since . . . we have arrived at a government that has metamorphosed into something that abuses citizens at home and destroys civilizations abroad. Whatever it is, it is not the republic our Revolutionary patriots gave us, nor what they envisioned. We have to start over, and *Dismantling the Republic* tells us why."

[33] President Andrew Johnson's veto on March 2, 1867. The First Reconstruction Act was passed by Congress in 1865 and vetoed by Johnson. Congress passed the bill again in April 1866 in support of 13th Amendment. Johnson again vetoed the bill. On March 2, 1867, Johnson vetoed the new Reconstruction Act. However, two-thirds majority in each chamber overrode the veto. The Act became law without presidential signature. Johnson's veto was drafted primarily by distinguished Philadelphia lawyer Jeremiah S. Black.

Chapter VIII A Shadow Darkens the Land...

I have examined the bill "to provide for the more efficient government of the rebel States" with the care and the anxiety which its transcendent importance is calculated to awaken. I am unable to give it my assent for reasons so grave that I hope a statement of them may have some influence on the minds of the patriotic and enlightened men with whom the decision must ultimately rest.

The bill places all the people of the ten States therein named under the absolute domination of military rulers; and the preamble undertakes to give the reason upon which the measure is based and the ground upon which it is justified. It declares that there exists in those States no legal governments and no adequate protection for life or property, and asserts the necessity of enforcing peace and good order within their limits. Is this true as matter of fact?

It is not denied that the States in question have each of them an actual government, with all the powers—executive, judicial, and legislative—which properly belong to a free state. They are organized like the other States of the Union, and, like them, they make, administer, and execute the laws which concern their domestic affairs. An existing de facto government, exercising such functions as these, is itself the law of the state upon all matters within its jurisdiction. To pronounce the supreme law-making power of an established state illegal is to say that law itself is unlawful.

. . . The bill, however, would seem to show upon its face that the establishment of peace and good order is not its real object . . . The excuse given for the bill in the preamble is admitted by the bill itself not to be real. The military rule which it establishes is plainly to be used, not for any purpose of order or for the prevention of crime, but solely as a means of coercing the people into the adoption of principles and measures to which it is known that they are opposed, and upon which they have an undeniable right to exercise their own judgment.

I submit to Congress whether this measure is not in its

whole character, scope, and object without precedent and without authority, in palpable conflict with the plainest provisions of the Constitution, and utterly destructive to those great principles of liberty and humanity for which our ancestors on both sides of the Atlantic have shed so much blood and expended so much treasure.

The ten States named in the bill are divided into five districts. For each district an officer of the Army, not below the rank of a brigadier-general, is to be appointed to rule over the people; and he is to be supported with an efficient military force to enable him to perform his duties and enforce his authority. Those duties and that authority, as defined by the third section of the bill, are "to protect all persons in their rights of person and property, to suppress insurrection, disorder, and violence, and to punish or cause to be punished all disturbers of the public peace or criminals."

The power thus given to the commanding officer over all the people of each district is that of an absolute monarch. His mere will is to take the place of all law. The law of the States is now the only rule applicable to the subjects placed under his control, and that is completely displaced by the clause which declares all interference of State authority to be null and void. He alone is permitted to determine what are rights of person or property, and he may protect them in such way as in his discretion may seem proper. It places at his free disposal all the lands and goods in his district, and he may distribute them without let or hindrance to whom he pleases. Being bound by no State law, and there being no other law to regulate the subject, he may make a criminal code of his own; and he can make it as bloody as any recorded in history, or he can reserve the privilege of acting upon the impulse of his private passions in each case that arises. He is bound by no rules of evidence; there is, indeed, no provision by which he is authorized or required to take any evidence at all. Everything is a crime which he chooses to call so, and

Chapter VIII A Shadow Darkens the Land...

all persons are condemned whom he pronounces to be guilty. He is not bound to keep and record or make any report of his proceedings. He may arrest his victims wherever he finds them, without warrant, accusation, or proof of probable cause. If he gives them a trial before he inflicts the punishment, he gives it of his grace and mercy, not because he is commanded so to do.

It is plain that the authority here given to the military officer amounts to absolute despotism. But to make it still more unendurable, the bill provides that it may be delegated to as many subordinates as he chooses to appoint, for it declares that he shall "punish or cause to be punished."

Such a power has not been wielded by any monarch in England for more than five hundred years. In all that time no people who speak the English language have borne such servitude. It reduces the whole population of the ten States—all persons, of every color, sex, and condition, and every stranger within their limits—to the most abject and degrading slavery. No master ever had a control so absolute over the slaves as this bill gives to the military officers over both White and colored persons.

I come now to a question which is, if possible still more important. Have we the power to establish and carry into execution a measure like this? I answer, Certainly not, if we derive our authority from the Constitution and if we are bound by the limitations which it imposes.

This proposition is perfectly clear, that no branch of the Federal Government—executive, legislative, or judicial—can have any just powers except those which it derives through and exercises under the organic law of the Union. Outside of the Constitution we have no legal authority more than private citizens, and within it we have only so much as that instrument gives us. This broad principle limits all our functions and applies to all subjects. It protects not only the citizens of States which are within the Union, but it shields every human being who comes or is brought under our jurisdiction. We have no right to do in one place more than in another that which the Constitution says we shall not do at all. If, therefore, the Southern States were in truth out of the Union, we could not treat their people in a way which the fundamental law forbids.

Some persons assume that the success of our arms in crushing the opposition which was made in some of the States to the execution of the Federal laws reduced those States and all their people—the innocent as well as the guilty—to the condition of vassalage and gave us a power over them which the Constitution does not bestow or define or limit. No fallacy can be more transparent than this. Our victories subjected the insurgents to legal obedience, not to the yoke of an arbitrary despotism.

Invasion, insurrection, rebellion, and domestic violence were anticipated when the Government was framed, and the means of repelling and suppressing them were wisely provided for in the Constitution; but it was not thought necessary to declare that the States in which they might occur should be expelled from the Union. Rebellions, which were invariably suppressed, occurred prior to that out of which these questions grow; but the States continued to exist and the Union remained unbroken. In Massachusetts, in Pennsylvania, in Rhode Island, and in New York, at different periods in our history, violent and armed opposition to the United States was carried on; but the relations of those States with the Federal Government were not supposed to be interrupted or changed thereby after the rebellious portions of their population were defeated and put down. It is true that in these earlier cases there was no formal expression of a determination to withdraw from the Union, but it is also true that in the Southern States the ordinances of secession were treated by all the friends of the Union as mere nullities and are now acknowledged to be so by the States themselves. If we admit that they had any force or validity or that they did in fact take the States in which they were passed out of the Union, we sweep from under our feet all the grounds upon which we stand in justifying

CHAPTER VIII A SHADOW DARKENS THE LAND...

the use of Federal force to maintain the integrity of the Government...

I need not say to the representatives of the American people that their Constitution forbids the exercise of judicial power in any way but one—that is, by the ordained and established courts. It is equally well known that in all criminal cases a trial by jury is made indispensable by the express words of that instrument...

An act of Congress is proposed which, if carried out, would deny a trial by the lawful courts and juries to 9,000,000 American citizens and to their posterity for an indefinite period. It seems to be scarcely possible that anyone should seriously believe this consistent with a Constitution which declares in simple, plain, and unambiguous language that all persons shall have that right and that no person shall ever in any case be deprived of it. The Constitution also forbids the arrest of the citizen without judicial warrant, founded on probable cause. This bill authorizes an arrest without warrant, at the pleasure of a military commander. The Constitution declares that "no person shall be held to answer for a capital or otherwise infamous crime unless on presentment by a grand jury." This bill holds every person not a soldier answerable for all crimes and all charges without any presentment. The Constitution declares that "no person shall be deprived of life, liberty, or property without due process of law." This bill sets aside all process of law, and makes the citizen answerable in his person and property to the will of one man, and as to his life to the will of two.

The United States are bound to guarantee to each State a republican form of government. Can it be pretended that this obligation is not palpably broken if we carry out a measure like this, which wipes away every vestige of republican government in ten States and puts the life, property, liberty, and honor of all the people in each of them under the domination of a single person clothed with unlimited authority?

The purpose and object of the bill—the general intent which pervades it from beginning to end—is to change the entire structure and character of the State governments and to compel them by force to the adoption of organic laws and regulations which they are unwilling to accept if left to themselves . . . If they do not form a constitution with prescribed articles in it and afterwards elect a legislature which will act upon certain measures in a prescribed way, neither Blacks nor Whites can be relieved from the slavery which the bill imposes upon them . . . I would simply ask the attention of Congress to that manifest, well-known, and universally acknowledged rule of constitutional law which declares that the Federal Government has no jurisdiction, authority, or power to regulate such subjects for any State . . .

The bill also denies the legality of the governments of ten of the States which participated in the ratification of the amendment to the Federal Constitution abolishing slavery forever within the jurisdiction of the United States and practically excludes them from the Union. If this assumption of the bill be correct, their concurrence cannot be considered as having been legally given, and the important fact is made to appear that the consent of three-fourths of the States—the requisite number—has not been constitutionally obtained to the ratification of that amendment, thus leaving the question of slavery where it stood before the amendment was officially declared to have become a part of the Constitution.

That the measure proposed by this bill does violate the Constitution in the particulars mentioned and in many other ways which I forbear to enumerate is too clear to admit of the least doubt.

It is a part of our public history which can never be forgotten that both Houses of Congress, in July, 1861, declared in the form of a solemn resolution that the war was and should be carried on for no purpose of subjugation, but solely to enforce the Constitution and laws, and that when this was yielded by the parties in rebellion the contest should cease, with the constitutional rights of the States and of individuals unimpaired. This resolution was adopted and sent forth to the world unanimously by the Senate and with only two dissenting voices in the House. It was accepted by the friends of the Union in the South as well as in the North as expressing honestly and truly the object of the war. On the faith of it many thousands of persons in both sections gave their lives and their fortunes to the cause. To repudiate it now by refusing to the States and to the individuals within them the rights which the Constitution and laws of the Union would secure to them is a breach of our plighted honor for which I can imagine no excuse and to which I cannot voluntarily become a party."

On July 19, 1867, Johnson, in a message to Congress, stated: "The veto of the original bill of the 2nd of March was based on two distinct grounds, the interference of Congress in matters strictly appertaining to the reserved powers of the States, and the establishment of military tribunals for the trial of citizens in time of peace."[34] Congress knew the nation was under martial law, and intentionally did not reveal this to the people. And they were under no obligation to do so. Treason? No. Deceit, yes. As a stratagem of war, such deceit is allowed under international law and the laws of war. To this day, the fact has never been revealed to the American people. Under martial law, the people are not entitled to full disclosure. The people are presumed to know the law. Ignorance of the law is not an excuse. But to the discerning, the truth is evident.

The motive of the banking cabal which controlled Congress was sinister . . . vengeance on a free people determined to exercise their sovereign right to self-determination; and complete control of the states, both North and South, under a centralized federal government, for their profit.

---

[34] See, President Andrew Johnson's veto message, parts of which are reproduced in the *Congressional Record*, p. 15643 (June 13, 1867).

Witnessing the dismantling of the South, General Robert E. Lee remarked to Texas former Governor F.W. Stockdale: "Governor, if I had foreseen the use these people desired to make of their victory, there would have been no surrender at Appomattox, no, sir, not by me. Had I seen these results of subjugation, I would have preferred to die at Appomattox with my brave men, my sword in this right hand."[35] Whatever the chaos of his beloved Virginia, Lee had no desire to leave: "I cannot desert my native state in the hour of her adversity," he remarked to a friend. "I must abide her fortune, and share her fate."

In spite of appearances, 14th Amendment to the Constitution was never lawfully ratified. According to the Constitution for the united States of America, a proposed amendment must be passed by two-thirds of both houses of Congress.[36] However, when Congress proposed the amendment, 23 senators were unlawfully excluded from the U.S. Senate in order to secure a two-thirds vote to adopt the amendment. Without the exclusion of both senators from the 11 Southern States and a senator from New Jersey, the amendment would not have passed. Further, in the House of Representatives, only 120 voted for the proposed amendment. However, 122 votes were required to total two-thirds of the 182 members seated. But, because there were 30 abstentions, it was declared to have been passed by a two-thirds vote of the House. Such chicanery mocked the Constitution, the bulwark of the Republic, and was unprecedented in American history. This was sufficient to invalidate the proposed amendment. Regardless, the 14th Amendment was sent to the states for ratification in June 1866.

By March of 1867, 20 states had ratified and 13 had rejected the proposed amendment. Therefore, it failed to become law:

> These totals do not include the actions of Tennessee, which is generally regarded as ratifying the proposed amendment. The Tennessee legislature was not in session when the

---

[35] General Robert E. Lee, CSA, as told to Texas ex-Governor F.W. Stockdale (August 1870). From the correspondence of General Robert E. Lee, in *The Life and Letters of Robert Lewis Dabney*, pp. 497-500.
[36] Article 5. Amendments may also be by proposed by a vote of two-thirds of the States.

proposed amendment was sent, so a special session of the legislature had to be called. The Tennessee Senate ratified the proposed amendment. However, the Tennessee House could not assemble a quorum as required in order to legally act. Finally, after several days and "considerable" effort, two of the recalcitrant members were arrested and brought into a committee room opening into the Chamber of the House. They refused to vote when their names were called, whereupon the Speaker ruled that there was no quorum. His decision, however, was overruled, and the amendment was declared ratified on July 19, 1866, by a vote of 43 to 11, the two members under arrest in the adjoining committee room not voting.[37]

Not dissuaded by the failure of the amendment, Congress passed the unconstitutional Reconstruction Act of March 2, 1867, which overthrew and invalidated the governments of the Southern States that had rejected the amendment. Recall President Johnson vetoed the bill. The lawfully constituted legislatures of the states were illegally removed by "military force" and replaced by illegitimate legislatures at the discretion of the military governors. And, as stated previously, the Act required the states to ratify the proposed the 14th Amendment before they would be readmitted to Congress. Such a condition is repugnant to a free Republic. Nowhere does the Constitution give Congress the authority to compel a State to ratify a Constitutional amendment, particularly by a legislature not elected by the people. Seven of these illegitimate legislatures eventually ratified the 14th Amendment. Andrew C. McLaughlin in his *Constitutional History of the United States*, wrote: "Can a State which is not a State and not recognized as such by Congress, perform the supreme duty of ratifying an amendment to the fundamental law? Or does a State—by congressional thinking—cease to be a State for some purposes but not for others?" Such an absurdity is preposterous.

---

[37] Flack, Horace Edgar, *Adoption of the Fourteenth Amendment*, p. 165 (1879, published 1906). See also, Tennessee House Journal (Extra Session), p. 25 (1866).

The Reconstruction Act violated several provisions of the *de jure* Constitution: Article 1, §9; Article 3, §3; Article 4, §3; Article 4; Article 5; and Amendment V. The congressmen who voted for the Act had taken a solemn oath to support and defend the Constitution. In voting for the Act, they committed perjury and treason.[38] Perhaps even more egregiously, SCOTUS abandoned its Constitutional and judicial responsibility to provide "checks and balances" to the other branches of the federal government. They refused to rule on the constitutionality of the Act. The precedent of *judicial statutory annulment* had been firmly established in 1803, when the court ruled: ". . . it is apparent that the framers of the Constitution contemplated that instrument as a rule for the government of courts, as well as that of the legislature. Why otherwise does it direct the judges to take an oath to support it?"[39]

The Reconstruction Acts, therefore, are null and void. SCOTUS settled the issue of unconstitutional acts, ruling: "An unconstitutional act is not a law; it confers no rights; it imposes no duties; it affords no protection; it creates no office; it is in legal contemplation as inoperative as though it had never been passed.[40]

And further:

> The general misconception is that any statute passed by legislators bearing the appearance of law constitutes the law of the land. The U.S. Constitution is the supreme law of the land, and any statute, to be valid, must be in agreement. It is impossible for both the Constitution and a law violating it to be valid; one must prevail. This is succinctly stated as follows: The General rule is that an

---

[38] The oath of office for all senators and representatives reads: "I, ___, do solemnly swear (or affirm) that I will support and defend the Constitution of the United States against all enemies, foreign and domestic; that I will bear true faith and allegiance to the same; that I take this obligation freely, without any mental reservation or purpose of evasion, and that I will well and faithfully discharge the duties of the office on which I am about to enter. So help me God." Article 6 Clause 3 of the Constitution states: "The Senators and Representatives before mentioned, and the Members of the several State Legislatures, and all executive and judicial Officers, both of the United States and of the several States, shall be bound by Oath or Affirmation, to support this Constitution . . ." Congress's defiance of the original objective of the War Between the States was a new war; a war against the States, the *de jure* Constitution, and our founding principles.

[39] *Marbury v. Madison*, 5 U.S. 137 (1803).

[40] *Norton v. Shelby County*, 118 U.S. 425 (1886).

unconstitutional statute, though having the form and name of law is in reality no law, but is wholly void, and ineffective for any purpose; since unconstitutionality dates from the time of its enactment and not merely from the date of the decision so branding it. An unconstitutional law, in legal contemplation, is as inoperative as if it had never been passed. Such a statute leaves the question that it purports to settle just as it would be had the statute not been enacted. Since an unconstitutional law is void, the general principles follow that it imposes no duties, confers no rights, creates no office, bestows no power or authority on anyone, affords no protection, and justifies no acts performed under it . . . A void act cannot be legally consistent with a valid one. An unconstitutional law cannot operate to supersede any existing valid law. Indeed, insofar as a statute runs counter to the fundamental law of the land, it is superseded thereby. No one is bound to obey an unconstitutional law and no courts are bound to enforce it.[41]

After passage of the Reconstruction Act, New Jersey and Ohio reversed their ratifications of the 14th Amendment. The final count of ratification, without considering the illegitimate governments of the Southern States, was 19 states for, 16 against, and two (California and Tennessee) not acting on the amendment. Ratification had failed . . . again.

However, on July 20, 1868, U.S. Secretary of State William H. Seward issued a proclamation listing the "official" results of ratification.[42] His tally showed 23 states that voluntarily ratified, six states that ratified under martial law, and two states that voluntarily (Ohio and New Jersey) reversed their ratifications. Even without considering the absurdity of the Southern States under an illegitimate legislature being compelled to pass the measure before their representatives would be seated in Congress, the amendment did not pass ratification.

---

[41] 16 Am Jur 2d, Sec 177 late 2d, Sec 256.
[42] Statutes at Large, v. 15, p. 706.

Seward was in a quandary. In his official proclamation, he wrote he was not authorized as secretary of state "to determine and decide doubtful questions as to the authenticity of the organization of State legislatures or as to the power of any State legislature to recall a previous act or resolution of ratification." He also stated the amendment was valid ". . . if the resolutions of the legislatures of Ohio and New Jersey, ratifying the aforesaid amendment, are to be deemed as remaining of full force and effect, notwithstanding the subsequent resolutions of the legislatures of these States." So much for state sovereignty. Seward also questioned the validity of ratification by States under martial rule.[43]

Congress, however, was not satisfied with Seward's proclamation, and on July 21, 1868, passed a joint resolution declaring three-fourths of the States of the Union had ratified the 14th Amendment, in spite of the reality.[44] On July 28, Seward yielded to Congress and declared three-fourths of the States had ratified the amendment. But the sordid saga was not over. In October 1868, the Oregon legislature, three months after Seward's proclamation of ratification, passed a rescinding resolution. The legislature argued the 14th Amendment had not been ratified by three-fourths of the States and the so-called ratifications in the Southern States were "usurpations, unconstitutional, revolutionary and void" and, "until such ratification is completed, any State has a right to withdraw its assent to any proposed amendment."[45]

So began the usurpation by government of the rights of the people. The so-called 14th Amendment is a disgrace to a free Republic and the rule of law. The banking cabal proved they would resort to any means, even unlawful, to destroy the Constitutional Republic.

The controversy regarding lawful adoption of the 14th Amendment continued in the ensuing years. On March 8, 1957, Congress approved a joint resolution introduced by Georgia: "A

---

[43] Note that the 14th Amendment did not need ratification by the states, since it was passed by a Congress exercising its military powers under martial law.
[44] House Journal, 40th Congress, 2nd Session, p. 1126.
[45] DiLorenzo, Thomas, J., "Truth About the Fourteenth Amendment" (*mises.org/library/truth-about-14th-amendment*).

CHAPTER VIII A SHADOW DARKENS THE LAND...

Memorial to Congress, Fourteenth and Fifteenth Amendments to U.S. Constitution Be Declared Void."[46] The resolution recounts the chronology of the purported ratification, and reads in part:

> Whereas, furthermore, when these invalid proposals were rejected by the General Assembly of the State of Georgia and twelve other Southern States, as well as of sundry Northern States, the so-called 39th and 40th Congresses, in flagrant disregard of the United States Constitution, by the use of military force, dissolved the duly recognized State Governments in Georgia and nine of the other Southern States and set up military occupation or puppet State governments, which compliantly ratified the invalid proposals, thereby making (at the point of the bayonet) a mockery of Section 4, Article IV of the Constitution, guaranteeing protection to "each of them against invasion" . . .
>
> The Congress of the United States is hereby memorialized and respectfully urged to declare that the exclusions of the of the Southern Senators and Representatives from the 39th, 40th and 41st Congresses were malignant acts of arbitrary power and rendered those Congresses invalidly constituted; that the forms of law with which those invalid Congresses attempted to clothe the submission of the 14th and 15th Amendments and to clothe the subsequent acts to compel unwilling States to ratify these invalidly proposed amendments, imparted no validity to these acts and amendments; and that the so-called 14th and 15th Amendments to the Constitution of the United States are null and void and of no effect.

In 1967, the House of Representatives, in a resolution entitled "The Amendment That Never Existed, The Non-Ratification of the United States Constitution, 14th Amendment," stated, in part; (quoting H. Con. Res. 208):

---

[46] Resolution No. 45, Senate Resolution No. 39, A Joint Resolution.

Whereas the purported 14th Amendment to the United States Constitution was never lawfully adopted in accordance with the requirements of the United States Constitution because eleven states of the Union were deprived of their equal suffrage in the Senate in violation of Article V, when eleven southern states, including Louisiana, were excluded from deliberation and decision in the adoption of the Joint Resolution proposing said 14th Amendment . . . Whereas the Reconstruction Acts of Congress unlawfully overthrew their existing governments, removed their lawfully constituted legislatures by military force and replaced them with rump legislatures which carried out military orders and pretended to ratify the 14th Amendment; and, Whereas in spite of the fact that the Secretary of State in his first proclamation, of July 20, 1868, expressed doubt as to whether three fourths of the required states had ratified the 14th Amendment, Congress nevertheless adopted a resolution on July 28, 1868, unlawfully declaring that three fourths of the states had ratified the 14th Amendment and directed the Secretary of State to so proclaim, said Joint Resolution of Congress and the resulting proclamation of the Secretary of State included the purported ratifications of the military enforced rump legislatures of ten southern states whose lawful legislatures had previously rejected the said 14th Amendment, and also included purported ratifications by the legislatures of the States of Ohio, and New Jersey although they had withdrawn their legislative ratifications several months previously, all of which proves absolutely that said 14th Amendment was not adopted in accordance with the mandatory constitutional requirements set forth in Article V of the Constitution and therefore the Constitution strikes with nullity the purported 14th Amendment.[47]

The Utah Supreme Court, in a case detailing the history of

---

[47] H7161, pp. 15641-6. See also, *Coleman v. Miller*, 307 U.S. 448, 59 S. Ct. 972 (June 13, 1967).

Chapter VIII A Shadow Darkens the Land...

the failed amendment, struck down the 14th Amendment in 1968.[48] And in 1975, the Utah Supreme Court again struck down the 14th Amendment, writing in its opinion: "I cannot believe that any court, in full possession of its faculties, could honestly hold that the amendment was properly approved and adopted."[49]

However, the 14th and 15th Amendments are not a part of the *de jure* Constitution for the united States of America, and are null and void under the restored Republic. Nevertheless, the unconstitutional 14th and 15th Amendments are clear examples of the usurpation of the federal government by the Global Elite. All amendments after the original Amendment XIII are merely bylaw amendments of the Constitution of the United States of America, the corporate charter. As bylaws, they do not need to be ratified by the States. Bylaws are approved by the board of directors of the corporate government, Congress, under the authority of the Board of Governors of the Fed.

The primary intent of the 14th Amendment was to make citizenship national, to create a special class of citizenship for the newly freed slaves, and to subvert the power of the States. This point was elucidated in a speech by James G. Blaine at a large gathering in Skowhegan, Maine on August 29, 1866:

> In the first place, we ask that they will *agree to certain changes in the Constitution of the United States; and, to begin with, we want them to unite with us in broadening the citizenship of the Republic.* The slaves recently emancipated by proclamation, and subsequently by Constitutional Amendment, have no civil status. They should be made citizens. We do not, by making them citizens, make them voters; we do not, in this Constitutional Amendment, attempt to force them upon Southern White men as equals at the ballot-box; but we do intend that they shall be admitted to citizenship, that they shall have the protection of the laws, that they shall not, any more than the rebels shall, be deprived of

---

[48] *Dyett v. Turner*, 439 P.2d 266, 272 (1968).
[49] *State v. Phillips*, 540 P.2d 936, 941 (1975).

life, of liberty, of property, without due process of law, and that they shall not be denied the equal protection of the law. This extension of citizenship, we are not confining the breadth and scope of our efforts to the negro (*sic*). It is for the White man as well. We intend to make citizenship National. Heretofore, a man has been a citizen of the United States because he was a citizen of some-one of the States: now, we propose to reverse that, and make him a citizen of any State where he chooses to reside, by defining in advance his National citizenship—and our Amendment declares that *"all persons born or naturalized in the United States, and **subject** to the jurisdiction thereof, are citizens of the United States and of the States wherein they reside."* This Amendment will prove a great beneficence to this generation and to all who shall succeed us in the rights of American citizenship; and we ask the people of the revolted States to consent to this condition as an antecedent step to their re-admission to Congress with Senators and Representatives.[50] [Emphasis added]

Blaine's words may have seemed noble, but were spoken with the tongue of a snake . . . filled with deception, lies, and innuendo. Rather than a "great beneficence to this generation and to all who shall succeed us . . ." the Amendment enslaved all Americans. The Republic, destroyed by Lincoln, was obliterated by the 14th Amendment; the *de jure* Constitution effaced by the Amendment's evil purpose. The nation was truly turned upside down.

The 14th Amendment begins:

Section 1. All *persons* born or *naturalized* in the United States, and *subject* to the jurisdiction thereof, are *citizens*

---

[50] Blaine, James G., *Political Discussions: Legislative, Diplomatic, and Popular, 1856-1886*, p. 61 (The Henry Bill Publishing Company, Norwich, CT, 1887). *The Reconstruction Problem, the Fourteenth Amendment as a Basis of Reconstruction*. James Gillespie Blaine (1830-93) was an American statesman and Republican politician who represented Maine in the U.S. House of Representatives (1863-76), served as speaker of the U.S. House of Representatives (1869-75), later served in the U.S. Senate (1876-81), and also served as secretary of state twice (1881, 1889-92).

CHAPTER VIII A SHADOW DARKENS THE LAND . . .

> *of the United States and of the state wherein they reside.* No state shall make or enforce any law which shall abridge the privileges or immunities of citizens of the United States; nor shall any state deprive any person of life, liberty, or property, without due process of law; nor deny to any person within its jurisdiction the equal protection of the laws. [Emphasis added]

The wording is egregiously deceptive, its true meaning obscured by the colloquial usage of the words. The word "person" is defined as: "In general usage [colloquial usage], a human being (i.e., natural person), though by statute the term *may include labor organizations, partnerships, associations, corporations, legal representatives*, trustees, trustees in bankruptcy, or receivers."[51] [Emphasis added] In the 14th Amendment (as in law today), the word is used to mean a corporate fiction, a non-substance corporate entity, and not the corporeal, living, flesh and blood people who were formerly the sovereigns in the land. Persons are not born; they are created by a superior corporation. The created is subject to its creator.

Naturalized means: "introduced from another region and persisting without cultivation. Planted so as to give an effect of wild growth. Cultivated. Domesticated. Established." The word is generally used to refer to a foreigner admitted to the citizenship of a country. It has nothing to do with the living, flesh and blood people.

The term "United States" as used in the 14th Amendment is defined in the U.S.C. as including only Washington, D.C. and the territories.[52] Later in this chapter, we will see that within a few short years following the alleged passage of the 14th Amendment, the "United States" government would become a legal corporation created by statute. The term in this case *does not* mean the *de jure* States united of the Republic.

---

[51] *Black's Law Dictionary* (sixth edition) p. 1142.
[52] See, 10 U.S.C. §113 (3): "In this subsection, the term 'United States,' when used in a geographic sense, includes the territories and possessions of the United States. Also, 5 U.S.C. §5911, 15 U.S.C. §1171, 26 U.S.C. §993, 26 U.S.C. §3121." Remember from Chapter VI a principle of law states that which is included *excludes* anything that is not included. In some definitions, the word "state" is used, meaning a territory, or sub-franchise, of the corporate federal government.

The wording, "subject to," denudes the people of their sovereignty and places them in the position of a "subject" (i.e., slave) of the new, all powerful, federal government. The term "citizen" was defined in Chapter VI, but will be repeated here: ". . . members of a political community who, in their associated capacity, have established or *submitted* themselves to the dominion of a government . . ."[53] [Emphasis added] Under the 14th Amendment, *citizens* have no rights, but merely *privileges* according to the dictates of an all-powerful federal government. The subjects can enjoy such privileges only as long as it suits the purpose of their master, the federal government. The 14th Amendment actually overthrows the lawful, *de jure* Constitution for the united States of America.

The phrase "citizens of the United States *and* of the State wherein they reside" has been overturned by the Court of Appeals of Maryland.[54] The court ruled a people *can* be a citizen of one of the states *without* being a U.S. citizen. And the term "reside" does not apply to the corporeal, living, breathing, flesh and blood people. The word comes from the Latin *res*, which means, "The thing. The subject of the matter—that is, an action concerning an object or property, rather than a person; the status of individuals."[55] The people, corporeal beings, do not *reside*; they live, or are domiciled, in a specific location within a State of the Union.

The Amendment also portended to strip the States of their sovereignty with respect to the federal government by dictating certain actions of the state: ". . . nor shall any state deprive any person of life, liberty, or property, without due process of law; nor deny to any person within its jurisdiction the equal protection of the laws." These clauses are a part of every State's Constitution, guaranteeing the rights of the people. In effect, the Amendment is

---

[53] *Black's Law Dictionary* (sixth edition) p. 244.
[54] *Crosse v. Board of Supervisors of Elections of Baltimore City*, 221 A.2d 431 (Md. 1966). The court stated: "Both before and after the Fourteenth Amendment to the federal Constitution, it has not been necessary for a person to be a citizen of the United States in order to be a citizen of his state. *U.S. v. Cruikshank*, 92 U.S. 542, 549 (1875); *Slaughter-House Cases*, 83 U.S. (16 Wall.) 36, 73-74 (1873); *Short v. State*, 80 Md. 392, 401-02, 31 A. 322 (1895); Spear, *State Citizenship*, 16 Albany L.J. 24 (1877)."
[55] *Black's Law Dictionary* (sixth edition) p. 1304: "Res. In the civil law, a thing; an object. As a term of the law, this word has a very wide and extensive signification, including not only things which are objects of property, but also such as are not capable of individual ownership."

usurping the sovereign power of the State Constitutions. But note the word "person" is used in the Amendment, which refers to non-sentient corporate beings.

Finally, Section 4 of the Amendment reads: "The validity of the public debt of the United States, authorized by law, including debts incurred for payment of pensions and bounties for services in suppressing insurrection or rebellion, shall not be questioned. But neither the United States nor any state shall assume or pay any debt or obligation incurred in aid of insurrection or rebellion against the United States, or any claim for the loss or emancipation of any slave; but all such debts, obligations and claims shall be held illegal and void." Note again there was no insurrection, no rebellion. The people merely exercised their divine right to secede from the Union in pursuit of self-governance, free from the dictates of an increasingly autocratic federal government.

Most egregious is that "The validity of the public debt of the United States . . . shall not be questioned." The Amendment made the people (enfranchised persons) accountable for the nation's debt. The sovereign voice of the people, the masters of their government, was muted, no longer able to express concern over a debt incurred on their behalf by ruthless bureaucrats not accountable to the people. The nation is currently burdened with an unsustainable and unpayable $28 trillion debt, and the people are silenced; liable for a debt they did not incur and with no standing to protest.

In summary, the 14th Amendment: strips the people of their sovereignty and God-given unalienable rights, treating them as legal entities (Section 1); establishes the people as *enemies of the state* (Section 2); public offices are illegitimate (Section 3); and the people cannot question the public debt (Section 4).

SCOTUS aptly summarized the effect of the 14th Amendment: "We have held also that in adopting the Fourteenth Amendment, the people *required the States to surrender a portion of the sovereignty* that had been preserved to them by the *original* Constitution, so that Congress may authorize private suits against nonconsenting States pursuant to its §5 enforcement power."[56] [Emphasis added] "By

---

[56] *Fitzpatrick v. Bitzer*, 427 U.S. 445 (1976).

imposing explicit limits on the powers of the States and granting Congress the power to enforce them, the Amendment fundamentally altered the balance of state and federal power struck by the Constitution."[57] "When Congress enacts appropriate legislation to enforce this Amendment (see, *City of Boerne v. Flores*, 521 U.S. 507 (1997)), *federal interests are paramount*, and Congress may assert an authority over the States which would be otherwise unauthorized by the Constitution."[58] [Emphasis added]

A dark shadow had indeed been cast over the land. But even more ominous and foreboding storm clouds appeared on the horizon, threatening to blot out the faintest glint of hope for the doomed Republic. The coup d'état by the Global Elite would soon be complete. In the chaos of war and its aftermath, the people unwittingly lost the Republic the Founding Fathers sacrificed their lives and fortunes for.

On February 21, 1871, Congress passed the "Act to Provide a Government for the District of Columbia," or "The District of Columbia Organic Act of 1871," known simply as the Act of 1871.[59] The Act created a *private municipal corporation* for D.C., giving Congress the authority under the existing martial law to govern the territory. The corporation was known as THE UNITED STATES and governed D.C. and the *territories* of the U.S. (Puerto Rico, Guam, Virgin Islands, et al.). The corporation subsequently trademarked the name "UNITED STATES GOVERNMENT," or the UNITED STATES CORPORATION. The corporation adopted a new Constitution as its articles of incorporation and corporate charter, which appeared identical to the Constitution for the united States of America, except that it omitted the *de jure* Constitution's Amendment XIII, and the 14th, 15th, and 16th Amendments of the *de jure* Constitution were respectively renumbered the 13th, 14th, and 15th Amendments.[60] The new corporate charter was named

---

[57] *Seminole Tribe of Florida v. Florida*, 517 U.S. 44 (1996), at 59. See also, *Alden et. al. v. Maine*, 527 U.S. 706 (1999).

[58] *Fitzpatrick, supra*, at 456.

[59] Acts of the Forty-first Congress, Section 34, Session III, chapters 61 and 62.

[60] The original Amendment XIII, also known as the "Title of Nobility" Amendment, reads: "If any citizen of the United States shall accept, claim, receive, or retain any title of nobility or honour, or shall without the consent of Congress, accept and retain any present, pension, office, or emolument of any kind whatever, from any emperor, king, prince, or foreign power, such person shall cease to be a citizen of

CHAPTER VIII A SHADOW DARKENS THE LAND...

THE CONSTITUTION **OF** THE UNITED STATES OF AMERICA [Emphasis added] . . . one small, simple word change and "all-capital" letters (a capitonym) distinguished the two documents.[61] The original *de jure* Constitution was vacated; rendered dormant. But it was not terminated. It still exists today, as made clear by SCOTUS Justice Marshall Harlan.[62] The new Constitution, or corporate charter, should have been ratified by the people, but it never was. Rather, the whole process was done in secrecy, behind closed doors, to dupe the people. An unwary, gullible people believe the *de jure* Constitution to still be in effect.

In passing the Act of 1871, Congress created an entirely new government for D.C. . . . an INCORPORATED government. In effect, the Act created a new nation, the District of Columbia Municipal Corporation, or UNITED STATES, INC. The UNITED STATES is a foreign nation with respect to the states and to the *united States of America*. It operates outside the *de jure* (organic) Constitution. The charter, a *de facto* Constitution, does not benefit the Republic. It is a mere corporate charter. It benefits only the corporation of UNITED STATES, INC. Its meaning can be changed to whatever the corporation determines is in its best interests and/or deems appropriate for its circumstances. This new nation is an illegal quasi-government. A corporation is merely an artificial entity which makes rules for its employees and its structural operation.[63]

---

the United States, and shall be incapable of holding any office of trust or profit under them, or either of them." The Amendment effectively barred attorneys (lawyers) certified by the International Bar Association (IBA), from serving in public office. The IBA was chartered by the King of England and headquartered in the City of London, and attorneys carried the title of "esquire," a title of nobility. Lawyers with the title of "esquire" were agents of a foreign power. Esquire was the main title of nobility that Amendment XIII intended to prohibit from public office. The Amendment also applied to judges, who are addressed as "Your Honor." The word "honor" meant anyone "obtaining or having an advantage or privilege over another." The Founding Fathers were adamant about prohibiting anyone, even government officials, from claiming or exercising a special privilege or power (an "honor") over other citizens. Attorneys today carry the title of esquire. Judges, lawyers, politicians, and many bureaucrats today have immunity from lawsuits (an "honor" or special privilege over other people), which is unconstitutional in the de jure Constitution. See more on the original Amendment XIII in
[61] A capitonym is a word that changes its meaning—and sometimes pronunciation—when capitalized. Note that in law, every word, letter, punctuation, and capitalization utilized in legal documents and proceedings has distinct legal meaning and significance.
[62] *Downes v. Bidwell*, 182 U.S. 244 (1901).
[63] This private corporation trademarked the names "United States," "U.S.," "US," "U.S.A.," "USA," and variations thereof.

The Act of 1871 reads, in part:

Section 1. ... That all that part of the territory of the United States included within the limits of the District of Columbia be, and the same is hereby, created into a government by the name of the District of Columbia, by which name it is hereby constituted a *body corporate for municipal purposes*, and may contract and be contracted with, sue and be sued, plead and be impleaded, have a seal, and exercise all other powers of a *municipal corporation* not inconsistent with the constitution and laws of the United States and the provisions of this act. [Emphasis added]

Section 18. That the legislative power of the District shall [129 U.S. 141, 144] extend to all rightful subjects of legislation within said District, consistent with the Constitution of the United States and the provisions of this act, subject, nevertheless, to all the restrictions and limitations imposed upon states by the tenth section of the first article of the Constitution of the United States; but all acts of the legislative assembly shall at all times be subject to repeal or modification by the congress of the United States, and nothing herein shall be construed to deprive congress of the power of legislation over said District in as ample manner as if this law had not been enacted.[64] [Emphasis added]

---

[64] See, *Stoutenburgh v. Hennick*, 129 U.S. 141 (1889). "Syllabus. Under the authority conferred upon Congress by §8, Article I, of the Constitution 'to make all laws which shall be necessary or proper for carrying into execution' the power 'to exercise exclusive legislation in all cases whatsoever over' the District of Columbia, Congress may constitute the District 'a body corporate for municipal purposes,' but can only authorize it to exercise municipal powers. The Act of the Legislative Assembly of the District of Columbia of August 23, 1871, as amended June 20, 1872, relating to license taxes on persons engaging in trade, business or profession within the District, was intended to be a regulation of a purely municipal character . . ." Also note; "And Whereas: On February 21, 1871, the Forty First Congress passed an act entitled 'An Act to Provide a Government for the District of Columbia,' legislating the organization of a municipal corporation to run the day to day affairs of the District of Columbia, the seat of government, which transferred the United States of America, the Republic, into 'a corporate entity' entitled UNITED STATES, in capital letters, having no jurisdiction outside the District of Columbia. And Whereas: Congress adopted the text of the federal constitution as the constitution or charter of this municipal corporation. This municipal corporation was granted the power to contract to provide municipal services to the inhabitants of the District of Columbia and necessarily as an operation of the privileges and immunity clause of Article Four of the Constitution, any other person who chooses to contract for its services."

Congress had no authority under the *de jure* Constitution to pass the Act of 1871. The Act was a strategic move by the Global Elite, specifically the Rothschilds of London, to gain a foothold into the united States by lending money to the nation, which was buried in debt and essentially bankrupt in the aftermath of the War. With Lincoln out of the way, the *de facto* Congress was free to accept loans from the Rothschild banking interests in exchange for the *people as collateral* for the debt of the newly formed corporation. The Rothschilds gained control of the former Republic. The UNITED STATES CORPORATION is privately owned by foreign interests, and operates in an economic capacity (relating to the economy, the system of production and management of material and financial wealth). It is a for-profit corporation of the City of London, courtesy of, and owned, by the Rothschilds.

The Southern States were never readmitted to the Union (Republic) as sovereign States. The Republic was no more. Rather, they became mere territories in the *de facto* federal government under martial law. Eventually, all states were incorporated as sub-franchises of the corporate UNITED STATES (the DISTRICT OF COLUMBIA MUNICIPAL GOVERNMENT). The Republic of Florida, or the Commonwealth of Virginia, for example, no longer existed except in ethereal form. They were now the STATE OF FLORIDA and the STATE OF VIRGINIA, *territories* of the UNITED STATES CORPORATION.[65] As *territories* of the UNITED STATES, they were under the jurisdiction of the UNITED STATES CORPORATION, a.k.a. the DISTRICT OF COLUMBIA MUNICIPAL GOVERNMENT.

How does a State lose its sovereignty? The Southern States lost their sovereignty by virtue of secession and conquest; the remaining states by voluntary submission to the corporate federal government. In his *Treatise on International Law*, Halleck stated: "The sovereignty of a state may be lost in various ways. It may be vanquished by a foreign power [the Southern States], and become incorporated into the conquering state as a province or as one of its component parts; or it may voluntarily unite itself with another is

---

[65] The name in all capital letters signifies their status as a corporation.

such a way that its independent existence as a state will entirely cease."⁶⁶

Halleck went on to write:

> If the hostile nation be subdued and the entire state conquered, a question arises as to the manner in which the conqueror may treat it without transgressing the just bounds established by the rights of conquest. If he simply replaces the former sovereign, and on the submission of the people, governs them according to the laws of the state, they have no cause of complaint. Again, if he incorporates them with his former states, giving to them the *rights, privileges, and immunities of his own subjects*, he does for them all that is due from a humane and equitable conqueror to his vanquished foes.⁶⁷ [Emphasis added]

Does that sound like the 14th Amendment? Yes; eerily so. The remaining sovereign States accepted the jurisdiction of UNITED STATES, INC., voluntarily uniting themselves with the corporate federal government.

Following the passage of the Act of 1871 and the 14th Amendment, each State legislature formed a limited liability corporation, chartered in a private, military, international, commercial, admiralty/maritime jurisdiction, entitled "STATE OF . . .," for example, STATE OF CALIFORNIA. This was evidenced by a new State seal and the creation of a new constitution, the Constitution of the State of California, 1879. The new Constitution established: a) "a general partnership agreement, hereinafter 'General Partnership,' exists between the California Republic (1849), and STATE OF CALIFORNIA (1879), with STATE OF CALIFORNIA acting as governmental controller"; and, b) "STATE OF CALIFORNIA acts as an agent/instrumentality of UNITED STATES INC., collecting whole life insurance premiums, known as 'taxes,' for the International Monetary Fund."

---

⁶⁶ Halleck, Henry Wagner, *International Law: Or, Rules Regulating the Intercourse of States in Peace and War*, (C.K. Paul & Co., London, 1878), Chapter 3, §23. Reprinted by Forgotten Books (2012).
⁶⁷ Ibid., Chapter 33, §3

Chapter VIII A Shadow Darkens the Land . . .

The new State Constitutions were never ratified by the people. But law is contract. The new Constitutions are constructive trusts, an implied contract, which can be ratified either by "acquiescence by silence" and/or by accepting "benefits" from the new government. Thus, the new status was confirmed over time by the presumption of jurisdiction. By 1970, **all** States had amended their Constitutions and statutes and formed private corporate entities under the name "STATE OF (X)" and vacated their original *de jure* government in favor of foreign ownership and control as sub-franchises of UNITED STATES INC. Thus, a general partnership was formed between the *de jure* State, i.e., Florida state (i.e., the Republic of Florida), and the private corporation, THE STATE OF FLORIDA, with the private corporation acting as general partner and administrator of governmental operations.

Why the need to incorporate government? Martial law governments are *fictional creations*. The doctrine of equal standing in law makes it clear only parties of equal standing can communicate in law. The maxim of law is *disparata non debent jungi*—"dissimilar things ought not to be joined."[68] Since the martial law government is a fictional creation, it can only deal with fictions. Therefore, the need to create legal fictions (corporations) for the Sates and the people. From the perspective of the corporate government, the people are no longer sovereign, sentient beings with unalienable rights, but non-sentient corporations with privileges.

The Act of 1871 gave the *de facto* corporate government rule over the territories of the united States. The *de jure* sovereign States succumbed to the power of an autocratic central government. Corporate law, operating under admiralty/maritime/international law,[69] replaced common law, muting the voice of the people. Corporate law denudes the people of their God-given unalienable rights. Corporate/commercial/public law is not private law. It is an agreement between two or more parties *under contract*. The common law of the sovereign

---

[68] *Bouvier's Law Dictionary* (Maxims of Law, p. 127, 1856).
[69] Also known as the "divine right of kings," which is based on the absolute authority of kings and queens. According to this a doctrine, kings derive their right to rule directly from God and are accountable only to God. The king is thus not subject to the will of the people, the aristocracy, or any other estate of the realm, including the church. Also known as the "law of the sea."

people is not commercial law; it is personal and private. Common law is the voice of the people, rendered silent under corporate law.[70]

The Act of 1871 lasted until 1874, when Congress passed "An Act for the Government of the District of Columbia, and for other purposes."[71] This Act abolished and replaced the 1871 government with a commission consisting of three persons. On June 11, 1878, Congress passed "An Act Providing a Permanent Form of Government for the District of Columbia."[72] This Act provided that D.C. remain and continue as a municipal corporation (brought forward from the Act of 1871), as provided in the Act of March 2, 1877, amended and approved March 9, 1878: ". . . But by the Act of June 11, 1878 (20 Stat. chap. 180), a permanent form of government for the District was established. It provided . . . that the commissioners therein provided for should be deemed and taken as officers of such corporation."[73]

With the Act of 1871 and its subsequent revisions, the coup by the Global Elite was complete. The people became irrelevant; subjects (a.k.a. U.S. citizens) of an all-powerful feudal . . . oops, I mean federal . . . government. The people were robbed of their sovereignty, their God-given unalienable rights, their property, and their dignity. The people were now indentured servants (slaves) of the federal corporation. The betrayal of the people by the Global Elite is both inexcusable and incomprehensible. With the Republic now firmly entrenched in the dustbin of history, could the situation possibly get worse for the American people? Read on. The scurrilous designs of the Global Elite would stop at nothing less than complete mastery and control over an unwary people.

---

[70] Note, however, the Uniform Commercial Code, though operating under corporate/commercial/public law, is compatible with common law. UCC 1-103.6. "The Code is complimentary to the Common Law, which remains in force, except where displaced by the code. A statute should be construed in harmony with the Common Law, unless there is a clear legislative intent to abrogate the Common Law."
[71] 18 Stat. at L. 116 (June 20, 1864).
[72] 20 Stat. 102 (June 11, 1878).
[73] *The District of Columbia v. Henry E. Woodbury*, 136 U.S. 472 (1890). See also, Volume 20: Corpus Juris Secundum §1785: "The United States government is a foreign corporation with respect to a State"; and *NY re: Merriam* 36 N.E. 505 1441 S. 0.1973, 14 L. Ed. 287

CHAPTER IX

The Darkness Deepens . . .
Federal Reserve Act and Trading with the Enemy Act

"The great enemy of the truth is very often not the lie—deliberate, contrived and dishonest—but the myth, persistent, persuasive, and unrealistic."
—John F. Kennedy

"For reporting a scientific finding, I was called a 'conspiracy theorist.' Only in America is scientific analysis seen as conspiracy theory, and government lies as truth."
—Paul Craig Roberts

"The real truth of the matter is, as you and I know, that a financial element in the large centers has owned the government of the U.S. since the days of Andrew Jackson."
—Franklin D. Roosevelt (letter to Colonel E. Mandell House)

The Founding Fathers were acutely aware of the dangers and evils of a central bank. In 1793, the new U.S. Congress actually took steps to keep the bankers out of the government by passing a law prohibiting them from serving in Congress. The law read: "Any person holding any office or any stock in any institution in the nature of a bank for issuing or discounting bills or notes payable to bearer or order, cannot be a member of the House whilst he holds such office or stock."[1]

Yet, in 1791, bankers succeeded in establishing a central bank in the united States. The First Bank of the United States was established largely due to the efforts of Alexander Hamilton, the

---

[1] Third Congress of the U.S. Senate, signed by President George Washington, December 23, 1793.

Rothschild's agent in the new Republic.[2] By the end of its 20-year charter, the central bank had almost ruined the nation's economy, while enriching bankers. Congress refused to renew the charter and restored a state-issued, asset-backed currency.

Thomas Jefferson warned:

> I believe that banking institutions are more dangerous to our liberties than standing armies. Already they have raised up a monied aristocracy that has set the government at defiance. If the American people ever allow private banks to control the issue of their currency, first by inflation, then by deflation, the banks . . . will deprive the people of all property until their children wake-up homeless on the continent their fathers conquered . . . The issuing power should be taken from the banks and restored to the people, to whom it properly belongs.[3]

James Madison stated: "History records that the money changers have used every form of abuse, intrigue, deceit, and violent means possible to maintain their control over governments by controlling money and its issuance."[4]

Daniel Webster later admonished: "Of all the contrivances for cheating the laboring classes of mankind, none has been more effective than that which deludes them with paper money . . . We are in danger of being overwhelmed with irredeemable paper, mere

---

[2] Alexander Hamilton was born Alexander Levine (or Lavien) out of wedlock in Charlestown, Nevis on January 11, 1755 (or 1757) to Rachel Levine. His mother later met and moved in with James Hamilton in St. Kitts, and the young Alexander changed his last name to Hamilton. James Hamilton later abandoned the family, leaving them destitute and impoverished. Hamilton's mother died at the age of 38 in 1768. He was taken in by and worked for a prosperous businessman, Nicolas Cruger, where he displayed acumen for business and finance. Cruger sent Alexander to America in 1773 to attend Kings College in New York, but he dropped out to support the colonies in the rebellion against Britain. In 1782, he was admitted to the New York Bar. In 1784, he established a legal practice in NYC as Alexander Hamilton, Esq. Hamilton wrote the charter for and founded the Bank of New York, as agent for the Rothschild banking empire. He was a staunch Federalist, and as secretary of the treasury under President George Washington, promoted the Rothschild's interest in establishing a central bank in the new government. He remained loyal to the Rothschild family and the Bank of England, owned by the Rothschilds.

[3] From the debate over the recharter of the Bank Bill in 1809. Part of the quote comes from an 1816 letter to John Taylor.

[4] *Writings of Madison*, Vol. 2, p. 14.

CHAPTER IX THE DARKNESS DEEPENS ...

paper, representing not gold or silver; no sir, representing nothing but broken promises, bad faith, bankrupt corporations, cheated creditors and a ruined people."[5] The sentiment was echoed by Vice President John C. Calhoun: "A power has risen up in the government greater than the people themselves, consisting of many, and various, and powerful interests, combined into one mass, and held together by the cohesive power of the vast surplus in the banks."[6]

President Andrew Jackson told a group of bankers in 1832:

> Gentlemen, I have had men watching you for a long time, and I am convinced that you have used the funds of the bank to speculate in the breadstuffs of the country. When you won, you divided the profits amongst you, and when you lost, you charged it to the bank. You tell me that if I take the deposits from the bank and annul its charter, I shall ruin ten thousand families. That may be true, gentlemen, but that is your sin! Should I let you go on, you will ruin fifty thousand families, and that would be my sin! You are a den of vipers and thieves. I intend to rout you out, and by the eternal God, I will rout you out.[7]

In December 1832, Jackson spoke before Congress. His message was succinct: "The bold effort the present bank had made to control government [Second National Bank of the U.S.], the distress it has wantonly produced ... are but premonitions of the fate that awaits the American people should they be deluded into a perpetuation of this institution or the establishment of another like it."[8] The charter of the Second National Bank was not renewed.[9]

Founding Father Thomas Jefferson rued one omission in the federal Constitution: "I wish it were possible to obtain a single

---

[5] Speech before the Senate on the question of renewing the charter of the Bank of the United States (1832).

[6] John C. Calhoun, 7th U.S. vice president. Richard Cralle, editor, *Speeches of John C. Calhoun*, p. 568 (D. Appleton & Company, NY, 1883).

[7] President Andrew Jackson discussing the bill to renew the charter of the National Bank with a delegation of bankers in 1832.

[8] Message to Congress, House *Congressional Record*, p. 506 (December 2, 1834).

[9] The Second Bank of the United States was located in Philadelphia, Pennsylvania. It was the second federally authorized Hamiltonian national bank in the U.S. during its 20-year charter (1816-36).

amendment to our constitution; I would be willing to depend on that alone for the reduction of the administration of our government to the genuine principles of its constitution; I mean an additional article taking from the federal government the power of borrowing. I now deny their power of making paper money or anything else a legal tender."[10]

Since its inception in 1913, the Fed (or central bank) has been the root of the evil that pervades the federal government today. As a malignant cancer spreading insidiously through the body, it has slowly and clandestinely—along with Lincoln and a complicit Congress years earlier—brought about the death of the Republic. It has placed an ever-tightening stranglehold on the freedom of the people, threatening to choke the last gasp of liberty from the near corpse once-thriving as Middle America.

The Fed is neither lawful nor constitutional. Through this evil monstrosity, international bankers have controlled the people, politics, and economy of the U.S. for their own personal goals, selfish interest, and gain. For over 100 years now, this evil has been perniciously stealing the wealth of the American people:

> States, most especially the large hegemonic ones, such as the United States and Great Britain, are controlled by the international central banking system, working through secret agreements at the Bank for International Settlements, and operating through national central banks (such as the Bank of England and the Federal Reserve) . . . The same international banking cartel that controls the United States today previously controlled Great Britain and held it up as the international hegemon. When the British order faded, and was replaced by the United States, the U.S. ran the global economy. However, the same interests are served. States will be used and discarded at will by the international banking cartel; they are simply tools.[11]

---

[10] November 26, 1798 letter from Thomas Jefferson to John Taylor.
[11] Marshall, Andrew Gavin, "Global Power and Global Government" (2009). Marshall is a research associate with the Centre for Research on Globalization.

CHAPTER IX THE DARKNESS DEEPENS...

In 1863, the Rothschilds stated: "The few who understand the [central bank] system, will either be so interested in its profits, or so dependent on its favors that there will be no opposition from that class, while on the other hand, the great body of people, *mentally incapable* of comprehending the tremendous advantages . . . will bear its burden without complaint, and perhaps without suspecting that the system is *inimical* to their best interests."[12] [Emphasis added]

Central banks have been a primary instrument used by the Global Elite in achieving their New World Order agenda. Montagu Norman, governor of the Bank of England, posited:

> Capital must protect itself in every possible way, both by combination and legislation. Debts must be collected, mortgages foreclosed as rapidly as possible. When, through process of law, the common people lose their homes, they will become more docile and more easily governed through the strong arm of the government applied by a central power of wealth under leading financiers. These truths are well known among our principal men, *who are now engaged in forming an imperialism to govern the world.* By dividing the voter through the political party system, we can get them to expend their energies in fighting for questions of no importance. It is thus, by discrete action, we can secure for ourselves that which has been so well planned and so successfully accomplished.[13] [Emphasis added]

Evidence of these tactics is abundant in society today. Symbols on the dollar bill blatantly display the agenda of the Global Elite . . . on the back of the bill is a pyramid with the *all-seeing eye* on top. The *all-seeing eye* is the Eye of Horus, which is the same as the Eye of Lucifer. It is also on the reverse side of the Great Seal of the United States. The motto *Novus Ordo Seclorum* ("New World Order,"

---

[12] Rothschild Brothers of London writing to associates in New York (June 25, 1863).
[13] 1924 address to the U.S. Bankers Association in NYC. The quote was printed in the *U.S. Bankers Magazine*, August 25, 1924, and reprinted in the *Idaho Leader* on August 26, 1924. It was adopted as the "Banker's Manifesto" in 1934 and was intended for the private circulation among leading bankers only (printed in *New American*, 1934).

or "A New Order of the Ages") is on the base of the pyramid, in plain sight, for all to see. President Franklin Roosevelt, a 32° Mason, was instrumental in the design. The *all-seeing eye* is also a symbol of Freemasonry.

The Fed must be audited, and subsequently abolished. It must not only be done away with, it must be obliterated by a Constitutional amendment ensuring this country will never again be at the mercy of a central national bank controlled by an elitist minority (even though a Constitutional amendment should not be needed to abolish an unconstitutional entity . . . read on).

The Fed is not part of the federal government. It is no more federal than Federal Express or the Federal Deposit Insurance Corporation.[14] Nor is there any "Reserve." The gold reserves in Fort Knox vaults have long been emptied. The Fed does not appear in Title 5 or Title 31 of the U.S.C.[15] Congressman John R. Rarick (D-LA), in the report "Deficit Financing," stated: "The Federal Reserve is not an agency of government. It is a *private* banking monopoly."[16] [Emphasis added] Furthermore, it is not really a bank; it is a *system* which places control of America's money and economy in the hands of its mostly non-Americans owners. As pointed out previously in these pages, the Fed is a privately held for-profit joint stock corporation owned by a consortium of 12 of the wealthiest families in the world. It was founded by members of the Global Elite which included U.S. Senator Nelson Aldrich (maternal grandfather to the Rockefellers), former Harvard University Professor of Economics Dr. A. Piatt Andrew, J.P. Morgan & Co. Partner Henry P. Davison, National City Bank President Frank A. Vanderlip, and Kuhn, Loeb & Co. Partner Paul M. Warburg, all part of the Rothschild Empire.[17]

The creation of the Fed began when this group of bankers met secretly beginning in 1910 on the privately owned Jekyll Island, Georgia, under the guise of a duck hunt, to formulate the plans for

---

[14] *Lewis v. U.S.*, 680 F.2d 1239 (9th Cir. 1982): ". . . we conclude that the Reserve Banks are not federal instrumentalities for purposes of the [Federal Tort Claims Act], but are independent, privately owned and locally controlled corporations."

[15] Title 5, Government Organization. Title 31, Money and Finance.

[16] "Deficit Financing," *Congressional Record*, 92nd Congress, First Session, Vol. 117, Part 1, p. 1260 (February 1, 1971).

[17] The Federal Reserve Charter is located within the Crown Templar of London (House of Rothschild).

Chapter IX The Darkness Deepens...

one of the greatest frauds that has ever been perpetrated on a people in the history of the world. As a result of their efforts, the Federal Reserve Act was passed on December 22, 1913, *without a quorum present*.[18] Many congressmembers had already left for the Christmas holiday. After several previous attempts to pass the bill had failed, the timing of this vote was quite intentional. Only select, handpicked members of Congress were present for the vote. Bankers had funded Woodrow Wilson's campaign for president, and as payback, Wilson signed the bill into law on December 23, 1913. Without a quorum, however, the Federal Reserve Act is unlawful. But little did Congress care, and people were oblivious to the machinations of the Global Elite.

On December 22, 1913, speaking in opposition to the Federal Reserve Act, Charles August Lindbergh addressed Congress:

> This [Federal Reserve] Act establishes the most gigantic trust on earth. When the President signs this bill, the invisible government by the Monetary Power will be legalized. The people may not know it immediately, but the day of reckoning is only a few years removed. The trusts will soon realize that they have gone too far even for their own good. The people must make a declaration of independence to relieve themselves from the Monetary Power. This they will be able to do by taking control of Congress. Wall Streeters could not cheat us if you Senators and Representatives did not make a humbug of Congress . . . if we had a people's Congress, there would be stability. The greatest crime of Congress is its currency system while the worst legislative crime of the ages is perpetrated by this banking bill. The caucus and the party bosses have again operated and prevented the people from getting the benefit of their own government.[19]

---

[18] Id. Griffin.

[19] Charles August Lindbergh (1859-1924) represented Minnesota's sixth congressional district in the U.S. House of Representatives from 1907 to 1917. He opposed the Federal Reserve Act and American entry into WWI.

Lindbergh later wrote in 1923:

> To cause high prices, all the Federal Reserve Board will do will be to lower the rediscount rate . . . producing an expansion of credit and a rising stock market; then when . . . business men are adjusted to these conditions, it can check . . . prosperity in mid-career by arbitrarily raising the rate of interest. It can cause the pendulum of a rising and falling market to swing gently back and forth by slight changes in the discount rate, or cause violent fluctuations by a greater rate variation and in either case it will possess inside information as to financial conditions and advance knowledge of the coming change, either up or down. This is the strangest, most dangerous advantage ever placed in the hands of a special privilege class by any Government that ever existed. The system is private, conducted for the sole purpose of obtaining the greatest possible profits from the use of other people's money. They know in advance when to create panics to their advantage. They also know when to stop panic. Inflation and deflation work equally well for them when they control finance.[20]

W. Loucks, in the book, *The Great Conspiracy of the House of Morgan*, wrote: "In the Federal Reserve Law, they [the financiers] have wrested from the people and secured for themselves the constitutional power to issue money and regulate the value thereof . . . The House of Morgan is now in supreme control of our industry, commerce and political affairs. They are in complete control of the policy making of the Democratic, Republican and Progressive parties."

The purpose of the Federal Reserve Act was to eliminate competition among banks. The banking cabal[21] would have complete

---

[20] Lindbergh, Charles August, *Lindbergh on the Federal Reserve* (Noontide Press, 1989, originally entitled *The Economic Pinch*, 1923).

[21] *Black's Law Dictionary* (sixth edition): "Cabal. A small association for the purpose of intrigue; an intrigue. This name was given to that ministry in the reign of Charles II, formed by Clifford, Ashley, Buckingham, Arlington, and Lauderdale, who concerted a scheme for the restoration of the Pope. The initials of these five names form the word 'cabal;' hence the appellation," p. 202. *Merriam-Webster's*

control over U.S. monetary affairs. It is sovereign with respect to the U.S. government. Its affairs are entirely private, closed from the scrutiny of the American people.

Yet Wilson expressed concerns over the lack of competition among banks, even in the years prior to signing the Act:

> A great industrial nation is controlled by its system of credit. Our system of credit is privately concentrated. The growth of the nation, therefore, and all our activities are in the hands of a few men who, even if their action be honest and intended for the public interest, are necessarily concentrated upon the great undertakings in which their own money is involved and who necessarily, by very reason of their own limitations, chill and check and destroy genuine economic freedom . . .
>
> We have restricted credit, we have restricted opportunity, we have controlled development, and we have come to be one of the worst ruled, one of the most completely controlled and dominated, governments in the civilized world—no longer a government by free opinion, no longer a government by conviction and the vote of the majority, but a government by the opinion and the duress of small groups of dominant men.[22]

Like Lincoln before him, Wilson was bought and paid for by the Global Elite to accomplish their spurious objectives. And, as Lincoln came to regret his decisions that led to the end of the Republic, there are sources that state Wilson came to regret the great harm his actions had done to the country.

Wilson's closest unofficial advisor was Colonel Edward Mandell House. House was instrumental in getting Wilson elected president, with the financial backing of the Rockefeller's National

---

online dictionary defines cabal as: "The contrived schemes of a group of persons secretly united in a plot (as to overturn a government); a group engaged in such schemes."

[22] Wilson, Woodrow, *The New Freedom* (Doubleday, Page & Company, NY, 1913). The first paragraph is from chapter 8, "Monopoly, or Opportunity." The second paragraph is from chapter 9, "Benevolence, or Justice?"

City Bank. In 1913, House exerted great influence in the selection of the charter members of the Federal Reserve Board. And, in a *private* meeting in 1913 with President Wilson at the White House, House gave a detailed outline[23] of the Global Elite's plans for a New World Order and to further enslave all Americans:

> [Very] soon, every American will be required to register their biological property in a national system designed to keep track of the people and that will operate under the ancient system of pledging. By such methodology, we can compel people to submit to our agenda, which will effect our security as a chargeback for our fiat paper currency. Every American will be forced to register or suffer being unable to work and earn a living. They will be our chattel, and we will hold the security interest over them forever, by operation of the law merchant under the scheme of secured transactions. Americans, by unknowingly or unwittingly delivering the bills of lading to us will be rendered bankrupt and insolvent, forever to remain economic slaves through taxation, secured by their pledges. They will be stripped of their rights and given a commercial value designed to make us a profit and they will be none the wiser, for not one man in a million could ever figure our plans and, if by accident one or two should figure it out, we have in our arsenal plausible deniability. After all, this is the only logical way to fund government, by floating liens and debt to the registrants in the form of benefits and privileges. This will inevitably reap to us huge profits beyond our wildest expectations and leave every American a contributor to this fraud which we will call "Social Insurance." Without realizing it, every American will insure us for any loss we may incur and in this manner; every American will unknowingly be our servant, however begrudgingly. The people will become helpless and without any hope for their redemption and,

---

[23] From the minutes of a meeting in the White House between President Wilson and Colonel House. Quoted in Stamper, Melvin, J.D., *Fruit from a Poisonous Tree*, p. 59. See also, Woodrow Wilson's *The New Freedom*. Original source is reported to be Wilson's private diary and notes of the meeting.

Chapter IX The Darkness Deepens . . .

we will employ the high office of the President of our dummy corporation to foment this plot against America.

These words were uttered in private, for obvious reasons. Lofty goals for the Global Elite, but words which would ultimately come to pass. Wilson later wrote: "Since I entered politics, I have chiefly had men's views confided to me privately. Some of the biggest men in the United States, in the field of commerce and manufacture, are afraid of somebody, are afraid of something. They know that there is a power somewhere so organized, so subtle, so watchful, so interlocked, so complete, so pervasive, that they had better not speak above their breath when they speak in condemnation of it."[24]

The owners of the 12 central banks in the U.S. are Rothschild Bank of London, Rothschild Bank of Berlin; Lazard Brothers of Paris; Israel Moses Seif Banks of Italy; Warburg Bank of Amsterdam; Warburg Bank of Hamburg; Lehman Brothers of New York (bankrupted in 2008); Kuhn Loeb Bank of New York; Goldman, Sachs of New York; Chase Manhattan Bank of New York. Alfred Owen Crozier, in testimony on October 23, 1913, before the Senate Committee on Banking and Currency, stated: "These 12 corporations together cover the whole country and monopolize and use for private gain every dollar of the public currency, and all public revenues of the United States."[25]

The policies of the Fed are dictated by the BIS, which sets the policy for every major central bank in the world, and also controls the IMF.[26] The BIS, like the Fed, is privately owned by the Global Elite. Quoting Carroll Quigley, noted Global Elite insider:

> The powers of financial capitalism had another far-reaching aim, nothing less than to create a world system of financial

---

[24] Id. Wilson.
[25] Alfred Owen Crozier (1863-1939) was a prominent attorney in Grand Rapids, Cincinnati, and New York. He wrote eight books on the political, legal, and monetary problems of the U.S., including *A Nation of Nations: The Way to Permanent Peace; A Supreme Constitution for the Government of Governments* (Stewart & Kidd Co., Cincinnati, OH, 1915).
[26] LeBor, Adam, *Tower of Basel: The Shadowy History of the Secret Bank that Runs the World* (Perseus Book Group, NY, 2014).

control in private hands able to dominate the political system of each country and the economy of the world as a whole. This system was to be controlled in a feudalist fashion by the central banks of the world acting in concert, by secret agreements arrived at in frequent private meetings and conferences. The apex of the system was to be the Bank for International Settlements in Basel, Switzerland; a private bank owned and controlled by the world's central banks which were themselves private corporations. Each central bank . . . sought to dominate its government by its ability to control Treasury loans, to manipulate foreign exchanges, to influence the level of economic activity in the country, and to influence cooperative politicians by subsequent economic rewards in the business world.[27]

The elite of the banking world meet once a month (except in August and October), to determine policies for all of the central banks, including the Fed; foreigners meeting far from the shores of America, determining monetary policies that will affect the lives of all people in the U.S., for good or bad.

Built in 1977, BIS headquarters stands in stark contrast to the medieval city it towers over, a modern technological marvel among buildings of antiquity. The ultra-luxurious 18-story circular building has become known as "The Tower of Basel," a place where decisions to fix the price of gold, set the value of the world's currencies, raise or lower short term interest rates, and determine the availability of credit are made. As the central bank of central banks, it houses the gold holdings of the European Elite. The elitist character of BIS is described by Edward Jay Epstein as having ". . . the advantages of luxurious space and Swiss efficiency. The building is completely air-conditioned and self-contained, with its own nuclear-bomb shelter in the sub-basement, a triply redundant fire-extinguishing system (so outside firemen never have to be called in), a private hospital, and some twenty miles of subterranean archives.

---

[27] Quigley, Carroll, *Tragedy & Hope: A History of the World in Our Time* (MacMillan Book Company, NY, 1966).

'We try to provide a complete clubhouse for central bankers . . . a home away from home,' said Gunther Schleiminger, the super-competent general manager . . ."[28] It is a supranational organization that strategizes and implements the global monetary policies of all central banks, including the Fed.

BIS is at the apex of the world's power structure. It operates in complete secrecy and confidentiality. Though accountable to its customers and shareholders, BIS controls their operations and is protected by "unalterable international treaties," writes Adam LeBor. It controls the "flow of credit and the volume of currency in circulation" across the globe, and is one of the largest holders of gold reserves in the world. Central bankers, according to *The Economist*, "seem more powerful than politicians, holding the destiny of the global economy in their hands."[29] In fact, they *are* more important than politicians. The ultimate goal of BIS is to construct a new global financial system through a single world currency.

Central bankers posture themselves as elite, as being far superior to the general population. According to LeBor:

> The BIS has the right to communicate in code and to send and receive correspondence in bags covered by the same protection as embassies, meaning they cannot be opened. The BIS is exempt from Swiss taxes. Its employees do not have to pay income tax on their salaries, which are usually generous, designed to compete with the private sector . . . The bank's extraordinary legal privileges also extend to its staff and directors. Senior managers enjoy a special status, similar to that of diplomats, while carrying out their duties in Switzerland, which means their bags cannot be searched (unless there is evidence of a blatant criminal act), and their papers are inviolable. The central bank governors traveling to Basel for the bimonthly meetings enjoy the same status while in Switzerland. All bank officials are immune under Swiss law, for life, for all the acts carried out during the

---

[28] Epstein, Edward Jay, "Ruling the World of Money," *Harper's Magazine* (November 1983).
[29] Quoted from Id. LeBor.

> discharge of their duties . . . Like many of those working for the UN or the IMF, some of the staff of the BIS, especially senior management, are driven by a sense of mission, that they are working for a higher, even celestial purpose and so are immune from normal considerations of accountability and transparency . . . The bank's opacity, lack of accountability, and ever-increasing influence raises profound questions—not just about monetary policy but transparency, accountability, and how power is exercised in our democracies.[30]

The arrogance of the banksters could not be more succinctly exemplified than in a statement by Lloyd C. Blankfein, then-Chairman and CEO of Goldman Sachs and Illuminati member. In a November 8, 2009 interview with *The Times* of London, Blankfein boasted: "We have a social purpose . . . and [we] are doing *God's work*." [Emphasis added] *Doing God's work! Not!* I wonder which "god" that is. Blankfein went on to state: "We're very important. We help companies to grow by helping them to raise capital. Companies that grow create wealth. This, in turn, allows people to have jobs that create more growth and more wealth. It's a virtuous cycle." Where is the virtue in fleecing people of their wealth? Or in making loans created solely with a key stroke on a computer, i.e., out of thin air, which must be paid back with interest? The article goes on to report the bank posted third-quarter earnings [in 2009] of $3 billion and plans to hand out more than *$16 billion* in year-end bonuses, a flagrant excess bordering on criminality. And that was after receiving $12.9 billion in bailout money during the 2007-8 financial crisis. Are they kidding? And I wonder: how much of that bonus is going to the rank-and-file workers? His words are the height of haughtiness, exemplifying egregious disdain for the common people.

Not only is the Federal Reserve Act *unlawful*, but it is also *unconstitutional*. The Act transferred the right to print currency from the U.S. Congress to an independent and privately owned

---

[30] Id. LeBor.

entity calling itself a bank, but which is in reality not a bank but a *system*. However, Article 1, Section 8 of the *de jure* Constitution states: "The Congress shall have Power To . . . Lay and collect Taxes, Duties, Imposts and Excises . . . To coin Money, regulate the Value thereof, and of foreign Coin, and fix the Standard of Weights and Measures; To provide for the Punishment of counterfeiting the Securities and current Coin of the United States . . ." The Constitution gives Congress, and *only* Congress, the power to lay and collect taxes, and to coin and regulate money. This power *cannot* be delegated to anyone or *anything*. Not only did Congress vacate this right, but it did so without a Constitutional amendment. This fraud was further cloaked in deception by the use of the word "federal," and the fact the Act makes no provision for the banks to be audited. The system operates under a dark cloak of secrecy and a total lack of transparency.

Just how does this Ponzi scheme work? When the U.S. government needs money, it borrows it from the Fed, generally in exchange for government-issued bonds. Since the Fed has the power to print money, it orders the currency from the U.S. Treasury Department, at a cost to the Fed of approximately 3¢ per $100 printed. At this point, the Fed has profited $99.97 for every 3¢ they invested to print the money which it pays to the U.S. government for the bonds. The Fed then charges the U.S. government interest on the money it has borrowed! The Fed is literally creating money out of thin air! Did you get that? The Fed is literally CREATING MONEY OUT OF THIN AIR! The Fed can then either keep the bonds it received for the currency (at almost no cost to themselves) and collect the interest the U.S. government owes them on the bonds, or it can sell the bonds to U.S. individuals or foreigners. The profit to the Fed, i.e., its owners, is TAX FREE![31]

In a landmark ruling from the 1968 *Credit River* case, the judge affirmed this truth, stating in his decision:

---

[31] See, Darland, Lloyd, *The Emperor's Clothes Cost Twenty Dollars* (*The Bob Livingston Letter*, Cullman, AL, 2018). This 71-page book was first published in August 1977, and is an excellent and easy-to-understand explanation, much of it written in an allegorical style, of the fraudulent Fed.

Plaintiff admitted that it, in combination with the Federal Reserve Bank of Minneapolis, which are for all practical purposes, because of their interlocking activity and practices, and both being Banking Institutions Incorporated under the Laws of the United States, are in the Law to be treated as one and the same Bank, did *create the entire $14,000 in money or credit upon its own books by bookkeeping entry.* That this was the Consideration used to support the Note dated May 8, 1964 and the Mortgage of the same date. The money and credit first came into existence when they created it. Mr. Morgan admitted that no United States Law Statue existed which gave him the right to do this. A lawful consideration must exist and be tendered to support the Note. See *Anheuser-Busch Brewing Company v. Emma Mason*, 44 Minn. 318, 46 N.W. 558. The Jury found that there was no consideration and I agree. Only God can create something of value out of nothing.[32] [Emphasis added]

The judge found that the money for the loan was created out of thin air, and there is no law which gave them the right to do that! As on other occasions, the truth was revealed to the people. But the people were asleep, too occupied with the routine of daily affairs to be concerned about their liberty . . . or truth.

As reported by the Grace Commission, 100% of federal income tax dollars paid by Americans goes to the Fed to pay the interest on the debt the U.S. government owes the Fed. The report states: ". . . 100% of what is collected is absorbed solely by interest on the Federal Debt and by Federal transfer payments. In other words, all individual income tax revenues are gone before one nickel is spent on the services taxpayers expect from government."[33] President Lincoln

---

[32] *First National Bank of Montgomery v. Jerome Daly* (Justice Court, Credit River Township, Scott County, MN, December 9, 1968). This case is critical to the understanding of the fraud that has been perpetrated by the Rothschild banking cabal. Judge Martin Mahoney's decision has been reprinted in its entirety in Appendix C. Melvin Stamper J.D., wrote of Mahoney's decision: "If we as a nation only had a few of these remarkable men in the judiciary we cannot even imagine the prosperity we would enjoy." Judge Mahoney died of mysterious causes several months after this decision.

[33] "The President's Private Sector Survey on Cost Control," p. 12, more commonly known as the Grace Commission Report (Peter Grace and Jack Anderson), submitted to President Ronald Reagan on January

stated: "The Government should create, issue, and circulate all the currency and credits needed to satisfy the spending power of the Government and the buying power of consumers. By the adoption of these principles, the taxpayers will be saved immense sums of interest." Remember from an earlier chapter, Lincoln's opposition to the Global Elite and his rejection of their offer of loans at usurious interest was a primary reason for his assassination.

Of the income tax collected by the Fed, through their collection agency, the IRS, the Federal Reserve charter reportedly allocates 67% of the income tax to the Crown Templar (House of Rothschild via the IMF), 23% to 300 shareholders of the Fed, and 10% be paid to the employees of the IRS to keep them quiet.

Although the Fed is required by the Federal Reserve Act to give back most of its profits to the U.S. Treasury, the Fed *cannot be audited*. Therefore, through "creative accounting," it retains the majority of the profits it receives by simply creating money out of thin air.

In 1920, Sir Josiah Stamp, a director of the Bank of England, admitted:

> The modern banking system manufactures money out of nothing. The process is perhaps the most astounding piece of sleight of hand that was ever invented. Banking was conceived in iniquity and was born in sin. The Bankers own the Earth. Take it away from them, but leave them the power to create deposits [money], and with the flick of a pen they will create enough deposits [money] to buy it back again. However, take it away from them, and all the fortunes like mine will disappear, and they ought to disappear, for this world would be a happier and better world to live in.

15, 1984. The report took two years to research and compile, and consisted of 21,000 pages in 47 volumes. It made 2,478 recommendations that would save taxpayers $424.4 billion over three years without cutting essential services or raising taxes. Note President Reagan was shot in an assassination attempt shortly after his criticism of the Fed. Six U.S. presidents have been assassinated for criticizing or not cooperating with the Fed, a.k.a. the international bankers (William Henry Harrison, Zachary Taylor, Abraham Lincoln, James A. Garfield, William McKinley, and John F. Kennedy). Reagan's attitude toward the Fed mysteriously, but not unexpectedly, changed after the assassination attempt.

But if you wish to remain slaves of the Bankers and pay for the cost of your own slavery, let them continue to create deposits [money] and control credit.[34]

The Fed itself admitted to its egregious sleight of hand: "When you or I write a check there must be sufficient funds in our account to cover the check, but when the Federal Reserve writes a check there is no bank deposit on which that check is drawn. When the Federal Reserve writes a check, it is creating money."[35]

Congressman Wright Patman of Texas, addressing Congress in 1941, stated: "The Federal Reserve bank buys government bonds without one penny . . ."[36] And the House Banking and Currency Committee emphasized the point in stating:

> When the Federal Reserve writes a check, it is creating money. This can result in an increase in bank reserves—a demand deposit—or in cash; if the customer prefers cash he can demand Federal Reserve notes, and the Federal Reserve will have the Treasury Department print them. The Federal Reserve is a total moneymaking machine. It can issue money or checks. And it never has a problem of making its checks good because it can obtain the $5 and $10 bills necessary to cover its check simply by asking the Treasury Department's Bureau of Engraving to print them.[37]

Henry Ford understood this degeneracy, saying: "It is well that the people of the nation do not understand our banking and monetary system, for if they did, I believe there would be a revolution before tomorrow morning."

Further, the Fed does not issue *lawful money*. The Federal Reserve Note (FRN) printed by the Fed is a private *debt* instrument,

---

[34] Quote attributed to Josiah Stamp, from an informal talk at the University of Texas in the 1920s, but source is unverified. Stamp (1880-1941) was an English civil servant, writer, and former director of the Bank of England.

[35] Boston Federal Reserve Bank pamphlet, "Putting it Simply."

[36] *Congressional Record* (September 30, 1941). John William Wright Patman (1893-1976) was a U.S. congressman chair of the House Committee on Banking and Currency (1963-75).

[37] "Money Facts" (1964), House Banking and Currency Committee, Wright Patman, chairman.

or legal tender. A note is a promise to pay, or an "I owe you." Notes represent debt. The corporate UNITED STATES is in bankruptcy and has no assets; it can only monetize debt. Legal tender is not asset-backed. Legal tender includes FRNs (dollar bills), bonds, and coinage (*tokens*, such as dimes, quarters, etc.) which have no inherent value, or other notes. "[Every circulating FRN] represents a one-dollar debt to the Federal Reserve system."[38] It is mere *currency* masquerading as lawful money. Paper currency that is not asset-backed by e.g., gold or silver, is fiat currency. It is inherently worthless. And because it is not asset-backed, there is virtually no limit on how much can be printed. The printing of asset-backed currency is limited to the amount of the asset, e.g., gold, on hand to guarantee its value.

"Neither paper currency nor deposits have value as commodities. Intrinsically, a 'dollar' bill is just a piece of paper. Deposits are merely book entries."[39] A dollar bill? Just a piece of paper? There is no more value in a dollar bill than a handful of dirt. It only has value in so much as someone is willing to accept it in payment for goods or services. Thomas Jefferson told us: "Paper is poverty. It is the ghost of money and not money itself." What happens when people lose confidence in the dollar? Our entire economic system, based on the Fed, collapses. The American people are bankrupt . . . the "banksters" rich beyond imagination. Paper money and credit created by the Fed is slowly and insidiously crushing the American people to insolvency.

The U.S. is the only country in the world which does not have its own national currency. What, you say? How can that be? FRNs are the "legal tender." However, they are a debt-based currency of a foreign international banking cartel owned by the Rothschilds through the IMF, which owns the Fed. Every time people use an FRN, they are using the currency of a foreign cabal, *and* paying interest on that note to the foreign cabal.

FRNs are backed by the full faith and credit of the United States of America (a.k.a. the UNITED STATES, INC.). But where

---

[38] Ibid.
[39] From "Modern Money Mechanics" workbook, Federal Reserve of Chicago (1975).

does this credit come from? It comes from the people. U.S. citizens are the collateral for all FRNs in circulation. When the government declared bankruptcy, U.S. citizens were pledged as collateral to pay off the debt. This includes all property of all U.S. citizens. According to U.S. Senate Resolution No. 62, 73rd Congress (April 1933): "The ownership of all property is in the state; individual so-called 'ownership' is only by virtue of the government, i.e., law, *amounting to mere user*; and use must be in accordance with law and subordinate to the necessities of the state."[40] [Emphasis added]

As stated by Bob Livingston:

> Paper money and credit are the licenses for all the evil that the human mind of man can conjure up and create. Central bankers have demonstrated in the past 100 years that with a stroke of a computer digit they can create trillions of dollars as easily as they can $1. Yes, they create these dollars out of nothing, but you have to work for your dollars. Printing-press money is the means and motivation for endless wars and endless death and suffering, courtesy of the banksters. This is banker blood money and with it they devalue all the money in circulation. It is an insidious confiscation of wealth that not one person in 1 million understands or is even aware of. Devaluation of the currency is the prime and silent purpose of banker-created money. Even at this hour, devaluation is impoverishing Americans by reducing and diluting the purchasing power of their money . . .[41]

Lawful money, on the other hand, is *asset-backed*. It includes silver coins (i.e., silver dollars, which contain 90% silver), gold coins containing 90% gold, and warehouse receipts or certificates, issued by the treasurer of the *de jure* united States of America, which are redeemable in gold or silver. Silver certificates or gold certificates are not money in itself, but are redeemable for a specified amount of lawful money; i.e., gold or silver.

---

[40] Senate Document No. 43, an article entitled "Contracts Payable in Gold; Money Banking History," 73rd Congress, 1st Session (April 1933).
[41] Livingston, Bob, "Do Bankers Kill Millions of People?" (*Personal Liberty Digest*, January 18, 2020).

Chapter IX The Darkness Deepens...

The fraud becomes even more egregious with the realization that all personal bank accounts have been converted to the ownership of the banks. Read that again: YOU DO NOT OWN YOUR BANK ACCOUNT! Notice the majority of bank accounts have the the account holder's name in all capital letters. JOHN Q. PUBLIC is not a people. It is a trust, a legal fiction, a corporate entity, a public trust. Bank accounts belong to a Puerto Rican estate trust owned and operated by agencies of the IMF, which itself is owned by the Crown Templar, a.k.a. the Global Elite. Therefore, the IMF surreptitiously owns ALL bank accounts. Take a close look, with a strong magnifying glass, at the signature line on your checks. It is not a line at all, but microprint endlessly repeating AUTHORIZED SIGNATURE. Now why would that verbiage have to be there, and why would it be obscured? Because the Global Elite don't want people to know the truth: that ownership of the accounts has unlawfully been converted to a Puerto Rican trust.[42] You are merely the "authorized user" of the account. And by your "authorized signature," you are authorizing the bank to consider you a "banker" pursuant to U.S.C. Title 12. The bank can then (mis)use their authority, by creating both the debt credit *and* the debt discharge, an illegal process known as "twinning." But, since there is no independent oversight or audit of the Fed, banks get away with this chicanery.

For example, the signed promissory note when taking out a mortgage is "legal tender." This fact is not revealed. After the loan is "funded," the bank (or mortgage broker) charges off the full value of the loan as being "accepted for value" against the bonded credit account of the borrower. But the bank nevertheless demands repayment of the debt, even though it has already *been discharged*, plus 30 years' interest and other charges. Fraud! The Fed has systematically raped and pillaged Americans of their resources and wealth for over 100 years.[43]

---

[42] Further, under the 2010 Dodd-Frank Wall Street Reform and Consumer Act, a bank's depositors are classified as unsecured creditors of the bank. Therefore, the bank and not the depositor owns the money on deposit with the bank. All money deposited with the bank can be lawfully confiscated by the federal government. Further, when you open a bank account, in the fine print, you agree to be surety for the national debt. See also, Public Law 111-203, H.R. 4173. With a bank bail-in, the bank can use the money of its unsecured creditors, including depositors and bondholders, to restructure their capital to keep it afloat in lieu of bankruptcy.

[43] See, U.S. Statutes at Large, Vol. 1, Public Acts, 3rd Congress, 2nd Session, Chapter 48.

Bank accounts are a commercial contract and therefore fall outside the protection of Amendment IV . . . that is, assuming the *de jure* Constitution was in effect. The Bill of Rights cannot interfere with the execution of commercial contracts. The IMF, or the Crown, views all bank accounts as their own private property, through the contract signed by the account holder when opening the account.

Americans who deposited their hard-earned money into a bank account thinking their money was safe, that the accounts were their own private property, have been egregiously deceived and defrauded. The nation is only one major catastrophe, manufactured or otherwise, away from your 401(k) or retirement savings vanishing into the ethers. And as the nation drifts closer and closer toward socialism and its redistribution of wealth mantra, people's bank accounts become more prone to confiscation. And if you are a proponent of socialism and think you will be on the receiving end of the redistribution, think again. Any so-called "redistribution" will go straight into the coffers of the banks and the Global Elite.

In a 1932 address to Congress, Louis McFadden elucidated the evils of the Fed:[44]

> Mr. Chairman, we have in this Country one of the most corrupt institutions the world has ever known. I refer to the Federal Reserve Board and the Federal Reserve Banks, hereinafter called the Fed. The Fed has cheated the Government of these United States and the people of the United States out of enough money to pay the Nation's debt. The depredations and iniquities of the Fed has cost enough money to pay the National debt several times over.
>
> This evil institution has impoverished and ruined the

---

[44] Louis McFadden served in the U.S. House of Representatives from Pennsylvania from 1915 to 1935. He was a banker by trade and held the position of chairman of the Banking and Currency Committee for more than 10 years. On May 23, 1933, McFadden brought formal charges against the Board of Governors of the Fed, the Comptroller of the Currency, and the U.S. Treasury secretary for numerous criminal acts, including but not limited to, conspiracy, fraud, unlawful conversion, and treason. A petition for articles of impeachment was referred to the Judiciary Committee and was never acted upon. McFadden paid with his life for his outspokenness and outrage. He lost his congressional seat in 1934, survived an assassination attempt when two bullets from a revolver narrowly missed, and later an attempted food poisoning. The third attempt on his life apparently succeeded. He died on October 3, 1936, of "intestinal flu" after attending a banquet in NYC. The "intestinal flu" was believed to be food poisoning.

CHAPTER IX THE DARKNESS DEEPENS...

people of these United States, has bankrupted itself, and has practically bankrupted our Government. It has done this through the defects of the law under which it operates, through the mal-administration of that law by the Fed and through the corrupt practices of the moneyed vultures who control it.

Some people who think that the Federal Reserve Banks are United States Government institutions. They are private monopolies which prey upon the people of these United States for the benefit of themselves and their foreign owners; foreign and domestic speculators and swindlers; and rich and predatory money lenders. In that dark crew of financial pirates there are those who would cut a man's throat to get a dollar out of his pocket; there are those who send money into states to buy votes to control our legislatures; there are those who maintain International propaganda for the purpose of deceiving us into granting of new concessions which will permit them to cover up their past misdeeds and set again in motion their gigantic train of crime.

These twelve private credit monopolies were deceitfully and disloyally foisted upon this Country by the bankers who came here from Europe and repaid us our hospitality by undermining our American institutions. Those bankers took money out of this Country to finance Japan in a war against Russia. They created a reign of terror in Russia with our money in order to help that war along. They instigated the separate peace between Germany and Russia, and thus drove a wedge between the allies in World War. They financed Trotsky's passage from New York to Russia so that he might assist in the destruction of the Russian Empire. They fomented and instigated the Russian Revolution, and placed a large fund of American dollars at Trotsky's disposal in one of their branch banks in Sweden so that through him Russian homes might be thoroughly broken up and Russian children flung far and wide from their natural protectors. They have since begun breaking up of American homes and the dispersal of American children. Mr. Chairman, there should be no partisanship in matters concerning banking and currency affairs in this Country, and I do not speak with any.

In 1912 the National Monetary Association, under the chairmanship of the late Senator Nelson W. Aldrich, made a report and presented a vicious bill called the National Reserve Association bill. This bill is usually spoken of as the Aldrich bill. Senator Aldrich did not write the Aldrich bill. He was the tool, if not the accomplice, of the European bankers who for nearly twenty years had been scheming to set up a central bank in this Country and who in 1912 has spent and were continuing to spend vast sums of money to accomplish their purpose.

We were opposed to the Aldrich plan for a central bank. The men who rule the Democratic Party then promised the people that if they were returned to power there would be no central bank established here while they held the reigns [sic] of government. Thirteen months later that promise was broken, and the Wilson administration, under the tutelage of those sinister Wall Street figures who stood behind Colonel House, established here in our free Country the worm-eaten monarchical institution of the "King's Bank" to control us from the top downward, and from the cradle to the grave.

The Federal Reserve Bank destroyed our old and characteristic way of doing business. It discriminated against our one-name commercial paper, the finest in the world, and it set up the antiquated two-name paper, which is the present curse of this Country and which wrecked every country which has ever given it scope; it fastened down upon the Country the very tyranny from which the framers of the Constitution sough to save us.[45]

---

[45] *Congressional Record*, p. 12595, et. seq. (June 10, 1932).

Chapter IX The Darkness Deepens...

Congressman Patman added:

When our Federal Government, that has the exclusive power to create money, creates that money and then goes into the open market and borrows it and pays interest for the use of its own money, it occurs to me that that is going too far. I have never yet had anyone who could, through the use of logic and reason, justify the Federal Government borrowing the use of its own money . . . I am saying to you in all sincerity, and with all the earnestness that I possess, it is absolutely wrong for the Government to issue interest-bearing obligations. It is not only wrong: it is extravagant. It is not only extravagant, it is wasteful. It is absolutely unnecessary . . .

Now, I believe the system should be changed. The Constitution of the United States does not give the banks the power to create money. The Constitution says that Congress shall have the power to create money, but now, under our system, we will sell bonds to commercial banks and obtain credit from those banks.

I believe the time will come when people will demand that this be changed. I believe the time will come in this country when they will actually blame you and me and everyone else connected with this Congress for sitting idly by and permitting such an idiotic system to continue. I make that statement after years of study.[46]

On March 17, 1993, U.S. Representative James Traficant Jr. of Ohio, addressing the House of Representatives, further exposed the evils of the Fed:

Mr. Speaker, we are here now in Chapter 11. Members of Congress are official trustees presiding over the greatest reorganization of any Bankrupt entity in world history, the U.S. Government. We are setting forth hopefully, a blueprint

---
[46] Congressman Wright Patman in a 1941 speech to Congress.

for our future. There are some who say it is a coroner's report that will lead to our demise. It is an established fact that the United States Federal Government has been dissolved by the Emergency Banking Act, March 9, 1933, 48 Stat. 1, Public Law 89-719; declared by President Roosevelt, being bankrupt and insolvent. H.J.R. 192, 73rd Congress in session June 5, 1933—Joint Resolution to Suspend the Gold Standard and Abrogate the Gold Clause dissolved the Sovereign Authority of the United States and the official capacities of all United States Governmental Offices, Officers, and Departments and is further evidence that the United States Federal Government exists today in name only.

The receivers of the United States Bankruptcy are the International Bankers, via the United Nations, the World Bank and the International Monetary Fund. All United States Offices, Officials, and Departments are now operating within a *de facto* status in name only under Emergency War Powers. With the Constitutional Republican form of Government now dissolved, the receivers of the Bankruptcy have adopted a new form of government for the United States. This new form of government is known as a Democracy, being an established Socialist/Communist order under a new governor for America. This act was instituted and established by transferring and/or placing the Office of the Secretary of Treasury to that of the Governor of the International Monetary Fund. Public Law 94-564, page 8, Section H.R. 13955 reads in part: "The U.S. Secretary of Treasury receives no compensation for representing the United States."

Gold and silver were such a powerful money during the founding of the United States of America, that the Founding Fathers declared that only gold or silver coins can be "money" in America. Since gold and silver coinage were heavy and inconvenient for a lot of transactions, they were stored in banks and a claim check was issued as a money substitute. People traded their coupons as money, or "currency." Currency is not money, but a money substitute. Redeemable currency must promise to pay a dollar equivalent

Chapter IX The Darkness Deepens...

in gold or silver money. Federal Reserve Notes (FRNs) make no such promises, and are not "money." A Federal Reserve Note is a debt obligation of the federal United States government, not "money." The federal United States government and the U.S. Congress were not and have never been authorized by the Constitution for the United States of America to issue currency of any kind, but only lawful money, gold and silver coin.

It is essential that we comprehend the distinction between real money and paper money substitute. One cannot get rich by accumulating money substitutes, one can only get deeper into debt. We the People no longer have any "money." Most Americans have not been paid any "money" for a very long time, perhaps not in their entire life. Now do you comprehend why you feel broke? Now, do you understand why you are "bankrupt," along with the rest of the country?

Federal Reserve Notes (FRNs) are unsigned checks written on a closed account. FRNs are an inflatable paper system designed to create debt through inflation (devaluation of currency). Whenever there is an increase of the supply of a money substitute in the economy without a corresponding increase in the gold and silver backing, inflation occurs.

Inflation is an invisible form of taxation that irresponsible governments inflict on their citizens. The Federal Reserve Bank who controls the supply and movement of FRNs has everybody fooled. They have access to an unlimited supply of FRNs, paying only for the printing costs of what they need. FRNs are nothing more than promissory notes for U.S. Treasury securities (T-Bills)—a promise to pay the debt to the Federal Reserve Bank.

There is a fundamental difference between "paying" and "discharging" a debt. To pay a debt, you must pay with value or substance (e.g., gold, silver, barter, or a commodity). With FRNs, you can only discharge a debt. You cannot pay a debt with a debt currency system. You cannot service a debt with a currency that has no backing in value or substance.

279

No contract in common law is valid unless it involves an exchange of "good and valuable consideration." Unpayable debt transfers power and control to the sovereign power structure that has no interest in money, law, equity or justice because they have so much wealth already.

Their lust is for power and control. Since the inception of central banking, they have controlled the fates of nations.

The Federal Reserve System is based on the canon law and the principles of sovereignty protected in the Constitution and the Bill of Rights. In fact, the international bankers used a "canon law trust" as their model, adding stock and naming it a "Joint Stock Trust." The U.S. Congress had passed a law making it illegal for any legal "person" to duplicate a "Joint Stock Trust" in 1873. The Federal Reserve Act was legislated post-facto (to 1870), although post-facto laws are strictly forbidden by the Constitution. [1:9:3]

The Federal Reserve System is a sovereign power structure separate and distinct from the federal United States government. The Federal Reserve is a maritime lender, and/or maritime insurance underwriter to the federal United States operating exclusively under admiralty/maritime law. The lender or underwriter bears the risks, and the Maritime law compelling specific performance in paying the interest, or premiums are the same.

Assets of the debtor can also be hypothecated (to pledge something as a security without taking possession of it) as security by the lender or underwriter. The Federal Reserve Act stipulated that the interest on the debt was to be paid in gold. There was no stipulation in the Federal Reserve Act for ever paying the principle.

Prior to 1913, most Americans owned clear, allodial title to property, free and clear of any liens or mortgages until the Federal Reserve Act (1913) "hypothecated" all property within the federal United States to the Board of Governors of the Federal Reserve, in which the trustees (stockholders) held legal title. The U.S. citizen (tenant, franchisee) was registered as a "beneficiary" of the trust via his/her birth certificate. In 1933, the federal United States further hypothecated all of the present and future properties, assets and labor of their "subjects," the 14th Amendment U.S. citizen, to the Federal Reserve System.

In return, the Federal Reserve System agreed to extend the federal United States Corporation all the credit "money substitute" it needed. Like any other debtor, the federal United States government had to assign collateral and security to their creditors as a condition of the loan. Since the federal United States didn't have any assets, they assigned the private property of their "economic slaves," the U.S. citizens as collateral against the unpayable federal debt. They also pledged the unincorporated federal territories, national parks forests, birth certificates, and nonprofit organizations, as collateral against the federal debt. All has already been transferred as payment to the international bankers.

Unwittingly, America has returned to its pre-American Revolution, feudal roots whereby all land is held by a sovereign and the common people had no rights to hold allodial title to property. Once again, We the People are the tenants and sharecroppers renting our own property from a sovereign in the guise of the Federal Reserve Bank. We the people have exchanged one master for another.

This has been going on for over 80 years without the "informed knowledge" of the American people, without a voice protesting loud enough. Now it's easy to grasp why America is fundamentally bankrupt.

Why don't more people own their properties outright?

Why are 90% of Americans mortgaged to the hilt and have little or no assets after all debts and liabilities have been paid? Why does it feel like you are working harder and harder and getting less and less?

We are reaping what has been sown, and the results of our harvest is a painful bankruptcy, and a foreclosure on American property, precious liberties, and a way of life. Few of our elected representatives in Washington, D.C. have dared to tell the truth. The federal United States is bankrupt. Our children will inherit this unpayable debt, and the tyranny to enforce paying it.

America has become completely bankrupt in world leadership, financial credit and its reputation for courage, vision and human rights. This is an undeclared economic war, bankruptcy, and economic slavery of the most corrupt order! Wake up America! Take back your country.[47]

In more recent years, Chuck Baldwin tried to warn the people:

Virtually our entire financial system is based on an illusion. We spend more than we earn, we consume more than we produce, we borrow more than we save, and we cling to the fantasy that this can go on forever. The glue that holds this crumbling scheme together is a fiat currency known as the Federal Reserve Note, which was created out of thin air by an international banking cartel called the Federal Reserve.

According to Congressman Ron Paul, in the last three years, the Federal Reserve has created over $4 trillion in new money. The result of all this "money-out-of-thin-air" fraud is never-ending inflation. And the more prices rise, the more the dollar collapses. Folks, this is not sustainable . . .

The only way to fix this economic mess that the international bankers have created is to return America to sound money principles, as prescribed in the U.S. Constitution. This means dismantling the Federal Reserve and the Internal Revenue Service, overturning the 16th Amendment and the personal income tax, and returning the American monetary

---

[47] *Congressional Record*, Vol. 33, p. H-1303 (March 17, 1993). To silence Traficant following the speech, members of Congress, who were bought and paid for by the Global Elite, had him imprisoned on trumped-up charges of corruption in what amounted to a kangaroo court. He was subsequently expelled from Congress. Traficant was sentenced to eight years in federal prison, and was released in 2009. He spent more than 17 years in public service, including being elected to Congress nine times. He died in 2014 from injuries sustained in a tractor accident on his Ohio farm. Traficant paid dearly for his honesty and patriotism.

system to hard assets: gold and silver. Anything short of this will only delay and worsen the inevitable collapse that has already begun.[48]

The *de facto* government's robbery of the people did not stop with the Federal Reserve Act. The Trading with the Enemy Act (TWEA) was passed and enacted on October 6, 1917.[49] The world was in the throes of WWI. The Act gave the president the power to oversee and restrict any and all trade between the U.S. and its enemies in times of war. The purpose of this Act was to "define, regulate, and punish trading with the enemy, and for other purposes." The Act gave Congress the authority to define the enemy, and gave the federal government complete authority over individuals considered to be the enemy. Section 5 (b) of the Act provided:

> During time of war or during any other period of national emergency declared by the President, the President may, investigate, regulate, or prohibit, under such rules and regulations as he may prescribe, by means of licenses or otherwise, any transactions in foreign exchange, transfers of credit between or payments by banking institutions as *defined by the President*, and export, hoarding, melting, or earmarking of gold or silver coin or bullion, currency or securities . . . by any person or with respect to any property, subject to the jurisdiction of the United States . . . [Emphasis added]

In essence, the Act gave the president the authority to take control of any and all commercial, monetary, or business transactions conducted by enemies within the U.S. The president has virtually unlimited powers to control the commercial transactions of the defined enemies.

The people of the U.S. were exempted from the provisions of the Act, which stated in Section 2 (c): ". . . other than citizens of

---

[48] Chuck Baldwin is currently pastor of Liberty Fellowship in Kalispell, Montana.
[49] 12 U.S.C. §95 and 50 U.S.C. App. §§1–44.

the United States." Seems innocent enough. Perhaps even appropriate for the time.

But by 1933, the federal government was bankrupt.[50] The stock market had crashed in 1929, and the nation was in the midst of the Great Depression. The uncertainty of the times caused a run on the banks. Bank deposits were still backed by gold at the time, and people were lining up at banks and demanding gold for their gold certificates (dollars). The problem was the banks did not have gold in their vaults. Why? The price of gold was legally limited to $35 an ounce in the U.S., but was selling for $60 an ounce in Europe. The banksters, a.k.a. the Global Elite, sold their gold to European banks for a nice profit, leaving American bank vaults virtually empty.

Bank closures were rampant. On February 14, 1933, Michigan declared an eight-day bank holiday. Within weeks, all other states declared bank holidays in order to avert runs on the banks. On March 4, Delaware became the last state to declare a bank holiday. On March 6, President Franklin Roosevelt declared a four-day *national* banking holiday, keeping all banks shut until Congress could act.

Prior to declaring the national banking holiday, on March 5, 1933, Roosevelt declared a National Emergency[51] and issued Proclamation 2038, calling Congress into a special extraordinary session. The proclamation stated:

> *Whereas* public interests require that the Congress of the United States should be convened in extra session at twelve o'clock, noon, on the Ninth day of March, 1933, to receive such communication as may be made by the Executive; *Now, Therefore, I, Franklin D. Roosevelt*, President of the United States of America, do hereby proclaim and

---

[50] The government was actually bankrupt since 1863, but President Roosevelt did declare the U.S. (corporation) bankrupt in 1933 by Executive Orders 6073, 6102, 6111 and by Executive Order 6260 on March 9, 1933. Congress confirmed the bankruptcy on June 5, 1933. See also, Congressman Traficant's speech above.

[51] *Black's Law Dictionary* (sixth edition): National emergency. A state of national crisis; a situation demanding immediate and extraordinary national or federal action. Congress has made little or no distinction between a "state of national emergency" and a "state of war." *Brown v. Bernstein*, D.C.Pa., 49 F.Supp. 728, 732.

declare that an extraordinary occasion requires the Congress of the United States to convene in extra session at the Capitol in the City of Washington on the Ninth day of March, 1933, at twelve o'clock, noon, of which all persons who shall at that time be entitled to act as members thereof are hereby required to take notice . . .

On March 9, 1933, Congress passed the Emergency Banking Act (EBA) (Amendatory Act),[52] "To provide relief in the existing national emergency in banking, and for other purposes." Title I, Section 1 states: "The actions, regulations, rules, licenses, orders and proclamations *heretofore or hereafter taken*, promulgated, made, or issued by the President of the United States or the Secretary of the Treasury since March the 4th, 1933, pursuant to the authority conferred by *subdivision (b) of Section 5 of the Act of October 6, 1917* [TWEA], as amended, are hereby approved and confirmed." [Emphasis added] In other words, *any* actions, orders, or proclamations made by the president after March 4, 1933, are approved and confirmed, *in advance*, regardless of the substance of the proclamation or order.[53] The Act effectively made the president a monarch/dictator in everything but name.[54] It also placed the president under the direction of the Fed.

---

[52] Emergency Banking Relief Act (EBA), Public Law 1, 48 Stat. 1 (March 9, 1933). See also, Title 12, U.S.C. 95 (b). The Act of March 9, 1933, is still in full force and effect today. The U.S. bankruptcy in 1861 placed the country under Emergency War Powers (12 Stat 319), which has never been repealed and exists in Title 50 U.S.C. §§212, 213, 215, Appendix 16, 26 C.F.R. Chapter 1 §303.1-6(a), and 31 C.F.R. Chapter 5 §500.701 Penalties. We are still under the "rule of necessity," in a declared state of national emergency. The rule of necessity is a common law rule permitting or requiring a judge or other official to adjudicate a case despite bias or personal interest when disqualification would result in the lack of any competent tribunal.

[53] This Trading with the Enemy Act is still in effect today, codified at 50 U.S.C., Chapter 53. See also, 12 U.S.C. §95(b). Further, every president since FDR has reaffirmed the "national emergency" and issued executive orders under 12 U.S.C. 95(a), continuing the U.S. bankruptcy and reorganization. §95(a): "In order to provide for the safer and more effective operation of the National Banking System and the Federal Reserve System . . . during such emergency period as the President of the United States by proclamation may prescribe . . ." This indicates the president acts for and under the direction of the Fed.

[54] Folsom, Burton W. and Anita, *FDR Goes to War: How Expanded Executive Power, Spiraling National Debt, and Restricted Civil Liberties Shaped Wartime America* (Simon and Schuster, NY, 2011). The book is an excellent expose of the abuse of power and *quid pro quo* by FDR during his presidency. Roosevelt was no more than a puppet of the Global Elite, his actions entirely directed by the Deep State. He was more responsible for the movement toward socialism in the U.S. than any other president, at least up until Obama. The book "exposes the negative impact of FDR's destructive wartime legacy on America's economic and foreign policies today."

The EBA gave the secretary of the Treasury (*not* listed as the *United States* secretary of the Treasury) new broad powers, including reporting directly to the creditors of the bankruptcy. It placed the American people under commercial law.[55] As a consequence of being under commercial law, all citizens are classified as *merchants*, and their records and affairs are completely subject to inspection and harsh penalties for any violations of mercantile law. The privacy of the people which was guaranteed by the *de jure* Constitution was obliterated.

Ah! But remember, the U.S. was still under martial law from the days of Lincoln. The president already had this authority under martial law. The TWEA and EBA were primarily for appearance only, to dupe the people into believing martial law was but a fallacious theory.

The 1973 U.S. Senate "Report of the Special Committee on the Termination of the National Emergency" clearly set forth the emergency powers granted the president by the EBA:

> Since March 9, 1933, the United States has been in a state of declared national emergency . . . These proclamations give force to 470 provisions of Federal law. These hundreds of statutes delegate to the President extraordinary powers, ordinarily exercised by the Congress, which affect the lives of American citizens in a host of all-encompassing manners. This vast range of powers, taken together, confer enough authority to rule the country without reference to normal Constitutional processes. Under the powers delegated by these statutes, the President may: seize property; organize and control the means of production; seize commodities; assign military forces abroad; institute martial law; seize and control all transportation and communication; regulate the operation of private enterprise; restrict travel; and, in a plethora of particular ways, control the lives of all American citizens.[56]

---

[55] Later formalized as the Uniform Commercial Code.
[56] Senate Report 93-549: "War and Emergency Powers Acts," November 19, 1973.

Chapter IX The Darkness Deepens...

In 1976, Congress passed the National Emergencies Act,[57] which ended all previous national emergencies and formalized the emergency powers of the president. However, the Act gives the president the authority to renew the emergency at the end of each year. Every president since has renewed the state of emergency. In addition to the emergency powers of the EBA, the Act allows the president to call up the National Guard and deploy troops overseas. This state of a declared national emergency has been in effect since 1933. Under the state of emergency, the president essentially has dictatorial powers.

The most egregious provision of the EBA is found in Section 2:

> Subdivision (b) of Section 5 of the Act of October 6, 1917,[58] as amended, is hereby amended as follows; [§5 (b)] (1) During time of war or during any other time of national emergency declared by the President, the President may, through any agency that he may designate, or otherwise, investigate, regulate, or prohibit, under such rules and regulations as he may prescribe, by means of licenses or otherwise, any transactions in foreign exchange, transfers of credit between or payments by banking institutions as defined by the President and export, hording, melting, or earmarkings of gold or silver coin or bullion, currency, or securities, and investigate, regulate, direct and compel, nullify, void, prevent or prohibit, any acquisition holding, withholding, use, transfer, withdrawal, transportation, importation or exportation of, or dealing in, or exercising any right, power, or privilege with respect to, or transactions involving, any property in which any foreign country or a national thereof has any interest, *by any person, or with respect to any property, subject to the jurisdiction of the United States* ... [Emphasis added]

The TWEA excluded U.S. citizens. But by including in this

---

[57] Pub.L. 94-412, 90 Stat. 1255, enacted September 14, 1976, codified at 50 U.S.C. §§1601-51.
[58] 40 Stat. L. 411.

amendment the phrase, "*any person . . . subject to the jurisdiction of the United States,*" U.S. citizens are now included in the definition of "enemies" of the U.S. The people became subject to the powers of the TWEA. In commercial, monetary, or business transactions, the people are now treated no different than enemies of the U.S. The government was given complete control over all transactions of U.S. citizens.

Roosevelt later used TWEA and EBA to justify the confiscation of gold from the American people.[59] On April 5, 1933, Roosevelt signed Executive Order 6102, "forbidding the hoarding of gold coin, gold bullion, and gold certificates within the continental United States." The order was made under the authority of TWEA, as amended by EBA. In effect, through executive orders and legislative decree, Roosevelt and Congress nationalized the people's money.[60]

But perhaps the most scurrilous act implemented by Roosevelt, was House Joint Resolution 192 of June 5, 1933.[61] The resolution reads:

> . . . Resolved by the Senate and the House of Representatives of the United States of America in Congress assembled: That (a) every provision contained in or made with respect to any obligation which purports to give the obligee the right to require payment in gold or a particular kind of coin or currency, or in an amount in money of the United States measured thereby, *is declared to be against public policy*, and no such provision shall be contained in or made with respect to an obligation hereafter incurred. Every obligation heretofore or hereafter incurred, whether or not any such provision is contained therein or made with respect

---

[59] People were compensated by the government for gold at the rate of $20.67 per troy ounce. Immediately after the forced surrender of gold, the Gold Reserve Act of 1934 raised the price of gold to $35 per ounce, resulting in a significant profit for the government. Also note that gold coins with numismatic value, and gold used in manufacturing, dentistry, and jewelry production were exempt. In addition, each person in a household could keep up to five troy ounces of gold bullion coins. Restrictions on the ownership of gold were removed on January 1, 1975.

[60] Nationalization is a violation of the "law of nations" and the public policy of Congress. See, *Hilton v. Guyot*, 159 U.S. 113 (1895).

[61] Joint Resolution "To Suspend the Gold Standard and Abrogate the Gold Clause," HJR 192, 73rd Congress, 1st Session (June 5, 1933).

CHAPTER IX THE DARKNESS DEEPENS...

> thereto, shall be *discharged* upon payment, dollar for dollar, in any such coin or currency, which at the time of payment is legal tender for public or private debts . . . [Emphasis added]

The resolution is blatantly unconstitutional according to the *de jure* Constitution for the united States of America.[62]

The only way lawful, Constitutional payment can be made on a debt is with gold or silver coin.[63] The government confiscated gold in 1933, followed by silver in 1934. And the Act declared payment in gold "against public policy." Therefore, the only way a debt can be paid is with FRNs, which are just promissory notes, supposedly backed by the government. Debts cannot be *paid*; debts can only be *discharged*. Of course, this was all by the design of the banksters, a.k.a. the Global Elite. In effect, the government was saying it would not redeem FRNs. FRNs have no substance;[64] they merely represent a permanent loan to the government, a debt which can never be paid.[65]

Joint Resolution 192 replaced legal tender (gold and silver) with *a legal obligation to use debt notes* belonging to the creditor, the Fed. The people have been rendered permanent debtors, barred from their lawful estate as free, sovereign beings. When people purchase goods or services with FRNs (a debt instrument), they forfeit all right to claim allodial title/ownership of the property.[66] They have no standing in substantive law. They are contractually obligated in perpetuity to the owner of the currency (the Fed, a.k.a.

---

[62] Note that courts ruled many of the provisions of EBA of March 9, 1933, unconstitutional. Roosevelt then stacked the courts with select chosen members of the BAR. The cases were sent back through and the rulings reversed.

[63] Between 1916 and 1933, FRNs and U.S. Notes were redeemable in gold. Debts could be paid off. A debt paid with gold or silver coin, or notes redeemable in gold, is completely eliminated. The creditor-debtor relationship is permanently and absolutely dissolved. No vestige of the debt remains.

[64] 26 U.S.C. 165(g) lists FRNs as "worthless securities." §165(g)(2)(C) defines as worthless security as, "a bond, debenture, *note*, or certificate, or other evidence of indebtedness, issued by a *corporation or by a government* or political subdivision thereof . . . [FRN]." [Emphasis added]

[65] Note also that the Federal Reserve Act stipulated that the interest on the debt was to be paid in gold. There was no stipulation in the Act for ever paying the principle.

[66] "There is a distinction between a 'debt discharged' and a debt 'paid.' When discharged, the debt still exists though divested of its charter as a legal obligation during the operation of the discharge, something of the original vitality of the debt continues to exist, which may be transferred, even though the transferee takes it subject to its disability incident to the discharge." *Stanek v. White*, 172 Minn.390, 215 N.W. 784.

Global Elite) that is used in commercial transactions, or used as the "good and valuable consideration" in contracts.

But it should be noted a *resolution* is merely advisory, not compulsory.[67] Resolutions only apply to those who make them. While having the appearance of law, resolutions do not have the force of law; they are merely Congress's opinion. They simply indicate what public policy may be, or what public policy is desired to be. Most people are deluded into thinking Congressional resolutions are law. And remember from previous chapters, Congress does not sit by Constitutional law, but by resolution, which is advisory, not compulsory. However, if a resolution is enacted by the president, in his authority under military law, the resolution will assume the form of law.

EBA also effectively robbed people of their property. The *Congressional Record* made this clear: "Under the new law the money is issued to the banks in return for government obligations, bills of exchange, drafts, notes, trade acceptances, and bankers acceptances. The money will be worth 100 cents on the dollar, because it is backed by the *credit of the nation. It will represent a mortgage on all the homes, and other property of all the people of the nation.*"[68] [Emphasis added]

As a consequence of EBA, the Fed agreed to extend the UNITED STATES, INC. all the credit it needed (via a money substitute, a.k.a. FRNs; not lawful money). Like any astute creditor, the Fed demanded collateral as a condition of the loan. However, the UNITED STATES was in bankruptcy and did not have assets. Therefore, the federal government hypothecated all property within the U.S. to the Board of Governors of the Fed, a private foreign

---

[67] *Black's Law Dictionary* (sixth edition) p. 1310: "Resolution. A formal expression of the opinion or will of an official body or a public assembly, adopted by vote; as a legislative resolution. Such may be either a simple, joint or concurrent resolution. The term is usually employed to denote the adoption of a motion, the subject-matter of which would not properly constitute a statute, such as a mere expression of opinion; an alteration of the rules; a vote of thanks or of censure, etc. Such is not law but merely a form in which a legislative body expresses an opinion. *Baker v. City of Milwaukee*, 271 Or. 500, 533 P. 2d 772, 775. The chief distinction between a 'resolution' and a 'law' is that the former is used whenever the legislative body passing it wishes merely to express an opinion as to some given matter or thing and is only to have a temporary effect on such particular thing, while by a 'law' it is intended to permanently direct and control matters applying to persons or things in general."
[68] HR 1491, p. 83 (March 9, 1933).

corporation.[69] This meant all the private property, present and future, of their subjects, U.S. citizens (via the 14th Amendment), was pledged as collateral against the unpayable federal debt. The unincorporated federal territories, national parks forests, birth certificates, and nonprofit organizations were also pledged as collateral. The U.S. citizen was registered as a "beneficiary" of the trust via his/her birth certificate. The people, and their property, are owned by the corporate federal government.

The road to slavery became even more opprobrious with the passage of the obscure "Buck Act" in 1940.[70] But first, a brief background to the Act.

In 1935, President Roosevelt signed the Social Security Act into law, creating the Social Security Administration. The Social Security Board (SSB) then created 10 Social Security "districts." The districts resulted in *federal areas* which covered the several states like a clear plastic overlay. The SSB assigned a Social Security Number (SSN), creating a contractual nexus between the people and the federal government. By accepting the SSN, people volunteered into the jurisdiction of the federal government, a.k.a. the District of Columbia Municipal Corporation (if they had not already volunteered into the system), and became UNITED STATES CITIZENS, or U.S. citizens (the 14th Amendment).

Next, in 1939 Congress passed the Public Salary Tax Act.[71] The Act is a municipal law for the District of Columbia Municipal Corporation, authorizing *taxing all federal and state government employees* and people who live and work in any "federal area" (or federal *territory*).

And that brings us back to the "Buck Act" of 1940. Section 110(e) of the Act authorized *any department* of the federal government to *create a federal area for imposition of the Public Salary Tax Act*

---

[69] *Black's Law Dictionary* (sixth edition) p. 742: "Hypothecate. To pledge property as security or collateral for a debt. Generally, there is no physical transfer of the pledged property to the lender, nor is the lender given title to the property; though he has the right to sell the pledged property upon default. *Moore v. Wardlaw*, C.C.A.Tex., 522 S.W.2d 552, 554. See also, Pledge; Rehypothecation."
[70] 54 Stat. 1059, October 9, 1940, codified at 4 U.S.C. §§105-10. Laws often acquire popular names as they make their way through Congress. 54 Stat. 1059 became known as the "Buck Act" for obscure reasons.
[71] Public Salary Tax Act of 1939, ch. 59, 53 Stat. 57. U.S.C. §111 (April 12, 1939).

of 1939.[72] Remember, the "Buck Act" authorized taxing all federal and state government employees and *people who live and work in any "federal area."* The SSB had already created "districts" which overlay the boundaries of the several states. The districts were defined as *federal areas*. Two relevant sections of the "Buck Act" read: "The term 'State' includes any Territory or possession of the United States"; and, "The term 'Federal area' means any lands or premises held or acquired by or for the use of the United States or any department, establishment, or agency of the United States; and any Federal area, or any part thereof, which is located within the exterior boundaries of any State, shall be deemed to be a Federal area located within such State."[73]

The "Buck Act" effectively extended the Public Salary Tax Act from D.C. into the states, which were legally redefined as territories or possessions of the U.S. People, by virtue of accepting the SSN and living in a Social Security district, were now subject to the Public Salary Tax Act. The Southern States were already territories of the U.S. as a conquered land in the War Between the States, in spite of the fact they were seated in the *de facto* Congress under the executive branch. The "Buck Act" and Social Security Act converted the remaining states into territories of the corporate federal government. State sovereignty, if not already a mere mirage, had been usurped to a foreign, privately owned corporation.

Again quoting H.G. Halleck on international law: "Complete conquest, by whatever mode it may be perfected, carries with it all the rights of the former government; or in other words, the conqueror [UNITED STATES, INC.], by the completion of his conquest, becomes the *absolute owner of the property conquered* from the enemy nation or state. His rights are no longer limited to mere occupation of what he has taken into his actual possession, but they *extend to all the property and rights of the conquered state*, including even debts as well as personal and real property."[74] [Emphasis added]

Halleck's principle was confirmed by SCOTUS in 1885:

---

[72] See, 4 U.S.C. Sec. 111.
[73] 4 U.S.C. §§110(d)(e).
[74] Id. Halleck, p. 839.

> It is a rule of public law, recognized and acted upon by the United States, that whenever political jurisdiction and legislative power over any territory are transferred from one nation or sovereign to another, the municipal laws of the country, that is, laws which are intended for the protection of private rights, continue in force *until abrogated or changed by the new sovereign* . . . Thus, upon a cession of political jurisdiction and legislative power—the latter is involved in the former—to the United States, the laws of the country in support of an established religion, or abridging the freedom of the press, or authorizing cruel or unusual punishments, and the like, *would at once cease to be of obligatory force without any declaration to that effect; and the laws of the country on other subjects would necessarily be superseded by existing laws of the new government upon the same matter.*[75] [Emphasis added]

The rule had previously been applied to U.S. foreign territories. The SCOTUS case extended the political jurisdiction and legislative power of the federal government to areas (territories) within the states over which the government acquired exclusive legislative jurisdiction. Therefore, when the federal government acquires legislative jurisdiction over a state, the state waives its sovereignty, and the laws of the state become federal laws.

This principle was supported by SCOTUS in *DeLima v. Bidwell*: "If the law or treaty making power enacts that the territory over which the military arm of the government has extended shall come under the permanent absolute sovereign jurisdiction of the United States, a new and different status arises. The former sovereign then loses all right of reverter, and the territorial limits of the United States are in so far enlarged."[76]

The states, as territories of the federal government, are under the permanent absolute sovereign jurisdiction of the U.S. corporate government. The president is, in effect, a dictator ruling as commander in chief under martial law.

---

[75] *Chicago, Rock Island & Pacific Railway v. McGlinn*, 114 U.S. 542 (1885).
[76] *DeLima v. Bidwell* 182 U.S. 179 (1900).

The property and unalienable rights of the people have been hypothecated by the Global Elite. Like it or not, the people are the property of the federal government, a.k.a. the Global Elite. No wonder the Deep State looks with disdain and contempt upon their former masters, a people who could be duped so easily and so completely.

In ensuing years, Congress made a feeble attempt to end the national emergency. Senate Report 93-549 of November 19, 1973, reads:

> Since March 9, 1933, the United States has been in a state of declared national emergency . . . These proclamations give force to 470 provisions of federal law. These hundreds of statutes delegate to the President extraordinary powers exercised by Congress, which affect the lives of American citizens in a host of all-encompassing manners. This vast range of powers taken together, confer enough authority to rule this country without reference to normal constitutional process. Under the powers delegated by these statutes, the President may: seize property; organize and control the means of production; seize commodities; assign military forces abroad; institute martial law; seize and control all transportation and communication; regulate the operation of private enterprise; restrict travel; and, in a plethora of particular ways, control the lives of all American citizens.

Congress acted upon the report and passed Public Law 94-112 on September 14, 1976: "To terminate certain authorities with respect to national emergencies still in effect, and to provide for orderly implementation and termination of future national emergencies." The stated objective of the law was noble-minded. However, there was one major exception to this Act. Section 502(a) states: "The provisions of this Act shall not apply to the following provisions of law, the powers and authorities conferred thereby, and actions taken thereunder: (1) Section 5(b) of the Act of October 6, 1917, as amended (12 U.S.C. 95a; 50 U.S.C. App. 5(b)." TWEA of 1917, amended in 1933, and EBA did not go away. Martial law and the state of emergency are still extant today.

CHAPTER IX THE DARKNESS DEEPENS...

In July 1944, the Bretton Woods Agreement was negotiated among 44 nations at the UN Monetary and Financial Conference held in Bretton Woods, New Hampshire. The Agreement established a new international monetary system, known as the Bretton Woods system, and also created the IMF and the World Bank.[77] As part of the Agreement, the UNITED STATES INC. was quitclaimed to the IMF (owned by the Rothschilds) as collateral for war debt. The UNITED STATES became entirely a foreign-owned, private corporation.[78] In exchange for the quitclaim deed, the president of the UNITED STATES INC. was given the right of seating and controlling the governors and general managers of the IMF and the World Bank.[79]

Finally, the former Republic gave up any remaining semblance of national sovereignty when the UNITED STATES signed the UN Treaty, making all Americans subject to the jurisdiction of the UN.[80]

According to a 1950 California 2nd District Court of Appeal ruling, the UN Charter has superseded the U.S. Constitution.[81] The court stated:

---

[77] July 12, 1944, Bretton Woods, New Hampshire. The U.S. became an IMF member in 1945. See, Title 22, Section 286 U.S.C. Under Bretton Woods, gold was the basis for the U.S. dollar, and all other currencies in the system were pegged to the U.S. dollar. The exchange rate at the time set the price of gold at $35 per ounce. Bretton Woods came to an end in the early 1970s when President Richard M. Nixon announced the U.S. would no longer exchange gold for U.S. currency.

[78] The UNITED STATES declared bankruptcy (again) and reorganization in 1950. The reorganization is located in U.S.C. Title 5 Annotated. The secretary of the Treasury was appointed as the "receiver" in bankruptcy. See, Reorganization Plan No. 26, 5 U.S.C.A. 903; Public Law 94-564, Legislative History, p. 5967. See also, "Explanation" at the beginning of 5 U.S.C.A.

[79] Codified at 22 U.S.C. §286.

[80] UNITED STATES INC. signed the UN Treaty (a.k.a. No. 147, UNITED NATIONS and UNITED STATES OF AMERICA) on June 26, 1947. The UN is a private corporation, incorporated in California, and owned by the Rothschilds via the Lucis Trust. It is currently headed by Baron Jacob Nathaniel Rothschild (NY) who is also identified as the head of the Khazarian mafia. The original charter of the UN is located in Switzerland, along with the charters of the IMF, the World Trade Organization, and BIS. According to the Lucis Trust website: "The Lucis Trust is dedicated to the establishment of a new and better way of life for everyone in the world based on the fulfillment of the divine plan for humanity. Its educational activities promote recognition and practice of the spiritual principles and values upon which a stable and interdependent world society may be based." Sounds noble, but pure evil in its design. Its premise is a One World Government under UN control. The "divine plan" is the plan of Lucifer. The website further states: "The Lucis Trust has Consultative Status with the Economic and Social Council of the United Nations (ECOSOC) and World Goodwill is recognized by the Department of Public Information at the United Nations as a Non-Governmental Organization (NGO)." On May 2, 2016, the United States of America Inc. went bankrupt when its Puerto Rico subsidiary defaulted on a $422 million payment. The bankruptcy legally placed the corporate UNITED STATES government under the control of the UN, headed by Baron Rothschild. Note the Lucis Trust was created in London in 1922 as Lucifer's Trust. The name was later changed for obvious reasons.

[81] The "Charter of the United Nations" was signed on June 26, 1945, in San Francisco, at the conclusion of the UN Conference on International Organization, and went into effect on October 24, 1945.

The efforts of our government [in supporting the rights of oppressed nations] reached fruition in the convention of representatives of the nations of the earth at which the Charter of the United Nations was adopted. It was promptly ratified by the Senate of the United States, thereby proclaiming allegiance to its principles and providing precedent and example for other countries. The United States has consistently regarded its treaties with other nations as inviolate. *The Charter has become "the supreme Law of the Land*; and the Judges in every State shall be bound thereby, any Thing in the Constitution or Laws of any State to the Contrary notwithstanding." U.S. Constitution, Art. VI, Section 2. The position of this country in the family of nations forbids trafficking in innocuous generalities but demands that every State in the Union accept and act upon the Charter according to its plain language and its unmistakable purpose and intent.[82] [Emphasis added]

The people have been betrayed by their so-called leaders since the days of Lincoln and the War Between the States.[83]

---

[82] *Sei Fujii v. California*, 38 Cal. 2nd 721 (April 24, 1950). The Supreme Court of California, however, modified this ruling, stating: "It is not disputed that the charter is a treaty, and our federal Constitution provides that treaties made under the authority of the United States are part of the supreme law of the land and that the judges in every state are bound thereby. (U.S. Constitution, Article VI) [1] A treaty, however, *does not automatically supersede local laws which are inconsistent with it* unless the treaty provisions are self-executing. In the words of Chief Justice Marshall: A treaty is 'to be regarded in courts of justice as equivalent to an act of the Legislature, whenever it operates of itself, without the aid of any legislative provision. But when the terms of the stipulation import a contract—when either of the parties engages to perform a particular act, the treaty addresses itself to the political, not the judicial department; and the Legislature must execute the contract, before it can become a rule for the court.'" (*Foster v. Neilson* (1829), 2 Pet. (U.S.) 253, 314 [7 L. Ed. 415] [Emphasis added] And further: "It is clear that the provisions of the preamble and of article 1 of the charter which are claimed to be in conflict with the alien land law are not self-executing. They state general purposes and objectives of the United Nations Organization and do not purport to impose legal obligations on the individual member nations or to create rights in private persons." *Sei Fujii*, Appellant, *v. The State of California*, Respondent, [L.A. No. 21149, *en banc*, April 17, 1952]. The court held that only "self-executing" treaties have application in domestic law without the need for a federal implementing statute.

[83] See also, Public Law 87-297. The law calls for complete disarmament of Americans (including the police) so the UN can "maintain internal peace." Also, there is no mention of God in the UN charter. The UN now owns 51 million acres of U.S. soil. The AIDS virus was induced by the UN for population control (HB 15090). HB 666 negates Amendment IV rights of the people. And Presidential Decision Directive 25 (PDD 25, February 22, 1996) places U.S. troops under the command of the UN: ". . . the President has the authority to place U.S. forces under the operational control of a foreign commander when doing so serves American security interests . . ." Members of Congress were not allowed to see PDD 25.

Chapter IX The Darkness Deepens . . .

On October 28, 1977, banks were placed under the control of the governor of the IMF. On that date, the UNITED STATES INC. officially declared insolvency.[84] The IMF is owned by the Crown Templar of the City of London (see Chapter X for information on the Crown Templar) and controls all the central banks of North America, including the Fed. U.S. banks were put under control of a foreign, for-profit corporation.

The conquest of the people by the Global Elite was complete. Americans surrendered, a vanquished foe, without firing a shot. The gold standard is no more. All property, real or personal, is now encumbered by the federal government. The people do not own or have a right to their labor. Money is *de facto*, a mere vapor in the air, an entry on a computer screen, controlled by a foreign private corporation. People willingly, yet unwittingly, bow down to their masters, agents of a foreign power. The plunder and consolidation of power by the federal government, a.k.a. the Global Elite, has been accomplished. America has indeed been turned upside down. This is nothing short of evil, in its most pernicious, unscrupulous form . . . evil, by agents of darkness who have no regard for human dignity or the sanctity of life, except their own.

As enemy combatants of the private creditors in bankruptcy, people have become nothing more than chattel owned by the creditors, the Global Elite. All enterprise and commercial activity between people as chattel/slaves of the creditors was made illegal, by operation of law, without first obtaining permission through a fee-based license. A marriage license is required to get married. A driver's license is required to travel. A business license is required to operate a business. A building permit is required to build a structure. A teaching certificate (license) is required to be a teacher. All are formerly unalienable rights now requiring permission of the all-controlling state. And most egregious of all . . . in order to work for an employer, allegedly requires a license in the form of an SSN.[85]

---

[84] See, 26 IRC 165 (g) (i); U.C.C. 1-201 (23); C.R.S. 39-22-103.5.
[85] Revelation 13:17: "And that no man should be able to buy or to sell, save he that hath the mark, even the name of the beast or the number of his name." *Black's Law Dictionary* (sixth edition) p. 970: "Marque. [mark] a license of reprisals." Reprisal is defined as "a retaliatory action against an enemy in wartime." People may unwittingly already have the Mark of the Beast.

An SSN is a commercial tracking number (Fed account number) enabling the Global Elite to tax and regulate their commercial chattel property, the American people.[86]

The right of the people to own property is an unalienable, natural right; not just ownership of material goods and land, but the right to one's speech, ideas, and labor. As expressed by James Madison: "The personal right to acquire property, which is a *natural right*, gives to property, when acquired, a right to protection, as a social right."[87] [Emphasis added]

When property rights are stripped away, tyranny is the result. Madison was even more concise in writing:

> This term [*property*] in its particular application means "that dominion which one man claims and exercises over the external things of the world, in exclusion of every other individual." In its larger and juster meaning, it embraces every thing to which a man may attach a value and have a right; and which leaves to every one else the like advantage. In the former sense, a man's land, or merchandize, or money is called his property. In the latter sense, a man has a property in his opinions and the free communication of them. He has a property of peculiar value in his religious opinions, and in the profession and practice dictated by them. He has a property very dear to him in the safety and liberty of his person. He has an equal property in the free use of his faculties and free choice of the objects on which to employ them [*his labor*]. In a word, as a man is said to have a right to his property, he may be equally said to have a property in his rights. Where an excess of power prevails, property of no sort is duly respected. No man is safe in his opinions, his person, his faculties, or his possessions . . . *Government is instituted to protect property of every sort*;

---

[86] On September 5, 1996, U.S. Patent & Trademark Office application No. 709471 was filed. This is a plan for marking the chattel of the Global Elite (i.e., every U.S. citizen) with a number for "inventory" purposes. Revelation 13:16: "And he causeth all, both small and great, rich and poor, free and bond, to receive a mark in their right hand, or in their foreheads . . ."

[87] Ketcham, Ralph (editor), *Selected Writings of James Madison* (Hackett Publishing, Indianapolis, IN, 2006).

Chapter IX The Darkness Deepens...

as well that which lies in the various rights of individuals, as that which the term particularly expresses. This being the end of government, that alone is a just government, which impartially secures to every man, whatever is his own.[88] [Emphasis added]

The right of property ownership has been stolen from the people, an act so egregious that it was unthinkable to the Founding Fathers.[89] As further stated by Madison: "That is not a just government, nor is property secure under it, where the property which a man has in his personal safety and personal liberty, is violated by arbitrary seizures of one class of citizens for the service of the rest."[90] And: "Where an excess of power prevails, property of no sort is duly respected. No man is safe in his opinions, his person, his faculties, or his possessions."[91]

In more recent years, Ayn Rand, speaking of socialism, wrote: "Just as man can't exist without his body, so no rights can exist without the right to translate one's rights into reality—to think, to work and to keep the results—which means: the right of property."[92]

Rand went on to write:

The right to life is the source of all rights—and the right to property is their only implementation. Without property rights, no other rights are possible. Since man has to sustain his life by his own effort, the man who has no right to the product of his effort has no means to sustain his life. The man who produces while others dispose of his product, is a slave. Bear in mind that the right to property is a right to action, like all the others: it is not the right to

---

[88] Madison, James, "Property," *National Gazette* (March 29, 1792).

[89] The right to property is also secured by Amendment IV to the Constitution for the united States of America: "The right of the people to be secure in their persons, houses, papers, and effects, against unreasonable searches and seizures, shall not be violated . . ." Though the word "property" is not used in Amendment IV, its implication is indisputable.

[90] *Letters and Other Writings of James Madison, Fourth President of the United States: Published by Order of Congress* Vol. 4 (1865).

[91] Madison, James, "Property," *National Gazette* (March 29, 1792).

[92] Rand, Ayn, "For the New Intellectual" (*The Ayn Rand Lexicon*, 1966, 1967).

an object, but to the action and the consequences of producing or earning that object. It is not a guarantee that a man will earn any property, but only a guarantee that he will own it if he earns it. It is the right to gain, to keep, to use and to dispose of material values.[93]

No man is free without the right to property . . . material, intellectual, and spiritual. As Rand expressed it, such a man is a slave, mere chattel existing at the pleasure of the master.

The American people have unwittingly sold their souls to the devil. Without ownership of property, including their own bodies and labor, they exist at the mercy of the Global Elite. The words of John Adams in the country's infancy should haunt people today: "The moment the idea is admitted into society *that property is not as sacred as the laws of God*, and that there is not a force of law and public justice to protect it, *anarchy and tyranny commence*. If 'Thou shalt not covet' and 'Thou shalt not steal' were not commandments of Heaven, they must be made inviolable precepts in every society before it can be civilized or made free."[94] [Emphasis added]

Indeed, tyranny is reaching its wicked tentacles over the land.

It bears repeating . . . the people have unknowingly returned to their pre-Revolutionary War feudal roots, serving fealty on the land to their masters. They are mere tenants on property they think they own, paying rent in the form of property taxes, and traveling in automobiles as a privilege at the pleasure of the true owner, the state (the certificate of title).

As a thief comes in the darkness of night, the Global Elite have burglarized our homes. They have robbed us of our wealth (Federal Reserve Act and IRS), confiscated our gold (TWEA, EO 6102), stolen our private property (H.R. 1491, the 14th Amendment, and the birth certificate),[95] deprived us of due process (admiralty/maritime law), and nullified our unalienable rights (the 14th Amendment). They have impinged upon our religious liberties. They have removed the Creator of the Universe from government and our halls of

---

[93] Rand, Ayn, *The Virtue of Selfishness* (Penguin Books, NY, 1961, 1964).
[94] Adams, John, "A Defense of the Constitutions of Government of the United States of America" (1787).
[95] Also, Senate Resolution No. 62, 73rd Congress, 1st Session (April 1933).

CHAPTER IX THE DARKNESS DEEPENS...

learning. They have labeled us as "domestic terrorists." They have destroyed memorials of our past. They have ripped pride in America from our hearts. They have made "We the People" enemies of our own government, albeit a *de facto* government. They have divided the people against themselves. They have enslaved the people as mere chattel. The Global Elite has stealthily destroyed the Republic. The people have been in a coma-like stupor as the intruder has quietly and surreptitiously ransacked everything American.

Like a cancer spreading silently and insidiously through the body, the Global Elite will not stop in their quest for complete control until the cancer metastasizes . . . until everything American is dead . . . until the total enslavement of all peoples everywhere is complete . . . until they have achieved their ultimate goal; a New World Order under a One World Government. A world with no borders, no walls, no due process, no personal initiative, no self-identity, and no self-expression. Autocratic rule enforced by the brute force of UN troops. Our freedom is an illusion; our realty a mirage. "We the People" are living the life of Truman, mere characters on the screen of life, mercilessly manipulated by an evil that postures itself as the elite . . . as beings superior to "We the People."

Evil is malicious. Evil is vile. But evil is also subtle. As a dense fog slowly rolls in over the land, a dark cloud has stealthily encompassed our demesne. The darkness deepens with every passing day. But, as the fog dissipates in the warmth of the rising Sun, so the darkness must be dispelled by the light of truth. Or vision will be lost, truth will be obnubilated, and the path to liberty enveloped in a blackness darker than a moonless, starless night. As a blind man without his cane, people will grope in the darkness, unable to find their way. Freedom will have succumbed to an ominous fate, plunging them into the depths of obscurity. Their only escape will be the parting of the clouds at the sound of the trumpet, as a blinding light descends from the Heavens to eviscerate the darkness once and for all.

In spite of the evil, the voice of the people is eerily quiet. Crickets chirp, owls hoot, frogs croak . . . the Sun rises and falls . . . birds sing their songs . . . against the backdrop of natural law, the Deep State flaunts its contempt of *"rights derived from the Great*

Legislator of the Universe" and *"liberties [that] are the Gift of God."* The government's repugnance of the law and the *de jure* Constitution is evidenced by its pugnacious actions. Yet in the face of abuse and tyranny, the voice of the people is silent . . . silent . . . so silent . . . muted in obedience to the master. The cacophony of silence is deafening. People cower in the halls of their homes, blindly obedient to the unspeakable evil of their Marxist master, seemingly not cognizant of their servitude.

Their silence merely emboldens the tyrannical government. The Deep State blatantly and seditiously continues its abusive efforts to subjugate them, in utter defiance and revulsion of common law, audaciously and belligerently proceeding with scorn and disdain for the sanctity of God-given *unalienable* rights and the value of human life. Their actions are so egregious as to be unthinkable in the context of freedom; an atrocity in the context of justice.

Where is the moral outrage? The righteous indignation? Where is the cry of protest? Wake up, people! The thief comes to steal, kill, and destroy. And We the People have wantonly opened our doors to the thief. We have left our homes unguarded; our doors unlocked. We have unwittingly adorned the shackles of servitude. When will enough be enough? When will We the People arise from our slumber, remove the intruder from our homes, and take back what is rightfully ours? This is our country! This is the Republic of "We the People!"

As poignantly written and sung by John Mellencamp:[96]

Well, I can stand beside ideas I think are right
And I can stand beside the idea to stand and fight
I do believe there's a dream for everyone
This is our country

There's room enough here for science to live
And there's room enough here for religion to forgive
And try to understand other people of this land
This is our country

---

[96] John Mellencamp, from the 2007 album *Freedom's Road*. (Debuted at No. 5 on the *Billboard 200*.)

Chapter IX The Darkness Deepens...

(Chorus) From the east coast to the west coast
Down the Dixie Highway
Back home
This is our country

And poverty could be just another ugly thing
And bigotry would be seen only as obscene
And the ones that run this land
Help the poor and common man
This is our country

Chorus

The dream is still alive
Some day it will come true
And this country
It belongs to folks like me and you
So let the voice of freedom
Sing out through this land
This is our country

Chorus

Yes. This is our country, bequeathed to "We the People" by our Founding Fathers. A gift of freedom won with the blood and courage of American patriots. Arise, America! Together, people of all colors, races, and creeds, with voices raised in unison against the pervasive evil, we can take our country back! Together, as one people, we can restore America to her glorious greatness! Together, we can restore the Republic. Together, America will once again be the land of the free and the home of the brave, from sea to shining sea!

To the misguided reprobates who prefer socialism, even in the face of Truth, I simply utter the words of Samuel Adams, previously quoted: "If ye love wealth better than liberty, the tranquility of servitude better than the animating contest of freedom, go home from us in peace. We ask not your counsels or arms. Crouch down and lick the hands which feed you. May your chains set lightly upon you, and may posterity forget that ye were our countrymen."

Under a socialist/communist regime, the day will surely come when you will be treated no better than a dog, licking the scraps under the master's table, scavenging for morsels of food in the master's trash. You will scour the fields for burlap and sackcloth to clothe your naked body. The stars overhead will be the roof of your slumber. Your children will be taken from you . . . or murdered in the womb of the mother. Internment camps for the dissident will be your only comfort. Wailing and weeping will be the music for your ears.

You laugh? Sound preposterous? Yeah, the people of Venezuela thought so, too. Once the wealthiest nation in South America, today its people live in abject poverty under a brutal dictator. But . . . healthcare is free, albeit with few doctors and even fewer medical supplies. And there is free college tuition for all, albeit with professors leaving in droves and few jobs for those who graduate.

Or ask the people of Cuba. Prior to the rise of Castro, Cuba was a developed country, ranking fifth in per capita GDP in the Northern Hemisphere. It was a popular tourist destination with luxury hotels, beaches, nightclubs, and casinos. Today, its people are poor (though generally not in poverty), and virtually devoid of the simplest luxuries of life, including Internet access. Just ask any Cuban American about life under the Castro regime. Ah . . . but Cubans have free college tuition, and free healthcare for all.

Still convinced socialism/communism is better than our Constitutional Republic? Canada welcomes you with open arms. The poverty of Cuba and Venezuela will be to your liking. Or perhaps China, Haiti, or Mexico . . . or some might say Denmark,[97] Sweden,[98] Finland, or Norway,[99] all bastions of so-called "democratic socialism"; countries in which government is "Big Brother" and

---

[97] See, "Brave New Denmark—A Model for the USA?" (*rense.com/general79/brave.htm*). For an interesting perspective of life in Denmark from a Dane, see the August 5, 2008 Internet post at *city-data.com/forum/europe/398666-denmark-sucks-happiest-nation-my-ass.html*.

[98] See, "Limits on Freedom of Expression: Sweden," Library of Congress (*loc.gov/item/2019668149*). See also, Jon Henschen's March 5, 2018 article, "Is Sweden Socialist? No, but . . ." (*fee.org/articles/is-sweden-socialist-no-but*). Swedes have no unalienable rights.

[99] Norway is a social democracy. Citizens pay high taxes and the government spends a lot of money on public projects such as schools, healthcare, and generous unemployment benefits. The price people pay (besides very high taxes) is a loss of unalienable rights. Many of the insights on Denmark apply to the people of Norway.

Chapter IX The Darkness Deepens...

unalienable rights are virtually extinct; countries already well on their way to succumbing to the servitude of the New World Order. You are not our brothers. America, the land of freedom, opportunity, and personal accountability, is not the land for you. Americans are a people of hard work, vision, ingenuity, self-reliance, self-persistence, self-control, and perseverance. Americans are a people of courage and sacrifice. True Americans eschew government handouts for their unalienable rights extant since the beginning of time. True Americans are repulsed by the overreach of power of an authoritarian government.

"He who passively accepts evil is as much involved in it as he who helps to perpetrate it. He who accepts evil without protesting against it is really cooperating with it."
—Martin Luther King Jr.

"I believe that liberty is the only genuinely valuable thing that men have invented, at least in the field of government, in a thousand years. I believe that it is better to be free than to be not free, even when the former is dangerous and the latter safe. I believe that the finest qualities of man can flourish only in free air—that progress made under the shadow of the policeman's club is false progress, and of no permanent value. I believe that any man who takes the liberty of another into his keeping is bound to become a tyrant, and that any man who yields up his liberty, in however slight the measure, is bound to become a slave."
—H.L. Mencken, "Why Liberty?" (January 30, 1927)

"The evils of tyranny are rarely seen but by him who resists it."
—John Hay (1872)

Appendix A

The 10 Planks of The Communist Manifesto

Author's note: Commentary by unknown author

1. Abolition of property in land and the application of all rents of land to public purposes.

   Zoning laws are the first step to government property ownership. The 14th Amendment of the U.S. Constitution (1868), and various zoning, school, and property taxes. Also the Bureau of Land Management. Abolition of allodial title to land. Title to property in fee simple (fealty).

2. A heavy progressive or graduated income tax.

   Misapplication of the 16th Amendment of the U.S. Constitution (1913), Social Security Act of 1936; Joint House Resolution 192 of 1933; and various state "income" taxes. They call it "paying your fair share."

3. Abolition of all rights of inheritance.

   Read: inheritance taxes. They call it federal/state estate tax (1916); or reformed probate laws, and limited inheritance via arbitrary inheritance tax statutes.

4. Confiscation of the property of all emigrants and rebels.

   Read: the accused, not the convicted; asset forfeiture laws, DEA, IRS, ATF etc. . . . We call it government seizures, tax liens, Public "Law" 99-570 (1986); Executive order 11490, sections 1205, 2002 which gives private land to the Department of Urban Development; the imprisonment of "terrorists" and those who speak out or write against the "government" (1995-6 crime/terrorist bills); and the **IRS confiscation of property without due process**.

5. Centralization of credit in the hands of the state, by means of a national bank with State capital and an exclusive monopoly.

> *Read: Federal Reserve, fiat paper money and fractional reserve banking. They call it the Federal Reserve which is a **private** credit/debt system nationally organized by the Federal Reserve Act of 1913. All local banks are members of the Fed system, and are regulated by the Federal Deposit Insurance Corporation. This private bank has an exclusive monopoly in money creation which in reality has ended the need for revenue from taxes.*

6. Centralization of the means of communication and transportation in the hands of the state.

> *Read: DOT, FAA, FCC, etc. We call it the Federal Communications Commission (FCC) and Department of Transportation (DOT) mandated through the ICC Act of 1887, the Commissions Act of 1934, the Interstate Commerce Commission established in 1938, the Federal Aviation Administration, Federal Communications Commission, and Executive Orders 11490, 10999, as well as state-mandated driver's licenses and DOT regulations. There is also the postal monopoly, AMTRAK and CONRAIL.*

7. Extension of factories and instruments of production owned by the state, the bringing into cultivation of waste lands, and the improvement of the soil generally in accordance with a common plan.

> *Read: "controlled" rather than "owned" or subsidized. They call it corporate capacity, The Desert Land Act and the Department of Agriculture. As well as the Departments of Commerce and Labor, Department of the Interior, the*

Environmental Protection Agency, Bureau of Land Management, Bureau of Reclamation, Bureau of Mines, National Park Service, and the IRS control of business through corporate regulations.

8. Equal liability of all to labor. Establishment of industrial armies, especially for agriculture.

Read: minimum wage and imprisoned or slave laborers, like in China (and here in U.S. prisons), our Most Favored Nation trade partner. They call it the Social Security Administration and the Department of Labor. The national debt and inflation caused by the Fed has caused the need for a two-income family. Women in the workplace since the 1920s, the 19th Amendment of the U.S. Constitution, the Civil Rights Act of 1964, assorted socialist unions, affirmative action, the Public Works Administration and of course Executive Order 11000.

9. Combination of agriculture with manufacturing industries, gradual abolition of the distinction between town and country by a more equitable distribution of population over the country.

Read: forced relocations and forced sterilization programs like in China. They call it the Reorganization Act of 1949, zoning (Title 17, 1910-1990), and super corporate farms, as well as Executive Orders 11647, 11731 (ten regions) and Public "Law" 89-136, the creation of "federal zones" via ZIP codes in place of the sovereign states.

10. Free education for all children in public schools. Abolition of children's factory labor in its present form. Combination of education with industrial production.

Read: all children will be indoctrinated and inculcated with government propaganda, like "majority rules" and "pay your fair share." The whole philosophical concept of "fair share" comes from the communist maxim: "From each according to their ability, to each according to their need."

This very concept is pure socialism. People are being taxed to support what are called "public" schools, which train the young to work for the communal debt system. We also call it the Department of Education, the NEA, and outcome-based education.

[Author's note: Politicians who believe in these things and pass more and more laws implementing these ideas are traitors to the *de jure* U.S. Constitution. The agencies and their agents that force these concepts upon the people of this nation are committing acts of war against the people and the nation.]

"None are more hopelessly enslaved than those who falsely believe they are free."
—Johann Wolfgang von Goethe

Appendix B

Excerpts from Our War

Excerpts from the book by June B. Goode, *Our War: An Account of the Civil War in Bedford, Virginia* (Warwick House Publishing, Lynchburg, VA, 2003).

In the book, Goode reprints in its entirety the diary of Letitia (Lettie) McCreary Burwell, the daughter of William McCreary Burwell and Frances Steptoe Burwell of Avenel Plantation in the town of Liberty (now Bedford), Virginia. Lettie was about 25-years-old when the war began. She was an intelligent and articulate woman, and her journal vividly portrays a picture of the people and life in Liberty during the first months of the war. Several excerpts from the journal give particular insight into the prevailing feelings at the time:

> April 19, 1861:
>
> For several days great excitement. Virginia has seceded at last. Seceded which it ought to have done long ago, and old Governor Letcher has waked up sufficiently to telegraph the different volunteer companies throughout the State to hold themselves in readiness in case of fighting.
>
> The telegraph yesterday brought news that Mr. James Allen had made an effort to secure the arms at Harpers Ferry, but his brave company had been defeated by Mr. Lincoln's troops who came over from Washington. I hope this is not true. No news from there today. Mr. Allen is a brave and sensible man and it was so gallant of him to try to seize the large store of arms at Harpers Ferry, as soon as he got the news that Virginia had left the Union.

But what a sad time is before us! The only thing we poor women can do is to weep when we think of the gallant lives that may be lost, and to pray without ceasing for them.

Very busy today packing Sister [Lettie's sister Kate] and Dr. B.'s [Dr. Thomas Bowyer] trunks in case of a dispatch from Richmond calling Dr. Bowyer's company. Sister has determined to go with them. She would be miserable up here. Papa is going too, although he is fifty years old. So Mama, Rosa, Fan and myself will be left alone. Cannot help hoping there will be no fighting although I feel so anxious the Northern fanatics shall have proof of the bravery of the South they have been abusing so long. I feel that the South should come out boldly now before the world and assert her independence. She should make such a brave stand for her rights and institutions that hereafter the civilized world will tremble and turn pale whenever it dares assert that the slave owners of the South are a set of villains and murderers. We should declare in Europe and every place to which "our Northern brethren" have had access, that it is time now for our people to come forward and put down this wide spreading sentiment even with the force of arms. This is very natural, if "our Northern Brethren" find so much fault with and abuse us so heartily that we should desire to set up a government for ourselves, especially as we have all of the resources requisite. This might be done peaceably, but the Northerners do not like the idea of losing so much good Southern money.

How strange to think we are in the midst of a Revolution. Who would have thought that in our time there would be such a thing?

A note from Sis Wingfield. Mary is at home at last, first time since she was married. Wish I could go to see her, but the weather is so disagreeable and we are helping Sister to get ready, so I don't expect I will see her.

Dr. Bowyer's company drilling in lot opposite our front gate. Such a fine looking set of men. He is quite proud of them. Commenced reading Froissart's Chronicles of the 15th Century. But so many things going forward in my own time I cannot confine my attention to Froissart and his times. Telegrams coming and going . . .

Saturday, April 20, 1861:
. . . I wish the Yankees would go home and let us do as we please with our own Southern States. We must have been a great source of revenue to them that they are so enraged at the prospect of us setting up for ourselves. The ladies in town are busy today finishing uniforms for Dr. Bowyer's company. I have never heard of such a mania for fighting. I believe if Dr. Bowyer and some of his company are not allowed an opportunity for fighting some Yankees in a few days they will go crazy. I am certain Sam and John Davis will go wild so intense is their desire, and so impatient are they to shoot some Abolitionists and Yankees. The idea of a Union of people who so cordially hate each other! How could such a Union have lasted so long!

Wednesday, April 24, 1861.
When I think of the dreadful events, which may follow in a few weeks, it fills me with grief so that I would just have to go to bed. But that would be wrong. We want all courage and encouragement now that we can give each other. And especially our sex should control their grief and do all to cheer up our brave hearted men. O! The bravery of our men! Was there ever anything like it! Each man, each boy, seems to be thrilled with a spirit to resist the enemy and fight them to the death so that I can but think we are to be victorious under God, who by His right hand and His holy arm will get Himself the victory. If ever there was a righteous cause, a holy cause, in which men had to fight, it is for their homes and families, their honor and their rights. The ladies offered to make up the undress uniforms for the Old Dominion Volunteers while they were out here this afternoon drilling. I wrote the offer of

the ladies and sent it down to them. It was read aloud and tremendous cheers rent the air for the ladies.

Too much excited all day to sew, and felt badly on account of loss of sleep. In the afternoon I went with Mrs. Donald to Mrs. Sale's. Sue Hobson very busy making red flannel shirts for some of the soldiers. All the ladies very busy. Mr. Davis came again to give me a lesson in shooting. Succeeded a little better. Fired six or eight times and did not hit the mark or anywhere near it but once. No news today. A letter from Papa. He could get no arms for Dr. Bowyer's company. Richmond so full of troops very difficult to get food for them. Still the troops are all flocking there from the country. The trains pass here, extra and regular trains, crowded with brave volunteers who just rush right down to Richmond to see at what points they may be wanted at and give themselves up to the orders of the Governor. Some of these volunteer companies are not armed but are so anxious to lend their aid that they will not remain at home any longer.

Tuesday, June 25, 1861:
Everyday pretty much alike. Read the newspapers a great deal. Think about the war all the time. Wonder if they are fighting and where. Go round to the neighbors and as soon as the train comes to hear if they have gotten any letters or news. Get ready something for the soldiers to eat at a minute's notice when the telegram tells us they are coming and are very hungry. Thus it is each day is passed in excitement and anxiety, for who can tell what may happen? All we can do is pray without ceasing that our Heavenly Father may give us strength for all that He may see fit to bring upon us and if it please Him in His mercy and goodness to put a final and speedy termination to this sad and unnecessary war by turning the hearts of our enemies that they may see the justice of our cause and leave us and our beloved South land to peace and prosperity.

Saturday, July 20, 1861:

Rumors all day that they are still fighting at Bull Run. The whole village in excitement and fearing that at any moment will bring the news of the death of some of the gallant young men from here. I pray that they may be spared and return to their homes and families.

Eight hundred soldiers stopped here for breakfast this morning. Everybody sent breakfast to the depot and we hear there was enough for them . . .

Another poignant and emotional entry was made on July 22, 1861, following the Battle of Bull Run:

What a day of excitement this has been! A telegram this morning stated that yesterday there was a terrible battle at Manassas. Another dispatch in the evening said we had gained a glorious victory but had lost many gallant men. A terrible slaughter on both sides, so much confusion it was impossible to tell how many had been killed of our men or the enemy. What an awful suspense after hearing this news before getting a telegram from Mr. Johnson telling us none of Colonel Preston's regiment was killed. Oh! This was a horrible day for us! Although we had won the victory each heart stood still that at the thought perhaps our dear ones had been killed. When the news came that our regiment was safe and only a few in it wounded, we returned our thanks to God, who in His mercy has spared us such an affliction. But our hearts bled for the thousands who will hear that their brothers, fathers, and friends have fallen in this dreadful battle to secure our victory. No letters from Papa or Dr. Bowyer. Our excitement is so great. The battle lasted ten hours, from morning to night. I do not expect Papa and Dr. Bowyer can write for a day or two.

We sat in Sister's room and she read us a chapter and a prayer, and we offered ourselves and our lives to do God's will and service the rest of our days, and promised to show forth our thanks for this merciful deliverance, not only with our lips but with our lives, praying that God will help us. It rained hard all day, and the rain refreshed many a dying soldier, and I expect, saved many a life on the battlefield. We could not sleep much after such excitement.

Though peace prevailed in the county, the war's horrors quickly became very real, even as hope for an end to any further bloodshed persisted, as revealed in this excerpt on Thursday, July 23, 1861:

> Another telegram from Mr. Johnson saying that Colonel R.T. Preston's regiment is safe, none killed and only a few wounded. What an awful thought that such a terrible battle has been fought in our land.
>
> After we have achieved a brilliant victory we are sad for nearly two thousand of our brave men have fallen. How I dread to read a list of the names of the killed! What a horrible calamity is ours! I even feel sorry for the ten thousand Yankees who were killed, though they don't deserve it.
>
> No letters, no mail from Manassas. I hardly expect a letter from any of them for the living must be very busy burying the dead and caring for the wounded.
>
> I worked in the yard all day to keep from thinking of the dreadful scenes on the battlefield this day and Sunday. How little we thought while we were so quiet here Sunday that our people were engaged all that day in this terrible conflict, and how can we realize anything so awful. In the afternoon I went to the courthouse where the ladies met and packed a bag with linen, lint, and clothes, pillows and everything to send to Manassas to the wounded.
>
> A number of rumors came to the village; some said from three to several thousand of our men killed and from seven thousand to fifteen thousand of the enemy. It is impossible to know the truth. I went over to Mr. Johnson's

after supper to talk with Mr. Hooper who had just come from Richmond. He thinks that after such a defeat the Yankees will not attack us again.

An entry for February 18, 1862, underscores how days were filled with routine, everyday tasks, yet clouded with fears of what the future may bring:

> Passed the morning writing and sewing. After dinner helped Mama ice cake, then went with Rosa up town to get china toys to put in bride's cake.
>
> Heard the sad news that Fort Donaldson was taken Sunday. Our men defended it bravely for five days but the Yankees had fresh reinforcements and became victors at last. The telegraph brought news too that Nashville, Tennessee, had capitulated to the Yankees. In that case they are not so far from our railroad and may get here very soon. This made us very gloomy and we felt little like fixing for a wedding. Perhaps we are only baking cake for the Yankees after all.
>
> We sat in Mama's room till bedtime, making plans in case the enemy should reach us and take our homes. It is too sad to think about and we just put our trust in God and hope and pray for victory. The mail brought a letter from Papa and a note from Lizzie (Mosby)."

Lettie Burwell's journal ended August 15, 1862, with the death of her sister, Fan, from typhoid fever. Fan's death was devastating for her, and combined with the anxiety brought about by the War, it was said she could no longer bear to keep a journal. Lettie never married, though she had several beaus through the years, and continued to live at Avenel as its "mistress" until she died in 1905. She is buried in Longwood Cemetery in Bedford with other members of her family.

Avenel was designed and built circa 1838 by Judge William

McCreary Burwell. Mr. Burwell married Frances Steptoe, daughter of the clerk of the Bedford County Court. He was the son of William A. Burwell, private secretary to President Thomas Jefferson, and later, a Virginia congressman. The house has a brick exterior, classical in style, with two feet-thick walls. The interior is equally massive, with large rooms, high ceilings, and a unique double stairway leading to the second floor. Intricate woodwork and ornate plasterwork adorn the interior. In 1838, the same year the house was completed, W.M. Burwell was elected to the Virginia House of Delegates. He was instrumental in bringing the railroad to Liberty in the 1850s. His friendship with the Jefferson family continued through the years, and the families visited back and forth often. Robert E. Lee was also a close family friend, and after the War, met with Confederate veterans in the front parlor of Avenel. The home has been preserved and is owned today by the Avenel Foundation.

Appendix C

Credit River Township Case

STATE OF MINNESOTA
COUNTY OF SCOTT

IN JUSTICE COURT
TOWNSHIP OF CREDIT RIVER
MARTIN V. MAHONEY, JUSTICE

First Bank of Montgomery,   Plaintiff,

vs.   JUDGMENT AND DECREE

Jerome Daly,   Defendant.

    The above entitled action came on before the Court and a Jury of 12 on December 7, 1968, at 10:00 A.M. Plaintiff appeared by its President Lawrence V. Morgan and was represented by its Counsel Theodore R. Mellby. Defendant appeared on his own behalf. A jury of Talesmen were called, impaneled and sworn to try the issues in this Case. Lawrence V. Morgan was the only witness called for Plaintiff and Defendant testified as the only witness in his own behalf.

    Plaintiff brought this as a Common Law action for the recovery of the possession of lot 19, Fairview Beach, Scott County, Minn. Plaintiff claimed titled to the Real Property in question by foreclosure of a Note and Mortgage Deed dated May 8, 1964, which Plaintiff claimed was in default at the time foreclosure proceedings were started.

    Defendant appeared and answered that the Plaintiff created the money and credit upon its own books by bookkeeping entry as the legal failure of consideration for the Mortgage Deed and alleged that the Sheriff's sale passed no title to Plaintiff.

The issues tried to the jury were whether there was a lawful consideration and whether Defendant had waived his rights to complain about the consideration having paid on the note for almost 3 years.

Mr. Morgan admitted that all of the money or credit which was used as a consideration was created upon their books, that this was standard banking practice exercised by their bank in combination with the Federal Reserve Bank of Minneapolis, another private bank, further that he knew of no United States Statute of Law that gave the Plaintiff the authority to do this. Plaintiff further claimed that Defendant by using the ledger book created credit and by paying on the Note and Mortgage waived any right to complain about the consideration and that Defendant was estopped from doing so. At 12:15 on December 7, 1968, the Jury returned a unanimous verdict for the Defendant. Now therefore, by virtue of the authority vested in me pursuant to the Declaration of Independence, the Northwest Ordinance of 1787, the Constitution of the United States and the Constitution and laws of the State Minnesota not inconsistent therewith;

IT IS HEREBY ORDERED, ADJUDGED AND DECREED:

1. That Plaintiff is not entitled to recover the possession of lot 19, Fairview Beach, Scott County, Minnesota, according to the Plat thereof on file in the Register of Deeds office.
2. That because of failure of a lawful consideration the Note and Mortgage dated May 8, 1964, are null and void.
3. That the Sheriff's sale of the above-described premises held on June 26, 1967, is null and void, of no effect.
4. That Plaintiff has no right, title or interest in said premises or lien thereon, as is above described.
5. That any provision in the Minnesota Constitution and any Minnesota Statute limiting the Jurisdiction of this Court is repugnant to the Constitution of the United States and to the Bill of Rights of the Minnesota Constitution and is null and void and that this Court has Jurisdiction to render complete Justice in this Cause.

6. That Defendant is awarded costs in the sum of $75.00 and execution is hereby issued therefore.
7. A 10 day stay is granted.
8. The following memorandum and any supplemental memorandum made and filed by this Court in support of this judgment is hereby made a part hereof by reference.

Dated December 9, 1968

BY THE COURT
MARTIN V. MAHONEY
JUSTICE OF THE PEACE
CREDIT RIVER TOWNSHIP
SCOTT COUNTY, MINNESOTA

MEMORANDUM

The issues in this case were simple. There was no material dispute on the facts for the Jury to resolve.

Plaintiff admitted that it, in combination with the Federal Reserve Bank of Minneapolis, which are for all practical purposes, because of their interlocking activity and practices, and both being Banking Institutions incorporated under the Laws of the United States, are in the Law to be treated as one and the same Bank, did create the entire $14,000.00 in money or credit upon its own books by bookkeeping entry. That this was the Consideration used to support the Note dated May 8, 1964 and the Mortgage of the same date. The money and credit first came into existence when they credited it. Mr. Morgan admitted that no United States Law of Statute existed which gave him the right to do this. A lawful consideration must exist and be tendered to support the note. See *Anheuser Busch Brewing Co. v. Emma Mason*, 44 Minn. 318. 46 N.W. 558. The Jury found there was no lawful consideration and I agree. Only God can create something of value out of nothing.

Even if defendant could be charged with waiver or estoppel, as a matter of Law this is no defense to the plaintiff. The Law leaves wrongdoers where it finds them. See sections 50, 51, and 52 of Am Jur 2d "Actions" on page 584 - "no action will lie to recover on a claim based upon, or in any manner depending upon, a fraudulent, illegal, or immoral transaction or contract to which plaintiff was a party."

Plaintiff's act of creating credit is not authorized by the Constitution and Laws of the United States, is unconstitutional and void, and is not lawful consideration in the eyes of the Law to support any thing or upon which any lawful rights can be built.

Nothing in the Constitution of the United States limits the jurisdiction of this Court, which is one of original Jurisdiction with right of trial by Jury guaranteed. This is a Common Law Action. Minnesota cannot limit or impair the power of this Court to render Complete Justice between the parties. Any provisions in the Constitution and laws of Minnesota which attempt to do so are repugnant to the Constitution to the United States and are void. No question as to the Jurisdiction of this Court was raised by either party at the trial. Both parties were given complete liberty to submit any and all facts and law to the Jury; at least in so far as they saw fit.

No complaint was made by Plaintiff that Plaintiff did not receive a fair trial. From the admissions made by Mr. Morgan the path of duty was made direct and clear for the Jury. Their Verdict could not reasonably have been otherwise. Justice was rendered completely and without denial, promptly and without delay, freely and without purchase, conformable to the laws in this Court on December 7, 1968.

December 9, 1968

BY THE COURT
MARTIN V. MAHONEY
JUSTICE OF THE PEACE
CREDIT RIVER TOWNSHIP
SCOTT COUNTY, MINNESOTA

Note: It has never been doubted that a Note given on a Consideration which is prohibited by law is void. It has been determined, independent of Acts of Congress, that sailing under the license of an enemy is illegal. The emission of Bills of Credit upon the books of these private Corporations, for the purposes of private gain is not warranted by the Constitution of the United States and is unlawful. See *Craig v. Mo.* 4 Peters Reports 912, This Court can tread only that path which is marked out by duty.

M.V.M.

Judge Mahoney's decision was as follows:

For the Justice fees, the First National Bank deposited with the Clerk of the District Court the two Federal Reserve Notes. The Clerk tendered the Notes to me. My sworn duty compelled me to refuse the tender. This is contrary to the Constitution of the United States. The States have no power to make bank notes a legal tender. See *American Jurist on Money*, sec. 13. Only gold and silver coin is a lawful tender.

Bank Notes are a good tender as money unless specifically objected to. Their consent and usage is based upon the convertibility of such notes to coin at the pleasure of the holder upon presentation to the bank for redemption. When the inability of a bank to redeem its notes is openly avowed they instantly lose their character as money and their circulation as currency ceases. (See 36 Am. Jur. on Money, Section 9).

There is no lawful consideration for these Federal Reserve Notes to circulate as money. The banks actually obtained these notes for cost of printing. There is no lawful consideration for said Notes.

A lawful consideration must exist for a Note. As a matter of fact, the "Notes" are not Notes at all, as they contain no promise to pay. (See 17 American Jurist section 85, 215).

The activity of the Federal Reserve Banks of Minnesota, San Francisco and the First National Bank of Montgomery is contrary to public policy and contrary to the Constitution of the United States and constitutes an unlawful creation of money, credit and the obtaining of money and credit for no valuable consideration. Activity of said banks in creating money and credit is not warranted by the Constitution of the United States.

The Federal Reserve Banks and National Banks exercise an exclusive monopoly and privilege of creating credit and issuing their Notes at the expense of the public, which does not receive a fair equivalent. This scheme is obliquely designed for the benefit of an idle monopoly to rob, blackmail, and oppress the producers of wealth.

The Federal Reserve Act and the National Bank Act is in their operation and effect contrary to the whole letter and spirit of the Constitution of the United States, for they confer an unlawful and unnecessary power on private parties; they hold all of our fellow citizens in dependence; they are subversive to the rights and liberation of the people.

These Acts have defiled the lawfully constituted Government of the United States. The Federal Reserve Act and the National Banking Act are not necessary and proper for carrying into execution the legislative powers granted to Congress or any other powers vested in the Government of the United States, but, on the contrary, are subversive to the rights of the People in their rights to life, liberty, and property. (See Section 462 of Title 31 U.S.C.).

The meaning of the Constitutional provision, "NO STATE SHALL make any Thing but Gold and Silver Coin a tender in payment of debts" is direct, clear, unambiguous and without any qualification. This Court is without authority to interpolate any exception. My duty is simply to execute it, as written, and to pronounce the legal result. From an examination of the case of *Edwards v. Kearsey*, 96 U.S. 595, the Federal Reserve Notes (fiat money), which are attempted to be made a legal tender, are exactly what the authors of the Constitution of the United States intend to prohibit. No State can make these Notes a legal tender. Congress is incompetent to authorize a State to make the Notes a legal tender. For the effect of binding Constitution provisions see *Cooke v. Iverson*. This fraudulent Federal Reserve System and National Banking System has impaired the obligation of Contract, promoted disrespect for the Constitution and Law and has shaken society to its foundations. (See 96 U.S.C. 595 and 108 M 388 and 63 M 147)

Title 31, U.S.C., Section 432, is in direct conflict with the Constitution insofar, at least, that it attempts to make Federal Reserve Notes a Legal Tender. The Constitution is the Supreme Law of the Land. Section 462 of Title 31 is not a law which is made in pursuance of the Constitution. It is unconstitutional and void, and I so hold. Therefore, the two Federal Reserve Notes are null and void for any lawful purpose in so far as this case is concerned and are not a valid deposit of $2.00 with the Clerk of the District Court for the purpose of effecting an Appeal from this Court to the District Court.

However, there is a second ground of invalidity of these Federal Reserve Notes previously discussed and that is that the Notes are invalid because on no theory are they based upon a valid, adequate or lawful consideration.

At the hearing scheduled for January 22, 1969, at 7:00 P.M., Mr. Morgan, nor anyone else from or represent the Bank, attended to aid the Court in making a correct determination.

Mr. Morgan appeared at the trial on December 7, 1969, he appeared as a witness to be candid, open, direct, experienced and truthful. He testified to 20 years of experience with the Bank of America in Los Angeles, the Marquette National Bank of Minnesota and the First National Bank of Minnesota. He seemed to be familiar with the operation of the Federal Reserve System. He freely admitted that his Bank created all of the money and credit upon its books with which it acquired the Note and Mortgage of May 8, 1964. The credit first came into existence when the Bank created it upon its books. Further, he freely admitted that no United States Law gave the Bank the authority to do this. There was obviously no lawful consideration for the Note. The Bank parted with absolutely nothing except a little ink. In this case the evidence was on January 22, 1969, that the

Federal Reserve Banks obtain the Notes for the cost of the printing only. This seems to be conferred by Title 12 U.S.C., Section 420. The cost is about 9/10ths of a cent per Note, regardless of the amount of the Note. The Federal Reserve Banks create all of the money and credit upon their books by bookkeeping entries by which they acquire United States and State Securities. The collateral required to obtain the Note is, by section 412 U.S.C., Title 12, a deposit of a like amount of Bonds—Bonds which the Banks acquire by creating money and credit by bookkeeping entry.

No rights can be acquired by fraud. The Federal Reserve Notes are acquired through the use of unconstitutional statutes and fraud. "The Common Law requires a lawful consideration for any Contract or Note. These Notes are void for failure at a lawful consideration at Common Law, entirely apart from any Constitutional Considerations. Upon this ground, the Notes are ineffectual for any purpose. This seems to be the principal objection to paper fiat money and the cause of its depreciation and failure down through the ages. If allowed to continue, Federal Reserve Notes will meet the same fate. From the evidence introduced on January 22, 1969, this Court finds that as of March 18, 1968, all Gold and Silver backing is removed from Federal Reserve Notes.

The law leaves wrongdoers where it finds them. See Amer. Jur. 2nd on Actions, Sections 50, 51 and 52.

Slavery and all its incidents, including Peonage, thralldom and debt created by fraud is universally prohibited in the United States. This case represents but another refined form of Slavery by the Bankers. Their position is not supported by the Constitution of the United States. The People have spoken their will in terms which cannot be misunderstood. It is indispensable to the preservation of the Union and independence and liberties of the people that this Court adhere only to the mandates of the Constitution and administer it as it is written. I therefore hold these Notes in question void and not effectual for any purpose."

Appendix C Credit River Township Case

January 30, 1969

BY THE COURT
MARTIN V. MAHONEY
JUSTICE OF THE PEACE
CREDIT RIVER TOWNSHIP
SCOTT COUNTY, MINNESOTA

Original court document:
mn.gov/law-library/assets/1968-12-09judgmentanddecree_tcm1041-115904.pdf

[Author's note: The implications of this case were enormous; however, the case was squelched in the media and eventually forgotten by the public. The decision was ultimately nullified on the grounds the ruling was beyond the jurisdiction of a justice of the peace. Therefore, the case has no value as a precedent. However, the nullity does not alter the truths revealed in the case.

On appeal, the federal court publicly ridiculed Mr. Daley for having the audacity to challenge the validity of Federal Reserve Notes, and subsequently had him "disbarred" (*U.S. v. Jerome Daly*, 481 F.2d. 28). The disbarment is overt evidence that the federal judiciary are agents of the Global Elite, a.k.a. International Banking Cartel.

Justice Martin V. Mahoney was murdered six months after entering the *Credit River* decision, although the death was officially listed as "under mysterious circumstances."]

Appendix D

Membership List of the Committee of 300

By Peter B. Meyer

"An Ex-Illuminati member posted a list of members of the Elite Secret Society and the Committee of 300. He was a high-ranking Illuminati member, who spent 47 years in a top-ranking position with the elite secret society, and says that he wanted to reveal everything about the secret society's plans after it all became 'too much to bear' for him."

"Membership of the Illuminati, or the Committee of 300, has always remained top secret. This is the first time that the full list of members' names has been exposed in this rare leak from this anonymous Insider."

The list of 300 (Illuminati 2016) criminals:

Abdullah II (King) of Jordan • Abramovich, Roman Arkadyevich • Ackermann, Josef • Adeane, Edward • Agius, Marcus Ambrose Paul • Ahtisaari, Martti Oiva Kalevi • Akerson, Daniel • Albert II of Belgium • Alexander, Crown Prince of Yugoslavia • Alexandra (Princess), The Honourable Lady Ogilvy • Alphonse, Louis, Duke of Anjou • Amato, Giuliano • Anderson, Carl A. • Andreotti, Giulio • Andrew (Prince), Duke of York • Anne, Princess Royal • Anstee, Nick • Ash, Timothy Garton • Astor, William Waldorf, 4th Viscount Astor • August, Ernst, Prince of Hanover • Aven, Pyotr • Balkenende, Jan Peter • Ballmer, Steve • Balls, Ed • Barroso, José Manuel • Beatrix (Queen of Netherlands) • Belka, Marek • Bergsten, C. Fred • Berlusconi, Silvio • Bernanke, Ben • Bernhard

Appendix D Membership List of the Committee of 300

(Prince) of Lippe-Biesterfeld • Bernstein, Nils • Berwick, Donald • Bildt, Carl • Bischoff, Sir Winfried Franz Wilhen • Blair, Tony • Blankfein, Lloyd • Blavatnik, Leonard • Bloomberg, Michael • Bolkestein, Frits • Bolkiah, Hassanal • Bonello, Michael C. • Bonino, Emma • Boren, David L. • Borwin, Duke of Mecklenburg • Bronfman, Charles Rosner • Bronfman, Edgar Jr. • Bruton, John • Brzezinski, Zbigniew • Budenberg, Robin • Buffet, Warren • Bush, George H.W. • Cameron, David William Donald • Camilla, Duchess of Cornwall • Cardoso, Fernando Henrique • Carington, Peter, 6th Baron Carrington • Carlos, Duke of Parma • Carlos, Juan, King of Spain • Carney, Mark J. • Carroll, Cynthia • Caruana, Jaime • Castell, Sir William • Chan, Anson • Chan, Margaret • Chan, Norman • Charles, Prince of Wales • Chartres, Richard • Chiaie, Stefano Delle • Chipman, Dr John • Chodiev, Patokh • Christoph, Prince of Schleswig-Holstein • Cicchitto, Fabrizio • Clark, Wesley Kanne Sr. (General) • Clarke, Kenneth • Clegg, Nick • Clinton, Bill • Cohen, Abby Joseph • Cohen, Ronald • Cohn, Gary D. • Colonna, Marcantonio, Prince and Duke of Paliano • Constantijn (Prince) of the Netherlands • Constantine II Greece • Cooksey, David • Cowen, Brian • Craven, Sir John • Crockett, Andrew • D'Aloisio, Tony • Dadush, Uri • Darling, Alistair • Davies, Sir Howard • Davignon, Étienne • Davis, David • de Rothschild, Benjamin • de Rothschild, David René James • de Rothschild, Evelyn Robert • de Rothschild, Leopold David • Deiss, Joseph • Deripaska, Oleg • Dobson, Michael • Draghi, Mario • Du Plessis, Jan • Dudley, William C. • Duisenberg, Wim • Edward (Prince), Duke of Kent • Edward (The Prince), Earl of Wessex • Elkann, John • Emanuele, Vittorio, Prince of Naples, Crown Prince of Italy • Fabrizio (Prince), Massimo-Brancaccio • Feldstein, Martin Stuart • Festing, Matthew • Fillon, Francois • Fischer, Heinz • Fischer, Joseph Martin • Fischer, Stanley • FitzGerald, Niall • Franz, Duke of Bavaria • Fridman, Mikhail • Friedrich, Georg, Prince of Prussia • Friso (Prince) of Orange-Nassau • Gates, Bill • Geidt, Christopher • Geithner, Timothy • Gibson-Smith, Dr. Chris • Gorbachev, Mikhail • Gore, Al • Gotlieb, Allan • Green, Stephen • Greenspan, Alan • Grosvenor, Gerald, 6th Duke of Westminster • Gurria, José Angel • Gustaf, Carl XVI of Sweden • Hague, William

- Hampton, Sir Philip Roy • Hans-Adam II, Prince of Liechtenstein • Harald V Norway • Harper, Stephen • Heisbourg, François • Henri, Grand Duke of Luxembourg • Hildebrand, Philipp • Hills, Carla Anderson • Holbrooke, Richard • Honohan, Patrick • Howard, Alan • Ibragimov, Alijan • Ingves, Stefan Nils Magnus • Isaacson, Walter • Jacobs, Kenneth M. • Julius, DeAnne • Juncker, Jean-Claude • Kenen, Peter • Kerry, John Forbes • King, Mervyn • Kinnock, Glenys • Kissinger, Henry • Knight, Malcolm • Koon, William H. II • Krugman, Paul • Kufuor, John • Lajolo, Giovanni • Lake, Anthony • Lambert, Richard • Lamy, Pascal • Landau, Jean-Pierre • Laurence, Timothy James Hamilton • Leigh-Pemberton, James • Leka, Crown Prince of Albania • Leonard, Mark • Levene, Peter, Baron Levene of Portsoken • Leviev, Lev • Levitt, Arthur • Levy, Michael, Baron Levy • Lieberman, Joe • Livingston, Ian • Loong, Lee Hsien • Lorenz (Prince) of Belgium • Louis-Dreyfus, Gérard • Mabel (Princess) of Orange-Nassau • Mandelson, Peter Benjamin • Manning, Sir David Geoffrey • Margherita, Archduchess of Austria-Este • Margrethe II Denmark • Martinez, Guillermo Ortiz • Mashkevitch, Alexander • Massimo, Stefano, Prince of Roccasecca dei Volsci • McDonough, William Joseph • McLarty, Mack • Mersch, Yves • Michael (Prince) of Kent • Michael of Romania • Miliband, David • Miliband, Ed • Mittal, Lakshmi • Moreno, Glen • Moritz, Prince and Landgrave of Hessen-Kassel • Murdoch, Rupert • Napoléon, Charles • Nasser, Jacques • Niblett, Robin • Nichols, Vincent • Nicolas, Adolfo • Noyer, Christian • Ofer, Sammy • Ogilvy, David, 13th Earl of Airlie • Ollila, Jorma Jaakko • Oppenheimer, Nicky • Osborne, George • Oudea, Frederic • Parker, Sir John • Patten, Chris • Pébereau, Michel • Penny, Gareth • Peres, Shimon • Philip (Prince), Duke of Edinburgh • Pio, Dom Duarte, Duke of Braganza • Pöhl, Karl Otto • Powell, Colin • Prokhorov, Mikhail • Quaden, Guy Baron • Rasmussen, Anders Fogh • Ratzinger, Joseph Alois (Pope Benedict XVI) • Reuben, David • Reuben, Simon • Rhodes, William R. • Rice, Susan • Richard Duke of Gloucester • Rifkind, Sir Malcolm Leslie • Ritblat, Sir John • Roach, Stephen S. • Robinson, Mary • Rockefeller, David Jr. • Rockefeller, Nicholas • Rodriguez, Javier Echevarria • Rogoff, Kenneth Saul • Roth, Jean-Pierre • Rothschild,

Appendix D Membership List of the Committee of 300

Jacob, 4th Baron Rothschild • Rubenstein, David • Rubin, Robert • Ruspoli, Francesco, 10th Prince of Cerveteri • Safra, Joseph • Safra, Moises • Sands, Peter A. • Sarkozy, Nicolas • Sassoon, Isaac S.D. • Sassoon, (Baron) James Meyer • Sawers, Sir Robert John • Scardino, Marjorie • Schwab, Klaus • Schwarzenberg, Karel • Schwarzman, Stephen A. • Shapiro, Sidney • Sheinwald, Nigel • Sigismund Grand Duke of Tuscany • Simeon of Saxe-Coburg and Gotha • Snowe, Olympia • Sofía (Queen) of Spain • Soros, George • Specter, Arlen • Stern, Ernest • Stevenson, Dennis, Baron Stevenson of Coddenham • Steyer, Tom • Stiglitz, Joseph E. • Strauss-Kahn, Dominique • Straw, Jack • Sutherland, Peter • Tanner, Mary • Tedeschi, Ettore Gotti • Thompson, Mark • Thomson, Dr. James A. • Tietmeyer, Hans • Trichet, Jean-Claude • Tucker, Paul • Van Rompuy, Herman • Vélez, Alvaro Uribe • Verplaetse, Alfons Vicomte • Villiger, Kaspar • Vladimirovna, Maria, Grand Duchess of Russia • Volcker, Paul • Von Habsburg, Otto • Waddaulah, Hassanal Bolkiah Mu'izzaddin • Walker, Sir David Alan • Wallenberg, Jacob • Walsh, John • Warburg, Max • Weber, Axel Alfred • Weill, Michael David • Wellink, Nout • Whitman, Marina von Neumann • Willem-Alexander, Prince of Orange • William (Prince) of Wales • Williams, Dr. Rowan • Williams, Shirley, Baroness Williams of Crosby • Wilson, David, Baron Wilson of Tillyorn • Wolfensohn, James David • Wolin, Neal S. • Woolf, Harry, Baron Woolf • Woolsey, R. James Jr. • Worcester, Sir Robert Milton • Wu, Sarah • Zoellick, Robert Bruce •

Source: *finalwakeupcall.info/en/2019/08/28/the-archon-bloodline-rulers*

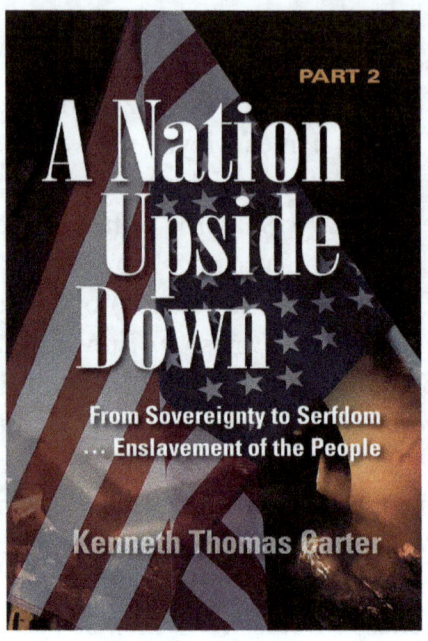

A Nation Upside Down **Part 2** continues the scintillating journey describing how America was subverted from the land of the free to the land of the serf. Your emotions will undoubtedly run the gamut from exhilaration to depression to anger. But the chapters offer hope: the hope of restoring the Republic of our Founding Fathers. The contrast could not be more stark; freedom or servitude, good or evil, unprecedented world peace and prosperity or the dire darkness of chains and servitude. Which will you choose? This is a read which will touch the very core of your being.

Chapter 10: The "Unholy" Trinity

A triumvirate of evil that has disgraced the shores of the U.S. for more than 100 years. This "Unholy" Trinity . . . the Federal Reserve System, IRS, and Bar Association . . . has taken control of and pervades virtually every aspect our lives. It has usurped control of the financial, political, social, educational, and moral fabric of American society. Through sleight of hand, masterful deception, and unbridled arrogance, the Global Elite has used these three *private corporations* to create an illusion of freedom, while cunningly destroying the principles the Republic was founded on and dismantling the vestiges of liberty. Yes, that's right . . . they are private corporations, owned by the Global Elite. They are not a part of the federal government. This chapter takes a detailed look at the machinations of these evil corporations, and will leave you stupefied at how the people could have been so masterfully deceived into believing the lie.

Chapter 11: Freedom is Not Free

Freedom is not free. It never has been, and it never will be. There is a cost. Throughout the ages, there has always been a cost, and there always will be a cost. Americans must be willing to pay the price that freedom demands. Or have they become so complacent in their evanescent comfort, drawing from the wellspring of government sustenance, that they willingly adorn the shackles of servitude for mere morsels of food and pennies paid out of the vast riches of the Global Elite? Americans addicted to government handouts may very well resist freedom for socialism. Tragically, these people already live their lives unknowingly in shackles, simmering in a cauldron of obfuscation oblivious to their coming peril. Government as tyrant is an anathema to freedom. This chapter explores the price Americans must be willing to pay to achieve enduring liberty. The price, however, is not steep. Every American must assume responsibility and accountability for their individual behavior, actions, and decisions. Freedom without morality and ethical behavior is an oxymoron. Moral law, or natural law, must be the framework that guides the lives of the people. Moral law is the foundation that will enable liberty to thrive.

Chapter 12: The Awakening

Freedom is rarely lost all at once. Throughout history, it has been usurped gradually, little by little, one step at a time, one law at a time, through the rise of tyrants or tyrannical governments. Its loss seems almost imperceptible. And so it has been for the American people. The people have been in a propaganda-induced coma, seemingly oblivious, or apathetic, to the encroachment upon their liberties and to the true agenda of their government. Most Americans are not aware they have exchanged their liberty for servitude. And the noose of enslavement is growing tighter and tighter around the necks of the people. What will it take to arouse the comatose from their slumber? The people must awaken to truth. Only then will they be able to destroy the evil that threatens to consume their souls. In this chapter, you will traverse the exhilarating road to Awakening.

Chapter 13: Restoring Liberty

Once armed with the light of truth, the people can reclaim their God-given unalienable rights and assume the task of restoring the Republic. Americans have ignored reality for too long, while being led deceptively down a primrose path to destruction by the ruling criminal cabal. The people have the right to liberty. But that right also incurs the *duty* to defend it with their lives and the *responsibility* to maintain it with their actions. Will they arise to the challenge? The people, and only the people, will determine their future. Embrace their sovereignty if they have the courage. Forsake it if comfort, security, and bondage leave them content. This chapter explores what it will take for liberty to be restored across America.

Chapter 14: NESARA

NESARA is a blueprint for restoring the Republic. It is already law: signed by President Clinton into law on October 10, 2000. But its implementation has been thwarted by the Global Elite, and it has never been revealed to the people. Key provisions of the Act include eliminating the Fed, abolishing the IRS, restoring the gold standard, and restoring common law to all courts and legal matters. This chapter takes the reader on a fascinating journey filled with drama and intrigue, from the roots of NESARA to its passage by Congress and presidential signature. But the Global Elite dug in their heels. They could not allow the Act's implementation, or their stranglehold over the people would be broken. The announcement of NESARA was to take place on September 11, 2001. But the so-called terrorist attack and the bombing at the Pentagon were used as ploys to subvert the announcement and bury NESARA deep in U.S. Supreme Court vaults. But knowledge reveals truth. Once enlightened, it will be incumbent upon the people to act . . . or perish.

Chapter 15: Reestablishing the *de jure* Constitutional Republic

Marcus Tullius Cicero gave us a blueprint 2,000 years ago for reestablishing our Constitutional Republic: "The Budget should be balanced, the Treasury should be refilled, public debt should be reduced, the arrogance of officialdom should be tempered and controlled, and the assistance to foreign lands should be curtailed, lest Rome will become bankrupt. The people should be forced to work and not depend on government for subsistence." Words spoken in antiquity, but words of wisdom nevertheless. Words just as relevant today as then. This chapter explores the steps that must be taken for restoring the Constitutional Republic of our Founding Fathers. But beware! Restoring the Republic will require a dramatic paradigm shift in the thinking of Americans. The people are the source of all power. They must assume their rightful authority over all government—state and national. Elections, voter registration, term limits, immigration, the media, education, socialism, and political parties are some of the topics that are addressed with respect to the restored Republic.

Chapter 16: The Reckoning

The country is in dire straits. People have never been more divided. THE UNITED STATES, INC. is bankrupt and insolvent. The educational system implemented by the Global Elite has succeeded in brainwashing the younger generations. Courts are owned by the Deep State. Corruption exists at every level in the federal government, particularly at the leadership level, which has been strategically infused with Global Elite agents. The nation is at a crossroads; the day of reckoning is nigh. Will the wings of angels or the winds of inequity prevail? The Deep State is desperate to maintain its power and usher in one world government. Toward that end, the Global Elite has perpetrated the most heinous acts, which are nothing short of crimes against humanity. The COVID-19 plandemic has been orchestrated and implemented for malefic and malicious purposes: to kill and maim millions of people worldwide, and render millions more "obedient idiots" controlled by AI (artificial intelligence) in a New World Order.

Chapter 17: A New Beginning . . . Or the End?

The COVID19 plandemic has been planned for a very long time, awaiting the right moment to be released. The goal? To bring the people to their knees in absolute subjection, and decimate the world's population through dangerous and deadly vaccines. But scientists, epidemiologists, and medical doctors throughout the world have exposed the fraud. A class action lawsuit is being brought before the International Court of Justice to hold these provocateurs of evil accountable for their crimes. The time is NOW for people across the land, from sea to shining sea, to awaken to the very present danger and reassert their God-given unalienable rights. The time is NOW for the People to once again assume the position of master over their servant, the government. The future of mankind hangs in the balance.

Order at *turningthetidepublishing.com*

**Turning the Tide Publishing • 6256 Bullet Drive • Crestview FL • 32536
(850) 689-8989**

www.ingramcontent.com/pod-product-compliance
Lightning Source LLC
Chambersburg PA
CBHW070046080526
44586CB00013B/931